EARLY SOUTHEAST ASIA VIEWED FROM INDIA

Nalanda-Sriwijaya Series

General Editors: Tansen Sen and Geoff Wade

The Nalanda-Sriwijaya Series, established under the publishing program of the Institute of Southeast Asian Studies, Singapore, has been created as a publications avenue for the Nalanda-Sriwijaya Centre. The Centre focuses on the ways in which Asian polities and societies have interacted over time. To this end, the series invites submissions which engage with Asian historical connectivities. Such works might examine political relations between states; the trading, financial and other networks which connected regions; cultural, linguistic and intellectual interactions between societies; or religious links across and between large parts of Asia.

1. *Nagapattinam to Suvarnadwipa: Reflections on the Chola Naval Expeditions to Southeast Asia*, edited by Hermann Kulke, K. Kesavapany and Vijay Sakhuja
2. *Early Interactions between South and Southeast Asia: Reflections on Cross-Cultural Exchange*, edited by Pierre-Yves Manguin, A. Mani and Geoff Wade
3. *Hardships and Downfall of Buddhism in India*, by Giovanni Verardi
4. *Anthony Reid and the Study of the Southeast Asian Past*, edited by Geoff Wade and Li Tana
5. *Portuguese and Luso-Asian Legacies in Southeast Asia, 1511-2011,* Vol. 1: *The Making of the Luso-Asian World: Intricacies of Engagement*, edited by Laura Jarnagin
6. *Portuguese and Luso-Asian Legacies in Southeast Asia, 1511-2011,* Vol. 2: *Culture and Identity in the Luso-Asian World: Tenacities & Plasticities,* edited by Laura Jarnagin
7. *Sino-Malay Trade and Diplomacy from the Tenth through the Fourteenth Century,* by Derek Heng
8. *Tradition and Archaelogy: Early Maritime Contacts in the Indian Ocean,* edited by Himanshu Prabha Ray and Jean-François Salles
9. *The Sea, Identity and History: From the Bay of Bengal to the South China Sea,* edited by Satish Chandra and Himanshu Prabha Ray
10. *Early Southeast Asia Viewed from India: An Anthology of Articles from the* Journal of the Greater India Society, edited by Kwa Chong-Guan

EARLY SOUTHEAST ASIA VIEWED FROM INDIA

An Anthology of Articles from the *Journal of the Greater India Society*

Edited by

KWA CHONG-GUAN

MANOHAR
2013

A collaborative project between the Nalanda-Sriwijaya Centre at the
Institute of Southeast Asian Studies, Singapore and
the Indian High Commission, Singapore

First published 2013

ISBN 978-93-5098-017-0

Published by
Ajay Kumar Jain *for*
Manohar Publishers & Distributors
4753/23 Ansari Road, Daryaganj
New Delhi 110 002

Typeset at
Digigrafics
New Delhi 110 049

Cover: Rabindranath Tagore at Borobudur on
23 September 1927. Tagore is flanked by Suniti Kumar Chatterji and
Keesje Bake-Timmer. Walking ahead is the archaeologist P. V. van Stein
Callenfels accompanied by Surendranath Kar and Sam Koperberg.
(*Photo courtesy of the Koninklijk Instituut voor Taal-, Land- en Volkenkunde*)

Printed at
Salasar Imaging Systems
Delhi 110 035

Contents

Foreword

Historically, it is a fitting moment to release this anthology of articles from the *Journal of the Greater India Society*. Never before has the world been so interdependent as today and we need to excavate those historical resources that enable us to view this—often invisible—inter-dependence, so nations can live by its imperatives, rather than through competition alone. Perhaps the most important historical experience of this phenomenon, certainly within Asia, was the regional world of maritime Asian trade and cultural flows which began early in the first millennium and flourished through to the first half of the second millennium. While to be sure there were wars and competition between powers who sought to dominate this trade, as Janet Abu-Lughod has shown, "goods were transferred, prices set, exchange rates agreed upon, contracts entered into, credit extended, partnerships formed and agreements that were made were kept on record and honored." Trade was contained "within the interstices of a larger collaboration in which goods and merchants from many places were intermingled on each others' ships and where unwritten rules of reciprocity assured general compliance. This system was not decisively challenged until the sixteenth century. . .".[1]

Kwa Chong-Guan has done us an immense service by bringing to light and introducing a selection from this journal that highlights how Indian scholars and historians from the first half of the twentieth century viewed the consequences of this extensive period of influence and exchange between India and Southeast Asia. He rightly points out that for the Indian scholars of that time, the "discovery" of Indic cultural and monumental influences served to boost their sense of national pride in Indian civilisational contributions outside the subcontinent. Often this blinded them to the extent of local or regional Southeast Asian achievements and other non-nationalist ways of viewing a circulatory history that changed substantially while it travelled throughout the wider Asian region.

The excitement about earlier civilisational achievements of colonised and semi-colonised countries like China and India was particularly marked at the end of World War I when a global disillusionment set in with the grand civilising mission of the West. Writer after writer, whether it was Oswald Spengler or Arnold Toynbee in the West, or Rabindranath Tagore or Liang Qichao in Asia, decried the barbarism that underlay Western civilisational ideals. Suddenly, notions of Asian civilisations representing alternative principles compatible

[1] Janet Lippman Abu-Lughod, "The World System in the Thirteenth Century: Dead-end or Precursor?" in *Essays on Global and Comparative History,* ed. Michael Adas (Washington DC: American Historical Association, n.d.), 9-11.

with modernity but which had lurked in the penumbra of Western civilisation, moved centre-stage and became joined to the nascent nationalist movements in these societies. In this context, studies on the peaceful interactions and exchanges between ancient Asian cultures and polities became popular among scholars in India and China.

At around the same time that the *Journal of the Greater India Society* was being established, Dai Jitao, an important intellectual and leader in the Guomindang in China was establishing *New Asia,* a journal and society designed to further Sun Yat-sen's ideas of Great Asianism and China's peaceful and central role in it that Sun presented in Japan just before he died in 1925. Although there were important differences between *New Asia* and the *Journal of the Greater India Society*, each shared a sense of its civilisational centrality in wider Asia and each was committed to playing a role in leading Asia to a new, more just world. Of course, the country where pan-Asianism became dominant during this time was Japan. There were many Japanese intellectuals and activists, such as Okakura Kakuzō, who worked for a truly participatory, alternative order in Asia. But the idealist rhetoric of pan-Asianism was seized by those committed to building a Japanese empire, most notably the military which, as is well-known, drove the region into catastrophic warfare that only ended with the conclusion of World War II.

Such a sobering history made Asian societies much more wary of pan-Asianism. It also prompts us to suggest that while it may be legitimate to feel national pride, it is more important to view the influence and circulation of culture through more scientific lenses. Research especially since the time of the *Journal* reveals, as Kwa points out, much greater participation and agency by Southeast Asians in the Indianisation process. More recently the eminent Sanskritist, Sheldon Pollock, has argued that Indianisation of Southeast Asia was not only not an expression of colonisation, but that there was also nothing monolithic about the Indian culture that circulated. Even more interesting, this kind of Sanskritisation/Indianisation was concurrent with and thus no different from the Indianisation of India. Indeed, in some parts of Southeast Asia this process may have occurred earlier and been more sophisticated than in many parts of the subcontinent.[2]

Such ideas and models of circulatory histories are not only more accurate, but they are much better suited to a world that was and may again be more equal and interdependent. As Kwa shows, there were, among those writing in the *Journal*, also scholars who became aware of the blinding effects of celebratory nationalism. H.B. Sarkar, who began with a nationalist view, ultimately resisted his nationalist environment and accepted the limitations of this perspective, settling for a view of interactive exchange between these societies. In that spirit, we hope that this volume will trigger more detailed

[2] Sheldon Pollock, *The Language of the Gods in the World of Men: Sanskrit, Culture and Power in Premodern India* (Berkeley: University of California Press, 2006), 530-2.

and scientific studies of the rich and productive interactions between South and Southeast Asia.

Singapore
October 2012

PRASENJIT DUARA
Raffles Professor of Humanities
Director, Asia Research Institute
Director of Research, Humanities & Social Sciences
Office of the Deputy President (Research & Technology)
National University of Singapore

Preface

This volume brings together a selection of articles written by a group of mainly Bengali historians to narrate how they came to envision early Southeast Asian polities and societies as ancient Indian colonies. The idea for such an anthology emerged in the course of a discussion on Indian historical writing during a lunch which the Nalanda-Sriwijaya Centre at the Institute of Southeast Asian Studies, Singapore, hosted for Professor Romila Thapar on 19 August 2011, after her lecture on "Historical Writing on Early India." I would like to thank Professor Tansen Sen and the Indian High Commissioner to Singapore Dr T.C.A. Raghavan for inviting me to compile this anthology from the *Journal of the Greater India Society* where these Indian perspectives of Southeast Asia were first incubated, hatched and nurtured. The intent of this anthology is thus to revisit the work of a pioneering group of Indian historians associated with the Greater India Society founded in 1926.

These historians looked east across the Indian Ocean and north to the deserts of Central Asia and saw the indelible impact of Hinduism and Buddhism on the historical landscapes of these regions. This anthology reprints a selection of their papers published in their *Journal* showing how these historians reconstructed a history of Southeast Asia focused on identifying Indian elements in that history and tracing the Indic inspiration and sources of those elements. The articles have been selected to indicate how these historians and philologists associated with the Greater India Society defined the historical sources and evidence, read the classical literature and epigraphy of Southeast Asia and viewed its monuments and art to reconstruct the history of early Southeast Asian polities as Indian colonies.

What is the relevance of these works today, fifty or more years after they were written, and in an age when it is so easy to critique them with the wisdom of hindsight and new evidence? The papers in the recent volume *Early Interactions between South and Southeast Asia: Reflections on Cross-Cultural Exchange* edited by Pierre-Yves Manguin, A. Mani and Geoff Wade,[1] for example, summarise the archaeological evidence accumulated in the past forty years which effectively challenges the views of the Greater India Society and their arguments for the dominance of Indian cultural influence in Southeast Asia. Today we perceive more the localisation of Indian cultural elements in Southeast Asia.

[1]Pierre-Yves Manguin, A. Mani and Geoff Wade, eds., *South and Southeast Asia: Reflections on Cross-Cultural Exchange* (Singapore and New Delhi: Institute of Southeast Asian Studies and Manohar, 2011). The volume comprises a collection of papers presented at a November 2007 "Conference on Early Indian Influences in Southeast Asia" held in Singapore.

But framing these papers from the *Journal of the Greater India Society* in the context of the time of their publication in the first half of the twentieth century helps us to understand what inspired this group of Indian historians to extend their vision of Indian history eastwards across the Indian Ocean, and how they constructed the idea of an ancient Indian colonisation of early Southeast Asia. New evidence and alternative readings of the evidence today challenges the Society's vision, but the contemporary relevance of that vision of an Indianisation of Southeast Asia cannot be overstressed. However politically incorrect the Society's name and arguments for a "Greater India" may sound today, the Society's legacy of focussing on the expansive influence of Hinduism and to a lesser extent, Buddhism, in the Indian Ocean and Central Asia in an earlier millennium lives on in India's understanding of its historical destiny as it once again "Looks East." Hopefully this anthology is a small step forward in helping us to understand how these reconstructions of Southeast Asia's past continue to shape Indian perceptions of its Asian destiny.

This anthology has been assembled on the premise that even though the arguments of a number of the articles have been negated by other and later evidence, they are still worth re-reading for how they shaped Indian thinking towards Southeast Asia. R.C. Majumdar's reconstruction of an Indian subcontinent homeland for the Malays was based on a hypothesis proposed by Sylvain Lévi, Jean Przyluski and others of a pre-Aryan and pre-Dravidian linguistic link between the Austroasiatic languages of India and the Austronesian languages of island Southeast Asia and Oceania. However, recent advances in our reconstruction of the linguistic history of the Asia-Pacific have shown the errors of this hypothesis. Despite this, Majumdar's article is reprinted in this anthology for the insight into how this group of Indian historians were defining their research issues and their relevance to the larger research programme and vision of India's historical links with Southeast Asia. More significant is the legacy of this belief in prehistoric linguistic links between India and Southeast Asia and its effects on Indian perception of Indic links with Southeast Asia, seen for example in Suniti Kumar Chatterjee's endorsement of Indonesia's choice of Indonesian as its national language because it revives this common ancestry of India and Indonesia.

The first group of ten articles in this anthology highlights the contributions of the Greater India Society scholars to reconstructing the Indian foundations of the classical kingdoms of early Southeast Asia. The next section of five articles provides an insight into how the Greater India Society scholars were reading Indic sources in the old Javanese literature and art of early Southeast Asia. The final selection, comprising seven articles, shows the insights and understanding that the Greater India Society scholars and associates like Kamaleshwar Bhattacharya could bring to our reading and understanding of Javanese and Khmer epigraphy. Nine articles documenting the Society's beginnings, its vision and the mindset it brought to research have been included to provide a context and understanding of what inspired the members of the

Greater India Society. The article by Kalidas Nag was published by the Society before it launched its *Journal* and has been included in this anthology as a significant programmatic statement of the Society's vision. The extracts of the minutes of the Society's twelfth Annual General Meeting have also been included in this anthology for their insight into the running of the Society. The Introduction to the anthology attempts, first, to locate these historians within the intellectual milieu of their time and identify the sources of their inspiration and ideas, and second, to critique them within the context of their time, pointing out the tacit assumptions underlying their research which they could or should have been aware of. Third and finally, the Introduction notes how the legacy of the Greater India Society's vision of a Greater India has become a part of Indian social memories today, shaping Indian perceptions of its strategic interests in the Indian Ocean as it "Looks East."

I first delved into the *Journal of the Greater India Society* some forty-five years ago, when I became interested in the art history of Borobudur and Angkor Wat and tried to make sense of the rival interpretations of these and other Indianised monuments in Southeast Asia. But my hopes of working on the analytical philosophy of disagreements in the art history of these Indianised monuments were diverted by other career concerns. I am therefore delighted with this invitation from Professor Sen and Indian High Commissioner Raghavan to revisit an old interest in the writing of Southeast Asian history.

I would like to thank Professor Sen and High Commissioner Raghavan for their continuing support of this anthology and seeing it through to completion. I need to especially thank Dr Geoff Wade for his meticulous correction of the proofs of this anthology and the compiling of the index. His commitment to, and work on this anthology has exceeded expectations of that of a General Editor of this Nalanda-Sriwijaya Series.

Singapore KWA CHONG-GUAN
October 2012

Introduction
Visions of Early Southeast Asia as Greater India

KWA CHONG-GUAN

L'Inde n'a produit ses chiefs-d'oeuvre definitifs que sous l'action de l'etranger ou sur la terre entrangere ... En architecture, c'est dans le lointain Cambodge et la lontaine Java qu'il chercher les deux merveilles issues du genie indien: Angkor et Boro-budur.

SYLVAIN LÉVI

On ne connait pas dans l'Inde de monument ressemblant, meme de loin, au Bayon d'Angkor Thom ou au Borobudur. Et cependant,ce sont de pures productions du genie hindou, don't le sens profound n'apparait qu'aux yeux de l'indianiste.

GEORGE COEDÈS

THE ORIGINS OF A VISION

Over a period extending from 1934 to 1959, the Greater India Society, based in Calcutta, published eighteen volumes of the *Journal of the Greater India Society.* The publication of this *Journal* was part of the Society's aims to "organize the study of Indian culture in Greater India [i.e. Serindia, India Minor, Indo-China and Insulindia], as well as in China, Korea, Japan and other countries of Asia." The *Journal* was to publish "the results into the history of India's spiritual and cultural relations with the outside world." [1] The Greater India Society was inaugurated on 10 October 1926 and included among its founding members a core group of University of Paris educated scholars lead by Kalidas Nag, Prabodh Chandra Bagchi, and Subodh Chandra Mukherji. The Vice-Chancellor of the University of Calcutta, Professor Jadunath Sarkar was elected President. Other members included staff of the University and the Calcutta Museum.[2]

[1] The "Aims and Objects" of the Greater India Society are stated on the cover of their *Journal.* Publication was interrupted from 1947 to 1954. The editors of the *Journal* were U.N. Ghoshal (1934-45), Kalidas Nag (1946) and Nalinaksha Dutt (1955-59). The eighteen volumes of the *Journal* were reprinted by Aditya Prakashan, New Delhi, in 1987 with a new Preface by Lokesh Chandra who also compiled an index to the key words in the titles of the articles and names of contributors in all the volumes. A more detailed author and subject index has been prepared by K.R. Bhattacharya, *Index to the Journal of the Greater India Society*.

[2] Handy in his "The Renaissance of East Indian Culture" provides a contemporary insight

An indication of the research which the Society intended to pursue and publish in its *Journal* is contained in the five *Bulletins* that the Society published in its initial years. The first was the text of a 1922 lecture delivered by Dr Kalidas Nag entitled *Greater India*, with the significant subtitle *A Study in Indian Internationalism.* The lecture, reprinted in this volume is, in effect, a visionary statement about the principles of universal tolerance and amity which guided India's "career of internationalism."[3] As Nag declaimed:

> from the beginning of the Christian era, India started playing her role of internationalism not only through her lofty academic philosophy or through the vigorous propagation of a royal personality, but as a whole people following mysteriously a divine impulse, an ecstatic [sic] inspiration to sacrifice the *Ergo* for the *All.* This grand movement of spiritual conquest, this noble dynamic of cultural imperialism—a legacy of Asoka—soon won for India the inalienable empire over the vast continent, right across Tibet and China to Corea and Japan on the one hand and across Burma and Indo-China to Java and Indonesia on the other. The history of this phenomenal progression has yet to be written.

It is towards the writing of this history of Indian "internationalism"—of India as "the heart of Asiatic Humanism"—that the Greater India Society was dedicated.[4]

The subsequent *Bulletins* focused on more matter-of-fact issues of relations between India and China and prospects for "Sino-Indian collaboration" by Dr Prabodh C. Bagchi,[5] and India's relations with Sumatra and Java under its Śrivijaya and Śailendra rulers by Dr Bijanraj Chatterjee and Dr Niranjan Prasad Chakravarti.[6] The latter also contributed to the third *Bulletin* surveying India's relations with Central Asia.[7] The fifth *Bulletin* carried a review of *Ancient Indian Culture in Afghanistan* by Dr Upendranath Ghoshal[8] who became the Secretary of the Society, editor of its *Journal* and a major contributor to it. In addition to these short *Bulletins*, the Society also published longer monographs, the first of which was by Ramesh Chandra Majumdar on *Ancient Colonies in*

---

into the place of the Society in the Bengali intellectual landscape of the 1920s. See also Louis Finot's note welcoming the founding of the Society in his "Chronique: Inde."

[3]Nag's humanism is prefigured in his doctoral dissertation supervised by Sylvain Lévi, *Les theories diplomatiques de l'Inde ancienne et l'Arthaçâstra* which argues for a humanist understanding of classical Indian statecraft culminating in Kautilya, who according to Nag, is not the Indian Machiavelli he is usually perceived to be.

[4]The Society published Hindi and Bengali translations of this *Bulletin*, suggesting the centrality of Kalidas Nag and his views in its vision. However, Nag was not a major contributor to the *Journal,* contributing only one article on Sylvain Lévi and obituaries for Gabriel Ferrand, Louis Finot and Rabindranath Tagore.

[5]Bagchi, *India and China*. Bagchi (1898-1956) established his reputation as a scholar of Sino-Indian cultural relations, on which see the selection of his essays compiled by Wang and Sen, *India and China.*

[6]Chatterjee, *Indian Culture*, published 1927.

[7]Chakravarti, *India and Central Asia,* published 1927.

[8]Ghoshal, *Ancient Indian Culture in Afghanistan,* published in 1928.

the Far East, vol. 1, *Champa.*[9] The subsequent two volumes of Majumdar's *Ancient Indian Colonies in the Far East* were published commercially. Kalidas Nag's 1941 survey of the extension of Indian influence into the Pacific World was also commercially published.[10] The Society's publications were not the only avenue for its members to circulate their ideas. They published widely, elsewhere and also lectured extensively.

The Society was inaugurated at a time of growing awareness in the Dutch East Indies and French Indochina of the colonial authorities' responsibility towards to the preservation of the historical monuments under their charge. Parallel with the appointment of John Marshall as the new Director General of the Archaeological Survey of India in 1902, which ushered in a new era in the conservation of archaeological sites, was the establishment of the École française d'Extrême-Orient in 1900 in Hanoi and the creation of a new Dutch East Indies' Oudheidkundige Dienst (Archaeological Service) in 1913 out of the rump of an old *Commissie* established in 1901. A consequence of the new era in the conservation of the region's archaeological heritage was an enhanced awareness of Indian influence on the art and architecture of Indonesia and Indochina. Early inventories of the epigraphy related to the historical monuments confirmed a Sanskrit foundation to many of the inscriptions.[11] Studies into the local literature and language of Java and Bali also showed the deep influence of Sanskrit, as summarised by Hendrik Kern[12] on his pioneering studies of Javanese and Balinese texts—"The Indian influence can be most clearly seen on Java and Bali. The Hindus have freely given all their knowledge and most valuable of their literature to the natives and in so doing they have laid the foundation to a great literature and a high development of their art."

It was to explain how and why Indian culture came to have such an impact on the lands south of China and east of India, and further into the Pacific as Nag was to argue for in his 1941 survey of Indian influence in the Pacific,[13] that the members of the Greater India Society devoted themselves. In this they were not the first. Others like Radhakumud Mookerji had earlier attempted to make the case that it was the Indian commercial spirit that secured for India the control of the seas for ages; of the "daring adventurers" who sailed from the ports of Kalinga on the subcontinent's east coast and Gujarat on the west coast to settle in Java, where they established thriving colonies which had a prosperous trade with the mother country, and from where came the artists to

[9] Majumdar noted in his preface to this book that he had started work on this comprehensive reconstruction of Cham history, religion and epigraphy several years before the founding of the Society.

[10] Nag, *India and the Pacific World.*

[11] Barth and Bergaigne, *Inscriptions sanscrites*; and Brandes and Krom, *Oud-Javaaansche oorkonden* are still standard reference texts today.

[12] Kern is quoted from his 1906 lecture "De invloed der Indische," p. 197.

[13] The review by U.N. Ghoshal reprinted in this volume summarises Nag's survey arguing for the extension of Indian influence to the Pacific.

erect the monuments of Java. In the "Temples of Barabudur" according to Mookerji, "Indian art reached its highest expression amid the Indian environment and civilization transplanted there."[14]

The remainder of this Introduction attempts to put in context why and how this group of essentially Bengali intellectuals and historians in the first half of the twentieth century became so convinced of an Indian mission to civilise Central and Southeast Asia, and the legacy of their vision today. This essay argues that it was Rabindranath Tagore's vision of an Indo-Asian humanism coupled with their ambition to write a nationalist history with Hinduism as the driving force that led them to claim an ancient Indian mission to civilize Southeast Asia. French scholars of India, in particular, of Sanskrit, provided the Greater India Society scholars with the methods of making this claim of an Indian colonization of Southeast Asia with the evidence being provided by French and Dutch colonial scholarship of Indochina and Indonesia.

CONSTRUCTING THE VISION

Rabindranath Tagore was a major inspiration to the founding members of the Greater India Society. They invited him to be the *purodha*, or "spiritual eminence" implied in the Sanskrit etymology of the word, of the Society. As *purodha,* Tagore outranked the Patrons of the Society, which included the Maharaja of Pithapuram, Sir J.C. Bose. Tagore accepted the Society's invitation to contribute a Foreword to the inaugural issue of the *Journal*, and his handwritten Foreword opens the inaugural issue of the *Journal* and is reprinted in this volume. The Society's respect for Tagore stemmed in part from his persona, but perhaps also from his views on the universality of Indo-Asian humanism.[15]

Tagore, as Sugata Bose points out, "was a powerful critic of worshipping the Nation as God and was horrified by the crimes committed by modern nation states. Yet he loved the land that had nurtured him and never abandoned a basic anti-colonial stance."[16]Tagore's only foray into political activism was to join the *Swadeshi* (meaning "one's country') movement to protest the 1905 partition of Bengal. For Bengal, *Swadeshi* was the watershed of a Bengali Renaissance which began with Rammohun Roy (1772-1833) and the Brahmo Samaj movement to reform Hinduism. But for Tagore, this was not his understanding of how to change the world, an understanding which he developed

[14]Mookerji, *Indian shipping*, pp. 5, 40f, 156. Similar views are expressed in the 1957 edition of this book, for which see pp. 4, 24, 109.

[15]See Hay's reconstruction in his *Asian Ideas of East and West*, pp. 21-25, where he portrays three strands of Tagore's Indo-Asian humanism: (1) that India and Asia were synonymous; (2) Asian humanism was distinguished by its spiritual profundity from Western materialism; (3) despite these differences, Asia and the West complemented each other.

[16]Bose, "Rabindranath Tagore and Asian Universalism," p. 11.

in his 1916 novel *Ghare Baire* (*Home and the World*).[17] Tagore stated his position more pithily in a 1908 letter, noting that, "I will never allow patriotism to triumph over humanity as long as I live. I took a few steps down that road and stopped; for when I cannot retain my faith in universal man standing over and above my country, when patriotic prejudice overshadows my God, I feel inwardly starved." Tagore's crusade against a narrow patriotic nationalism for a broader and more inclusive humanism was developed in controversial lectures he delivered in Japan and America in 1916 and 1917.[18]

To promote his vision of the oneness of Asian humanism, in 1921 Tagore transformed the *ashram* and old school complex at Sāntiniketan which he inherited from his father into a "university" which that he named "Visva-Bharati" which may refer to "India in the World" or "The World in India." Tagore attracted to Visva-Bharati a stream of European Indologists including Sylvain Lévi, Moriz Winternitz, Giuseppe Tucci, and Charles Freer Andrews. Of significance to the development of the *ashram* at Sāntiniketan as a centre of inter-Asian exchange was a visitor from Japan, the art historian and critic, Okakura Tenshin (1863-1913).[19] From his sojourns at the *ashram* came two classic texts, *The Ideals of the East*, published in 1903 and later, *Awakening of Asia.* Even today, the impassioned opening paragraph of *Ideals of the East* resonates:

> Asia is one. The Himalayas divide, only to accentuate, two mighty civilisations, the Chinese with its communism of Confucius, and the Indian with its individualism of the Vedas. But not even the snowy barriers can interrupt for one moment that broad expanse of love for the Ultimate and Universal, which is the common thought-inheritance of every Asiatic race, enabling them to produce all the great religions of the world, and distinguishing them from those maritime peoples of the Mediterranean and the Baltic, who love to dwell on the Particular, and to search out the means, not the end, of life.[20]

Perhaps an equally, if not more, influential voice for an Indo-Asian humanism at Sāntiniketan was Swami Vivekananda's Irish disciple, Margaret Nobel who as Sister Nivedita (the dedicated one) helped Okakura draft if not rewrite much of his *Ideals of the East.* The "Introduction" she contributed to *Ideals of the East* appropriated and extended Okakura's documentation of the Buddhist inspiration of Japanese art to contend that "the thing we call Buddhism cannot

[17] See Sarkar, "Nationalism and 'Stri-Swadhinata,'" for a reading of Tagore's novel as not only a critique of nationalism, but an exploration of issues of masculinity and feminist issues in the struggle for freedom.

[18] The texts of Tagore's lectures on nationalism have become part of the corpus of Tagore's classic works, and are much reprinted. See the Penguin Books India 2009 reprint with an introduction by Ramachandra Guha, in which Tagore's 1908 letter is quoted at p. xii.

[19] Bharucha, *Another Asia*, provides a nuanced critical reading of the Tagore-Okakura relationship and their different understandings of "Asia," nationalism and cosmopolitanism.

[20] Okakura, *The Ideals of the East*. Okakura published in 1906 another classic entitled *The Art of Tea* which has also shaped the way we think about Japanese culture.

in itself have been a defined and formulated creed, with strict boundaries and clearly demarcated heresies, capable of giving birth to a Holy Office of its own. Rather must we regard it as the name given to the vast synthesis known as Hinduism. . ." Nivedita then claims that it was "not the Buddhaising but the *Indianizing* of the Mongolian mind, was the process actually at work." She concludes that because of "the genius of a wandering monk—the Swami Vivekananda . . . [o]rthodox Hinduism has again become aggressive, as in the Asokan period." She quotes Vivekananda that the creed "of the despised Hindu may yet dominate the world," and anticipates that "what took a thousand years at the beginning of our era may now, with the aid of steam and electricity, repeat itself in a few decades and the world may again witness the Indianising of the East."[21] Tagore was apparently attracted to Nivedita and her ideas. The circle of the Greater India Society would be similarly attracted to Nivedita's ideas.

The Society may also have found the ideas of Ananda Coomaraswamy[22] interesting. This Sinhalese art historian also spent time with Tagore and his circle during his visits to India between 1901 and 1913.[23] In Bengal he became involved in the *swadeshi* movement and its implications for Indian craftsmanship, on which he wrote several essays which formed the basis of *Art and Swadeshi* which helped establish his reputation as more than an art historian. More importantly, it was at Sāntiniketan that Coomaraswamy developed his views of the underlying unity of Asian art and culture captured in Okakura's "Asia is one" call. Coomaraswamy's 1927 *History of Indian and Indonesian Art* is still a classic statement on the underlying cultural and spiritual unity of Indian, Indonesian and much of East Asian art.[24]

Tagore's influence on the Greater India Society included not only the reputation he brought as *purodha* of the Society, but the intellectuals and scholars he attracted to Sāntiniketan and the seepage of their ideas of Asian

[21] Bharucha probes the layers of meanings in Nivedita's "Introduction" to *Ideals of the East* in the context of their relationship and ultimately conflicting visions of "Asia" in *Another Asia,* pp. 34-43.

[22] See Frost, *That Great Ocean of Idealism* for the Calcutta context of Coomaraswamy's and Okakura sojourns at Santiniketan.

[23] Roger Lipsey, *Coomaraswamy, 3: His Life and Work,* Bollingen Ser. LXXXIX (Princeton: Princeton University Press, 1977), chap. 7 on this phase of Coomaraswamy's life.

[24] Coomaraswamy's *History of Indian and Indonesian Art* published to much acclaim in 1927, remains a classic statement of the underlying stylistic and aesthetic unity of Indian and Indonesian art. Coomaraswamy envisioned the underlying unity of Asian art in a deep *vedānta* version of Hinduism evident in the one article he contributed to volume 3 of the Society's *Journal,* on "The Source of, and a Parallel to, Dionysius on the Beautiful," in which he sought a Vedic parallel to Dionysius. Evidently there was little in common between Coomaraswamy's metaphysics of Indian art and the politics of the Greater India Society circle. However, Coomaraswamy's text was the start point of another classic study of *The Art of Indian Asia* by Heinrich Zimmer.

unity and humanism through the members of the Greater India Society. Tagore's well-publicised overseas journeys, especially his 1924 visit to China and 1927 travels through Singapore to Malaya and on to Bali and Java must have influenced the Society's outlook on its activities. Kalidas Nag was invited to join Tagore on his 1924 journey to China and Japan. Tagore's 1927 tour of Malaya, continuing on to Bali and Java, included the linguist Suniti Kumar Chatterji, a committee member of the Society, as secretary. Chatterji's notes of the journey suggest that Tagore and his delegation were surprised and awed by the Balinese and Javanese transformation of the Hindu culture they were familiar with.[25]Of the letters and eighteen poems and songs Tagore wrote during this three-months tour of Malaya and Indonesia, the poem *Shribijaylakshmi* composed on 19 August enroute sailing from Singapore to Java is an allegory of India's millennium-long spiritual relationship with Java, and encapsulates well the visions of a Greater India

In the distant unrecorded age
We had met, thou and I

When my speech became entangled in thine and my life in thy life. . .

The East Wind had carried thy beckoning call
Through an unseen path of the air. . .

The Great god Vishnu spoke to me,
And spoke Uma, the ten-armed goddess:

Make ready thy boat, carry the rite of our worship
Across the unknown sea. . .

Kalidas Nag's fulsome obituary of Tagore in the *Journal* has then to be read as the gratitude of a community of scholars to its *purodha*.

A second stream of inspiration for these founding members of the Society were the theories and methods of the pioneering group of French scholars of oriental studies, especially of Indian and Sanskrit studies. Two names stand out, the doyen of French Sanskrit Studies, Sylvain Lévi[26] and Jean Przyluski. Lévi was Nag's *professeur* at the Collège de France and his fulsome obituary of Lévi reprinted in this volume is an expression of homage to his guru. Tagore also paid tribute to Lévi "as the first of the European scholars who readily responded to my call and came to train our own students and scholars [at Sāntiniketan] in the scientific techniques of historical research. . ." What Nag and his colleagues appreciated in Lévi and his predecessors Abel Bergaigne and Eugène Burnof was their wider *l'Inde transgangétique* view of Indian

[25]Bose, "Rabindranath Tagore and Asian Universalism," for an insightful reading of Tagore's impressions of his travels in Malaya and Indonesia, and Das Gupta, "Rabindranath Tagore in Indonesia" for a more analytical reconstruction. Also see Chaudhuri, *Tagore looks East.*

[26]See especially on this issue, Bayly, "India's 'Empire of Culture,'" for a careful excavation of Lévi's influence on the Greater India Society.

studies, in contrast to the orientalism of their German and British colleagues concerned with the evolution of the "classical" Sanskrit texts and their Vedic roots. Lévi's passage on this *Transgangétique* perspective of Indian studies became a rallying call for this Greater India understanding of India's past:

> From Persia to the Chinese Sea, from the icy regions of Siberia to the islands of Java and Borneo, from the Oceanea to Socotra, India has propagated her beliefs, her genius, her tales and her civilization. She has left indestructible imprints on one-fourth of the human race in the course of a long succession of centuries. She has the right to reclaim, in universal history, the rank that ignorance has refused her for a long time and to hold her place amongst the great nations, summarising and symbolising the spirit of humanity.

For Lévi, this greater vision of an "Eastern Humanism" developed as part of a larger personal life agenda which Nag and his contemporaries, because of their proximity to Lévi and awe of him as their *professeur*, may not have been aware of. Lévi came to Indian studies from a Jewish background and was destined to enter Jewish studies, but instead chose to go for oriental studies and eventually opted for Indian studies. Here he was challenged by "Aryanist scholarship" of German Indologists arguing that it is in the Vedas, and Sanskrit as its derivative, that the origins of the Aryans and their homeland are to be sought. This would provide the Aryanists a more venerable genealogy than Judaic begining origins. Lévi's response was to stress the salience of the *brahmanas* (over that of the Vedas) and its *Transgangétique* dimensions, with Buddhism as an offshoot of the *brahmanas*.[27]

Lévi understood brahmanic Hinduism to be a *religion particulières*[28] defined by its rituals, especially of the sacrifice, which enabled Hinduism's survival by "embodying" our experience of the sacred in social spaces such as the "family house" and embedding itself in local rituals. In contrast, Buddhism as an offshoot of Brahmanism, is a *religion universelles* which (like Christianity and Islam) divorced itself from its Indian roots and contexts to develop a more universal appeal and in the process, lost its identity that eventually proved disastrous for the faith in India. As a socially disembodied entity, Buddhism was then perceived by the nineteenth-century Orientalists and Indologists as a religion similar to Christianity, without particularities of a local context. Embodied religions survive, but disembodied, like Buddhism (and possibly Judaism), they could only wither and die, as happened to Buddhism in India (and Judaism in Europe). Consequently brahmanic Hinduism's survival in Transgangetic lands was because it could be selectively appropriated, adapted and embodied in the local experience, creating new forms.[29]

local agency

[27] See Laurens, "Sylvain Lévi"; Weill, "Entre l'Orient et l'Occident."

[28] Lévi, "Religions universelles."

[29] Lévi's case for the centrality of the rituals of the sacrifice in creating the gods, who then create the world, is made in *La doctrine du sacrifice*. Lévi equates Prajapati (the primeval Creator) with the sacrifice: "Prajapati, the sacrifice, is the father of the gods and the Asuras . . . and its son." (p. 27). See Malamoud, "Sylvain Lévi.".

Lévi's techniques for reconstructing this *transgangétique* past of brahmanism's diffusion and embodying of the local was, as Jean Przyluski explains in his memorial of Lévi reprinted in the present volume, through the science of onomastics, the linguistic study of how the meanings of proper names (of persons, places, things) change in time and space and social context. Not only the scholars of the Greater India Society, but later generations of Southeast Asian historians have continued this onomastic search for Sanskrit etymologies, allusions or synonyms of Southeast Asian names or phonetic correspondences between Indian and Chinese references to Southeast Asian names. For example, Lévi's argument for the equivalence of the classical Chinese reference to *kun-lun* with the Sanskrit *dvīpāntara* evoked a response (chapter 18 in this volume) from K. A. Nilakanta Sastri (1892-1975), arguing for a more localised rooting of *dvīpāntara* to the Malay Peninsula, than the more generic equivalence of the South China Sea implied in the Chinese *kun-lun*.

Beyond Lévi, the founding members of the Society also appreciated the support and acknowledgment of other French scholars, especially those attached to the École française d'Extrême-Orient. Kalidas Nag penned an effusive obituary to its founding Director Louis Finot (chapter 9 in this volume) which focused on his support for the Society and its work. Interestingly, Nag also chose to remember Gabriel Ferrand (chapter 8 in this volume) not so much for his work on Arab texts on Southeast Asia, but rather for his monograph drawing together the Chinese, Arab and Indian texts on Śrīvijaya, and his contribution of rare books to Tagore's Visva-Bharati. The philologist and scholar of Buddhism Jean Przyluski (1885-1944) was another savant whom the Society esteemed. His article on "Indian Influence on Western Thought Before and During the Third Century A.D." was the lead contribution to the inaugural issue of the *Journal*.

Przyluski contributed six other articles to the *Journal*. The papers which he, Lévi and Jules Bloch (1906-55) wrote on the possibility of an underlying linguistic link between the Austronesian languages of island Southeast Asia and the Pacific with the Austroasiatic languages of mainland Southeast Asia, including the Munda and Santhal languages of northwest India in a wider "Austric" language group were welcomed by the Greater India Society scholars. A compilation and translation of these papers by P.C. Bagchi[30] became the basis for speculations of an earlier pre-Aryan migration of Dravidian sea-faring indigenes from northeast India or Bengal, to Southeast Asia. R. C. Majumdar made these speculations the basis of an argument for India as the homeland of the Malays in his article for the *Journal* (chapter 25 in this volume). It was these beliefs in a deep Austric linguistic link between Indonesia and India that

[30]Bagchi, ed. and trans., *Pre-Aryan and Pre-Dravidian*. These ideas of an "Austric" language group first proposed by the missionary and anthropologist Wilhelm Schmidt in 1906 continues to be disputed up to today. On this see Reid, "The Current Status of Austric."

led Suniti Kumar Chatterji to welcome Indonesia's choice of Indonesian as the national language because it revived this ancient kinship link between the two countries (chapter 29 in this volume)

Much of the Society's work appearing in its *Journal* was not only inspired by, or in response to, the work of Lévi and other French and Dutch scholars, but was built upon the "empiric orientalism" practised by the École française, and the Oudheidkundige Dienst of *in situ* research by colonial officials to conserve the monuments, record the epigraphy and collect the old texts and manuscripts.George Coedès, the long-serving Director of the École française, pointed out that

> curiously, India quickly forgot that her culture had spread over such vast domains to the east and southeast. Indian scholars have not been aware of this fact until very recently; it was not until a small group of them, having learnt French and Dutch, studied with the professors of the Universities of Paris and Leyden, that they discovered, in our works and those of our colleagues in Holland and Java, the history of what they now call, with justifiable pride, 'Greater India.'[31]

Paul Mus, Coedès' colleague and secretary-librarian at the École française and, for a short time, covering the duties of Director in the early 1930s, also pointed out that R.C. Majumdar was able to publish his compilation of *Inscriptions of Kambuja* in *devanāgari* font because the École française had helped with rubbings and photostats of the inscriptions.[32]

In drawing on the work of the French and Dutch scholars, the Greater India scholars often went beyond what the French or Dutch scholars claimed for Indian influence. O.C. Gangoly took the opportunity of reviewing a small book by the Dutch archaeologist W.F. Stutterheim on *Indian Influences in Old Balinese Art* (chapter 22 in this volume)to push the argument for an Indian origin of Balinese art much further than Stutterheim did. He also criticised the Angkor conservator Henri Parmentier's 1925 study of the pre-Angkor roots of Angkor architecture, claiming that "there was a tendency, somewhat unscientific, on the part of the French archaeologist to regard Cambodian art as the autochthonous and original products of Khmer genius – and to discount, if not disregard, the part of Indian art." [33]

H.B. Sarkar (1905-90) also stressed the Indian elements and influence on the literature of Java and Bali in his *Indian Influences on the Literature of Java and Bali*, which the Society published.[34] He could do this because generations of Dutch officials and scholars had systematically collected many

[31] Coedès in his preface to his 1944 "synthesis," entitled *Histoire ancienne des états hindouisés d'Extrême-Orient,* and repeated in subsequent editions of this work entitled *Les états hindouisés d'Indochine et d'Indonésie,* pg. 4 and in its English translation as *The Indianized states of Southeast Asia* pp xvii.

[32] Mus' book review in *Journal of the American Oriental Society* of Majumdar, *Inscriptions of Kambuja.*

[33] Gangoly, review in *Rūpam.*

[34] As its Publication no. 6 in 1934, reprinted in New York by AMS Press in 1981.

of the old Javanese and Balinese texts and transcribed them. But his strong emphasis on the Indian influences in these texts provoked a lengthy critical review by the leading Dutch scholar of old Javanese literature, C.C. Berg,[35] which challenged Sarkar to issue a reply (seen in chapter 21 in this volume). Sarkar's epigraphic studies such as that of the 828 Śaka era copper-plate of Borobudur (chapter 27 in this volume), culminating in the two-volume *Corpus of the Inscriptions of Java* published in 1972,[36] builds upon earlier transcriptions and translations of the inscriptions by Dutch scholars. Sarkar became one of the Society's most prolific scholars, producing from the 1950s onwards along series of nuanced papers, monographs and books that did not quite follow the more strident calls of his teacher, R.C. Majumdar and his other Greater India Society colleagues for recognition of an ancient Indian colonization of Southeast Asia.[37]

To position itself and its work in relation to the "empiric orientalism" of the French and Dutch colonial institutions, the Society had to keep very close track of what they were doing. Every issue of the *Journal* carried detailed notices or reviews of new publications and listing of the contents of the leading journals in Southeast and Central Asian studies. In addition, the *Journal* also commissioned more detailed retrospective reflections of the state of the art in "Greater India research." U.N. Ghosal's "Progress of Greater India Research during the last 25 Years (1917-1942)" is a remarkable compilation for what it highlights of how closely the members of the Society monitored colonial research in their colonies and their interests. For example on Borobudur, Ghosal highlights reports on the conservation of the monument and what can be inferred of its Indian origins. Lévi's work on tracing the reliefs of the buried base of the Borobudur to the *Karmavibhāga* is highlighted as a new discovery, while Paul Mus' large study of the deep symbolism of the monument is mentioned only in passing, probably because it was seen as presenting no new information, and was only a synthesis of current ideas of Buddhist art, archaeology and theology, in which the Society appeared to have little interest.

The members of the Greater India Society were then interested only in the "facts" of the diffusion of Indian influence across the Indian Ocean and further which they could derive from the "empiric orientalism" of colonial scholarship.

[35] Berg's review in *Annual Bibliography of Indian Archaeology*. For other reviews, see Th. Pigeaud in *Djawa* and Gonda in *Indische Gids*.

[36] *Corpus of the Inscriptions of Java*. Sarkar says that publication of this compilation of old Javanese inscriptions was a task left to him by his teacher, R. C. Majumdar (*Cultural Relations*, p. 75) who had intended to undertake it as a follow-up to his 1953 compilation of *Inscriptions of Kambuja*.

[37] A collection of his papers edited by Kumar as *Glimpses of Early Indo-Indonesian Culture* was published in 2001. Other book length studies by Sarkar include: *Some Contribution[s] of India*; *Literary Heritage of South-East Asia*; *Cultural Relations between India and Southeast Asian Countries*; and *Trade and Commercial Activities*.

They sought through toponymy to identify the ports from which Indian mariners and traders started their voyages across the Indian Ocean and the locations they arrived at to establish trading settlements which grew into colonies, in a manner perhaps not too different from the Dutch and British a millennium later. They attempted to identify the Indic roots of the Sanskrit words in the Angkor and old Javanese epigraphy, search for the Indian Urtext of the old Javanese literature or sources of the art of Śrīvijaya or Java and Angkor, in order to establish that culturally Śrīvijaya, Śailendra Java, Angkor, and Champa were Hindu colonies, ruled according to the laws of Manu. This proposed reconstruction of an Indian *mission civilatrice* to create a Greater India was however part of a larger historiography project to rewrite Indian colonial history into a more nationalist history in parallel with India's struggle for independence.

Ramesh Chandra Majumdar (1888-1980) led the writing of a nationalist history of India which incorporated Southeast Asia as Hindu colonies. Majumdar's major work was his large three volume study entitled *Ancient Indian Colonies in the Far East*. Volume I on Champa was published by the Greater India Society in 1927 while volumes II and III on Indonesia, entitled *Suvarnadvipa,* were published in 1937 and 1938. Majumdar apparently planned to, but did not succeed in writing further volumes on Angkor[38] and Siam as Indian colonies. Instead he became involved in the co-editing of a large eleven-volume *History and Culture of the Indian People* from 1951 to 1977, and wrote a three-volume *History of the Freedom Movement in India.* In this nationalist framing of India's past, Indian influence spread across the Indian Ocean through Southeast Asia to create an Indianized cultural empire during the Golden Age of Indian history from the Mauryas in the third century BCE to the Guptas in the seventh century CE. This culture empire was terminated by the forces of an expanding *dār al-islām* crossing into Sind and inaugurating a "medieval" era in India's past which lasted until the eighteenth century. The struggle for freedom from British colonialism, according to Majumdar, originated not in the Sepoy Mutiny and revolt of 1857, but in the middle-class resistance to the 1905 partition of Bengal which ushered in a new era of Indian history driven by the "nationalization of Hinduism."[39]

For Majumdar and his peers, this nationalization of Hinduism was necessary to challenge the prevailing evangelical Christian perception of Hinduism by British Protestant missionaries, especially William Carey and William Ward, and their negative impressions and assessments of Hinduism which was accepted by the Benthamite Utilitarian political theorist James Mill (1773-1836) in his study entitled *The History of British India.*[40] The long section of

[38] His views on Angkor are contained in a series of lectures *Kambuja-deśa or An Ancient Hindu Colony*.

[39] As argued by Chatterjee, "History and the Nationalization of Hinduism."

[40] The book, online at http://oll.libertyfund.org/?option=com_staticxt&staticfile=show.php%3Ftitle=1867,became a textbook for East India Company officials when it was published

ten chapters on Hinduism in the first volume of the book became the dominant understanding of Hinduism for East India Company and colonial officials governing India. For Mill, Hinduism was a "backward" culture notable for its superstition, ignorance and apathy. The Indian nationalist historians countered this antagonistic British colonial understanding of Hinduism by turning to alternative, more sympathetic and affirmative, colonial readings of the Hindu texts, as initiated by William Jones (1746-94), which became the basis for the construction of a new Hinduism which Romila Thapar has dubbed "syndicated Hinduism."[41] It was on this modern construct of a universalizing and proselytizing Hinduism that the members of the Greater India Society based their reconstruction of an Indian colonization of Southeast Asia.

Unfortunately this ancient Indian colonisation of the "Far East" (as Majumdar termed it), came to an end with the Islamic conquest of India. The middle stanzas of Tagore's *Shribijaylakshmi* express this sense of loss:

> The time wore on, the dark night came upon us,
> and we knew not each other
>
> The seat we shared was buried under the dust
> Raised by Time's chariot wheels
>
> By the receding flood of oblivion I was borne back
> To my own lonely shore
> My hands bare, my mind languorous with sleep. . .

The members of the Greater India Society apparently also sensed this loss and terminated their narrative of an Indian colonisation of the "Far East" with the construction of Borobudur and Prambanan in Central Java and Angkor Wat. The East Javanese temples were seen to be a degenerate expression of the Hindu spirit which survives in a variant form on Bali today and surprised Tagore on his 1927 visit to the island.

THE LIMITATIONS OF A VISION

It was a young Dutch socio-economic historian by the name of Jacob Cornelis van Leur who had the temerity to challenge his seniors' reconstruction of Indonesian history as a narrative of Dutch colonization in his 1934 doctoral dissertation *Eenig beschouwingen betreffende den ouden Aziatischen handel* and widen his case against an earlier Indian colonization assumed by some Dutch

---

in 1818 and thereafter went through several editions and revisions. Majumdar provided a six-page discussion and summary of Mill's *History* in his 57-page *Historiography in Modern India* and concludes that "no comment of mine is necessary upon this extraordinary anti-Hindu outburst of a British historian of repute," before quoting Horace Hayman Wilson's critical comments on Mill in his updating of Mill's work.

[41] Thapar, "Syndicated Moksa," p. 21, an updated version of which can be found in Sontheimer and Kulke, eds., *Hinduism Reconsidered*.

archaeologists and scholars to explain the construction of the Borobodur and other Indian-influenced monuments in Java.[42] Arguing against the thesis that the "flag follows trade,"[43] Van Leur documented the difficulties the Dutch flag had following the traders of their East India Company, and claimed that likewise, Indian settlers did not follow their traders to established Indian kingdoms:

> There were, then, no 'Hindu colonization' in which 'colonial states' arose from intermittent trading voyages followed by permanent trading settlements; no 'Hindu colonies' from which the primitive indigenous population and first of all its headmen took over the superior civilization from the west; and no learned Hindus in the midst of Indian colonists as 'advisers' to their countrymen.

The alternative narrative van Leur proposed begins with the Brahmanization of South India that was occurring around the beginning of the Christian era. As South India, more than any other part of the subcontinent was the trading region for Indonesians, van Leur projected that:

> By means of that trade, whether carried on as Indonesian shipping, or through the intermediary of Indian shipping, the Indonesian rulers and aristocratic groups came in contact with India, perhaps seeing it with their own eyes. In the same sort of attempt at legitimizing their interests involved in 'international trade' (in the first place *vis-à-vis* Indian traders themselves), and (though this was probably of secondary importance) organizing and domesticating their states and subjects, they called Indian civilization to the east—that is to say, they summoned the Brahman priesthood to their courts.[44]

For van Leur, the historical analogy is that "one must imagine that Southeast Asia was 'Hinduized' in the same way the German civilization of the middle ages extended its influence far beyond the limits of German group colonization, in the same way the Graeco-Byzantine hierocracy set its stamp on the civilization of Russia."[45]

Van Leur's strident calls for the rewriting of Indonesian history on its own terms, rather than within the framework of Dutch or, for an earlier era, ancient

[42] Van Leur's major publications have been translated and published as *Indonesian Trade and Society*. Van Leur died in action as a volunteer naval officer during World War II at the age of 34.

[43] The underlying issue is our understanding of the nature of trade in the first millennium. Was it a "peddling trade" as van Leur proposed, following Max Weber's reconstruction of trade in medieval Europe as a peddling trade of traders moving from town to town with their stock of goods? Or was it some kind of non-market driven trade for status products or redistribution of scarce resources and commodities as Karl Polanyi has proposed in his "Traders and Trade." See also Webb, "The Flag Follows Trade," for an analysis of issues in linking trade to state formation in the premodern world.

[44] *Indonesian Trade and Society*, p. 98.

[45] *Indonesian Trade and Society,* p. 104. Van Leur reiterated his critique of his colleagues' writing of Hindu immigration and colonization of Indonesia in a critical book review of Staple, ed., *Geschiedenis van Nederlandsch Indië*, translated in *Indonesian Trade and Society,* pp. 249-60.

Indian history, raises profound issues[46] about the feasibility of such a project, a concern which continues to bedevil historians today.[47] What does it mean to write an "autonomous" history of Indonesia when *first* the materials are Dutch archival records and Sanskrit texts for that earlier era of Indonesian history? Can the Dutch archival records or the Sanskrit texts be read to support the alternative narrative of an autonomous world of Southeast Asia with its own history, which van Leur is proposing?[48] *Second,* how is the historical significance of events for a narrative alternative to Indian colonization or Dutch colonialism in Indonesia to be assessed? Was Mahmud of Ghazni's campaign of destruction and plunder in northern India from 1000 CE the beginning of the end of Hindu rule and its colonization of the Far East? Was Vasco da Gama's arrival at Calicut on 27 May 1498 the nadir of the long medieval epoch of Indian history and the inauguration of 500 years of Western domination of Asia which truncated India's relations with Southeast Asia even more, as Indian nationalist historians[49] accept? *Third* and more difficult are the moral judgments underpinning the writing of an Indonesia-centric history. How are European claims of their responsibility to "civilise" the natives and liberate them from the tyranny of their despotic rulers, as James Mill argues as a justification of utilitarian British rule over India, to be evaluated? The paradox is that the Greater India Society scholars apparently saw no contradiction between their struggle for freedom from British colonialism and imperialism and their justification for an earlier Indian colonization of Southeast Asia.

The moral argument of the Greater India Society scholars was that in contrast to the violence of European colonialism to subjugate the colonised, Indian colonization of the Far East was peaceful, humane, benign and welcomed by the pre-literate natives. Majumdar declared this in his first major work published by the society:

[46] Resink, "Lets over Europacentrische," pp. 26ff on the debate which van Leur sparked within Dutch academic circles and first introduction of the perspective of history he was attacking: "Europe-centric history." The English translation of van Leur's writings launched another debate about revising the writing of Southeast Asia's history to examine it from within, on which, see Machin, "Colonial Post-mortem."

[47] See especially Wolters, *History, Culture, and Region* for a deep insight into what is involved in reading Southeast Asia's premodern past from within.

[48] C.C. Berg in a long series of studies beginning in the 1930s attempted to go beyond the classical philological editing of texts to developing a deep reading of their meanings, trying to read the text through the eyes of the priest or court poet writing it. His last major work, *Maya's hemelvaart in het Javaanse Buddhisme,* is a dense reading of the thirteenth century *Deśawarṇa* (*Nāgarakṛtāgama*) by Mpu Prapañca. Berg provides a brief English introductions to his thinking in his contribution to Soedjatmoko et al. eds., *An introduction to Indonesian Historiography* and Hall, ed., *Historians of South-East Asia*. Wolters, *History, Culture and Region* is also deeply preoccupied with how to read local writings and in his 1999 revised edition provides a critical survey of other attempts to read local writings.

[49] See K. M. Panikkar's still debated study entitled *Asia and Western Dominance.*

[The] . . . regeneration of the Cham power in the second century AD was due to the introduction of a new element in her politics, viz, the Indian colonists. From this time forward . . . [the Chams] . . . cheerfully submitted to their foreign masters and adopted their manners, customs, language and religion. They were politically merged in the Indian elements and there was a complete cultural fusion between the two races.[50]

Such views raise the spectre of the inequality of human races[51] as moral justification for colonialism. Majumdar and his generation of historians must have been aware of the consequences of interplaying race, language and ethnology in the search for India's origins in an Aryan immigration into India. They would have studied how such a racist framing and meta-narrative of Indian civilization as the outcome of a clash and subsequent intermixture of fair-skinned civilized "Aryan" invaders (related to the Europeans) and the dark savages native to India was developed by colonial Indology at Kolkata in the nineteenth century for the colonial state.[52] But in their writing of a national history for an independent India they did not challenge the "empiric orientalism" underpinning this meta-narrative of British colonialism,[53] which was then extended to explain and justify an Indian colonization of the Far East.

Within such an understanding of race, language and ethnology underpinning colonialism Majumdar and his Bengali colleagues stoutly rejected any role for local creativity or "genius" in adopting and adapting Indian culture. For them Borobudur was the apogee of Gupta art. But the architecture of the Borobudur—a stūpa surrounded by 72 latticed stupas, each containing a Buddha statue on top of a large five terraced truncated pyramid—has no parallel anywhere in the Indic world. Majumdar however is convinced that it is an Indic stupa and his explanation of the discrepancy between the Indic architectural norms for a stupa and the Borobudur is that:[54]

The whole structure was intended as a *stūpa*, pure and simple, but the disproportion between the actual *stūpa* on the top and the massive support in the shape of nine terraces is difficult to explain and has given rise to a great deal of explanation. It has been viewed as a novel principle of construction, but then we have neither any precedent nor any imitation of it. Mystic meaning has been attributed to the shape of the entire structure, but it is too speculative. Perhaps the simplest and the most rational explanation is furnished by the nature of the soil. When the first terrace was constructed as the real base of the great dome, it sank considerably and showed that the soil was unable to bear the weight of a huge solid domical *stūpa* as was originally contemplated. Hence the size of the *stūpa* was considerably diminished and the addition of successive terraces was a constructional necessity rather than the introduction of a new style.

[50] Majumdar, *Ancient Indian Colonies in the Far East,* vol. 1: *Champa*, p. 21, n. 9.

[51] First raised by the Frenchman Comte de Gobineau (1816-1862) in his polemical *Essai sur l'inégalité des races humaines.*

[52] See Thomas R. Trautmann's unpacking of this "racial theory of Indian civilization" in his *Aryans and British India.*

[53] Documented by the archaeologist Dilip K. Chakrabarti in a polemical plea for more archaeological spadework to counter this racist meta-narrative of Indian history in his *Colonial Indology*. Note his scathing comments on Majumdar on pp. 3-4 and 213.

[54] In his *Ancient Indian Colonization in South-East Asia,* p. 83.

The massive monuments in the different Hindu colonies, even in their most developed forms of diverse types, are clearly evolved, step-by-step, from the original Indian prototype, and even the best sculptures of Java show the indelible stamp of Indian style. Broadly speaking, this colonial art shows definite influences of the Gupta, Pallava and Pala styles of art, though they were modified, to a greater or less degree, by the local genius in most cases.

At stake is the issue of whether Javanese society was a dormant mass that the "awakened Indian spirit fecundated . . . thus procreating a new life that was predestined to develop into a new independent organism in which foreign and native elements were to merge into an indissoluble entity," as the long-serving head of the Oudheidkundige Dienst F.D.K. Bosch argued.[55] In a similar biological metaphor, the École française Director George Coedès saw "the early civilizations of Indochina and Indonesia as branches springing directly from the main trunk of Indian civilization . . . that India supplied much more than a graft, . . . that it was the whole plant that was exported, and that according to the nature of the ground where it flourished, the same plant bore fruits of varying flavour."[56] Bosch has widened his argument for the centrality of fundamental Indic cosmological ideas about the origins of life in the interplay of the primordial elements of fire and water becoming embedded in this deep cultural infrastructure of Javanese society and is reflected in its rituals up to today.[57]

However, not all Dutch and French scholars agreed with their more Indianist colleagues. W.F. Stutterheim, who succeeded Bosch as Director of the Oudheidkundige Dienst and Paul Mus, a member of the École française, detected a more vibrant local society in Southeast Asia characterised by a pervasive belief in the prowess of their ancestors to shape their lives and as such, requiring their veneration in various monuments and sculptures.[58] This deification of kings to be worshipped after their death in what Mus felicitously terms "substitute bodies" or "living tombs" was not usual practice in the

[55]Bosch is quoted from his 1946 inaugural address on "The Problem of the Hindu Colonization of Indonesia" as Professor of Archaeology and Ancient History of Southeast Asia at the University of Leiden, translated in his *Selected Studies in Indonesian Archaeology,* p. 20.

[56]Coedès is quoted from the English translation of *The Making of South-East Asia*, p. 55. He has elaborated his ideas in "Le substrat autochtone et le superstructure," and "L'osmose Indienne en Indochine et en Indonésie."

[57]Bosch's ideas were first worked out in a 1919 article, of which a translation entitled "A Hypothesis as to the Origin of Indo-Javanese art," was published in the art journal *Rūpam* edited by O. C. Gangoly. Bosch further developed his ideas in a 1948 study which has become a seminal text, The *Golden Germ*.

[58]For example, Stutterheim in his "Lets over Prae-Hinduistische" and others have documented this pervasive cult of ancestors in their fieldwork. Mus and other French ethnologists observed it in their work among the Chams, on which see Bayly, "French Anthropology," for how this fieldwork shaped French thinking about Indian influence in Southeast Asia.

Sanskrit cultures of north India. The Greater India Society scholars had problems accepting that Borobudur or Angkor Wat may have been more tombs than temples.[59]That kings could be deified as a *devarāja* was another Southeast Asian practice the Indian scholars struggled with, and sought Indian analogies and precedents to explain it. [60]The 1053 CE Sdok Kak Thom inscription located near the Thai-Cambodian border town of Aranyaprathet has attracted special attention for its description of the rituals for the installation of a *devarāja.*[61]

For Stutterheim and Mus, Borobudur and other monuments were less Indian inspirations and creations, and more local adaption and application of the Hindu architectural models to express these deep local beliefs about ancestors.[62] Mus in a massive 800-page study[63] argued that the Borobudur is a complex use of Mahayana theologies and cosmologies to express very local beliefs. In another remarkable short monograph on Champa,[64] Mus argued for an indigenous Cham society absorbing and adapting Indian concepts to create their temples before reverting to their local forms. Understandably, Mus' call for "India to be seen from the East" did not evoke any response from Indian scholars. It was to these views of the Dutch and French scholars who were adopting a very local perspective of the monuments in their studies that Majumdar was responding.

However, it was not only with this issue of local creativity and "genius" in adapting and utilizing Indian culture for their needs and interests that the Greater India Society scholars had difficulties. They also appeared ambivalent about the role of Buddhism. On the one hand, the members of the Society appear to have accepted Alexander Cunningham's (1814-93) reconstruction that Theravada and Mahayana Buddhism enjoyed its heyday under the Mauryan ruler Aśoka, and by the seventh century CE was in deep decline. But on the

[59] For example, Chatterjee, in "Recent Advances in Kambuja Studies," where he discusses Coedès' attempts to reconcile conclusions by Przyluski and others that the Khmer monuments were more tombs.

[60] See Sengupta, *God & King*.

[61] See Chakravarti's study, *The Sdok Kak Thom Inscription*. Kamaleshwar Bhattacharya has attempted a new translation of the Sanskrit portion of the inscription in his *A Selection of Sanskrit inscriptions from Cambodia* ([Siem Reap]: Centre for Khmer Studies, 2009), pp. 123ff.

[62] On this tension between the outlook of the Indianist / Indologists and the "sociologists" in interpreting the Cham and Angkor monuments as reflected in the work of Paul Mus during his time at the École française, see Manguin, "Un <sociologue> parmi les orientalistes." See also the contributions by Mabbett, "L'Indologie de Mus: Sociologie ou cosmologie?" and Yves Goudineau, "Génologie des forms."

[63] Stutterheim's short monograph on "Chandi Barabudur," was the start for Paul Mus' massive 800-page synthesis *Barabudur*. Mus' 302-page introduction to the 1935 publication of his book has been translated by Macdonald, *Barabudur*.

[64] Mus, "Cultes indiens et indigenes au Champa," was reprinted with the significant title *L'Inde vu de l'Est: cultes indiens et indigenes au Champa* and has been translated and edited by Mabbett and Chandler as *India Seen from the East*.

other hand, they were also aware that in its Tantric forms emanating from Pala Bengal between the eighth and twelfth centuries CE, Buddhism had left a legacy in not only Southeast Asia, but also China and Tibet. How to reconcile this Pala legacy abroad with their narrative of Muslim termination of Hindu rule and its relations with its colonies in Greater India was an issue the Society's scholars did not appear to resolve.[65]

Indian trading contacts and cultural influence in Southeast Asia did not begin with Aśoka or end with Mahmud of Ghazni's campaign of destruction and plunder in northern India from 1000 CE. Indian shipping continued under the Mughals as Mookerji has documented. Indian trade with Southeast Asia continued with Tamil merchants and their guilds in the southern Thai port of Takuapa and north Sumatra. The Arabic texts edited by G. Ferrand suggest growing Arab and Persian shipping and trade in the Bay of Bengal and the South China Sea from the eighth, if not the seventh century, constructing a new Indo-Islamic trading world—*al-bahr al hindi*—which drew the Indian subcontinent and West Asia tighter together with Southeast Asia to form a new trading world. It may not be a coincidence that Borobudur, Angkor and the Ananda temple in Bagan were all constructed during this era of *al-bahr al-hindi* when Southeast Asians were drawn closer to India. Hinduism in its new south Indian *bhakti* variations and Buddhism in its Vajrayana variations continued to shape India's relations with Southeast Asia.

Whether viewed from the shores of Kalinga or the rice fields of Angkor, Southeast Asia was part of a wider Hindu world with Sanskrit as its language. Sanskrit, as Sheldon Pollock has shown,[66] exerted a dominant homogenizing influence on this Hindu world from Sind to Bali, creating a Sanskrit cosmopolis for much of the first millennium of the Christian era. That cosmopolis did not die at the close of the millennium as the nationalist historians of India feared, but, as Pollock controversially argued, was transformed by the emergence of local identities appropriating and expressing the classical Sanskrit idioms in new vernacular forms.[67] Sarkar and others were aware of this transformation in their study of the development of old Javanese literature. However, the issue is that, where Pollock and other Sanskritists see a millennium long monolithic and normative uniformity, others see heterogeneity and local innovation in creating distinct regional centres of Sanskrit before its "vernacular millennium." Issues of identifying centres and defining peripheries in this Sanskrit cosmopolis become complicated with the Sanskrit epigraphy of Angkor rivalling if not better than any Indian epigraphy,

[65]The Greater India Society scholars appear to have faced the same quandary as the British Orientalists and archaeologists of how to define the later Buddhist images of Eastern India, which Janice Leoshko discusses in her *Sacred Traces,* Chapter 4.

[66]Pollock, *The Language of the Gods*.

[67]On the relevance of Pollock to our understanding of Sanskrit in Southeast Asia, Bronkhorst, "The Spread of Sanskrit"; Ali, "The Early Inscriptions of Indonesia"; and Romain, "Indian Architecture" in Manguin et al., eds., *Early Interactions*.

Vasco da Gama's arrival at Calicut in 1498 was not a turning point in Indian history as William Moreland taught his Indian students.[68] The various merchant empires of Europe may have controlled Asian trade to Europe, but they did not control much of the trade within Asia. [69] That trade remained in the control of Asian merchants and their networks which European traders had no access to except through a series of middlemen the Portuguese called *compradors.* Indian trade with Southeast Asia continued in *bazaars* they dominated through networks of Gujarati; Chulia and Malabar traders with their Indonesian and Chinese counterparts.[70] The Sanskrit cosmopolis, as Pollock points out,[71] was again transformed in a "second vernacular revolution" and continued to define the forms of knowledge in early modern Asia. None of these events and trends was however in the historical mindscapes of most of the Greater India Society members. Tagore could therefore write that

Thy call reaches once again
Across hundreds of speechless years

I'll come to thee, look in thine eyes,
And seem to see there the light of the wonder
Of our first meeting in thy forest glade
Of the gladness of a promise.

It will have to remain a counterfactual issue whether the Society could have avoided or reduced these strictures on its vision and work if they had heeded more carefully the teachings of Sylvain Lévi and other French scholars they looked to. As Susan Bayly[72] points out, the Greater India Society admirers of Lévi "oversimplified" his ideas on Indian humanism and its diffusion to the Transgangetic lands. Where Lévi detected a process of "give and take" in this interaction of cultures and civilizations, a process of acculturation that the French anthropologists and archaeologists and their Dutch colleagues in Indonesia saw,[73] but the Greater India Society scholars did not perceive.

The Society could perhaps also have more closely followed their *Purodha*

[68] Moreland's views were adopted by nationalist historians like K.M. Panikkar, author of *Asia and Western Dominance*, who saw in it a convenient justification and start point for their critique of some 500 years of Western colonization of Asia. Moreland's ideas continue to be discussed today, e.g. Das Gupta, "Moreland Hypothesis," pp. 20-22.

[69] See Chaudhuri's pioneering study of Asian commercial capitalism, *Trade and Civilization.*

[70] Om Prakash's edited volume *The Trading World of the Indian Ocean* represents the shift in historiographical focus from an India turning inwards from the 16th century to an India actively responding to external regional and wider global change in the Indian Ocean.

[71] See Pollock's arguments for Sanskrit continuing as the language of science and scholarship into early modern times in his *Forms of Knowledge.*

[72] Bayly, "Imagining 'Greater India,'" pp. 720ff.

[73] Strenski, "Zionism, Brahmanism and the Embodied Sacred." See also Bayly, "French Anthropology."

Tagore as the metaphoric "fox" of the Greek poet Archilocus, "who knows many things" in the search for universal humanity in all of us.[74] Instead, the Society's members chose to follow M.K. Gandhi as Archilocus' metaphoric "hedgehog" who focuses on only "one big thing," a non-violent (*satyagraha*) nationalist struggle for freedom. For Tagore, with his flowing robes and beard, Gandhi in his coarse loincloth and bald pate was his antithesis: the "Mahatma," the "Great Soul" of India's nationalism, which Tagore abhorred. For Gandhi, Tagore was the "Great Sentinel" warning us "against the approaching enemies called Bigotry, Lethargy, Intolerance, Inertia and other members of that brood." Arguably, the Society members' "hedgehog" preoccupation with documenting India's hegemonic cultural influence on Southeast Asia as part of its glorious past to a prelude of India's new future did not match Tagore's punitive empathy for others. They should have explored more Tagore's elliptical comments on the spirit of civilizations and not subverted it to serve their nationalism. The Society's members may have done better to follow Tagore in looking at Bali and Java for what they could learn about themselves, rather than what they could give.

THE LEGACY OF A VISION

Reviewing the work of his peers, H.B. Sarkar assessed in 1985 that:

> It is doubtless true that the works of RCM[ajumdar] and of some of those who had banded themselves together under the Greater India Society had made great impact on the scholarly world of the time. The works of Kalidas Nag and P.N. Bose were not however noted for their depth, but those of U.N. Ghoshal and P.C. Bagchi in Afghanistan and Central Asia respectively, were marked by deep scholarship. The output of B.R. Chatterji is not much, being mainly limited to a work on Cambodia and another on *India and Java* (the second edition of this book is called *History of Indonesia*), but the works of RCM and K.A. Nilakanta Sastri have left their impact on succeeding generations of scholars; I think this will continue for many years to come. . . . The chief value of the work of RCM lies, in my opinion, in bringing the subject to the desk of scholars who have not the linguistic equipment to read Dutch or French.[75]

Sarkar may have said the same of himself and his attempt to translate N.J. Krom's 1931 *Hindoe-Javaansche geschiedenis*.[76] But the sub-text of his comments on Majumdar appears to be an attempt to salvage the academic reputation of his teacher by disassociating him from the more ideological

[74] See Larson's "The Hedgehog and the Fox" for this insightful application of Sir Isaiah Berlin's reworking of this elliptical reference from a fragment of Achilocus into a classic analysis of Tolstoy's view of history. I would like to thank Dr T.C.A. Raghavan for presenting me with a copy of this publication.

[75] Sarkar, *Cultural Relations*, p. 84.

[76] Sarkar only managed to translate and publish the first three chapters of 129 pages of Krom's 467-page book. In hindsight, Sarkar may have been over-ambitious, and perhaps should have tried to translate instead Krom's 180-page chapter on "De Hindoe-Javaansche tijd."

agenda of the Greater India Society. Sarkar's own deep scholarship may have led him to be aware that Kalidas Nag's visions lacked depth and were ultimately untenable. As Sarkar noted, "After the achievement of independence, both the Greater India Society and its *Journal* ultimately became defunct. The term 'Greater India' though sanctioned by ancient and medieval usage, is no longer in fashion in India or elsewhere and has been replaced by the expression 'Indianized States'."[77]

Sarkar's comment on the Society's dissolution appears to be a carefully considered depreciation of the Society's achievements. As one of longest surviving founding members of the Society, Sarkar must have realized that the Society's dissolution was in large part a realization that new approaches to the accumulating archaeological evidence and alternative readings of the epigraphy and classical texts were seriously disconfirming the Society's reconstructions of Southeast Asia's past and attempts to view it from India. Sarkar may also have realized that the reasons for the Society's establishment in 1926 were very much a reflection of the times and that the Society contained within its vision the seeds of its own destruction.

Calcutta at the time of the Greater India Society's founding was in a state of intellectual ferment. Although it had lost its status as the capital of Britain's Indian empire to New Delhi in 1911, Calcutta was still the second city and gateway linking the empire's hinterland with the Indian Ocean trading world. Improved sea communications, expanding educational facilities and increasing circulation of published materials widened the intellectual horizons of the local intelligentsia in their reflections on Bengal's past and future. New understandings of Asia and its civilizations were developed by Swami Vivekenanda, Tagore and Bhudev Mukhopadhyay among others in response to perceptions of the decline of a materialistic Western civilization, especially after the Great War.[78] This vision of India rising to lead Asia into a new Asian Renaissance inspired the founding fathers of the Greater India Society to project an earlier cycle of Indian humanism and spiritualism emanating from Bengal across the Indian Ocean to civilize the indigenes of Southeast Asia. The founding fathers of the Society could not have anticipated how their efforts to embed their version of

[77] Sarkar, *Cultural Relations,* p. 76. The preceding and subsequent pages of this chapter of Sarkar's work are a remarkable piece of self-reflection and assessment of the work of his peers. On the term "Greater India," Sarkar was more defensive of its use in 1970 when he wrote in the "Introduction" to his *Some Contribution[s] of India to the Ancient Civilization of Indonesia and Malaysia* that "the term [Greater India] refers to a time when any other designation would have been most inappropriate. Even a few years ago, we were accustomed to hear of Indo-China, Indian Archipelago, Further India, etc., in serious works written by European scholars, and the practice has not entirely disappeared. The term Greater India fills up a bigger canvas; it is quite appropriate and there is no better substitute for it."

[78] For other contemporary Indian constructions of East and West and Indo-Asian humanism, see Hays, *Asian Ideas of East and West,* pp. 246ff. For a similar Chinese debate on "civilizations" see Duara, "The Discourse of Civilizations and Pan-Asianism."

Bengal's wider and longer history as a sub-plot of the emerging national history of India would become appropriated as a major theme of India's post-independence national past.

Neither could they have anticipated that their emphasis on a dynamic, if not muscular, Hinduism as inspiration and driving force for India's first millennium cultural empire in Southeast Asia would be appropriated by groups advocating a more strident Hindu-driven nationalism. The term *Hindutva* to express this fusion of religion, ethnicity and territoriality in an encompassing Indian nationalism was proposed by V.D. Savarkar in 1923. Like Gandhi, Tagore and others, Savarkar was struggling to redefine Hinduism in response to colonial constructs of Hinduism as a religion. But Savarkar also could not anticipate how his 1920s attempt to contextualize Hinduism would become a controversial text in the politics of post-1975 imposition of Emergency rule by Indira Gandhi.[79] This assertiveness of Hindu nationalist forces today is probably captured in the intentions of one group, the Mahavir Mandir Trust of Patna, to build what the Trust has claimed will be the largest Hindu temple in the world in the style of Angkor Wat on a 110-acre site in Vaishali district of north Bihar, where they believe the god Ram visited the ancient kingdom of Vaishali on the banks of the Ganges. The Trust has retracted its initial announcements that the temple it proposed will be a replica of Angkor Wat, and now proclaims on its website that "in respect to the sentiments of the Cambodian people" it will change the name of its temple from Viraat Angkor Wat Ram Temple to Viraat Ramayan Mandir. The Trust declares that it hopes its temple "will cement further the strong bond between the two culturally rich countries India and Cambodia. This strong bond has existed between the two countries for a period of two millennia."[80] The old Greater India Society's vision of Angkor Wat as one of the pinnacles of Hindu art has taken on a new reality.

By the time of its demise, the Greater India Society had developed a way of thinking and looking at Southeast Asia from the shores of India. The authority of such perspectives of Southeast Asia was reinforced by the leading members of the École française who were reaching similar conclusions. The long-serving director of the École française George Coedès may have been the most successful in consolidating an "Indianist" perspective of Southeast Asia in his 1944 "synthesis" entitled *Histoire ancienne des états hindouisés d'Extrême-Orient*. The 1948 second edition carried the title *Les états Hindouisés d'Indochine et d'Indonésie,* and its 1964 third edition was translated into

[79] See Sharma's "On Hindu, Hindustān, Hinduism and Hindutva" on how the etymologies of these terms impact on modern Indian political discourse.

[80] See http://www.mahavirmandirpatna.org/Viraat%20Ramayan%20Mandir.html The Trust justifies its decision to build a replica of Angkor Wat or a temple in its style on the grounds that there is no copyright on historic monuments. The Mahabodhi temple of Bodh-gaya, the Trust points out, has been replicated at least ten times in Thailand, Myanmar, Sri Lanka, India and the United States.

English as *The Indianized States of Southeast Asia.* In its various reprints the text continues to serve as the standard reference for new generations of students of Southeast Asia's early history. Coedès' "synthesis" is today the classic elaboration of Sylvain Lévi's assertion that India "produced its definitive master-works only through the activity of the foreigner or on foreign soil. . . . In architecture, it is in distant Cambodia and Java that we must seek the two marvels born of the Indian genius: Angkor and the Borobudur." Echoing Lévi, Coedès reiterates that "we know of no monument in India resembling even remotely the Bayon or Angkor Thom or the Borobudur. And yet these monuments are pure productions of the Indian genius, the deep meaning of which is apparent only to the eyes of the Indianist."[81]

Such visions of India's deep and extensive cultural influence on Southeast Asia have pervaded Indian social memories and its perceptions of Southeast Asia up to today. Jawaharlal Nehru's reflections on his *Discovery of India* while imprisoned from 1942-45 is a significant expression of these social memories. He recalled his amazement and excitement when he first read about "Champa, Cambodia and Angkor, Śrivijaya and Majapahit [which] suddenly rose out of the void, took living shape, vibrant with that instinctive feeling which makes the past touch the present." Reflecting on India's condition in 1942, Nehru thought that there is still "a feeling of respect and friendship for India, for old memories endure and people have not forgotten that there was a time when India was a mother country to these [*sic*] and nourished them with rice fare from her own treasure-house. Just as Hellenism spread from Greece to the countries of the Mediterranean and in Western Asia, India's cultural influence spread to many countries and left its powerful impress upon them." [82] It is a moot issue whether Nehru's discovery of Greater India shaped his thinking about India's destiny to lead not only Southeast Asia, but also other ex-colonial states in a non-aligned movement during the Cold war. Nehru was wise enough to recognize the contradictions between India's post-independence foreign policy of pan-Asianism and assumptions of an ancient Greater India.[83]

The historian, scholar and statesman-politician K.M. Panikkar (1895-1963) has also drawn freely on these social memories of a first millennium Indian

[81] Coedès, *The Indianized States of Southeast Asia,* p. 255. It may be worth recalling that the 1944 edition of this text was intended to be a complement to a history of India by Vallée-Poussin, *Dynasties et histoire de l'Inde.* On the significance of this text in the annals of the École française, see the evaluation and critique by Clémentin-Ojha and Manguin, *Un siècle pour l'Asia*, pp. 130f.

[82] Nehru, *The Discovery of India* (available online at http://www.scribd.com/doc/31927774/The-Discovery-of-India-Jawaharlal-Nehru), pp. 201 and 209. Nehru concludes his reflections on India's ancient relations with Southeast Asia by appreciatively quoting Lévi's "From Persia to the China Sea" passage.

[83] Keenleyside, "Nationalist Indian Attitudes Towards Asia"; and also Bayly, "Imagining 'Greater India,'" p. 736.

maritime domination of the Indian Ocean to argue for a post-Independence naval strategy of reasserting Indian naval control over the Indian Ocean. [84] More recently the former Indian Chief of Naval Staff, Admiral Arun Prakash has revived Panikkar's insights to frame a "grand historical narrative" of an Indian maritime identity justifying India's creation of a robust Navy to safeguard its maritime interests today.[85]

Indira Gandhi may have recalled these memories of India's cultural empire from her correction of her father's *Discovery of India* when in 1982 she responded to appeals from the then new Cambodian government led by Heng Samrin for help in preserving Angkor, and approved the despatch of teams of Archaeological Survey of India archaeologists to survey and study the feasibility of restoring Angkor Wat. K.M. Srivastava, the Archaeological Survey of India archaeologist who led the 1982 team to survey and report on the feasibility of restoring Angkor Wat had no doubt about what motivated India to come "forward to assist the new [Cambodian] regime in every possible manner, in order to revive the age-old ties of close relationship. We stood as brothers since the first century of the Christian era, for a brother must stand to extend help in the hour of calamity." [86] Based on these reports, the Archaeological Survey of India undertook the conservation and restoration of Angkor Wat between 1986 and 1992.[87]

In 2006 the Indian Ministry of External Affairs entered into another agreement to support the Archaeological Survey of India to conserve the thirteenth century Ta Prohm temple. Indian Ambassador to Cambodia Pradeep Kumar Kapur writes of how his

> visits to these [Angkor] temples made us aware of the depth of our bonding from ancient times. India has had close cultural links for millennia with several countries of Southeast Asia. What is unique about our links with Cambodia is the fact that India has been involved with the nation from its very inception and conception. . . .There was perhaps a continuous stream of architects, teachers, scholars, preachers, and others who came from India to settle in Cambodia. It cannot be ruled out that the Cambodians themselves visited India to explore the cultural artefacts most suited to their civilization. There seems to have been an extraordinary blossoming of talent due to this fusion of synergies between the two countries.[88]

[84] Panikkar, *India and the Indian Ocean.*

[85] Quoted from Prakash, *India's Maritime Growth.* See also Prakash's call for more Indian awareness of their naval history , "At Sea about Naval History."

[86] Srivastava, *Angkor Wat.*

[87] A very brief summary of the Archaeological Survey of India's work is available online at http://asi.nic.in/asi_abroad.asp. For a summary of the controversy surrounding this Indian restoration, see Ciochon and J. James, "The Battle of Angkor Wat."

[88] Kapur's "My Encounter with Cambodia" provides the historical context to the monument and an argument for what defines authenticity in the restoration of historical monuments, an issue in the restoration of Angkor monuments among various countries with diverse philosophies of what constitutes authenticity in restoration. The Archaeological Survey of India (with the hindsight wisdom of its work on Angkor Wat) has published its plans in *Ta Prohm Temple.*

In June 2012, the Indian Ministry of External Affairs also responded to a Vietnamese request for assistance to help conserve parts of the old Cham capital at Mỹ Sơn and, on the basis of an Archaeological Survey of India team survey, committed US $3 million to the restoration of Mỹ Sơn.[89] In offering to help conserve Ta Prohm and Mỹ Sơn, India is not only joining a global effort to preserve World Heritage Sites, but more specifically, heritage sites which it perceives to be part of its patrimony the Greater India Society was the first to stake out.

A new generation of Indian institutions and scholars are today continuing the legacy of the Greater India Society's search for the origins of Indian influence in Southeast Asia and promoting awareness of this influence . The Indira Gandhi National Centre for the Arts has been publishing a series of translations of classic French and Dutch studies on Southeast Asia.[90] The International Academy of Indian Culture founded by Raghu Vira has for some time been publishing annotated translations of the old Javanese texts in its Śata-piṭaka Series.[91] The ambitious Project of History of Indian Science, Philosophy and Culture under the Centre for Studies in Civilizations has dedicated one part of the first volume of its "History of Science, Philosophy and Culture in Indian Civilization" to India's *Interaction with Southeast Asia.* The editor G.C. Pande attempts in his Introduction to dissociate himself and his colleagues from the "discourse established by Majumdar and Coedès", arguing instead for "the development of common and parallel civilizational trails in India and Southeast Asia through a long process of interchange. For a time classical Indian languages, religions and art were creatively adapted and developed in Southeast Asia." [92]

In conclusion, it is not only through continuing academic studies and publications that a younger generation of Indians are reminded of the deep roots of India's "Look East" Policy today, but perhaps more significantly through festivals like the annual *bālijātra* celebrated in Orissa's old capital of Cuttak, on the Gabagadia Ghat of the Mahanadi River and the Mahavir Mandir Trust's plans to construct a replica of Angkor Wat in north Bihar. A society remembers itself not only in inscribed records and historiography, but also

[89] http://news.in.msn.com/national/article.aspx?cp-documentid=5570373 for the 6 November Indian news report and http://english.thesaigontimes.vn/Home/travel/aroundcountry/24226/for the 9 September Vietnamese report.

[90] A translation of Stutterheim's *Rāma-legends and Rāma-reliefs in Indonesia* was published in 1989, as one of its earliest publications. Other publications include Mus' extended introduction to his Borobudur study (see n. 63 above) in 1998; and Mireille Bénisti's (1909-1993), *Stylistics of Early Khmer Art* in 2003.

[91] Including, *inter alia,* the old Javanese *Sutasoma* by Soewito Santoso in 1975 ; *The Indonesian Mahābhārata* by I Gusti Putu Phalgunadi in 4 volumes from 1990-1997; and Jan Gonda's benchmark reference *Sanskrit in Indonesia,* which went into a second edition in 1973.

[92] Pande, "Introduction," p. xxviii.

through its oral traditions and in its social memories of non-inscribed ritual performances, bodily practices and in the construction of the landscape around it.[93] The *bālijātra* festival[94] which invites participants to launch model ships commemorating the start of voyages across the Indian Ocean to Bali is the enactment of an imagined past, as is the proposed reconstruction of a replica of Angkor Wat. Both the *bālijātra* ceremonies and the plans for a new Angkor Wat are expressions of a rising India "Looking East" and derive from the visions of the Greater India Society earlier looking East across the Indian Ocean. The legacy of the Greater India Society is a living and dynamic heritage which diverse groups in successive decades are reinterpreting for incorporation into their different agendas.

[93] See Connerton's *How Societies Remember* on how we remember who we are and express ourselves more in commemorative ceremonies and other ritual performances than in literary texts. Connerton's analysis of memory as embedded in what we perform follows from the work of Maurice Halbwachs (1877-1945) who was the first to point out that our personal memories of who we are and the world around us are very much defined by our participation in larger social and collective memories of the social groups we are members of. Halbwachs' major 1925 text has been translated as *On Collective Memory* by Lewis A. Coser. Halbwachs also showed how our perceptions of our landscape like the Holy Land of Christianity is shaped and constructed by the collective memories of pilgrims, which changes over time. In this tradition of French scholarship on social memory, Pierre Nora and his team have in his *Rethinking France* detailed how French identity and values are very much shaped by the social memories of its ceremonies, symbols, landscapes and other "memory sites."

[94] The *bālijātra* is today a major trade fair and festival in the Orissa annual festival cycle.

REFERENCES

Ali, Daud. "The Early Inscriptions of Indonesia and the Problem of the Sanskrit Cosmopolis." In *Early interactions between South and Southeast Asia: Reflections on Cross-cultural Exchange,* edited by P-Y Manguin et al., pp. 277-98. Singapore: Institute of Southeast Asian Studies and New Delhi: Manohar, 2011.

Anonymous. "India helps My Son-Cham Tower Complex Restoration." Available online at http://english.thesaigontimes.vn/Home/travel/aroundcountry/24226/.

___. "Vietnam Seeks ASI Help in Restoring Ancient Temples." 6 November 2011. Available online at http://news.in.msn.com/national/article.aspx?cp-documentid=5570373.

Archaeological Survey of India. *Ta Prohm Temple: A Conservation Strategy*. New Delhi: Director General Archaeological Survey of India, 2006.

Bagchi, P[rabodh] C[handra]. *India and China*. Calcutta: Greater India Society, 1927.

Bagchi, Prabodh Chandra, ed. and trans. *Pre-Aryan and Pre-Dravidian in India*. Calcutta: University Press, 1929.

Barth, A. and A. Bergaigne. *Inscriptions Sanscrites du Cambodge: Inscriptions Sanscrites de Campa*. Paris: Imprimerie nationale, 1893.

Bayly, Susan. "French Anthropology and the Durkheimians in Colonial Indochina." *Modern Asian Studies* 34, no. 3 (2000): 581-622.

___. "Imagining 'Greater India': French and Indian Visions of Colonialism in the Indic Mode." *Modern Asian Studies* 38, no. 3 (2004): 703-44.

___. "India's 'Empire of Culture': Sylvain Lévi and the Greater India Society." In *Sylvain Lévi (1863-1935): Etudes Indiennes, Histoire Sociale Bibliothèque de l'Ecole des Hautes Études, Sciences Religieuses*, edited by L. Bansat-Boudon and R. Lardinois, pp. 193-212. Turnhout, Belgium: Brepols Publishers, 2007.

Bénisti, Mireille. *Stylistics of Early Khmer Art*. New Delhi: Indira Gandhi National Centre for the Arts and Aryan Books International, 2003.

Berg, C. C. "Review of Sarkar's *Indian Influences on the Literature of Java and Bali*." *Annual Bibliography of Indian Archaeology* 9 (1936): 37-50.

___. "Javanese Historiography—A Synopsis of Its Evolution." In *Historians of South-East Asia, Historical Writings on the Peoples of Asia*, edited by D.G.E. Hall, pp. 13-23. London: Oxford University Press, 1961.

___. "The Javanese Picture of the Past". In *An Introduction to Indonesian Historiography*, edited by Soedjatmoko et al., pp. 87-117. Ithaca: Cornell University Press, 1965.

___. *Maya's Hemelvaart in het Javaanse Buddhisme,* Verhandelingen der Koninklijke Nederlandse Akademie van Wetenschappen, afd. Lett., n.r. 74. Amsterdam: Noord-Hollandsche Uitgevers, 1969.

Bharucha, Rustom. *Another Asia: Rabindranath Tagore & Okakura Tenshin*. New Delhi: Oxford University Press, 2006.

Bhattacharya, Kakali Ray. *Index to the Journal of the Greater India Society*. Kolkata: Centre for Archaeological Studies & Training, Eastern India, 2009.

Bhattacharya, Kamaleswar. *A Selection of Sanskrit Inscriptions from Cambodia*. Siem Reap: Centre for Khmer Studies, 2009.

Bosch, F.D.K. "A Hypothesis as to the Origin of Indo-Javanese Art." *Rūpam* 17 (1924): 6-61.

___. *The Golden Germ: An Introduction to Indian Symbolism*. 's-Gravenhage: Mouton, 1960.

___. "The Problem of the Hindu Colonization of Indonesia." 1947 Inaugural Address as Professor of Archaeology and Ancient History of Southeast Asia at the University of Leiden), translated in *Selected Studies in Indonesian Archaeology,* Koninklijk Instituut voor Taal-, Land- en Volkenkunde, *Translation Series 5*. 's-Gravenhage: Martinus Nijhoff, 1961.

Bose, Sugata. "Rabindranath Tagore and Asian Universalism." In *An Age in Motion: The Asian Voyages of Rabindranath Tagore*: *Selected Speeches and Writings on Rabindranath Tagore*, pp. 10-18. Singapore: Nalanda-Sriwijaya Centre, [2011]. Available online at: http://nsc.iseas.edu.sg/others/tagore_booklet.htm

Brandes, J.L.A. and N.J. Krom. *Oud-Javaaansche Oorkonden; Nagelaten Transscripties,* Verh. Bataviaasch Genootschap van Kunsten en Wetenschappen, dl. LX. Batavia: Albrecht, 1913.

Bronkhorst, J. "The Spread of Sanskrit in Southeast Asia." In *Early Interactions Between South and Southeast Asia: Reflections on Cross-cultural Exchange,* edited by P-Y Manguin et al., pp. 263-76. Singapore: Institute of Southeast Asian Studies and New Delhi: Manohar, 2011.

Chakrabarti, Dilip K. *Colonial Indology: Sociopolitics of the Ancient Indian Past*. New Delhi: Munshiram Manoharlal Publishers, 1997.

Chakravarti, Adhir. *The Sdok Kak Thom Inscription* (2 volumes). Calcutta Sanskrit College Research Series no. CXI-CXII. Calcutta College: Sanskrit College, 1978-80.

Chakravarti, N.P. *India and Central* Asia. Calcutta: A.C. Sarkar, 1927.

Chatterjee, B.R. *Indian Culture in Java and Sumatra,* pt. I, *Text;* pt. II, *Inscriptions* (with N. P. Chakravarti). Calcutta: A.C. Sarkar, 1927.

Chatterjee, B.R. "Recent Advances in Kambuja Studies." *Journal of the Greater India Society* 6, no. 1 (1940): 138-48.

Chatterjee, Partha. "History and the Nationalization of Hinduism." *Social Research* 50, no. 1 (1992), 111-49; reprinted in *The Oxford India Hinduism Reader*, edited by Vasudha Dalmia and H. von Stietencron, pp. 231-61. New Delhi: Oxford University Press, 2007.

Chaudhuri, K.N. *Trade and Civilization in the Indian Ocean: An Economic History from the Rise of Islam to 1750*. Cambridge: Cambridge University Press, 1985.

Chaudhuri, Sukanta. *Tagore Looks East*. Nalanda-Sriwijaya Centre Working Paper Series No. 2 (May 2011). Available online at http://nsc.iseas.edu.sg/documents/working_papers/nscwps002pdf).

Ciochon, R. and J. James. "The Battle of Angkor Wat." *New Scientist* 1686 (14 October 1989): 52-57. Available at http://www.newscientist.com/article/mg12416864.000-the-battle-of-angkor-wat-cambodias-national-symbol.html.

Clémentin-Ojha, Catherine and Pierre-Yves Manguin. *Un siècle pour l'Asia: L'École française d'Extrême-Orient, 1898-2000*. Paris: Les Editions du Pacifique and EFEO, 2001.

Coedès, George. *Histoire ancienne des états hindouisés d'Extrême-Orient*. Hanoi: Imprimerie d'Extrême-Orient, 1944.

___. "Le substrat autochtone et le superstructure indienne au Cambodge et la Java." *Cahiers d'histoire Mondial* 1, no. 2 (1953): 368-77.

___. "L'osmose Indienne en Indochine et en Indonésie." *Cahiers d'Histoire Mondiale* 1, no. 4 (1954): 827-38.

___. *The Indianized States of Southeast Asia,* edited by W. F. Vella and translated by S.B. Cowing. Honolulu: University of Hawai'i Press, 1968.

___. *The Making of South-East Asia*. London: Routledge, 1966.

Comte de Gobineau, Arthur. *Essai sur l'inégalité des races humaines*. Paris: P. Belfond, 1967.

Connerton, Paul. *How Societies Remember*. Cambridge: University Press, 1989.

Coomaraswamy, A[nanda] K[entish]. *History of Indian and Indonesian Art*. Reprint, New York: Dover Publications, 1965.

Das Gupta, A. "Rabindranath Tagore in Indonesia: An Experiment in Bridge Building." *Bijdragen tot de Taal-, Land- en Volkenkunde* 158 (2002): 451-77.

Das Gupta, Ashin. "Moreland hypothesis." In *Mariners, Merchants and Oceans: Studies in Maritime History*, edited by K. S. Mathew, pp. 19-24. New Delhi: Manohar, 1995.

Duara, Prasenjit. "The Discourse of Civilizations and Pan-Asianism." *Journal of World History* 12, no. 1 (2001): 99-130.

Finot, Louis. "Chronique: Inde." *Bulletin de l'École française d'Extrême-Orient* 27 (1927): 504-07.

Frost, Mark R. *That Great Ocean of Idealism: Calcutta: The Tagore Circle and the Idea of Asia, 1900-1920*. Nalanda-Sriwijaya Centre Working Paper Series No. 3 (June 2011). Available online at http://nsc.iseas.edu.sg/documents/working_papers/nscwps003.pdf.

Gangoly, O.C. "Review of W. F. Stutterheim's *Indian Influences in Old Balinese Art*." *Rūpam* 32 (1927): 138.

Ghoshal, U. P. *Ancient Indian Culture in Afghanistan*. Calcutta: Greater India Society, 1928.

Gonda, Jan. "Review of Sarkar's "*Indian Influences on the Literature of Java and Bali*." *Indische Gids* 57 (1935): 637-43.

___. *Sanskrit in Indonesia*. New Delhi: International Academy of Indian Culture, 1973.

Goudineau, Yves. "Génologie des Forms et Scenarios Rituels dans l'Asie des Moussons: L'orientalism de Paul Mus Entre Sociologie et Iconologie." In *L'espace d'un regard: L'Asie de Paul Mus (1902-1969)*, edited by David Chandler and Christopher E. Goscha, pp. 129-42. Paris: Instut d'Asie Orientale, Les Indes savants, 2006.

Halbwachs, Maurice. *On Collective Memory*, edited and translated by Lewis A. Coser. Chicago: University of Chicago Press, 1992.

Handy, E. S. Craighill. "The Renaissance of East Indian Culture: Its Significance for the Pacific and the World." *Pacific Affairs* 3, no. 4 (1930): 362-69

Hay, Stephen N. *Asian Ideas of East and West: Tagore and his Critics in Japan, China, and India*. Cambridge: Harvard University Press, 1970.

Kapur, Pradeep K. "My Encounter with Cambodia." In *Ta Prom: A Glorious Era in Angkor Civilization*, edited by Pradeep Kumar Kapur and Sachchidanand Sahai, pp. xxiii-xxvi. Bangkok: White Lotus Press, 2007.

Keenleyside, T. A. "Nationalist Indian Attitudes towards Asia: A Troublesome Legacy for Post-independence Indian Foreign Policy." *Pacific Affairs* 55, no. 2 (1982): 210-30.

Kern, Hendrik. "De Invloed der Indische Beschaving op Java en Omliggende Eilanden." In *Verspreide Geschriften*, edited by Hendrik Kern, pp. 182-3. 's-Gravenhage: Martinus Nijhoff, 1928.

Kumar, Bachchan, edited. *Glimpses of Early Indo-Indonesian Culture: Collected Papers of Himansu Bhusan Sarkar*. New Delhi: Aryan Books International and the Indira Gandhi National Centre for the Arts, 2001.

La Vallée-Poussin, Louis de. *Dynasties et Histoire de l'Inde depuis Kanishka Jusqu'aux Invasions Musulmanes*. Paris: E. de Boccard, 1935.

Larson, G. J. "The Hedgehog and the Fox; Metaphors for the Intellectual Life of Gandhi and Tagore." In *Something Old, Something New: Rabindranath Tagore 150 Birth Anniversary Volume, Marg* 62, no. 3, edited by Pratapaditya Pal, pp. 96-107. Mumbai: Radhika Sabavala for the Marg Foundation, 2011.

Laurens, Henry. "Sylvain Lévi, la Palestine, les États-Unis et l'avenir du Judaïsme." In *Sylvain Lévi (1863-1935): Etudes Indiennes, Histoire Sociale*, edited by L. Bansat-Boudon and R. Lardinois, pp. 289-300. Turnhout, Belgium: Brepols Publishers, 2007.

Leoshko, Janice. *Sacred Traces: British Explorations of Buddhism in South Asia*. Aldershot: Ashgate Publishing, 2003.

Lévi, Sylvain. *La Doctrine du Sacrifice dans les Brâhmanas*. Paris: Ernest Leroux, 1899.

___. "Religions Universelles et Religions Particulières." In *Mémorial Sylvain Lévi*, edited by Sylvain Lévi and Louis Renou, pp. 126-32. Paris: P Hartmann, 1937.

Lipsey, Roger. *Coomaraswamy, 3: His Life and Work,* Bollingen Ser. LXXXIX. Princeton: Princeton University Press, 1977.

Mabbett, Ian. "L'Indologie de Mus: Sociologie ou Cosmologie?" In *L'espace d'un Regard: L'Asie de Paul Mus (1902-1969)*, edited by David Chandler and Christopher E. Goscha, pp. 117-28. Paris: Instut d'Asie Orientale, Les Indes savants, 2006.

Mabbett, I.W. and D.P. Chandler, ed. and trans. *India Seen from the East: Indian and Indigenous Cults in Champa*, Monash Papers on Southeast Asia, no. 3. Monash University: Centre of Southeast Asian Studies, 1975.

Macdonald, A.W., trans. *Barabudur: Sketch of a History of Buddhism Based on Archaeological Criticism of the Texts*. New Delhi: Indira Gandhi National Centre for the Arts and Sterling Publishers, 1998.

Machin, G.I.T. "Colonial Post-mortem: A Survey of the Historical Controversy." *Journal of Southeast Asian History* 3, no. 2 (1962): 129-38.

Majumdar, R[amesh] C[handra]. *Ancient Indian Colonies in the Far East,* vol. 1: *Champa.* Lahore: The Panjab Sanskrit Book Depot, 1927.

___. *Kambuja-deśa or An Ancient Hindu Colony in Cambodia: Sir William Meyer Lectures 1942-43.* Madras: University of Madras Press, 1944.

___. *Ancient Indian Colonization in South-East Asia.* The Maharaja Sayajirao Gaekwad Honorarium Lecture, 1953-54. Baroda: Maharaja Sayajirao Gaekwad University Press, 1955.

___. *Historiography in Modern India,* Heras Memorial Lectures 1967. Bombay: Asia Publishing House, 1970.

Malamoud, Charles, "Sylvain Lévi, Les Etudes Védiques et la Doctrine du Sacrifice." In *Sylvain Lévi (1863-1935): Etudes Indiennes, Histoire*, edited by L. Bansat-Boudon and R. Lardinois, pp. 103-10. Turnhout, Belgium: Brepols Publishers, 2007.

Manguin, Pierre-Yves. "Un <Sociologue> Parmi les Orientalistes: Paul Mus à l'École Française d'Extrême-Orient." In *L'espace d'un Regard: L'Asie de Paul Mus (1902-1969)*, edited by David Chandler and Christopher E. Goscha, pp. 109-116. Paris: Instut d'Asie Orientale, Les Indes savants, 2006.

Mill, James. *The History of British India*, 6 vols. (3rd edition). London: Baldwin, Cradock, and Joy, 1826). Available online at http://oll.libertyfund.org/?option=com_staticxt&staticfile=show.php%3Ftitle=1867

Mookerji, Radhakumud. *Indian Shipping: A History of the Sea-borne Trade and Maritime Activity of the Indians from the Earliest Times*. Bombay: Longmans, 1912; 1957.

Mus, Paul. "Cultes Indiens et Indigenes au Champa." *Bulletin de l'École française d'Extrême-Orient* 33 (1933): 367-410. Reprinted as *L'Inde vu de l'Est: cultes indiens et indigenes au Champa,* translated and edited by I. W. Mabbett and D. P. Chandler.

___. "Review of Majumdar's *Inscriptions of Kambuja.*" *Journal of the American Oriental Society* 77, no. 2 (1957): 150-1.

___. *Barabudur: Esquisse d'une Histoire du Bouddhism Fondée sur la Critique Archéologique des Texts*. Reprint, Paris: Arma Artis, 1990.

Nag, Kalidas. *Les Theories Diplomatiques de l'Inde Ancienne et l'Arthaçâstra*. Paris: Jean Maisonneuve, 1923.

___. *India and the Pacific World.* Calcutta: Book Company, 1941.

Nehru, Jawaharlal. *The Discovery of India*. Delhi: Oxford University Press, 1989. Available online at http://www.scribd.com/doc/31927774/The-Discovery-of-India-Jawaharlal-Nehru.

Nivedita. "Introduction." In *Ideals of the East: With Special Reference to the Art of Japan*, by K. Okakura, pp. ix-xxi. London : J. Murray, 1920.

Nora, Pierre. *Rethinking France = Les lieux de mémoire* , translated by Nary Trouille. Chicago: University of Chicago Press, *c.* 2009-2010.

Okakura, Kakuzo. *The Book of Tea*. Reprint, New York: Dover Books, 1964.

___. *The Ideals of the East: With Special Reference to the Art of Japan*. Reprint, Berkeley: Stone Bridge Classics and Tokyo: IBC Publishing, 2007.

Pande, Govind Chandra. "Introduction." In *India's Interaction with Southeast Asia,* edited by Govind Chandra Pande, pp. . History of Science, Philosophy and Culture in Indian Civilization, vol. I, part 3. New Delhi: Centre for Studies in Civilizations, 2006.

Panikkar, K. M. *Asia and Western Dominance: A Survey of the Vasco da Gama Epoch of Asian History 1598-1945*. Reprint, London: Allen & Unwin Ltd., 1959.

___. *India and the Indian Ocean*. George Allen & Unwin Ltd., 1962.

Phalgunadi, I Gusti Putu. *The Indonesian Mahābhārata*. New Delhi: International Academy of Indian Culture and Aditya Prakashan, 1990.

Pigeaud, Th. "Review of Sarkar's *Indian Influences on the Literature of Java and Bali.*" In *Djawa* 15 (1935): 97-98.

Polanyi, Karl. "Traders and Trade." In *Ancient Civilization and Trade*, edited by J.A. Sabloff and C. C. Lamberg-Karlovsky, pp. 133-54. Albuquerque: University of New Mexico, 1975.

Pollock, Sheldon. *The Language of the Gods in the World of Men: Sanskrit, Culture, and Power in Premodern India*. Berkeley: University of California, 2006.

___, ed. *Forms of Knowledge in Early Modern Asia: Explorations in the Intellectual History of India and Tibet, 1500-1800*. Durham: Duke University Press, 2011.

Prakash, K.M. "At Sea about Naval History." *Sunday Tribune*, 2 September 2007. Available online at http://www.bharat-rakshak.com/NAVY/History/1600s/Prakash.html.

___. *India's Maritime Growth: Rationale and Objectives*. National Maritime Foundation Policy Paper No. 1. New Delhi: National Maritime Foundation Varuṇa Vāk Series, July 2011.

Prakash, Om, ed. *The Trading World of the Indian Ocean, 1500-1800*. History of Science, Philosophy and Culture in Indian Civilization, vol. III, part 7. Delhi: Pearson Education in South Asia for the Centre for Studies in Civilizations, 2012.

Reid, Laurence. "The Current Status of Austric: A Review and Evaluation of the Lexical and Morphosyntactic Evidence." In *The Peopling of East Asia: Putting Together Archaeology, Linguistics and Genetics*, edited by Laurent Sagart et al., pp. 134-62. London: RoutledgeCurzon, 2005.

Resink, G. J. "Iets over Europacentrische, Regioncentrische en Indoncentrische Geschiedeschrijving." *Oriëntatie* 37 (1940): 22-30.

Romain, J. "Indian Architecture in the 'Sanskrit Cosmopolis': The Temples of the Dieng Plateau." In *Early Interactions Between South and Southeast Asia: Reflections on Cross-Cultural Exchange,* edited by P-Y Manguin et al., pp. 299-316. Singapore: Institute of Southeast Asian Studies and New Delhi: Manohar, 2011.

Santoso, Soewito. *Sutasoma: A Study in Javanese Wajrayana*. New Delhi: International Academy of Indian Culture, 1975.

Sarkar, Himansu Bhusan. *Some Contribution[s] of India to the Ancient Civilizations of Indonesia and Malaysia*. Calcutta: Punthi Pustaka, 1970.

___. *Corpus of the Inscriptions of Java (Corpus Inscriptionum Javanicarum) (up to 928 A.D.* Calcutta: Firma K.L. Mukhopadhyay, 1971-2.

___. *Literary Heritage of South-East Asia*. Calcutta: Firma KLM, 1980.

___. *Indian Influences on the Literature of Java and Bali*. Reprint New York: AMS Press, 1981.

___. *Cultural Relations between India and Southeast Asian Countries*. New Delhi: Indian Council for Cultural Relations and Motilal Banarsidass, 1985.

___. *Trade and Commercial Activities of Southern India in the Malayo-Indonesian World (up to A.D.1511)*. Calcutta: Firma KLM, 1986.

Sarkar, Sumit. "Nationalism and 'Stri-Swadhinata,' The Contexts and Meanings of Rabindranath's *Ghare-Baire."* In *Beyond Nationalist Frames: Relocating Postmodernism, Hindutva, History*, edited by Sumit Sarkar, pp. 112-52. Delhi: Permanent Black, 2002.

Sengupta, Arputha Rani, ed. *God & King: The Devarāja cult in South Asian Art and Architecture*. New Delhi: Regency Publications, 2005.

Sharma, Arvind. "On Hindu, Hindustān, Hinduism and Hindutva." *Numen* 49, no. 1 (2002): 1-36.

Srivastava, K.M. *Angkor Wat and Cultural Ties with India*. New Delhi: Books & Books, 1987.

Strenski, Ivan. "Zionism, Brahmanism and the Embodied Sacred: What the Durkheimians Owe to Sylvain Lévi." In *The Sacred and its Scholars: Comparative Methodologies for the Study of Primary Religious Data*, edited by Thomas A. Idinopulos and E.A. Yonan, pp. 19-35. Leiden and New York: E.J. Brill, 1996.

Stutterheim, Willem Frederik. "Lets over Prae-Hinduistische bijzettingsgebruiken op Java." *Mededelingen der Koninklijke Nederlandse Akademie van Wetenscappen* afd. Lett., n.r. 2. Amsterdam: Noord-Hollandsche uitgeversmaatschappij, 1939.

Stutterheim, Willem Frederik. "Chandi Barabudur: Name, Form and Meaning." In *Studies in Indonesian Archaeology*, pp. 1-62. Koninklijk Instituut voor Taal-, Land- en Volkenkunde, *Translation Series*. 's-Gravenhage: Martinus Nijhoff, 1956.

___. *Rāma-legends and Rāma-reliefs in Indonesia*, translated by C.D. Paliwal and R.P. Jain. New Delhi: Indira Gandhi National Centre for the Arts and Abhinav Publications, 1989.

Tagore, Rabindranath. *Nationalism*. New Delhi: Penguin Books India, 2009.

Thapar, Romila. "Syndicated Moksa." *Seminar* 313 (Sept. 1985), p. 21; also in *Hinduism Reconsidered*, edited by Sontheimer & H. Kulke, pp. 54-81. New Delhi: Manohar Publishers, 1997 revised edition.

Trautmann, Thomas R. *Aryans and British India*. Berkeley: University of California Press, 1997.

van Leur, Jacob Cornelis. *Indonesian Trade and Society: Essays in Asian Social and Economic History,* Selected Studies on Indonesia by Dutch Scholars, vol. 1. den Haag and Bandung: W. van Hoeve Ltd, 1955.

___. "Review of F.W. Staple's, *Geschiedenis van Nederlandsch Indië*," translated in *Indonesian Trade and Society,* pp. 249-60. The Hague: W. Van Hoeve Publishers, 1967.

Wang, Bangwei and Tansen Sen. *India and China: Interactions through Buddhism and Diplomacy: A Collection of Essays by Professor Prabodh Chandra Bagchi*. London: Anthem Press.

Webb, M.C. "The Flag follows Trade: An Essay on the Necessary Interaction of Military and Commercial Factors in State Formation." In *Ancient Civilization and Trade*, edited by Sabloff and Lamberg-Karlovsky, pp. 155-93. Albuquerque: University of New Mexico Press, 1975.

Weill, Georges. "Entre l'Orient et l'Occident: Sylvain Lévi Président de l'alliance Israélite Universelle (1920-1935)." In *Sylvain Lévi (1863-1935): Etudes Indiennes, Histoire Sociale*, edited by L. Bansat-Boudon and R. Lardinois, pp. 391-420. Turnhout, Belgium: Brepols Publishers, 2007.

Wolters, O.W. *History, Culture, and Region in Southeast Asia*. Ithaca, N.Y.: Southeast Asia Program Publications, Southeast Asia Program, Cornell University, 1999, revised edn.

Zimmer, Heinrich. *The Art of Indian Asia*, edited by Joseph Campbell. Bollingen Series XXXIX. 2nd edn., New Jersey: Princeton University Press, 1960.

PROGRAMMATIC STATEMENTS OF THE SOCIETY AND ITS VISION

Foreword

To know my country in truth one has to travel to that age when she realised her soul, and thus transcended her physical boundaries; when she revealed her being in a radiant magnanimity which illumined the Eastern horizon making her recognized as their own by those in alien shores who were awakened into a great surprise of life; and not now when she has withdrawn herself within a narrow barrier of obscurity, into a miserly pride of exclusiveness, into a poverty of mind that dumbly revolves round itself in an unmeaning repetition of a past that has lost its light and has no message to the pilgrims of the future.

Rabindranath Tagore

Foreword
Journal of the Greater India Society

To know my country in truth one has to travel to that age when she realised her soul, and thus transcended her physical boundaries; when she reveals her being in a radiant magnanimity which illumined the Eastern horizon making her recognized as their own by those in alien shores who were awakened into a great surprise of life; and rot now where she has withdrawn herself within a narrow barrier of obscurity, into a miserly pride of exclusiveness, into a poverty of mind that durably revolves round itself in an unmeaning repetition of a past that has lost its light and has no message so the pilgrims of the future.

RABINDRANATH TAGORE

Source: *Journal of the Greater India Society* (I/1, 1934, 1).

CHAPTER 1

Greater India: A Study in Indian Internationalism

KALIDAS NAG

INDIAN ATTITUDE TOWARDS HISTORY

India enjoys the precarious privilege of possessing no systematic history well defined by Time and Space. She has passed, like every other country, through all the phases of historical evolution—sociological and religious, intellectual and political; yet with a peculiar obstinacy India has hitherto refused to develop a hierarchy of orthodox historians and a consistent tradition of national history. No doubt she has acknowledged from very ancient times the value of chronicles (Itihasa-Purana) as an intellectual discipline, yet such compositions have remained, down to the appearance of the Muhammadan historians, as subsidiary to her proverbially rich contributions to Religion and Ethics.

To Western scholars, trained in methods of precision applied to the intensive study of national histories, the apparent apathy towards the preservation of what they call "national glories" seems not only to be a little disconcerting but even derogatory to the prestige of the Indians as an intellectual people. Diagnosis of this peculiar malady led to the development of diverse theories: lack of political cohesion and comprehension of national solidarity, oriental fatalism and obsession of hereafterism—all seemed to have combined to weaken the Hindu faculty of precision and thereby sap the foundation of historical science in India. The present degradation of India was considered to be the cumulative effect of these national perversities and well-wishers of India, both outside and inside, have sought to cure it by reconstructing her history on a national basis.

Without discounting the value of possessing a systematic national history or disputing India's poverty in that department of literature, one may still plead that the judgement passed on the Indian people from that standpoint is nevertheless superficial and unjust. A people that could evolve at least forty

This paper was read in connection with a *Symposium* on "The Role of Internationalism in the Development of Civilisation", invited by the Peace Congress of Lugano (Switzerland) in August 1922 which was attended by the master spirits of modern Europe like Romain Rolland, Bertrand Russel, Hermann Hesse and others. I beg to express in this connection my best thanks to my friends of the "International League of Women for Peace and Freedom" for provoking this study and for publishing a *French version* of this monograph in the Rassegna Internationale (Rome, April 1923)—K.N.

Source: Greater India Society Bulletin, no. 1, 1926.

centuries ago, the earliest collection of human lyrics in the form of the Vedic Hymns, may be credited with a certain amount of creative imagination. A people that could present to the world about 2,500 years ago a scientific treatise on grammar like that of Panini may aspire to a certain amount of analytical power and capacity for system-building. A people that could perpetuate through millenniums, the traditions of its religious, social and intellectual life—not through writing but by a phenomenal memory, may claim to possess some sort of instinct for precision and preservation. So it still remains a problem why such people did not develop a tradition of national history in the special sense of our days. This is a paradox which has not been explained by condescending theorists of the historical school.

It may not be an improbable hypothesis that the Hindus somehow felt history, with its interminable details of wars and treaties, of triumphs and dissolutions, as a poor portraiture of the real national life and a very unsatisfactory and imperfect reflection of its creative activities. They boldly challenged the validity of the *world of phenomena* and tried to discover the *world of permanence* immutable beyond all phenomena. Revulsion from things transient and temporal produced almost an obsession of the Absolute and the Eternal. Thus India neglected History and developed Philosophy; or rather, she considered the quest of the spirit for the Eternal Verity as the real history of Humanity (*cf.* Nag: "The Humanisation of History", *Modern Review*, February 1923). Thus whilst her next door neighbour China was (quietly) laying the foundation of early science and inventions; while Babylonia was developing the earliest astronomy and legal code; while Egypt was composing her *Book of the Dead* and was trying to triumph over Death by her titanic architecture—India was quietly scaling the supernal heights of Human Philosophy—the Himalayas of Thought—and was filling the world with the reverberations of profound questions about Existence and Non-existence, Death and Immortality—fundamental problems of human life—through the Vedic Hymns:

There was not the Non-existent nor the Existent then,
There was not the air nor the heaven which is beyond,
What did it contain ? Where ? In whose protection ?
Was there water, unfathomable, profound ?
There was not Death nor Immortality then,
There was not the beacon of Night nor of Day,
That one breathed, windless, by its own power
Other than *That* there was not anything beyond.

Rigveda IV.i.112

Descending from the heights of primitive speculation when India was confronted with the problems of complex life, in and through the expansion of her Society, she subordinated *Economics* to her science of Equity and Jurisprudence and *Politics* to her science of Ethics. Thus she developed her *Dharmasastra* and *Raja-dharma* with *Dharma*, the Eternal as the mainstay of her secular history. This obsession of the Eternal in her temporal life has its counterpart in the obsession of the Universal in her national history and that of the Formless in her aesthetic discipline, creating mystic forms and symbolic art-languages. So Hindu apathy towards History is the effect of a malady that is deeper than the diagnosis of our modern historians. It is a triple complex which some future psycho-analyst may analyse to satisfy our curiosity! Meanwhile I beg leave to trace the influence of the Universal on the history of India, to indicate the landmarks of Internationalism in her national evolution and to point out, by suggestions and implications if possible, the specific contributions of India to the development of International History. In an age wherein international hatred threatens unfortunately to be the order of the day, such a study may not be without profit, not simply for the transvaluation of historical values but for ascertaining the warning-gesture of the profound Past to our muddling Present.

I. RETROSPECT ACROSS THE FIRST MILLENNIUM (*c*.1400-500 BC)

EXPLOSION OF THE "SPLENDID ISOLATION" THEORY

The first fiction and unfortunately the most tenacious fiction of Indian History is the glaringly unhistorical hypothesis that India grew up in "splendid isolation". For the fabrication of this fiction we have to be thankful as much to the narrow outlook of late Hindu orthodoxy as to the erroneous picture of primitive Indian society drawn by the early school of occidental philologists. While acknowledging fully the value of the works of these scholars in the decipherment of the ancient texts, we cannot forget that the outlook of these new types of *Pundits* were generally limited by those very texts which engrossed their attention. Thus frequently too much emphasis was laid on particular aspects of Indian life as suggested by some special terms or words, and too little regard paid to the general historical evolution. Words are valuable as landmarks in the progress of society, but for that very reason they are but *static symbols* of the ever-changing and ever-expanding life. So the picture of caste-ridden India, cut-off from the rest of the world by the external barriers of the Ocean and the Himalayas, as well as by the internal prohibitions of a morbid, all-excluding cult of purity, India ever-chanting Vedic hymns or celebrating occult sacrifices, weaving transcendental philosophies or absurd reactionary principles of life—this fancy picture of India fades away as soon as we view it from the vantage ground of History.

VEDIC GODS IN WESTERN ASIA

Truth is not only stranger but thousand times stronger than fiction. The chance stroke of the spade of an archaeologist makes short work of heaps of scholarly theories. So the discovery of the inscription of Boghaz Keui in 1907 by the German archaeologist Hugo Winckler led to the explosion of the "Isolation" theory and expanded to an unexpected extent the horizon of Indian history. Here, for the first time, we read the startling fact that in far off Cappadocia, in the fourteenth century BC, two belligerent tribes, the Hittites and the Mitannis, invoking the Vedic Gods, Mitra, Varuna and Indra, while concluding a treaty; moreover, the special twin-gods, Nasatyas were invoked to bless the new marriage-alliance concluded between the two royal families (cf. Dr. Sten Konow: "The Aryan Gods of the Mitanni People", *Modern Review*, December 1921, pp. 683-4).

India's Symbolic Role: The Peace-maker of Ancient History

Thus, by a curious coincidence, this first concrete document in the history of Indian internationalism, represents the Indian gods as the peace-makers and harmonisers of conflicting interests; and as such, we consider the Boghaz Keui inscription, not only as a landmark in Asiatic history but also as a symbol of India's role in the development of internationalism through *peace* and *spiritual unity*. This is, as we shall try to show, quite different from the *economic internationalism* of exploitation (e.g., Phoenician) or the *imperialistic internationalism* of compulsion (e.g., Assyrian and Roman). We cannot forget that when the Indian gods appear for the first time in their symbolic role of Peace-makers in Cappadocia, Egypt is proudly proclaiming her world-conquests through the famous Victory Ode of Thutmosis III, cataloguing with sublime egotism the vanquished nations and countries. Further westwards, we hear about the same time (1500 BC), the Achæans thundering on the ramparts of the Aegian capital Knossos (Crete), the collapse of the Minoan hegemony in the Mediterranean and the peaceful penetration of the crafty Phoenicians connecting the East and the West with a subtle tie of economic exploitation. The Achaean ascendency, already weakened by the fateful Trojan war (1200 BC) as well as the Phoenician commercial empire began to give way before the onrush of the virile Dorians who, with iron weapons, inaugurated the Iron Age in Europe (1000 BC), vanquishing their predecessors of the Bronze Age; while in Asia the Assyrians played the same role as that of the Dorians, pulverising the decadent nations with superior military organisation and efficiency.

Aryo-non-Aryan Compromise

What was happening in India in that epoch of transition from, the pre-classical to the classical period of Western history with its interlude of the Epic Age, we have no definite political records to ascertain. But we have invaluable literary documents to attest the rapid development of Indian life and thought. From the *Rigveda* (the earliest literary monument, if not of humanity, at least of the Indo- European people) to the earliest *Brahmanas* (1000 BC), Indian life had traversed quite a long path of sociological evolution. The Vedic Aryans were confronted with the same problem, presented to the Egyptians and the Assyriaus, the Achaeans and the Dorians—of an autochthonous people barring the way of a more virile expanding power. And herein lies the originality of the Indian Aryans, that they solved the problem in the only lasting manner possible—by recognising the title of their rivals *to exist*, not merely as enemies but as collaborators in the building of a civilisation which we may call today as much Aryan as non-Aryan (Indo-Mesopotamian or Dravidian as we like (*cf.* my note on the "Aryo-Dravidian Compromise", *Modern Review*, January 1922, pp. 31-3).

The Vedic literature being essentially sacerdotal, records but poorly this march of India along the path of historical synthesis. Yet we get glimpses of the complexity of the picture here and there, the background is already polychrome; the crowding of the canvas is already Epic. From the very beginning we notice the *white* Aryans engaged in tussle with the *dark* aborigines. Surely, the social and political problems thus raised were not removed by the simple utterance of Vedic *mantras*. There were occasional conflicts and outbursts of cruelties. The path was often red with "blood and iron". The atmosphere was often dark with horror and the Vedic poets seemed to have given vent to their feeling of suspense and agony during those awful nights, in their semi-symbolical hymn to Ushas, the goddess of Dawn to be born in the womb of primeval Darkness:

> Arise ! the breath, the life again has reached us !
> Darkness has gone away and Light is coming.
> She leaves a path for the sun to travel,
> We have arrived where men *prolong existence* !—
>
> *Rigveda* V.i.113

Indian Principle of "Live-and-Let-Live"

Yes, the aim of the Indian Aryans was to prolong existence not to extinguish it. And long before the formulation of the doctrine *ahimsa* (non-injury) by Mahavira and the Buddha, India demonstrated her *profound respect for life* by realising that in her early history. The Aryo-Dravidian synthesis will ever remain as the first and the foremost glory in her career of international amalgamation. Two nations, quite different in race, language and culture were fused to give birth to a virile stock of people and to lay the foundations of a great civilisation.

Ideals of "World-Conquest" in the Epics

Needless to say that this was achieved through many conflicts and catastrophies which prepared the way for the Indian *Epic Age* with its formulation of the principles of *world power* and *world-empire* (though the geography of that world was singularly different from our own). Hence in the later Vedic literature as well as in the *Brahmanas*, we read frequently of *samrajyas* (vast empires) aud *sarva-bhaumas* (great emperors). From that doctrine it is an easy and normal transition to the concepts of *digvijaya* (conquest of world-quarters) and that of *raja-chakravartin* (super-sovereign of the diplomatic circle). That naturally brought in its train, wars on an epic scale, and martial ballads came to be composed by contemporary bards and minstrels. And just as Homers and pseudo-Homers appeared several centuries after the Trojan war to give epic form to the floating legends and ballads, so the actual great epics of India, the *Ramayana* and the *Mahabharata* were composed by our Valmikis and Vyasas, many centuries after the traditional wars between Rama and Ravana or between the Pandavas and the Kauravas.

War as a Sociological Experiment—its Lessons

So, whilst the Vedic age was a period of tribal warfare and unconscious fusion of tribes and races, the Epic age was a period of strife between more extensively organised kingdoms and empires, striving after suzerain power. In this epoch the old principle of *amalgamation* underwent its hardiest test. In both the Epics, we road a great deal about war, but in none of them we miss the *lessons of war* as they were imprinted on the heart of the ancient Hindus; the ultimate victory is always on the side of the righteous and even then, victory in a game like war is too much like defeat! That shows clearly that even in the process of testing the principle of concord and amalgamation, in the very act of experimenting with a new method of discord and dissolution, Indian mind was wide awake and open to conviction. Hence the poet of the *Ramayana* makes the victor Rama stand humbly by the side of his dying enemy to have his parting advice. Hence also, in the *Mahabharata*, we find the triumphant Yudhisthira sitting at the feet of the dying hero Bhisma, to listen to the Canto of Peace as the only fitting conclusion to an War Epic. Thus, confronting the actualities of war as a sociological experiment, its terrible consequences and tragic legacies, Indian mind pronounced its verdict on war through the formulation of new doctrines later on embodied in systematic treaties like the Santiparvan and the *Bhagavad Gita*. This sanity and this self-knowledge are really admirable. India tried the path of "blood and iron" and shuddered back in horror and disgust. No doubt one school of thought continued to refine the philosophy of mutual suspicion and of the inevitability of war as a means of aggrandisement, and thus gave rise to the science of *sadgunya* (sextuple methods of Diplomacy) culminating in the atomistic politics of the *mandala* of the *Arthasastra* of Kautilya which dominated the political thoughts of India in her periods of disintegration (Nag: *Les Theories Diplomatiques de l'Inde Ancienne et l'Arthasastra*, p. 115). Another school attempted to explain away the war philosophically, by transforming local war into an allegory of cosmic war, thus giving rise to the grand philosophical poem of the *Bhagavad Gita*. While a third school candidly preached Peace to be the only true sublimation of War and thus gave us the famous Santiparvan (the Canto of Peace).

Emergence of the Principles of Universal Tolerance and Amity

The soul of India seemed to have been undergoing a travail for New Birth. The atmosphere was surcharged with a new agony and a terrific gloom which reminded us very much of the age of the Vedic groping in the dark. Suffocating under that atmosphere of narrow egotism and shocking carnage, one section of the Indian mind sought and found liberation in the serene region of emancipated individualism (the gravitation of the Hindu mind) and cried out through the deathless voices of the sages of the Upanishads, the message of this fresh Revelation: "Listen to me, O ye children of immortality . . . I have come to know the Great Person, like the Sun, beyond the darkness !"

This solemn call was sent to the whole universe (*visva*), for it was the result of the realisation of Him who is the All-feeling one (*sarvanubhuh*). And this new aspiration did not remain a mere ecstatic dream but soon became flesh in an actual *Purusha*, a historical personality, the Buddha, whom India created out of the depth of her universal Charity. Truth that was burning in the heart of India became incarnate. Dispelling with the radiance of Divine Amity, the dark smokes arising out of the bloody altars of sacrifice, both sacerdotal and political, Buddha proclaimed the sublime paradox that *to gain all one must give all*, to avoid suffering one must eradicate the all-devouring Ego, the root of all suffering, and that real illumination is in the quenching of the flames of passion (*nirvana*).

The Age of the Buddha and the Soul of Asia

Political history of Humanity is full of absurd gaps, stupid silences and illogical *lacuna*. That is why we cannot explain satisfactorily the real significance of such grand historical revelations. But the history of human thought expresses itself by suggestions probably too subtle for our chronological apparatus. The unerring universalism of the Upanishads, the divine cosmopolitanism of the Buddha, surely proceeded from some *super-historical*, if not historical need of Humanity. That is why, towards the end of our first millennium (*c.* 1400-500 BC), we find the Buddha dedicating himself to Humanity; Mahavira, the founder of Jainism, preaching *ahimsa* (non-injury) as the noblest principle of religion; that in dark days of the Chow dynasty of China, Lao-tse and Confucius (500-478 BC) evolving respectively their grand systems: the Tao-kiao (School of the Way) and Ju-kiao (School of the Knowers), emphasising the same principles of life non-interference, suppression of ego, and purification of heart. So also in the land of the Iranian cousins of the Indians, the reformation of faith had been started a little earlier by Zoroaster; and now we are startled to read for the first time in an imperial autobiography on stone—in the famous Behistun and Nakshi Rustam inscriptions of Darius the great (550-485 BC):

> Days Darius the King: for this reason Ahuramazda bore me aid, and the other gods which are, because I was not an enemy, I was not a deceiver, I was not a despot. . . .

The last words of the Emperor of Asia were equally significant for the age:

O man, what (are) the commands of Ahuramazda, may he make them revealed to thee do not err, do not leave the right path, do not sin. . . .

II. RETROSPECT ACROSS THE SECOND MILLENNIUM (*c.* 500 BC-AD 500)

India, the Pioneer in Practical Internationalism.

"*. . . rastam ma avarada ma starava*"—right (path) relinquished not, do not sin—these are the last words of the greatest figure in world politics towards the end of our millennium. They signalised a new departure in the history of the epoch we are going to survey. The Persian empire under Darius the Great, touching India on the one side and Greece on the other, marked the apogee of the history of antiquity and the connecting watershed of the streams of the Ancient and the Modern history. It awakened the lyre of the first tragedian of Hellas, Æschylus fighting in the field of Marathon (490 BC) and composing his drama, "The Persians". It evoked also the genius of Herodotus, the father of European history. Pursuing the age-old method of pulverisation, Persia battered at the decaying fabrics of ancient empires of Egypt and Mesopotamia and they tumbled down like houses of cards. So the Achemenian art under Darius represented in traditional style the throne of the world-emperor carried by long rows of vanquished soverigns. At the same time the traditional political legacy of the *dream of world-empire* hypnotised Greece, the first rival of Persia in Europe. From Greece the chronic infection contaminated Rome. Greece chocked the military advance of Persia but had neither the political sagacity nor the spiritual insight to arrest the disintegrating politics of antiquity, represented in its last phase by the Persian imperialism. The Peloponnesian war destroyed miserably the noble prospect of consolidation opened by the Confederacy of Delos. Hellas, and with her Europe, preferred the fateful path of empire-building. Athens, Sparta, Thebes, all attempted by turn, till at last Alexander of Macedon succeeded in traversing the same path of conquest from Greece to India. What appears as a splendid turning of the table on Persia is really an ephemeral imitation of the Persian emperors; and Persian influence on Alexander is acknowledged by all, for it was highly resented by his hellenic compatriots. World-empire may be a new ideal with the occident but it is a dangerously old institution of antiquity. In spite of the unmistakable warning of ancient history as to the inevitable self-disintegration of such gigantic edifices resting on the precarious foundation of *force*, Greece under Alexander and Rome under her republican proto-cæsars and imperial cæsars, attempted the dangerous experiment, met with the usual tragic disaster and, even in the very failure, left the fateful legacy of empire-building to all of their "Barbarian" successors who are struggling down to this day, with varying degrees of success and permanency, with the same impossible, antiquated experiment of antiquity—of building a world-empire—a machinery of gain for a *few* at the sacrifice of the *many*, based on the quick-sand of selfishness and propelled by the inhuman energy of brute force.

With phenomenal originality, nay with divine inspiration, India under Asoka the Great (273-242 BC) suddenly developed an ideal of *Empire of Peace and Progress* for all. Within 250 years of the appearance of the great Buddha, India produced another historic personality. *Dharmasoka* not only contradicted with an unparalleled historical sagacity, the entire politics of antiquity up to his age, but also, like a Spiritual Columbus, discovered a new world of constructive politics which unfortunately, remains as yet only an aspiration and a dream for humanity. Behind him stretches the dead ruin of ancient empires; before him unfolds the tableau of lamentable duplication of the same selfish politics in our modern history; and in the centre lies the spiritual oasis of Asokan imperialism. It shines as a beacon light in the path of the political evolution of humanity, explaining the inevitable decay of old empires and putting to shame the retrospective laughter of the cynical imperialists of our modern age. Thus the empire of Asoka, with its new philosophy of conquest by Righteousness (*dharma-vijaya*) and its now foundation of universal well-being (*kalyana*), stands as the central climacteric of human history—at once a fateful warning and a divine inspiration for Humanity.

Starting his career as an orthodox emperor engaged in the conquest of a territory (Kalinga) to the east of India, entailing the death of millions, Asoka had his first conversion as the result of that tragic contact with the actualities of politics. In a moment he discovered his mistake; and not stopping there, like a truly great soul, admitted his mistake with a sincerity and penitence rarely paralleled by any other character of history. His edict of Kalinga is the noblest monument of his magnanimity; he made his repentance a perpetual lesson to posterity by carving on the rocks of the ravaged Kalinga an account of his Imperial blunder. Through that awful suffering he arrived at that noblest of political revelations that "true conquest consists in the conquest of men's hearts by the law of Dharma". From that conversion and that revelation issued twenty years (261-242 BC) of humanitarian activities touching the frontiers of the Hellenic world on the one hand and of the Mongolian world on the other, building the *first great causeway of Love and Illumination* between the Orient and the Occident, the first code of progressive imperialism and the first basis of constructive internationalism. The great truth of Universalism which flashed as a *revelation* upon the Souls of the *rishis* of the Upanishads, which appeared as an *incarnation*, in the personality of the first World-man, Buddha, translated itself into the Cosmopolites of this first practical internationalist of history—Dharmasoka Piyadasi, the well-wisher of all, proclaiming with divine simplicity, "*Sava munisa me paja*"—whole humanity is my children—an echo of his master Buddha's saying.

India is generally known, represented and accepted as physically isolated and psychologically exclusive, and in a way that is true. But how could such an India evolve such cosmic personalities, remains still a paradox of history. Between the Boghas Keui inscription and the Behistun inscription—for nearly thousand years, the history of India's relations with the external world is full of tantalising guesses and absurd gaps. Latest researches, however, seem to discover "specific evidence for supposition that by 15th century BC, tribes of Aryan stock held influence over the wide area extending from Northern Asia Minor and North-western Babylonia to Media".[1] Coming nearer home we find that there was a period of intimate historical contact between India and Iran, postulated and proved by philologists analysing the *Rigveda* and the *Avesta*. So Indo-Iranian period is a definite chapter of Asiatic history. Yet concrete historical facts are so few! The invasion of India by the Assyrian Queen Semiramis is only a legend though Arrian (Ch. 5) records that some Indian tribes were subjects of the Assyrian sovereigns. The simultaneous occurrence of the legend of the great Deluge in the Babylonian record and in the *Satapatha Brahmana* (*c.* 1000 BC) is probably more definite as an evidence of contact of India with the Mesopotamian culture. Some astronomical notions and the use of iron are said to have been derived from Babylonia.[2]

The occurrence of Indian apes and peacocks in the Old Testement is admitted by some and disputed by others.[3] But Rawlinson and Kennedy (*JRAS*, 1898) demonstrate that there are evidences of very early commercial relations between southern India and the western regions. The Semitic races were great pioneers in connecting isolated countries through commercial relations, one of the earliest motives of human amalgamation. Another great service rendered to humanity by the Semitic races was the *diffusion of alphabet*, at first probably for commercial facilities but later on converted into one of the greatest machineries for the propagation of Humanism. India is said to have derived her first alphabet from Semitic sources about the same time as Greece did (800 BC). And even if we do not accept the possibility of the march of Cyrus the Great to Indian frontiers we cannot help admitting that another script of India, the Kharosthi was established through the instrumentality of the Iranian rulers of north-western India. Darius was the first king to bring India to historical clarity. He sent one Skylax of Karyanda (510 BC) who discovered a water passage from Persia to the mouth of the Indus, and as the result of that survey the Indian satrapy of Darius was acquired. According to Herodotus it was the richest and the most populous of the Persian provinces. From that time the relation between India and Persia became steady. Indian soldiers fought with the Persians under Mardonius against the Greeks on the field of Platæa (479 BC) and the Mauryan empire and art bear here and there traces of this Persian contact, though the categorical assertions of a "Zoroastrian period of Indian history" and Zoroastrian influences on Asoka are extravagant.[4]

But all these are phases of primitive aggression or imperialistic exploitation—the earliest and the latest features of human politics. To elevate that politics

[1] P. Giles, "The Aryans", *Cambridge History of India* (1922).

[2] *Indian Antiquary*, XXXIV.

[3] Sylvain Lévi, "Baveru Jataka", Keith, *Cambridge History of India*, Chap. V.

[4] V. Smith, "Oxford History of India", 1919, pp. 79, 95.

into the dignity of a medium of humanistic ministrations and to transform that primitive instinct of aggrandisement into creative cosmopolitanism—that was done for the first time by the Buddhist Emperor Dharmasoka fulfilling the Brahmanical prophecy of *dharma-rajya* (Kingdom of Righteousness) contained in the *Mahabharata*. Thus in the same epoch that Rome, the mother and model of European imperialism, was pulverising her last oriental enemy, Carthage, in the Punic wars, Asoka had been celebrating the Spiritual Matrimony between countries and continents. This was undoubtedly a new departure in world-politics and the opening of a new page in the history of humanity. Not satisfied with preaching his new revelations *inside* India, Asoka sent his missionaries of humanism to Syria (then under Antiochos Theos), to Egypt (under Ptolemy Philadelphos), to Cyrene (under Magas), to Macedonia (under Antigonus Gonatus), and to Epirus (under Alexander). Apart from these names inscribed on his Rock Edicts of 257-256 BC, we have strong traditions about his missions to Ceylon visited by his own son (or brother) Mahendra and daughter Sanghamitra and even of his mission to far-off Burma (Suvarna-bhumi). Thus for the first time in history, humanity witnessed the *humanisation of politics*, and India, through the hands of Asoka, showered her blessings of Peace and Progress over this symbolical union of Asia, Africa, and Europe with ties of true internationalism.

By the side of this grand achievement of Asoka, the military adventures of Alexander the Great, in spite of their voluminous, nay garrulous expatiations, appear quite mediocre so far as the sublimity of conception and originality in execution of a *world idea* are concerned. Alexander, while acting as a splendid "Scourge of God", punishing the decadent powers of antiquity, followed the traditional method of conquest in achieving the traditional ideal of autocratic empire. Thus, accidentally, he happened to be the founder of the Greek colonies which helped in the propagation of Hellenism, but consciously he might seldom be said to have worked out any definite order of human welfare. All the legends collected by later chroniclers about Alexander and the Indian Gymnosophists show, how the Indian mind was not only not affected by the so-called martial glories of Alexander in India, but showed a somewhat disdainful pity at the sight of the cruel exploits of that Grand Barbarian. As a matter of fact, as soon as his army, demoralised by over-exhaustion and by the dread of the great Gangetic empire of Magadha, turned its back on India, the so-called Hellenic conquest of Alexander was dissipated from the mind of the Indians as an evil dream. Soon after, Chandragupta Maurya (330-298 BC) the grandfather of Asoka, cleared the country of all foreigners and taught a good lesson to the second Greek invader, Seleukos Nikator, who was forced to cede the provinces of Paropanisadai, Aria, Arachosia and Gedrosia. A treaty to this effect was concluded about 300 BC, strengthened by a matrimonial alliance—a Hindu emperor marrying a Hellenic wife, in spite of the so-called caste rigidities. The Syrian court sent Megasthenes as an ambassador to the court of Chandragupta. Megasthenes left a valuable book—his *Indika*, and was replaced by Deimachos in the reign of the next emperor Bindusara (298-273 BC), who also received another envoy Dionysios sent by Ptolemy Philadelphos of Egypt (285-247 BC), an ally of Bindusara and of his son Asoka.

Thus down to the end of the reign of Asoka, the Hellenic people looked up to India as a strong ally and a civilising power and thus the Greeks seldom aspired to impose upon the Indians in contact with the Hellenistic world, a civilisation of their own.

Asoka's Missions: Their Historical Consequences

Historically this was the commencement of the period of steady decadence of Hellas rendering the Hellenism of this epoch a dangerous solvent of the victorious Roman society. Both in art and literature the Greeks were betraying unmistakable signs of exhaustion and atavism. So, when Hellenism under Heliodorus and Menander made headway for the second time into the very heart of Hindusthan, we find some of these Hellenic adventurers already devotees of Hindu faith. The famous Besnagar Column (*c.* 150 BC) announces the conversion of a Greek ruler to Vaishnavism of the Bhagavata sect; while the Buddhist classic *Milinda Panho* (the Questions of Milinda or Menander) stands as the proof of the assertion of Buddhist thought against Greek mind. This process continued also in the realm of art, when the Greek converts to Buddhism, collaborating with their Hindu fellow believers, developed the *Graeco-Buddhist art* which exerted such a profound influence on the art evolution of Central Asia and the *Far* East (*cf.* Nag, "Indian Iconography", *Modern Review*, January 1922).

Thus India, through various political vicissitudes, through victory or defeat, was ever transforming the weapons of brute force into instruments of human progress—art and literature, philosophy and religion. Her north-western frontier lands remained ever as a veritable laboratory of *Cultural Chemistry*. India has demonstrated so far, that the political nomenclatures like the *Victor* or the *Vanquished* are misnomers. The real thing that counts and lasts for ever is human creation, in and through human amalgamation.

Barbarian Invasions and the Problem of tiie "Open Door"

But now came the period when this principle of amical international assimilation was put to the severest test. During the first half of this millennium (500 BC downwards) India had to encounter two nations that had a civilisation of their own—Persia and Greece. Fusion with them was comparatively an easy problem. But throughout the second half of this millennium (down to AD 500) India was confronted with the problem of meeting the real Barbarians from Central Asia, surging down the Himalayas, and threatening to submerge civilisation in a deluge of savagery ! Was India to make no distinction between the civilised and the non-civilised ? Was she to follow still her policy of "open door" ? With supreme faith in her principle of *international amity*, India answered in the affirmative. Yes, she must allow every species of humanity to participate in her life and to test her principle. A law is either universal or nothing. Thus India remained faithful to her spiritual tradition whatever might have been the fluctuations of her political destiny.

Instincts of Conservation and Assimilation

So when the barbarian Sakas began their trial of India's faith, India accepted them, as she did accept and assimilate, the other branches of the barbarous races—the Kushans and the Huns. No doubt the instinct of conservation manifested itself in the stricter social legislation. The simpler social laws of the early law-books, the Dharma-sutras, were amplified, sometimes showing inordinate rigidity (not always, however, ensuring or enforcing practice). Thus the great codes of Manu and Yajnavalkya, of Vishnu and Narada were all compiled in a systematic fashion by AD 500, and through them the Hindu mind betrayed its pre-occupation with the "untouchable Mleccha problem". But actual history always defies the codification of social Legislators as well as the admonition of religious Censors. Sacerdotal blockade or imperial barricade were futile against subtle sociological fusion. Thus the Four Orders of Society—the *chaturvarnas*, in spite of their being very ancient and quite orthodox as contended by Oldenburg (*ZDMG*, vol. 51), remained generally and especially in this period, *in a state of fluidity*, and Senart had good reasons to assert that the *Caste System* was largely a social fiction (Emile Senart, "Les Castes dans l'Inde: les Faits et la Systeme", 1896). Hence we find frequently, glaring exceptions and anomalies, e.g., Mleccha kings or laymen, our Usabhadatas and Rudradamans posing as the Pillars of Orthodoxy! This has been conclusively proved with reference to concrete epigraphic documents by Prof. D.R. Bhadarkar in his paper, "The Foreign Elements in Hindu Population" (*Indian Antiquary*, 1911).

Salvation through Faith: The Bhakti Marga and the Mahayana

The sudden invasion and the continuous infiltration of these savage foreigners into India, produced at first an ethnic confusion (*varnasamkara*) and cultural disturbance which threatened to be cataclysmic. It is the phenomenal adaptability or vitality of Hinduism that enabled India to sustain that shock. It produced no doubt at first a laxity in her lofty discipline by the inevitable enfranchisement of diverse religious and social norms. But in another way that apparent lowering of her standard led to a grand enrichment of her cultural life and an unparalleled *democratisation of her culture*. India had already developed the discipline of Faith (*Bhaktimarga*), through the Bhagavata sects of Vaishnavism (second century BC), for the foreign converts. (Vide. Sir R.G. Bhandarkar, *Vaishnavism Saivism*, etc.) The *Bhagavad Gita* offered, through its philosophical muse, salvation through one God:

Leaving everything else aside.
Betake thyself to my unique protection.

And about the same time that the divine prophet of Judaea was putting to shame the whole decadent culture of the Greco-Roman world by his profound expiation for Humanity, India also was transcending her "little path" (Hinayana) of individual salvation arid inaugurating her career along the "grand path" (Mahayana) through her divine solicitude for the All-Being (*sarva-sattva*). Her great poet-philosopher Asvaghosha, who composed a magnificent poem on the life of Buddha the first inculcator of universal amity (*maitri*), also developed the philosophy of the All-Being as the ultimate goal of individual discipline, in his "Awakening of Faith (*Sraddhotpada Sastra*) which may be accepted as a landmark in the history of Indian internationalism. Moreover, it was composed by a philosopher who himself was carried away as a part of a tribute imposed on his native city by the barbarian conqueror Kanishka.

Pan-Asiatic Expansion

Thus, from the beginning of the Christian era, India started playing her role of internationalism not only through her lofty academic philosophy or through the vigorous propagation of a royal personality, but as a whole people following mysteriously a divine impulse, an ecstatic inspiration to sacrifice the *Ego* for the *All*. This grand movement of spiritual conquest, this noble dynamic of cultural imperialism—a legacy of Asoka—soon won for India the inalienable empire over the vast continent, right across Tibet and China to Corea and Japan on the one hand and across Burma and Indo-China to Java and Indonesia on the other. The history of this phenomenal progression has yet to be written. It is full of profound lessons for students of internationalism. We can only suggest here a few lines of approach. It was a period of rare give-and-take in human history—between Buddhism and Mazdaism, Taoism and Confucianism, Manichaeism and Christianity. It is through years of international collaboration that we may hope to reconstruct this long-forgotten history and to trace the specific contributions of India in this grand Passion-Play of Humanity.

Scholars like Richard Garbe and Vincent Smith agree with regard to the theory that Buddhism influenced the early development of Christianity[5] which in its turn coloured some of the later Hindu doctrines and creeds. "Although (Asoka's) missionary effort did not succeed in planting Buddhist Churches in foreign countries (excepting Syria) its effects may be traced," says V. Smith, "obscurely both on the history of Gnostic and Manichæan sects of Christianity." So the great Egyptologist Flinders Petrie remarks after having discovered portraits of Indian men and women at Memphis: "These are the first remains

[5] Cf. also Kennedy, "Buddhist Gnosticism", *JRAS*, 1902.

of Indians known on the Mediterranean. Hitherto there have been no material evidence for that connection which is stated to have existed both by embassies from Egypt and Syria to India and by the great Buddhist missions sent by Asoka as far west as Greece and Cyrene. We seem now to have touched the Indian Colony in Memphis and we may hope for more light on that connection, which seems to have been so momentous for western thought!"[6]

From Gandhara Khotan and Central Asia to China.

But the most important result of the formulation of the new doctrine of the Grand Vehicle (Mahayana) was not so much on the Western Countries as on the Eastern Asiatic world. Arrian, writing about this epoch, notes in his *Indika* that "a *sense of justice* prevented any Indian king from attempting conquest beyond the limits of India". While remaining true to this tradition with regard to political expansion, Mahayana India set about a *spiritual* conquest that remains to this day a marvel of history. Shaking off the narrow individualism of the old *Theravada* school, India elaborated (in *Gandhara*, that crucible of her cultural experiments) the doctrine of *Sarvastivada*, asserting that everything external as well as internal is *real*. The classical works of this new school of philosophy, the *Vibhasa* and the *Maha-Vibhasa* were composed by Katyayaniputra one of the masters of Asvaghosha.[7] The Vaibhasika sect of the *Sarvastivadins* were strong in the border-lands of the north-western India, in Kashmir, in Gandhara and through Udayana, Kashgar, Khotan and Persia[8] it entered China. In fact, there are strong traditions about the persistent attempt of China to reach India. In 217 BC in the reign of Emperor Tsin Shih Huaung-ti, 18 Buddhist monks are said to have been brought to the Chinese capital. It is a fact well established that the Chinese Colombus in this respect was Chang Kien who succeeded for the first time to penetrate through the barbarian zones of the Hiueng-nu to the West of China, and to bring definite information about Ta-hia (Bactria) and Shen-tu (Sindfau-Hindu) by his intrepid adventures between 128-115 BC (*cf.* Nag, *Les Theories Diplomatiques de l'Inde Ancienne et l'Arthasastra*, Paris).

About the beginning of the Christian era Yue-chi ambassadors to the Chinese Court are said to have brought some Buddhist Scriptures, proving thereby that Buddhism had already spread over a part on Central Asia. Lastly, in AD 67 under Emperer Ming-ti we hear about the official introduction of Buddhism into China, not only with Buddhist scriptures but statues and also two Indian monks, Kasyapa Matanga and Dharmaraksa, the former translating the first

[6] "Man", vol. VIII (1906).
[7] Takakusu, "Sarvastivadins."
[8] Stein, *Geographical Journal*, May and August 1916.

Chinese Buddhist text: "The 42 sayings of Buddha." In the then capital Loyang, the famous Pai-ma temple was built in the Honan province and many Taoist and Confucian nobles were said to have boon converted to Buddhism by AD 71.

Asvaghosha and Nagarjuna

This period coincides with the great Kushan empire in India, which witnessed such a grand development in religion, art and literature that this foreign Mleccha Dynasty underwent a sort of canonisation. Its greatest King Kanishka appeared as a second Asoka. So the principles of the Great Vehicle suggested by Asvaghosha was given a tremendous impetus by its second great philosopher-scientist Nagarjuna living about this age of illumination with its centre in the court of Emperor Kanishka who was also a great patron of the Græco-Buddhist art of Gandhara which came gradually to be a sort of international art-language for the whole of Central Asia. So Taxila became a great centre of scientific and artistic activities with Charaka as the master of the medical school, Katyayani-putra its great philosopher, and Asvaghosha as its poet and musician.

Expansion by Sea: Champa, Camboj, Sumatra, Java

But the expansion was not only along the land routes. In this marvellous century Hippalus discovered the Trade-winds, the "monsoons" (AD 79) and thereby facilitated sea voyage. "Periplus of the Erythræan Sea", an invaluable journal of some nameless navigator of this age, saved for us by chance, proves the magnitude of the international trade in that epoch extending from Africa *via* India and the Malay Peninsula to far off China. Bold Indian mariners were starting to found their culture-colonies in Champa and Camboj in Indo-China, and in the Malay Archipelago as far as Java. For Ptolemy in his *Geography* (second century AD) already calls the Island of Java by its Indian name Jabadiu. So Professor Pelliot in his researches into the history of Fu-nan (ancient Cambodia) finds traces of Indian culture there, already in the third century AD and also notices the frequent mention of big ships crossing the seas. (Vide Le Fou-nan, *Bulletin. Ecole F. Ex. O.*, vol. III.)

Indian legends stories and art traditions were already penetrating the Far East by these Sea Routes, as Indian religious and philosophical texts were entering by the Land Routes; and in course of a few years we find China using both the routes in her grand cultural commerce with India. So, on the one hand, the material wealth of India was rapidly developing an active commerce between India and the Western World through the Roman Empire, and on the other hand, the invaluable spiritual treasures of India wore inducing her far stabler relations with the Eastern World. So Bakaria (port of Kottayam, Travancore) and Bharukaccha (Broach), Vidisa and Vaisali, Tamraparni and Tamralipti, were big centres in this grand international circulation, so well reflected in the wonderful anthologies of popular tales and legends; the Jatakas, the Avadanas and the Katha literature of India.

Common People as Civilising Agencies

By the side of this marvellous development of internationalism through free economic relations and spiritual exchange, the rise and fall of self-centred governments and nationalistic empires seem to be quite second rate in importance. The profoundest changes in the life-history of nations are often effected silently by agencies distinctly non-political. So we watch the simultaneous collapse of the Kushan empire in India and the Han empire in China (*c.* AD 225); we observe the rise of the Sassanian empire in Persia (AD 226), the establishment of the Gupta empire in India (AD 300) and the dawnfall of the Western Roman empire as the result of the Barbarian invasions (AD 487). But through all these rises and falls of empires, continues the silent fertilising current of International Commerce—economic as well as spiritual—leading to a phenomenal quickening of human thought and sympathy. Thus through all those periods of political trials and vicissitudes, India went on quietly with her work of internationalism; and about the same time that the Huns were to open another chapter of savage onslaught on her bosom, India was sending her sons Kumarajiva and Gunavarman to China to preach Buddhism, while Chinese pilgrims like Fa-hien, Chih-mong and Fa-mong were coming to India to drink at the fountain head of spiritual wisdom. All the barriers of geography and ethnography have been swept away by the inundation of international amity. India realises herself in a new way by transcending her narrow national limits. That is probably why the greatest poet of this epoch (fifth century AD) Kalidasa, the brightest of the "Nine gems" of geniuses adorning the court of Vikramaditya, gives deathless expression to this profound longing of India for the world beyond the Himalayas, through his immortal poem of the "Cloud Messenger" (*Megha-duta*) addressed to the Beloved in the Great Beyond—almost symbolical of this cosmic passion of India in this golden age of Indian internationalism.

III. RETROSPECT ACROSS THE THIRD MILLENNIUM (*c.* AD 500-1500)

India, the Heart op Asiatic Humanism

The cry of the hero of Kalidasa's "Cloud Messenger" for his Beloved beyond the barriers of the Himalayas, was a veritable cry of India at that age, for the Great Beyond—the Greater India. Out of the sheer fulness of her heart, India had already twice before, under Asoka and Kanishka, plunged into the vast world outside her narrow geographical limits. Each time India transcended her national boundaries, she had developed a civilisation as permanently *national*, in the best sense, as *international* in its beneficial operation. Now, for the third time we witness the *overflow of Indian Humanism* fertilising the whole of Asia, at the same time, developing an indigenous culture unparalleled in her history. The more names of Kalidasa and Varahamihira, Gunavarman and Vasubandhu, Aryabhatta and Brahmagupta, are sufficient to mark this epoch as an apogee of Indian culture. Our political historians try to explain this grand development by referring to this or that emperor of this or that dynasty. The Guptas or the Vardhanas of India, the Wei or the T'ang dynasty of China are supposed to have worked the whole miracle. But thanks to the indisputable evidences recovered, as the result of the international crusades of archæology in Central Asia, we know that this wonderful transformation was effected by factors far from being political; its progression was mostly along the peaceful *silk-roads* from China and *manuscript-roads* from India rather than along the path of aggressive imperialism. The Russian archæological missions under Klementz and Kazoloff, French missions under Dutreuil de Rhins and Paul Pelliot, English missions under Dr Iloernle and Sir Aurel Stein, German missions under Grunwedel and von Le Coq and Japanese missions under Count Otani and Tachibana, have brought to light a treasure of archæological and artistic finds, masses of inscriptions and manuscripts which, when thoroughly analysed and digested, would revolutionise our conception about the migration of early culture in Eurasia, now viewed generally from the false perspective of isolated national histories of the different countries. With gratitude to the researches of those *savants* I beg to present a rough sketch of this grand movement of cultural exchange between nations and nations.

India and China

Down to the period of the missionary activities of Kumarajiva (AD 344-413), Buddhism and Indian culture penetrated China mainly through the Central Asian routes. Most of the early Sino-Buddhist texts coming down from the Loyang School, were from the pen of the Yuch-chi, Parthian or Sogdian converts to Buddhism, working in collaboration with the Chinese Buddhists. In Mahayana texts like the *Chandragarbha* and the *Suryagarbha sutras* as well as in *Mahamayuri* texts, we find a curious admixture of Indian, Khotanese, Iranian and Chinese spirit. Linguistic test also demonstrates that most of these translations were not done directly from Indian classical languages like Sanskrit and Pali but from popular dialects (Prakrits) of the various parts of India.

Fa-Hien, a Pilgrim from China

With the appearance of Fa-hien (AD 399-414) one of the earliest of the Chinese Buddhist pilgrims to India, the great period of *direct* Sino-Indian collaboration was opened. Classical Buddhist texts like *Dhamma-pada* and *Milinda-panho* came to be translated or adapted *directly* from Indian originals. Fa-hien studied in Pataliputra (Patna) under the great savant Revati, master of Buddhaghosha who soon carried the torch of Truth to Ceylon. Since then the history of India and Ceylon are so intimately connected that we shall not attempt here a separate treatment of Indian influences on Ceylon. India in this age was the veritable land of illumination and attracted countless ardent spirits like Fa-hien who took tremendous risk in those days to cross the Taklamakan (Gobi) desert, Khotan and the Pamir ranges to reach the land of his heart's desire. Visiting the great intellectual centres of Taxila and Purushapura (Peshawar), studying for three years at Pataliputra and two years at Tamralipti, Fa-hien returned to China, having stopped for some time in the Indian colonies of Ceylon and Java on his way.

Kamarajiva, a Missionary from Kucha

Kumarajiva[9] (344-413), a monk from an Indian family domiciled in Karashahr (Kucha), was brought to China as a captive by a Chinese general. This Buddhist captive repaid his captors by working for more than ten years in China, attracting by his phenomenal talent the best Chinese brains of that age. The most veteran men of letters collaborated with Kumarajiva in his work. No wonder that the translations from his pen are recognised today as classics of Chinese literature and his version of the "Lotus of the Good Law" (*Saddharma-pundarika*) still stands as the most valued text of the Chinese-Buddhist scriptures. By sheer genius and devotion Kumarajiva succeeded in reuniting temporarily the Northern (Turco-Mongolian) and the Southern (Indigenous) schools of Chinese Buddhism which had by that time made a tremendous progress amongst the mass of the people.

Buddhabhadra, Founder of the Dhyana School in Cihna

About the same period another Buddhist missionary, Buddhabhadra, arrived in China by the *sea route* (Shantung), and by his purity of life, great discipline and meditation influenced profoundly the southern Chinese people, poetic and transcendental in spirit. Here Buddhabhadra found a field of work congenial to him; and by fusing Buddhist meditativeness with Chinese quietism, he laid the foundation of the *Shan-no* (Dhyana) school of Chinese philosophy and poetry, callaborating with the group of monks, poets and philosophers of the monastery of Mount Lu Shan associated with the name of the great Hui-yuau (AD 416).

Prince Gunavarman, the Painter Missionary from Kashmir

Simultaneously with Kumarajiva and Buddhabhadra appears the noble figure of the Prince-monk Gunavarman[10] who refused his throne of Kashmir, prompted by his zeal for the mission work. Ho visited Ceylon in AD 400 and then crossed

[9] Cf. Sylvain Lévi, *Journal Asiatique*, 1913.
[10] Cf. E. Chavannes, "Gunavarman", *T'oung Pao*, vol. V.

over to the island of Java where he found the first Buddhist monastery converting the King and the Queen-mother. Then he appeared in Canton (AD 424) and in Nanking, propagation his faith as much by his wonderful religious paintings as by his learned translations. He founded two *viharas* in Nanking, introduced the strict Vinaya system of ordination after the Indian School, and organised the first congregation of Chinese nuns. After his death in China (AD 431) we read of the arrival of two batches of nuns from Ceylon under Tissara (?) organising the Chinese nunneries after Sinhalese model. So during this epoch the relation between India and China through Ceylon and Java by the sea route was quite intimate; and Dr. Takakusu opines (*JRAS*, 1896) that the great Indian missionary Buddhaghosha also visited China from his base of work in Ceylon. No wonder that China acknowledges her gratitude by translating (AD 472 from an Indian original now lost) and cherishing the "Lives of Twenty-three Indian Patriarchs", comprising the careers of great Buddhist saints like Kasyapamatanga, Asvaghosha, Nagarjuna, Vasubandhu and others. But while a few such names have been fortunately preserved, hundreds are lost. And we are as much thankful to those nameless and unknown workers of humanity as to the group of the more fortunate known. The precious researches of Edouard Chavannes and Sylvain Lévi have recovered for us from oblivion many such grand yet long forgotten personalities: Chih-mong and Fa-mong (contemporary of Fa-hien, AD 400) from China, and Sanghasena and Guna-vriddhi from India (AD 492).

Bodhidharma, the Silent Missionary

In the sixth century we witness a phenomenal development in sea-communication between India and China *via* Malay Archipelago. The first notable case of sea voyage from India was that of Bodhidharma who came to south China in AD 520, and worked in the same field as Buddhabhadra, amongst the mystic population of China. Bodhidharma is said to have remained silent for the first *nine years* ! Yet he exerted a profound influence on the Chinese mind and "opened a powerful stream of meditative naturalism in China and Japan".

Paramartha, founder of the Yogachara School in China

The second case of sea voyage was that of the Indian savant Paramartha, the famous biographer of the Buddhist philosopher Vasubandhu (AD 420-500). Having arrived in China in AD 540, Paramartha was cordially invited to Nanking in AD 548. He was not only the translator of the works of Asanga and Vasubandhu, the pillars of the *realistic school* of Buddhist Idealism, but was also the first propagator of the Yogachara school of thought before Hiuen-Tsang.

The Golden Age of Sino-Indian Collaboration

With the unification of the North and the South under the auspices of the T'ang Dynasty (AD 617-910) recovering control over Central Asia, there opened the most glorious period of Asiatic Art and Philosophy through the vigorous collaboration of India and China. The invaluable records left by the two great Chinese pilgrims Hiuen-Tsang (AD 629-45) and I-tsing (AD 700), bear testimony to the fact that India had come to be the very heart of Asiatic Humanism. That explains partly the jealous attacks on the Buddhist organisations in China from contemporary Taoist and Confucian rivals. Yet it must be admitted that through every phase of this evolution, India had been shaping vigorously the whole fabric of Chinese thought and aesthetics. On the one hand, the Indian spirit was so marvellously naturalised in China that the Sino-Indian texts, even today, "form an intergral part of the Chinese language and literature". On the other hand, the recent discoveries of Grunwedel and von Le Coq in Central Asia and of Sir Aurel Stein and Paul Pelliot in, the wonderful grottos of Touen Houang, prove the phenomenal fusion of Hellenic and Iranian, Christian and Manichaean streams of thought and culture under the grand transforming agency of Buddhism. "Anything that came from India brought with it a high prestige." Indian models of Buddhist art were closely followed; Indian imagery and symbolism, Indian ideals of form were taken over by Chinese masters and therefore their Buddhist pictures show a striking contrast to their secular drawings and paintings. The Touen Houang pictures show the wonderful fusion of Sino-Indian styles and the T'ang masters of Touen Houang were closely followed by the early Japanese masters. Thus the chance discovery[11] of this desert grotto with its polyglot library and wonderful art treasures, has contributed so much to our knowledge of the history of international intercourse. Touen Houang, situated on the great highway stretching across Asia from China to the Mediterranean where it intersected the main routes from Mongolia in the north and Tibet and India in the south—naturally shows the relics of the historical fusion of the Orient and the Occident, and that is why the Chinese Buddhist paintings of the T'ang period are considered, by experts like Raphaeal Petrucci and Laurence Binyon, to inaugurate "one of the greatest periods of creative art in world history".

India and Korea

From China, Buddhism naturally entered Korea. As early as AD 374 two monks A-tao and Shun-tao, both foreigners, were invited from North China to the capital of Koryo (modem Pien-yang). In AD 384 certain Matananda (a curious Indian name) was welcomed by the court of the Paikchai (middle Korea) and was backed by a fresh batch of Indian and Chinese missionaries. Towards the middle of the fifth-century Buddhist propaganda advanced to the south and an ascetic called the "Black Foreigner" preached the doctrine of the *Tri-ratna* (triple gem), after having been famous by curing with his wonderful science a princess of the Silla kingdom which recognised Buddhism officially in 528.

[11]Cf. Sir Aurel Stein, *Ruins of Desert Cathay* and *Serindia* also Paul Pelliot, *Touen Houang*.

Between AD 540-76, we read about a king and a queen of Korea taking to the robes of monks and nuns. In AD 551 a sort of Buddhist Patriarchate was created with a Korean priest as the archbishop of the realm, and Buddhism continued to shine with incomparable radiance down to the tenth century when Korea was under the Koryo dynasty (AD 918). So Korea still remains a rich and virgin field of Buddhist archaeology largely unexplored. We may hope that some day the friendly collaboration of Chinese, Korean and Japanese scholars would unfold to the world the complete history of Korean Buddhism.

India and Japan[12]

The small country of Korea had the unique privilege presenting to Japan one of its greatest civilising agencies—continental Buddhism. Chinese learning had penetrated Japan as early as the fifth century AD; but it was Korea that made the first official presentation in AD 538 of a gilt statue of Buddha, some beautiful banners and sacred texts to the Japanese court, as a sign of homage and friendship. The accompanying message from Korea was also noble, declaring that "Buddha dharma the most excellent of all laws which brings immeasurable benefit to its believers . . . had been accepted in all lands laying between India and Korea."

The opposition of the conservative party only accentuated the zeal of progressive Japan and with the fall of the anti-Buddhist party in AD 587, Prince Umayado or Shotoku (AD 593-622) the Constantine of Japan, made Buddhism the state religion of Japan. He invited Korean monks to teach the sciences like astronomy and medicine to his people and sent Japanese students to China to study Buddhism. With the influx of Buddhist monks and savants came artists, artisans and physician-philanthropists as the rear guard of religion. And here, as everywhere, Buddhism built its influence on the solid foundation of the philanthropic and aesthetic instincts of the believers. Thus there grew up asylums, hospitals, dispensaries as well as the great treasures of Art: painting, sculpture and architecture, wherever the new Faith went. We hear of Chinese missionary Kan-jin (AD 754-63) organising medical missions and founding botanical gardens. So the Indian missionary Bodhisena, a Brahmin of Bharadwaja *gotra*, came to Japan in AD 736 with his Cham (from the Hindu colony of Champa) and Chinese followers, many of whom were artists and musicians; and Bodhisena worked as the Buddhist Bishop of Japan till his death in AD 760, always known as the "Brahmin Bishop".

These missionaries not only introduced but developed many useful arts, knowing full well that art is a great handmaid to religion. Indian lyre (*rina*) and other musical instruments as well as bas-reliefs in the Graeco-Buddhist

[12]Cf. Anesaki, "Buddhist Mission", in *Encyclopædia of Religion and Ethics*; also Takakusu, "What Japan owes to India", in *Young East*, vols. II-VI.

style are preserved in the Imperial treasury of Japan dating from the eighth century AD. With profound respect for individual development, these Buddhist workers never imposed anything by force; so that everywhere their advent was followed by a phenomenal growth of native arts and crafts. Thus the medical and the artistic missionaries played almost as great a part as saints and learned scholars in the propagation of the Indian faith.

During the whole of the eighth century, the famous Nara Period (AD 708-94), the movement of Peace and Illumination spread from the capital city to the provinces where many people now began to endow religious and philanthropic institutions and these humanitarian works soon "converted the whole of Japan into Buddhadom". Japanese sculpture and painting began to awaken to its career of world famous creation, while the constant contact with China brought from time to time different schools of Buddhistic thought. The mystic *Mantra* sect, introduced into China in the eighth century by Subhakarasiraha and Amoghavajra, entered Japan in the ninth century and even some of the esoteric sects like the Dharmalakshana, organised by Asanga, while losing hold on India and China, were preserved in the Japanese school of Buddhist philosophy. Far from imposing a foreign system to the detriment of the independent development of the indigenous peoples, Buddhism liberated the dormant springs of individual creative activities. So within two centuries of the official introduction of Buddhism, we find the Japanese people developing cults, sects, schools of philosophy and art-traditions of their own. The brightest stars of Japan in the ninth century like Saicho and Kobo were pioneers of real Japanese Buddhism independent of continental influences: Saicho (AD 767-822) founded the famous sect called *Tendai-shu*, preaching "Buddha the historical revealer of Truth as the full enlightenment, and the realisation of such Buddhahood in one's own consciousness as the supreme object of all mysteries, virtues and wisdom". Another sect called the *Shingon-shu* was founded by Kobo or Kukai (AD 774-835). He preached: "the Universe is Buddha externalised and that the Buddha within us may be called forth by the practice of the mystery in heart, in conduct and in speech".

The *Tendai* and *Shingon* sects exerted powerful influence amongst the refined and cultured aristocracy of Japan. But the stoic military class and the superstitious mass also were evolving their own suitable systems out of Buddhism. Since the beginning of the twelfth century, internal troubles and disasters of Japan slowly developed a pessimism which wanted less philosophical and more emotional from of religion to satisfy the people. So Horen (AD 1133-1212) appeared denouncing all philosophy as effete and all mysteries as useless. He preached the doctrine of *Sukhavati*, the Japanese Jodo or "The Western Paradise" according to which any creature, ignorant or wise, high or low, could be saved by simple faith in the boundless grace of Amitabha.

Side by side, we watch the marvellous transformation of the primitive Shintoism under Buddhist influences, when men like Chika-fusa (AD 1339) developed a new syncretism representing all popular animistic gods of Shintoism as the *avataras* of Buddha.

Lastly, the stoical *samurai* military class found its firm support in the philosophy of the Zen (*Dhyana*) sect introduced into Japan in AD 1250, by some disciples of the old *Shan-no* (*Dhyana*) sect of China, organised by Indian missionaries like Buddhabhadra and Bodhidharma. Thus while India herself, on accout of her pre-occupation with narrow domestic problems forgot all about her far-off cultural colonies of Korea and Japan, the devoted philosophers and master artists of Japan were worshipping the ineffable personality of Buddha-Amitabha and covering temple after temple with the marvellous figure of the Indian saint, *Pindola Bharadwaja*.

India and Tibet

Tibet was rather late in emerging from its state of savage isolation. It is significant that the very first king who brought Tibet up to Asiatic importance, was in close contact with India and China: King Srong-btsan-Gampo (AD 630-98) married an Indian (Nepalese) princess as well as a Chinese one; the former introduced the Hindu-Buddhist cult of Tara along with other occult practices, while the latter brought Chinese Buddhism and priests. Not stopping there, Gampo sent his able minister Thummi Sambhota to India where he studied and gradually evolved out of Devanagari script, the present Tibetan alphahet. The next King Khri-Srong-de-blsan (AD 740-86) invited learned scholars from India and with their noble collaboration, the Tibetans soon managed to have a scripture and literature of their own. The names of Indian savants like Padmasambhava and his disciple Pagur Vairochana are ever memorable in Tibetan history. Translations and adaptations of Indian texts continued vigorously down to the appearance of the great personality of Dipamkara Srijnana or Atiśa (AD 1038) from Bengal, who effected a veritable reformation in the religious history of Tibet.

Naturally primitive and gross by temperament the Tibetans did not develop any independent system of their own as was done by the Chinese or the Japanese. Most of their standard compilations like the *Kandjour* (book of revelation—words of Buddha) and the *Tandjour* (book of tradition) stand today as curious collections of religion and magic, science and poetry. No doubt they translated from time to time, classical works of Indian literature like the famous lexicon of *Amarakosha* and the *Meghaduta* "Cloud Messenger" of Kalidasa, the grammar of Chandragomin and the treatise on painting and iconography like the "Chitralakshana"—yet we cannot help noticing that the Tibetans showed almost a morbid preference for the mystical and magical texts of later debased Buddhism: the Vajrayana, the Kalachakrayana, etc., which went to the formation of Lamaism. Here we find the alchemist-philosopher Nagarjuna tacitly preferred to the Buddha himself. So the savage pre-Buddhistic Shamanism of the Bon cult, the crude magic and devil-charming rituals common to the mountainous tribes, came to be mixed up with Indian Buddhism. Still it effected a miracle by gradually transforming the mentality of the people. Waddel who lived amongst the Tibetans for a long time and who is one of the leading authorities on Tibetan history, writes:

> The current of Buddhism which runs through its tangled Paganism has brought to the Tibetan most of the little civilisation which he possess and has raised him correspondingly in the scale of humanity, lifting him above a life of semi-barbarism, by setting before him higher hopes and aims, by giving milder meanings to his demonist mythology, by discountenancing sacrifice of animal lives and by inculcating universal charity and tenderness to all living things.

India and the Turco-Mongolian Peoples

With the conquest of China and Central Asia by the Mongol chief Chengiz Khan (died AD 1227) and his successor Kubilai Khan (AD 1260), Tibetan Buddhism was established as a sort of theocracy by Lama Phagspa, the Tibetan ally of Kubilai. Through the intermediary of Tibet, the arts and crafts of India and Nepal (especially *Bronze casting*) reached the courts of the Buddhist Mongolian emperors of China and were always prized as works of rare craftsmanship and great value. Phagspa[13] (Tibetan for Arya) died in AD 1250 and was succeeded by Lama Dharmapala in the office of the Imperial Chaplain of the Mongol emperors of China. The noble activities of these Buddhist workers, in this epoch, connected the Tibetans, the Mongols, the Tunguse and the Ouigur Turks (in the frontiers of Siberia) and other Samoyed races, in one bond of spiritual union.[14]

India and South-eastern Asia

The whole of the eastern Asiatic world may be linguistically divided into three main sections: (i) Koreo-Japanese (ii) Sino-Tibetan and (iii) Malay-Polynesian. We have, so far, traced the influence of Indian humanism on the nations of the first two groups. Now, passing on to the third group, we remember the border land of Burma. From Burma we march through Siam, Cambodia (in fact the whole of the Trans-Gangelic peninsula) to the Malay Archipelago (with Sumatra, Java, Madura, Bali, Lombok, Borneo and other islands) till at last we are in the heart of Indonesia. The whole history of this vast area was enveloped in deep obscurity till very recont times. Thanks to the researches of the French and the Dutch scholars who are pioneers in this branch of investigation, we havo how a fairly clear view of the history of South-eastern Asia. With every fresh archaeological discovery or philological analysis, we are more and more convinced of the fact, that down to quite late-periods (thirteenth-fourteenth centuries) when Islam penetrated this area, the greatest

[13] Paul Pelliot, *Lectures on Lamaism in College de France* (1922-3).

[14] Huth (G), *Geschichte des Buddhismus in der Mongolei* (1893).

formative influence on the life and history of the peoples of south-eastern Asia was that of India, backed by China in certain parts.

Epochs of Hindu Colonisation

The archaeological finds in this part of the world are of a comparatively late period. So the scholars of the last generation were rather sceptic with regard to the possibility of early penetration of Indian influence. But we should consider that long before a king feels inclined to get a grandiloquent panegyric of his career inscribed on a rock or a copper-plate, that long before a community is capable of rearing a great architectural monument, a people discovers another people quite normally, propelled by the *spirit of adventure*, economic or spiritual. So it is not *prima facie* improbable that Indian missionaries reached south-eastern Asia by the sea route, about the same period that they had been penetrating the Far-Western and the Far-Eastern regions by the land route.

The very fact that Ptolemy (second century AD) names many of the places in his *Geography* of this region in an Indian way up to Java, proves that the Indians were already in the field. The earliest inscriptions of Champa (Indo-China) bearing evidences of Indian (simultaneously Brahmanic and Buddhistic) influence, go as far back as the third century AD. Prof. Paul Pelliot, one of the greatest living authorities on the history of this area, believes that apart from the great Central Asian route, there were *two other old roads* of communication for the Eastern Asiatic peoples: one was the land-route from India *via* Assam and Burma to China and another was the sea-route *via* Indo-Chinese coasts. And Pelliot discovers in Chinese documents that India appears in the history of Funan (ancient Cambodia) as early as third century AD. Thus, although the materials are as yet scanty, we may state that in course of their *first movement of expansion* about the beginning of the Christian era, the Indians left unmistakable traces of their influence on Pegu, Burma and Champa, Cambodge, Sumatra and Java, though the despatching of Asokan missionaries to Burma may be a later fabrication.

The *second wave of cultural colonisation* was in the fifth century AD—a period of great internal prosperity and intellectual maturity in the history of India. During this century not only Champa and Cambodge were thoroughly Hinduised, but fresh Hindu colonies appear in the Malay Peninsula, in ancient Siam, in Laos, in Borneo, Sumatra and Java. This is the epoch when Aryabhatta (b. AD 479) and Varahamihira (AD 505-87) were assimilating the Hellenic sciences, when Gunavarman (dying in Nanking AD 431) was converting Java to Buddhism, when the famous frescoes of Ajanta were recording in their exquisite language the fusion of Aryo-Dravidian and Indo-Persian culture. In this grand epoch of *Hindu renaissance*, there was no exclusive *caste* prohibitions and no intolerant sectarianism. Hence we find Brahmanism and Buddhism, in fact all sects and denominations, flourishing peacefully in these cultural colonies of India in South-eastern Asia. The history of the movement of Hindu syncretism and cultural synthesis in this region of *Magna India*, has yet to be written.

Burma and Ceylon

Burma is linguistically related to Tibet but it came in touch with Indian civilisation much earlier. The introduction of Buddhism by Asokan missionaries (third century BC) may or may not be true; but it is strongly urged by native tradition that Buddhaghosha established the Hinayana Buddhism in Burma from Ceylon about AD 450. Meanwhile sinologists have discovered in the Chinese *Tai Annals*, sufficient evidences to assert that even Buddhaghosha, the champion of the Ceylonese Hinayana was not the first in this field. He had his predecessors in the missionaries of the Mahayana and of the Brahmanical systems in Burma. This is corroborated by the interesting collection of *Pyu* inscriptions (fifth century AD) which bear traces of borrowing from Sanskrit vocabulary through the medium of *living dialects* (Prakrits) of eastern India and not through the canonical language Pali. So there is every possibility of early contact with Sanskrit Mahayana through eastern Bengal and Assam. From that period down to the present day, Burma, like Ceylon, remains in religion and culture, essentially a part of India.

Champa, Cambodge, Siam and Laos

The Indian colonies of Champa and Cambodge are, like Ceylon, too important to be treated summarily; special studies would be devoted to them.

Siam was also formally converted during the later period of Hindu expansion. Buddhism was introduced into Siam from Cambodia and like Cambodia it remained faithful to the Ceylonese or the southern Pali Buddhism. A splendid Buddha image, a rare specimen of Ceylon bronze-casting, has been discovered amongst the ruins of Champa. Mon. Cabaton, an authority on the history of these peoples affirm that until the advent of the Portuguese navigators (sixteenth century), Siam was completely within the cultural influence of India:

> It received its first civilisation from the Brahmins of India and then from the merchants from the Malabar and the Coromandel (coast); and along with Cambodia and Laos, Siam remained permeated with Indian civilisation until the east coast of Indo-China (Annam) accepted Chinese civilisation. There are still extant, noteworthy archaeological witnesses of this primitive *hinduisation* of Siam in the monuments of its former capitals, *Savankhalok*, *Sukhokai* and *Lopburi*. The former and present religions of Siam (*i.e.*, Brahmanism and Buddhism) its secred language, its civil institutions, its writing, its arts, and its literature, came from India. In the thirteenth century the *Thai* alphabet, the prototype of the present alphabet was invented by the help of *Brahmin gurus* on the model of the Indian writing already in use in the country. All this civilisation has been preserved and diffused up to the present day by the monks who are, as a rule, the educators of the people. . . .

From the Indian to the Pacific Ocean

Leaving aside the as yet obscure problem of pre-Aryan, even pre-Dravidian contact of India with the Mon-khmer and, the Malay-Polynesian world, we may still safely say that there were very early maritime communications between the peoples across the Indian Ocean, connecting the African Archipelago including Madagascar with the Malay Archipelago. The island of Ceylon or Taprobane was a sort of a halting stage in his grand oceanic traffic. The very frequent confusion between Indian Malay and African place-names made by classical travellers and geographers is highly significant. It is now beyond doubt that audacious Indian mariners reached Madagascar, Ceylon as well as Sumatra, Java and Borneo in early times. Fa-hien and Gunavarman (AD 400) followed only the traditional maritime routes of Indian Oceanic migration. The Malay Peninsula served both as a *great causeway* for the migrations from the Asiatic continent and as a *rendezvous* for merchants and peoples from widely separated countries. In Sumatra the Malayan races were moulded by Indian influences into a comparatively civilised condition before they crossed over to the Peninsula. The oldest foreign loan-words in Malay are Sanskrit, including words for religious, moral and intellectual ideas, with some astronomical, mathematical and botanical terms, a court vocabulary and a large number of everyday words. In their pantheon the greater gods are Hindu while the lesser gods are Malay. Their cosmology is also Hindu. Only in one branch, in their arts, both industrial and ornamental, some of the Indonesian peoples, while deriving the ideas and inspiration from India (China did not play a great part here before the T'ang period, sixth century AD), could preserve their distinct individuality. Both in the evolution of the architectural and of the decorative motifs, the Javanese and the Khmer peoples will always occupy a big place in the general history of Asiatic art.

The Empire of Sri-Vijaya in Sumatra

So it is not at all surprising to note that the famous Chinese-Buddhist pilgrim I-tsing twice visited in AD 671 and 698 Sumatra (then known as the kingdom of Sri-Vijaya),[15] studying and translating Indian texts. More than 1,000 monk-savants studied there all the subjects that were taught in Indian centres of learning. In fact, this daughter university of Sumatra had already become so important that Dharmapala, the celebrated Mahayana professor of the great Nalanda University before the visit of Hiuen-Tsang, went to Suvarnadvipa (Sumatra) in his old age, most probably as a veteran Director of Indian Studies. Between the age of I-tsing (AD 700) and that of the Mahayana Buddhist king Adityavarman of Middle Sumatra (AD 1350) we have as yet very few records. In the fourteenth century, Sumatra, under king Adityavarman was still erecting the statue of Jina Amoghapasa, a Tantric incarnation of Avalokiteswara in the temple of Padang Chandi, with an inscription in barbarous Sanskrit. But already the north of Sumatra had been converted to Islamism which soon overwhelmed the whole of the island.

[15]Coedes, Le Royaume de Dri Vijaya, *B.E.F, Ex. O.* 1917.

Java, Madura, Bali, Lombok and Borneo

Java was from very early times noticed in Indian literature. *Ramayana* describes Java (and probaly also Sumatra, known as the Suvarnadvipa), as rich in gold mines. Fa-hien found it necessary to pay a visit to this island in the early fifth century. Like Sumatra, Java was the stronghold of the Buddhist sect of the Mula-Sarvastivadins. Their scriptures being in Sanskrit was much valued locally, but those texts frequently checked the spontaneous development of Javanese-Buddhist art which remained a little too faithful and rigidly documentary as was noticed by Mon. Foucher in his monograph on the Buddhist temple of Borobudur. In the eighth century, Mahayana Buddhism gained a firm footing in Java. In AD 778 a king of the Sailendra dynasty of the Sri-Vijaya kingdom of Sumatra, commemorates the erection of a statue and a temple of Arya Tara, *sakti* of Avalokiteswara by an inscription in Sanskrit language and in a north Indian script, not in Kawi or old Javanese. H. Kern, the great Dutch savant, expressed his opinion to the effect that the Tantric-Mahayanists came to Java from Western Bengal. The temple of Arya Tara is now in ruins known as Chandi Kalasan. The splendid monuments of architecture, which appear in Java about the ninth century, bear the impress of Mahayana Buddhism. But the later Javanese art as well as the Javanese literature and inscriptions are largely Hindu Saiva. That seems to show that a great bulk of the people in the Hindu colonies like Champa, Java and especially in the island of Bali were allowed to practise and profess other cults of Hinduism even when the ruling houses were officially adopting Buddhism. Down to the middle ages, the relation between official Buddhism and non-official popular Hinduism, was marked by perfect tolerance and friendliness which produced a wonderful fusion of religious thought and art-styles.

In the ninth century we witness the *third grand wave* of cultural colonisation mainly from south India. The kingdom of Sri-Vijaya (Sumatra) suddenly becomes a great civilising agency extending its influence over Java as well as a part of south India and its name appears in an inscription of Devapala recently discovered in Nalanda. Impregnated with the spiritual and aesthetic ideals of India, Java now created the wonderful temple of Borobudur, a marvel of oriental architecture. Buddhism was a favourite religion with the Javanese sovereigns from King Sree Isanavijaya Dharmottungadeva (AD 950) to Tribhuvanottunga Devi, the queen ruling over the whole of Java (AD 1350).

Indo-China and Indonesia Spiritually Connected

Other forms of Brahmanical religion, especially Saivism were tolerated and widely practised by a large part of the population of Java, Madura, Bali, and Lombok. That is why probably during the tenth, eleventh and twelfth centuries when the Indonesian art reached its apogee, we find in Java, the great Prambanam and Panataram temples consecrated to Brahmanical deities like Brahma, Vishnu, Siva, Durga, etc., as well as brilliant stone pictures (bas-reliefs) of the *Ramayana* and the Krishnayna. So we find in Cambodia, the famous Mon-Khmer monuments, the Saiva temple of Angkor Thorn (ninth century) and the Vaishnava temple of Bapuon, as well as the marvellous monument of Angkor-Vat (completed AD 1150) dedicated to Vishnu, by the Cambodian king Parama Vishnuloka. "These monuments," remarks Mon. Cabaton, "give evidence to this day of cultural and artistic gifts so incompatible with the intellectual apathy of the Khmers, that some scholars are inclined to think that the grandeur of the empire was due to a Hindu colony which governed the country (Champa-Cambodge) from the eighth to the fourteenth century." However, the Sino-Tibetan invasions of the Annamites and the Siamese during the twelfth and thirteenth centuries led to a gradual decadence, and the downfall of the great Hindu colonies of Champa and Cambodge was complete when Islam swept over the whole area like a hurricane.

Malay-Polynesian World

Leaving aside the question of the reciprocal influence of the Hindu and the Islamic history, we shall note summarily the main features of India's role in the history of South-Eastern Asia. Unlike the thoroughly pacific cultural penetration of India in Serindia, China and Japan, her expansion over South-eastern Asia was not unaccompanied by occasional political conquests or military occupations. However, what India brought as her real contributions to these regions, were not the conquering armies or dynasties long forgotten, but a veritable *fertilising influence* in the domain of intellectual and artistic creation. That is why a veteran philologist like Dr. Skeat found after an elaborate analysis that the oldest loan-words in this linguistic group are "words for *religious*, *moral* and *intellectual* ideas coming from India". So in the highly interesting monograph on the "Indonesians" Mr. Kruijt notices how the name for *God* in most of the languages of this Malay-Polynesian world, is derived from the Indian word *devata*:

> In Siau the highest god is called *Duata* which is also found among the Macassars and Buginese as *Dewata*, among the Dayaks of Borneo as *Jabata Jata*, among the Mongondouians as *Duata*, and among the people of the Philippine islands as *Divata*, *Davata*, *Diuata*.

So the Sanskrit word *bhattara* is found in more or less changed forms, in many Indonesian languages in the sense of God, e.g., *batara guru* who appears with Saripada and Manalabulan as the three most important deities of the Malay Archipelago, as pointed out by H. Kern. And what is still more amazing is the recent discovery of Indian influence on the formation of early Polynesian poetry and mythology. A.H. Keane's remarks in this connection deserve quoting:

> At times the Polynesian singers appear to soar into the ethereal spaces and to realise the concept of a Supreme Being. . . . Tangaroa is spoken of as Toivi, the Eternal or else like the Hindu *Brahma* or the Dodonian Zeus that 'was is and shall be' . . . described in the loftiest language as dwelling 'in the limitless void of space, when the world was not yet,

nor the heavens nor the sea, nor man.' Such sublime conceptions, such subtle theosophies, such personifications of Chaos, Immensity, Gloomy Night and other pure abstractions in these children of nature, excite wonder and remain inexplicable in their present fragmentary state. Everywhere we find Heaven, Earth, the Universe, the Afterworld, recurring under diverse names and forms, personified by language embodied in theocratic and anthropomorphic philosophies—*echoes as it were of the Vedic hymns* reverberating from isle to isle over the broad Pacific waters. The question arises: *Have there been Vedic contacts*? It is a chronological question which cannot be answered until the date is approximately determined of the eastward migration of the Indonesians from Malaysia. Did the migration precede or follow the arrival of the Hindu missionaries in that region?

Service and Fellowship: Key-Notes of Greater Indian History

Thus listening to these profound hymns of the Polynesian Vedas amidst the vast expanse of the Pacific Ocean, we seem to catch the real secret of India's success in her career of internationalism. In spite of occasional lapses to militarism on the part of individual sovereigns, the *Indian people as a whole, stuck substantially to the principle, of Peace and Progress*. They respected the individuality of the races and nations which came into contact with them, offering their best and evoking the best in others. Thus India managed to leave a record of collaboration in the realm of the Sublime and the Beautiful, quite remarkable in world history. The political conquerors and economic exploiters might have been there too; but they never played a dominant role in this grand drama of Creative Unity. That is why, when the names of the great kings and emperors were forgotten, the people of these cultural colonies cherished with gratitude the memory of the services rendered by the innumerable Indian monks and teachers, artists and philanthropists—selfless workers for human progress and international amity.

CHAPTER 2

Sylvain Lévi and the Science of Indology

KALIDAS NAG

It requires no apology to-day to claim the title of science on behalf of the systematic study of Indian culture and antiquities. The ninteenth century had witnessed the enfranchisement of a few more *ologies* in her already bulky list of sciences. Along with Egyptology, Assyriology and Sinology, Indology also claims her place in the scale of her comparative culture history of humanity.

Like every other science, Indology now presents a long list of devoted workers. Inasmuch as Sylvain Lévi's career epitomises and symbolises the progress of this new science, we presume to present an outline of the life and activities of this French *savant* for the benefit of the fresh recruits in the field of Indology.

Sylvain Lévi entered the arena of Indian studies just one century after its inauguration: 1784 witnessed the foundation of the Asiatic Society of Bengal under the initiative of Sir William Jones and in 1884 we find Sylvain Lévi sitting at the feet of Abel Bergaigne, one of the rarest type of the teachers of Sanskrit in Europe. Thus a hurried glance across the list of Lévi's predecessors and contemporaries would help us to have a correct perspective and to ascertain the specific character of Lévi's contribution to the development of the science.

India attracted the attention of the world through ages: Alexander to Albouquerque, Kadphises to Nādir Shāh—what a history of feverish search for the wealth of India! As late as the mid seventeenth century we find Milton singing of "the wealth of Ormuz and of Ind" in his *Paradise Lost*—no doubt a poetic paraphrase of the history of Portuguese exploitation. A century after we notice a curious phenomenon. The foremost intellect of France, the arch-rationalist Voltaire eagerly searching for the *Ezour Vedam* of the Hindus not knowing that the papers were forgeries of a Portuguese Jesuit priest. What is more wonderful is that France in another of her sons offers the first audacious discoverer of the authentic records of Indian culture. Anquetil Duperron, eager to discover the Vedas of the Hindus, joined the service of the French East India Company in 1754, and succeeded in offering to the Bibliothèque Nationale of Paris, the first nucleus of an Oriental Library in the form of the manuscripts of the Vedas and the Avesta. Duperron signalised a new departure in the history of Europe's quest for India (vide Lévi: Preface to M.R. Schwab's *Anquetil*

Source: *Journal of the Greater India Society* (III/1, 1936, 3–17).

Duperron, Paris, 1934). It is not only the physical wealth but the cultural and spiritual legacy of India that is attracting Europe. This *orientation* (in the literal and metaphorical sense of the term) of the occidental outlook is as mysterious as, and coincides strikingly with, the startling declaration of American Independence and the epoch-making phenomenon of the French Revolution. The West suddenly felt the need of the East—a need which, as future history would show, is deeper than economics and wider than politics. The pioneers of Indian studies like Jones and Chézy were passionate admirers of *Śakuntalā*. The masterpiece of immortal Kālidāsa by a characteristic touch of poetic justice secured the cooperation of the English, the French and the German schools of Indology. Thus the new science went on gaining fresh votaries to her temple. After Jones and Chézy came Colebrooke and Burnouf—both remarkable for their intensity of study and variety of achievements. Colebrooke studied the Vedas and Indian philosophy, the lexicon and Indian law with equally fruitful results; while Burnouf proved himself to be a veritable prodigy—the first great genius of the science of Indology. Not satisfied with an extensive, study of Sanskrit and Pāli, Burnouf applied himself to the mastery of Tibetan, Siamese, Burmese and Avestan languages, thereby attaining a rare maturity of judgment and accuracy of intuition. *Introduction à l'historie du Buddhisme Indien* still stands as a marvel of scholarship and a deathless monument to his genius. Working at the Duperron MSS on the one hand and the Hodgson MSS on the other, Burnouf sounded the keynote for the French School of Indologists: not narrow specialisation in one particular branch but the opening, up of ever-widening vistas of Indian Culture History. Hence it was as it were in the fitness of things that Burnouf should bless the pioneers of the forthcoming generation of workers by his personal initiation. Both Bopp and Max Müller sat at the feet of Burnouf, while Christian Lassen was deeply influenced by him. Thus gradually we reach the period of *scientific excavations*, when in Germany appear workers like Bopp and Weber, Böhtlingk and Roth and in France Regnaud and Bergaigne, Barth and Senart whose appearance was characterised by Lévi as "*la naissance d'une pleiade d'Indienistes*".[1]

It was when this pleiad was shining bright on the firmament of the French School that Sylvain Lévi appeared on the horizon. Thus his career, stretching as it does across the nineteenth to the twentieth century, touches the luminous line radiating between Burnouf and Bergaigne on the one hand and the luminaries of the coming generation like Foucher and Pelliot on the other. Hence his career is of immense historic interest to all students of Indology.

Born in Paris, 28 March 1863, Sylvain Lévi seemed to have finished undergoing the university discipline with such a phenomenal rapidity that we almost miss Lévi the maturing student in Lévi the finished savant. He was a *licencié* (1882) and an *agregé des lettres* (1883) when he was barely twenty. Men like Ernest Renan and James Darmesteter had always an eye on this remarkable young scholar. Lévi manifested at this time a strong predilection

[1]Lévi, *l'Indienisme*, 1915.

for the Classics. In fact, he was meditating to join the French School at Athens, when Renan rendered unconsciously a signal service to the cause of Indology by deeding the decisive push which won Lévi permanently for the Indian science. Lévi was brought in touch with Abel Bergaigne, one of the greatest teachers of Sanskrit in Europe. It is an irony of fate no doubt that almost immediately after Lévi's affiliation into the classes of Bergaigne, James Darmesteter, the great Avestan scholar, paid him a visit to win him as an assistant to his Avestan studies. But India and not Iran was the predestined sphere of Lévi's work. And thus we find him preparing for his memorable researches under the instruction of his master, Bergaigne. That great scholar had then been publishing his researches into the Vedic literature and the documents of Cambodgian history published in the *Journal Asiatique* (1882-3). Lévi learned his elements of Sanskrit rhetoric and prosody not from academic Indian treatises on the subject but from concrete epigraphical documents discovered in Cambodge. Thus from the very beginning Lévi had a vision of Indian history and culture not circumscribed by the *modem political delimitation of India*. We thankfully remember the names of Burnouf and Bergaigne who were responsible for this grand vision of *Magna India* which radiates from every page of Lévi. Here Lévi proved a worthy disciple of worthy masters and continued the grand traditions of the French School of Indologists, ever expanding the frontiers of the new science, ever widening the horizon of Indian history.

Towards the end of the year 1885 the first paper of Lévi was honoured with a place in the foremost oriental journal of France: *La Bṛhatkathā-Mañjarī de Kṣemendra* was published in *Journal Asiatique* (1885-6). Lévi was appointed maitre des conferences of the Ecole des Hautes Etudes on the retirement of Hauvette Besnault (1886). To the conferences of this professor prodigy of twenty-three were attracted men who have left their mark on many departments of research—men illustrious in the later history of French scholarship—to mention among others, A. Meillet the great philologist and A. Foucher the illustrious writer on Buddhist art and archaeology, now representing Indology in the French Academy. While Lévi was thus continuing his work with a unique devotion and passion, Bergaigne, who was a great lover of mountains met his tragic death in course of one of his excursions (1889). The loss of his beloved *guru* was an awful blow to the youthful enthusiasm of Lévi. Everyone knew how he used to adore his master. M. Emile Senart paid a visit to Lévi to cheer him up. Gradually Lévi accepted this new challenge of fate in a spirit at once characteristic and admirable. The master is gone but his work remains. He devoted his whole energy to the perpetuation of that noble work of interpreting India to Europe. The Société Asiatique requested Lévi to fill up the place of his late lamented master in the Council (1889) and in 1890 we notice his second paper—"*Abel Bergaigne et* l'Indianisme" (*Revue Bleue*, 1890)—a noble tribute to the memory of a noble master.

In 1890 Lévi became a full-fledged Docteur ès lettres presenting two theses, one in Latin—*Quid de Graecis Veterum Indorum Monumenta Tradideriut*

(What About Greece Ancient Indian Monuments conserved) and another in French, *Le Theatre Indien*—which still stands as the most authoritative treatise on Hindu drama. Almost at the same period he was honoured with a place in Faculté des Lettres of the University of Paris and was promoted to the rank of the directeur adjoint of the Ecole des Hautes Etudes (1892-3) working with brilliant pupils like Meillet, Finot, Foucher and de La Vallée Pouasin. The year 1894 witnessed the appointment of Lévi to the Chair of Sanskrit in the College de France, nearly 80 years after creation of the first French Chair of Sanskrit with Chézy. Vide Lévi: *L'entrée du Sanscrit au College de France* (1932). This was the crowning of his academic career: A young man of thirty started his works on Indology as the colleague of Darmesteter, Maspero and Gaaton Paris.

This was undoubtedly a point of departure in the career of Lévi. He was lecturing on *Vedānta-Sāra* and *Uttara-Rāmacarita*, he was discussing the inscriptions of Piyadasi and contributing valuable articles on India in the *Grande Encyclopaedic*. Not satisfied with these, he organised a class for a systematic study of Chinese and Tibetan along with Sanskrit and Pali texts under the direction of M. Specht. At the same time he had been dreaming of the possibility of founding a French School of Indology in Chandernagore and in consultation with M. Guièysse, the then minister of Colonies, entrusted Foucher (in course of his first mission) to enquire about the possibilities of such a foundation. The scheme, however, matured when Lévi himself visited India (1897-8) and laid indirectly the foundation of the Ecole Française d'Extrême Orient with the help of Leon Bourgeoise (a former pupil of M. Bergaigne), the then Governor-General of Indo-China.

Thus Greater India loomed large on the horizon of Lévi. He had already published his first studies on the *Buddha-carita* of Aśvaghoṣa (*JA*, 1892) and soon discovered and transliterated 150 stanzas of the hymns of Mātriceta. But the most important event at this period is his friendship with Edouard Chavannes, the great French Sinologist, through their common friend of the Ecole Normale, M. Foucher. That friendship was fruitful with several years of most important publications in collaboration—the earliest being the *Iténeraries d'Ou-K'ong* (*JA*, 1895). Within two years we find Lévi sent on a mission to the Extrême Orient (1897-8), in course of which he visited India, Nepal, Indo-China and Japan. This tour widened his sphere of research to such an extent that in spite of his isolated monograph on *La Doctrine du Sacrifice dans les Brāhmaṇas* (1898). Lévi might be said to have settled down on the broader and far more complicated problems of extra-Indian Indology. On his return from the East he was elevated to the rank of the Director of the Ecoles des Hautes Etudes (1898), working with brilliant young savants like Huber, Pelliot and Jules Bloch. Soon after, the *Bulletin* of the *Ecole Française d'Extrême Orient* was founded under the direction of Finot and the *T'oung Poo* came under the editorship of Lévi's friend, Chavannes, and these important journals evoked some of the most original papers of Lévi on Sino-Indian culture. This is the branch of study which the French scholars have made their own. From the time of Abel Rémusat and Stanislas Julien to that of Chavannes and Pelliot there is a continuity of tradition in the parallel study of the documents of two of the oldest and yet living nations of Asia. This study has revolutionised our conception of Asiatic history. Lévi was the first Indologist who brought his marvellous knowledge of Indian things to bear on the elucidation of many intricate problems of that forgotten history. His collaboration with Chavannes and Meillet has more than mere academic significance; it symbolises the inauguration of the comparative study of Sino-Indian and Serindian life and culture. But he was ever close to his India. The same year that he lectured (while Bergson opened his inaugural lecture on *Volonté* in College de France, 1907) on Dharmapada in its Sanskrit and Chinese recensions, he lectured also on Śakuntalā and while he discussed the *Kotikarṇa Avadāna* in its Sanskrit, Chinese and Tibetan versions, Lévi analysed the beauty and sublimity of the Great Epics.

The year 1908 saw the maturity of his studies on the History of Nepal in three grand volumes in the Annals of the Musée Guimet. The very same year Pelliot started on his mission of exploration in Central Asia. Just as the archaeological mission of Chavannes threw a flood of light on the history of ancient China, so Pelliot's mission brought to light a collection of MSS., the value of which we are just beginning to realise. Lévi was the first to give his attention to this rich collection. While busy editing the translating the *Sūtrā-laṃkāra of Asaṅga* and giving Tibetan lessons to young savants like Bacot, Hackin, and Gauthiot, Prof. Lévi formed a smaller seminar for an intensive study of the documents of the Pelliot Mission (1910). In course of this investigations, he found in his former pupil and friend M. Meillet a noble collaborator and thus ensued his brilliant contribution to the decipherment of the Tokharian, Sogdian and Koutchean dialects of Central Asia. Thus for a while the greatest living Indologist of France joined hands with her greatest Sinologist Chavannes and her greatest living Philologist Meillet. But the premature death of Chavannes was a great blow to this momentous union. Lévi, however, continued with Meillet to render signal service to the study of the Central Asian languages. No wonder Lévi was honoured with the place of the President of the Société Linguistique of which Meillet was the prime mover and also with the Presidentship of the *Société Asiatique* of Paris, after the death of Emil Senart.

Apart from these, prodigious activities in the line of scholarship, Lévi was a lay worker of quite inexhaustible energy. How many public institutions of France were indebted to him for his unstinted service. Moreover he bore the heavy burden of responsibility as the president elect of the Alliance Israelite Universelle which has hundreds of educational and philanthropic institutions in the old as well as in the new world and which imposed upon him in the last days the heavy task of succouring the thousands of Jewish scholars expelled from Germany. Even at an advanced age Lévi showed an enthusiasm and capacity for work that was almost phenomenal. In India he would be specially remembered because of his undertaking the noble task of training generations of Indian scholars in the science of which he was the accredited master. That is why he was the first to be invited to occupy the seat of the Ācārya in a truly national institution like the Viśvabhāratī of Rabindranath Tagore joined hands with Lévi, the East collaborated with the West for the cause of Truth and Humanity and we expressed our hope in the language of our poet Kālidāsa that through this spiritual cooperation each served as a purifying factor to the other.

"अन्योन्यपावनमभूदुभयं समेत्य"

Between 1921, when Sylvain Lévi visited India as the first guest-professor of Viśvabhāratī, and the end of his career (30 October 1935), he left a record of research that may fill the lives of several scholars. Organizing oriental studies in the University of Strassbourg (since 1918) and Tibetan and Chinese Studies at Śāntiniketan with brilliant Indian scholars like Mm. Pandit Vidhusekhara Sastri, Pandit Kshitimohan Sen and Prabodh Chandra Bagchi (1921-2) Lévi visited Japan on his return trip, was nominated by Sir Ashutosh Mookerjee, Reader of the University of Calcutta, President of the Second All-India Orientalists, Conference, Calcutta (1921), corresponding member of the Imperial Academy of Tokyo, a foreign member of the Russian Academy of Sciences, a member of the governing body of the Institute of Indian Civilisation (Paris University) and finally President of the *Société Asiatique*. Invited by the Imperial Universities of Tokyo and Kyoto, Prof. Lévi visited Japan for the second (1922-3) and third times (1926-8); lecturing on Buddhism and helping in the completion of the *Hobougirin*, or the *Encyclopaedic Dictionary of Buddhism*, in collaboration with eminent Japanese scholars like Takakusu, Anesaki, Inoue, Sugiyama and others (vide *The Young East*, vol. V, no. 4, Tokyo). Between November 1926, and May 1928, he acted as the Director of the *Maison Franco-Japonaisie* in Tokyo and on their return trip through India, Prof. and Madame Lévi were accorded grand receptions by the *Greater India Society* and the *Sociététe Indo-Latine*, founded by his Indian pupils and admirers who with the modest resources at their disposal are trying for the last ten years to develop Greater Indian Studies in India inspired by his example. Lévi visited the Dutch East Indies in 1928 and made a selection of Hindu texts from Bali recently published by the Gaekwad Oriental Series. Another study on the Javanese *Mahābhārata* was communicated by him to the *Golden Book, of Tagore* (1931) published in honour of his old friend Rabindranath Tagore. So his second and third visits to Nepal provoked him to publish new texts of Vasubandhu (Viṃśatikā and Triṃśikā as well as the variorum edition of the Mahā-karma-vibhaṅga and other valuable documents published by Ernest Leroux (Paris) as well as by the *Journal Asiatique* to which he was contributing for nearly half a century. The forthcoming number of the *Journal Asiatique* will publish an exhaustive and authoritative bibliography of his works by our esteemed friend M.L. Renou. Meanwhile in this special number of our *Journal of the Greater India Society*, we publish bibliographic notes up to 1925 requesting our readers to refer to the *necrologie* of Sylvain Lévi published in the *Journal Asiatique* and other learned French publications.

Series of studies are necessary to do justice to Lévi the savant. The tentative bibliography of his works which we publish below will suffice to demonstrate how almost every branch of Indology feels the impress of his genius. In this short article we have tried only to supply a commentary to this bibliography for the convenience of Indian scholars. We shall conclude by giving two extracts from Lévi's writings illustrating his attitude towards Indian History. In 1890 he concluded his article on *Abel Bergaigne et l'Indienisme* with these words:

> From Persia to the Chinese Sea, from the icy regions of Siberia to the islands of Java and Borneo, from the Oceanea to Socotra, India has propagated her beliefs, her genius, her tales and her civilization. She has left indestructible imprints on one-fourth of the human race in course of a long succession of centuries. She has the right to reclaim, in universal history, the rank that ignorance has refused her for a long time and to hold her place amongst the great nations, summarising and symbolising the spirit of humanity.

As a pupil of the great Vedic scholar Bergaigne, Lévi has given us his studies on the Vedic rituals, as a master teacher of the Sanskrit language he has given us a history of the Hindu Drama, as an intellectual descendant of Burnouf he has given us invaluable studies on Buddhism, as an exponent of scientific method in historical composition he has given us three splendid volumes on Nepal, as an audacious seeker of the relics of Indian genius outside India he has given us the Sūtrālaṃkāra of Asaṅga and the collation of Dharmapada texts—yet all these are side issues and bye-products. Lévi the silent worker is probably greater than his works. This is a fact which can only be attested by those who had the privilege of knowing him intimately. By his life of silent *tapasyā* dedicated to the resuscitation of Indian history and culture, he gained a synthetic vision of that history rarely found in writers on India. It is exactly here that Sylvain Lévi stands as an inspiration and a dream for the young school of Indian Indologists whom he blessed unconsciously through his noble utterances on the mission of India in the scheme of universal history:

> The *multiplicity* of the manifestations of Indian genius as well as their *fundamental unity* gives India the right to figure on the first rank in the history of civilised nations. Her civilisation, spontaneous and original, unrolls itself in a continuous time across at least thirty centuries, without interruption, without deviation. Ceaselessly, in contact with *foreign elements*, which threatened to strangle her, she persevered victoriously in absorbing them, assimilating them and enriching herself with them. Thus she has seen the Greeks, the Scythians, the Afghans, the Mongols pass before her eyes in succession and is regarding with indifference the Englishmen—confident to pursue, under the accidents of the surface, the normal course of her high destiny. (Lévi's article on "*India*" in the *Grande Encyclopaedie*)

BIBLIOGRAPHY

ABBREVIATIONS

JA—Journal Asiatique
BEFEO—Bulletin de l'Ecole Française d'Extrême-Orient
TP—T'oung Pao
BEHE—Bibliothéque d'Ecole des Hautes Etudes
CMG—Conference de Musée Guimet

1885—*La Bṛhatkathāmañjarī de Kṣemendra—JA.*
1886—*La Bṛhatkathāmañjarī et Vetālapañcaviṃśati—JA.*
1889—*Deux chapitres du Sarvadarśana-saṃgraha: le systeme Pāśupata et le systeme Śaiva—BEHE*, vol. I. Articles on Indian subjects contributed to the *Grande Encyclopœdic*:
(a) *Brahmanisme*, (*b*) *Brahmoisme*, (*c*) *Calendrier*, (*d*) *Castes*, (*e*) *Hindouisme*, (*f*) *Hiouen Tsang*, (*g*) *Inde.*
1890—*Abel Bergaigne et l'Indianisme—Revue Bleue*, Paris. *Le Theatre Indien—BEHE.*
Quid de Groecis Veterum Indorum Monumenta Tradiderint (Latin thesis for the doctorate).
Notes sur l'Indes: Chronologie indienne—JA.
1891—*Le Boudhisme et les Grecs: Revue de l'Ḥistoire des Religions*, Paris.
La Grece et l'Indes: Revue des Etudes Grecques, Paris (1891-2).
1892—*Science des Religions et les Religions de l'Inde—Programme de l'Ecole des Hautes, Science Religieues.*
Le Buddhacarita d'Aśvaghoṣa—JA.
1893—*Un nouveau document sur le Milinda-praśna—Comptes rendus de l'Academie des Inscriptions*, Paris.
Un project de cartographie historique de l'Indes—Transactions of the 9th International Congress of Orientalists, London.
Un Journaliste Indien: Benjamin Malabari—Revue Bleue.
1894 *Note préliminaire sur l'inscription de Kui-yong-Koan par Śylvain Lévi et Chavannes—JA.*
Notes sur la chronologie du Nepal—JA.
1895—*L'Iteneraire d'Ou-K'ong par Chavannes et Lévi—JA.*
Une poesie inconnue du roi Harṣai Śilāditya—Actes du dixieme Congrése des Orientalistes, Genéve.
Le Theatre Indien à Paris (*le chariot de terre cuite—Revue de Paris.*
1896—*Les Donations religieus des rois de Valabhi—BEHE.*
Notes sur diverses inscriptions de Piyadasi (*with Rāhula Sutra*)*—JA.*
Notes sur les Indo-Scythes—JA. (1896-7).
Deux peuples méconnu (*Cañcūka et Muruṇḍa*). *Melange Charles de Harlez Leyden.*
Translation of Wassilieff's paper on *Buddhism—Revue de l'Histoire des Religions.*
1898—*La doctrine du Sacrifice dans les Brāhmaṇas—BEHE.*
1899—*Rapport de M. Sylvain Lévi sur sa mission dans l'Inde et en Japon—Comptes rendus* de l'Academie des Inscriptions et Belles Letters.
De Nagasaki à Moscow par la Siberie—Annates de Geographie.
1900—*Les Missions de Wang Hieuen-Ts'e dans l'Inde—JA.*
1902—*Sur quelques terms employés dans les inscriptions des Kṣatrapas—JA.*
Notes Chinoises sur l'Inde: (*i*) *l'ecriture Kharoṣṭrī et son berceau;*
(*ii*) *une version Chinoise du Bodhicaryavatāra—BEFEO.*

1903—*(iii) la date de Candragomin—BEFEO.*
La legende de Rāma dans un avadāna Chinois: *Album Kern* (1903), Leyden.
1904—*Le Pays de Kharoṣṭra et l'ecriture Kharoṣṭrī—BEFEO.*
Anciennes inscriptions du Nepal—JA.
La Transmigration des ames—CMG.
The Transformation of Sanskrit Studies in course of the 19th century: *Congress of Arts and Sciences*, St. Louis, 1904.
[*French version published in Revue des Idées*, 1906].
Le Saṃyuktāgama Sanskrit et les feuillets Grünwedel—TP. 1904.
1905—*Le Dhartnaśarīra Sūtra* (avec M. Chavannes)—*TP.*
Documents sur le Bouddhisme dans l'Asie Centrale—BEFEO.
Criticism of Vincent Smith's History of India (Oxford 1905)—*Journal des Savants*, 1905.
1906—*Des Préverbes chez Pāṇini, sūtras* 1.4, 80-83—*Memorie de la Societe Linguistique*, XIV.
1907—*Anciennes Inscriptions du Nepal—J A.*
Les Elements de formation du Divyāvadāna—TP.
La Formation religieuse de l'Inde Contemporaine—CMG.
Mahāyāna Sūtrālaṃkāra d'Asaṅga (Sanskrit text) Champion, Paris (1907).
1908—*Aśvaghoṣa: Le Sūtrālaṃkāra et ses sources—JA.*
Le Nepal (3 vols.)—*Annales de Musée Guimet* (1905-8).
Numismatique Hindou: *Review of V. Smith's Catalogue of Coins in the Indian Museum—Journal des Savants.*
L'original Chinoise du Sūtra Tibetan sur la Grande Ourae—TP.
1909—*Les Saintes Ecritures du Bouddhiame—CMG.*
1910—*L'enseignement de l'orientalisme en France—Revue de Synthèse Historique*, Paris, 1910.
Textes Sanskrit de Touen-Houang—JA.
1911—*Les Etudes Orientales*: *leurs lecons, leurs resultats—CMG.*
Compte rendu de la Valleé Poussin: *Bouddhisme*—Gottengische Gelehrte Anzeigen, 1911.
Mahāyāna Sūtrālaṃkāra d'Asaṅga (*Traduction*), Paris, 1911—*BEHE.*
Etudes sur les documents Tokhariens de la mission Pelliot—JA.
1912 —*Wang Hiuen-tse et Kanaṣka—TP.*
Un fragment Tokharien du Vinaya des Sarvāstivādins—JA.
L'apramādavarga—etude sur les recensions des Dhammapada—JA.
Observation sur une langue précanonique du Buddhisme—JA.
Une legende du Karuṇapuṇḍarīka en Tokharienne: *Melange Vilhelm Thomsen*, 1912 (Leipzig).
Les noms de nombres en Tokbarien B.—Memoire de la Societe Lingiatique, Paris, 1912.
1913—*Remarques sur les formes grammaticales de quelques textes en Tokharien B par Lévi et Meillet. Memoire de la Societe Linguiatique*, Paris, 1912.
Le Tokharien B langue de Koutcha—JA.
Les grandes hommes dans l'histoire de l'Inde—CMG.
1914—*Autour du Bāveru Jātaka—Annuaire E. Hautes Etudes* (1913-14).
Central Asian Studies—Journal of the Royal Asiatic Society (London).
1915—*L'Indianisme dans la Science Française* (Larousse, Paris).
Le Catalogue Geographique des Yakṣa dans la Mahāmāyūrī—JA.
Sur la récitation primitive des textes Bouddhiques—JA.

Quelques titres enigmatique dons la hierachie Bouddhique. (Lévi et Chavannes).—*JA*.

1916—*Les Sieze Arhat protecteurs de Loi* (avec Chavannes)—*JA*.

Kuchean fragments edited by Sylvain Lévi in Hoernle's Manuscript Remains of Buddhist Literature in E. Turkisthan (Oxford). Cf. also Tokharian Prātimokṣa Fragment, *JRAS* (1913), and *Nīlakaṇṭhadhārani*, *JRAS* (1912).

1917—*Tato jayam udîrayet*—Bhandarkar Memorial Volume, 1917.

1918—*Pour l'histoire du Rāmāyaṇa*—*JA*.

Une Renaissance juive en Palestine—Le Temps, Paris, 1918.

1919—*Sphūṭārtha*: *Abhidharmakoṣa-vyākhyā of Yaśomitra with the collaboration of Prof. Stcherbatsky*, Petrograd, 1918-19.

1920—*Nala et Damayantī* (Traduction), Paris.

1921—*La part de l'Indienisme dans l'oeuvre de Chavannes*—*Bulletin Archeologique due Museé Guimet*.

Miscellaneous: Articles, reviews criticisms, etc. in

(*a*) *Revue Critique*, Paris, since 1885.

(*b*) *Revue d'Histoire des Religions*.

1923—*Pré-Aryen et Pré-Dravidien dans l'Inde* (*JA*).

1925—*Gonatda, le berceau du Gonardiya*—*Sir Asutosh Memorial Volume, III, Calcutta* (1925).*

*Based on a paper published in the *Modern Review*, December, 1921, when Prof. Lévi, accompanied by his *sahadharmiṇī* Madame Lévi visited India at the invitation of Rabindranath Tagore inaugurating the research department of Viśva Bhāratī.

The writer begs to record his thanks in this connection to his esteemed friend and *satīrtha* Louis Renou, now the Director of the Ecole des Hautes Etudes, for his kind courtesy in sending me advance proofs of his exhaustive bibliographical study on our common *guru*. It reached me unfortunately too late to be utilized for my tribute prepared for our *Greater India Society's Journal*. But I recommend to all admirers of Prof. Lévi's works, the most exhaustive and up to date analysis of Renou: *Sylvain Lévi et son oeuvre scientifique*, to be published soon in the *Journal Asiatique*, Paris.

CHAPTER 3

Greater India and the Work of Sylvain Lévi

J. PRZYLUSKI

In 1885, Sylvain Lévi, then aged twenty-two was appointed lecturer at the "École Pratique des Hautes Etudes". The period was still a Golden Age for Vedic studies. A generation of Indianists had attempted to retrace the formation of the Indo-European religion through an interpretation of the Veda according to the method of comparative mythology. E. Senart and H. Kern had endeavoured to explain by the same means the legend of the Buddha. Sylvain Lévi, undecided at first as to the course he should follow, turns resolutely from the Vedic period. He keeps to the strictly philological method only and during the most productive years of his life, he concentrates his activity upon the period where the great Indian epics were elaborated. Let us examine how such a decision can be explained and justified.

In the last part of his article "*Pour l'historie du Rāmāyaṇa*", Sylvain Lévi wrote: "The great epics mark a critical moment for the Indian soul; like the human hero of the *Bhagavad-gītā*, it was hesitating yet between the exigencies of practical duty, and the seductions of inertia."[1] Here lies already a psychological reason to take a special interest in the epics.

Sylvain Lévi had a deep sense of the intercourse which took place between India and the other Asiatic countries, and he was one of the first to grasp the importance of a great fact: the expansion of Indian civilization. And it is close to the birth of the Christian era—probably at the origin of the epic age—that both the continental and the naval expansion of India began. North-west, the invasion of the Śaka, then later on that of the Yue-chi, establish new communications between India and Upper Asia, and allow Buddhism to spread over the Iranian marches, Turkestan and China; south, the development of the high-sea trade draws the ships up to Indo-China and to the East-Indies.

But other motives attracted Sylvain Lévi towards this remarkably rich period. At the mere start of his career, he had been won to the genius of Aśvaghoṣa, and to the end he was fascinated by the charm of this poet. Basing his belief upon the fact that certain tales picture Aśvaghoṣa in the presence of Emperor Kaniṣka, Sylvain Lévi believed that he could admit the synchronism and decided to make of the great poet a contemporary of the great king. Thus,

[1] *JA*, janv. fév., 1918, p. 153.

Source: *Journal of the Greater India Society* (III/1, 1936, 18–22).

his admirations, his tastes, his historical preoccupations, everything carried him back to the epic period.

But, in order to co-ordinate these views, some chronology became necessary. To build up one, Sylvain Lévi makes use of two kinds of facts: the events which the texts relate, and onomastics. Being offered but a meagre harvest of historical events by the Sanskrit literature, his active curiosity explores the foreign literatures, like the Chinese and Tibetan texts. All the results of these investigations do not possess the same value. The knowledge that we gather in the texts is often no more than a legendary and therefore unreliable tradition. Comparisons between them confirm the existence of a tradition, but do not prove its veracity. Sylvain Lévi was led to think that Kaniṣka's reign began some time before the Christian era[2] and that Aśvaghoṣa must have been his contemporary. The latter part of this thesis is uncertain; the former has not been confirmed by the latest works upon the subject; today, almost every historian places the reign of Kaniṣka in the second century of the Christian era.[3]

But his handling of onomastics really displayed the talent of Sylvain Lévi, and his immense learning. The method is the following: by the onomastics of a text, he determines, with all achievable precision, the geographical and chronological horizon of its writer. Indian names have changed often, because cities were deserted, or given a new name, and because the populations replaced one another in the more troubled periods. It is possible, therefore, to determine by the names of the people and of the places the approximate date of the text and of the events which are mentioned in it. This method is based upon the following proposition: India is the land of the present moment; the old writers have never been attracted by historical research; a writer would never "have been tempted to look in the ashes of the past for the traces" of the small populations or the minor localities long disappeared.[4]

By this method, Sylvain Lévi has tried to establish a number of guiding-marks in the history of Indian literature, and we must not forget that, in this past without a chronology, the historian's most pressing task must be to determine the age of the texts. He shows that our *Rāmāyaṇa*, in its many recensions, had its origin in an edition published around the Christian era.[5] He establishes that "if the (*yakṣa*) list of the *Mahāmāyūrī* answers through many concording indications to the image of India as it was during the 3 or 4 earlier centuries after Christ, the *Mahābhārata*, which resembles this list so closely, was given its definitive redaction about the same time".[6] Then, in 1925, he proves in an article on *Ptolémée, le Niddesa et la Bṛhatkathā*, that one of the most important texts in Pali discloses a state of naval science "which is not likely to have existed in another age than that of Ptolémy". And he places in

[2]"Notes sur les Indo-Scythes", *JA*, 1897, I, 1ff

[3]L. de la Vallée-Poussin, *L'inde au temps dee Mauryas*, pp. 343-74.

[4]*JA*, janv. fév. 1915, p. 121.

[5]*JA*, 1918, I. p. 149.

[6]*JA*, 1915, I. p. 122.

the two earlier centuries of the present era the poet Guṇāḍhya who, according to the words of Lacôte, "is the third of the epic triad", and his *Bṛhatkathā* which ranks with the *Rāmāyaṇa* and the *Mahābhārata*.[7]

In short, Sylvain Lévi has constantly traced the ways for the future study of Greater India. But the exploration remains unfinished, and the synthesis is yet to be made. If we instal Kaniṣka in the second century AD we must perhaps ascribe to the influence of the Yue-chi some important features of a period particularly active in the political, economical and literary domains. It is the time of the Indo-Scythian hegemony, and of the expansion of Buddhism. Greater India is then in its full bloom, and the development of the sea-trade, first observed by Pliny and the Periplus, later on testified to by Ptolémy in his *Geography*, takes place. During this period, several great *diascévastes* set to work upon the old rhapsodies and build up the monumental epics, whilst a poet of genius, Aśvaghoṣa, endows the legend of the Buddha with the prestige of his unparalleled talent. One of the tasks of the near future must be to study this period of Indian history, with the help of all the resources that can be found in epigraphy and archaeology, philology and onomastics, ethnology and the science of religions.

Sylvain Lévi was a very learned man already when he started upon the travelling career which was to give the last maturity to his talent. He added then to his science of the past the vision of the sites and of the things, the divination of the paths which the merchants, the conquerors and the apostles had followed. And it is chiefly upon notes and studies made by him in Nepal, that he constructed his valuable monograph in three volumes on this Himalayan kingdom.

Like every orientalist in his time, Sylvain Lévi was dazzled by the result of the excavations made in Central Asia about the beginning of the century. So many monuments, paintings and texts brought to light, allowed the hope of a marked progress in science and stimulated the workers. Sylvain Lévi undertook the task of deciphering an unknown language, to which we give, with impropriety perhaps, the name of "Tokharian". The study of these documents inspired his several publications, the most important of which for the history of Central Asia, is probably *Le Tokharien B, langue de Koutcha*.[8]

His creative mind, his priceless gifts, have allowed Sylvain Lévi to leave his personal mark in all the domains where his indefatigable activity exerted itself. He formed a great number of pupils; among those who promised to do him the utmost credit, ed. Huber and F. Lacote have died early. Quite recently he had been deeply affected by the loss of L. Finot, who had been one of his earlier auditors, and who contributed more than anyone else to the creation of the Indo-Chinese History. Both in Europe and in Asia, however, many disciples prove to this day the persistence and the richness of his influence.

[7] *Etudes asiatiques publiees a l'occasion du vingt-cinquieme anniversaire de l'Ecole francaise d'Extreme-Orient*, II, p. 52.

[8] *JA*, 1913, II.

CHAPTER 4

India and the Pacific World*

U.N. GHOSAL

The author's aim, as he tells us in his informative Introduction, is to correlate "the monumental and artistic materials" of Pacific culture with "their anthropological and pre-historic contexts", "to trace the history of the Far Eastern civilization from the age of the Peking Man and the Java Man to the age of the modern antiquarians". He modestly disclaims the intention of delineating the history of Man in Asia as "a harmonious series of frescoes", and he offers his present volume as an "attempt to work the diverse materials and their interpretations into some sort of a mosaic". That a work of this compass was urgently needed to broaden the painfully narrow outlook of our people cannot be gainsaid for a moment. As Ramananda Chatterji writes in course of his appreciative foreword,

> The real position of India in ancient pre-historic and proto-historic times with the world, particularly with Asia and America as the background, has still to be perceived even by scholars.... The cultures which grew up in Oceania and Polynesia and generally in countries washed by the Pacific Ocean and which most probably influenced the aboriginal American cultures, are not yet adequately recognised. Still less recognised is India's part in the bringing about of inter-continental contacts and the fusion to a greater or less extent, of cultures separated by oceans as regards their places of origin.

Such being the importance of the theme, it must be admitted that the author has enjoyed almost unique opportunities for doing justice to his task. Deriving his inspiration from the master-mind of Rabindranath Tagore to whom the work is aptly dedicated, the author was enabled by a happy concourse of circumstances to make frequent visits between 1924 and 1938 to the lands and peoples of the Pacific practically as one of India's cultural ambassadors.

The present work consists, besides a well-written Introduction and Conclusion, of twelve chapters having the following titles: The Pacific Basin—A Cultural Survey, Cultural Migrations in Oceania, Maori Land and Culture, The Polynesian World, The Peoples and Cultures of the Philippines, India and the Archaeology of Malaysia and Indonesia, Art and Archaeology of Thiland, Art and Archaeology of Indo-China, Art and Archaeology of Sumatra, Java in

*Kalidas Nag, with Foreword by Ramananda Chatterji, Book Company Ltd., Calcutta, 1941, pp. viii + 295.

Source: *Journal of the Greater India Society* (IX/1, 1942, 39–41).

Asiatic History and Culture, China in Asiatic History and Culture, Japan in Asiatic History and Culture. There are besides three Appendices, a map and a good Index.

A glance at the above list of contents is enough to convince even the casual reader of the enormous range of the author's studies which extend over the whole region of the Pacific world from pre-historic down to quite modern times. Not only the pre-history and proto-history, but also the art and archaeology during the historical period of the countries dealt with in turn are described with a truly amazing amount of documentation. The author lays under contribution an enormous mass of publications extending to the most authoritative and up to date works many of which are almost inaccessible in this country. Frequently he gives adequate bibliographies and lists of museums and other centres of study and research in the Pacific lands which he describes so well. His personal reminiscences not only give him an opportunity for remembering with gratitude the scholars, art-critics and public men of many lands and nationalities who helped to make his tours fruitful, but also lend to his descriptions a touch of vividness which no amount of mere book-learning would have conveyed.

The author's views of the relation between Indian and Pacific cultures, which indeed form the theme of his work, can best be expressed in his own eloquent words which we quote from his concluding chapter (pp. 283-4):

> The expansion of Indian culture into the Pacific world is a grand chapter of human history.... What parts of this cultural complex could reach the Eastern Pacific basin and New World are problems for future anthropologists and antiquarians.... This colossal cultural drama is reappearing to us like an ancient mutilated play with many acts and interludes still missing which future research alone would probably restore and reconstruct. But whatever portions have already been recovered inspire us with awe and admiration.... There was no sordid chapter of economic exploitation or political domination in the development of Greater India which, coming as a legacy from Emperor Asoka of third century BC continued for over 1000 years to foster the fundamental principles of *maitrī* (fellowship) and *kalyāṇa* (universal well being) which form the bed-rocks of Hindu-Buddhist idealism.

We have no doubt that every reader of this arresting volume will share the author's firm conviction so well stated in his concluding sentence, that "Civilized Humanity will ultimately triumph over all the savage instincts of destruction", for, as he finely says in words that might come from the lips of Rabindranath Tagore, "Drowning the temporary typhoons of wars and violent conquests, the voice of the Universal Man is ever ringing in our ears, and the corridors of History are reverberating [with] the music of human sympathy".

THE SOCIETY'S VIEWS OF ITSELF AND OTHERS

CHAPTER 5

Annual Report of the Greater India Society for 1939

GENERAL

"The Greater India Society completed the 12th year of its existence in 1939. The Society's record of work during the year under review is on the whole one of progress, although the international situation could not but adversely affect its interests.

MANAGEMENT

"No change took place in the constitution of the Managing Committee during the year. The same was the case with the personnel of the Journal Sub-Committee. The Honorary Secretary continued to discharge the duties of Honorary Editor of the Society's Journal over and above his other work. The business of both committees was disposed of, as the occasion arose, by circulation among the members.

OFFICE

"No change took place in the office establishment..........The typing for office work was done *gratis* as in former years, by Mr. Ramesh Kumar Ghoshal, M.A., Mr. P. K. Sen very kindly acted as Honorary Auditor of the Society's accounts for the year. The Committee takes this opportunity to convey its heart-felt thanks to this last-named gentleman for the offer of his valuable services for three years in succession.

MEMBERS AND SUBSCRIBERS

"The number of members on the Society's roll on the 31st December 1939 remained nearly the same as on the corresponding date of 1938. . . .The number of subscribers to the Society's Journal showed a slight decrease. . . .The Committee has the pleasant duty of thanking as in former years the various Provincial Governments in India and Burma, the different Indian Universities, the Director-General of the Archaeological Survey of India and the Superintendents of various Archaeological circles, the Government Epigraphist

Source: *Journal of the Greater India Society* (VIII/1, 1940, 152–6).

for India and the enlightened Governments of Baroda, Mysore Travancore, Gwalior and Indore for their continued patronage of the Society's Journal.

FINANCE

"The closing balance of the: Society's accounts on the 31st December 1939 was Rs. 1355-7-8 as compared with Rs. 1148-9-8 the corresponding figure for the previous year. As against this favourable state of the society's finances must be set its commitments namely, the cost of publication of the two under-mentioned works, Prof. Tucci's *Travels of Tibetan Pilgrims in the Swat Valley* and the English version of Dr. N. J. Krom's *Hindoe-Javaansche Geschiedenis*. On the receipt side the Committee has again most gratefully to acknowledge the kind grant of Rs. 400 from the National Council of Education (Bengal) and Rs. 100 from Dr. Narendra Nath Law, an esteemed member of the Managing Committtee of the Society. During the period under review receipts under the head Sale of Books and Pamphlets amounted to Rs. 184-1-6 with which may be compared the figure for the preceding years; Rs. 415-12-6 (1936-37), & Rs. 543-8-9 (1935-36). This serious setback is partly to be attributed to the present international situation and partly to the failure of the Society to get free advertisements of its publications as before. . . .On the expenditure side the charges under Publications proved as usual to be the heaviest item, accounting for not less than Rs. 448-0-9 with which may be compared the corresponding figures from the last Annual Report namely, Rs. 911-5-0 (from 1st April 1937 to 31st December 1938). The next heaviest item consisted of Allowances to Staff namely, Rs. 165-3-0. This included the typist's and proof-reader's charges for the two issues of the Journal. This figure compares favourably with the corresponding figure in the preceding report namely, Rs. 208-0-0. The postal charges during the year under review amounted to the modest sum of Rs. 86-7-6, the corresponding figures from the last Annual Report being Rs. 193-14-3.

LECTURES

"As in previous years the Society arranged a number of popular lectures in accordance with the terms of its agreement with the National Council of Education, Bengal. The range and variety of the lectures may be realised from the under-mentioned lists: (1) Art and Archaeology in the North-West-Frontier Province (Dr. Kalidas Nag), (2) Early Buddhism in Burma (Dr. Nihar-Ranjan Ray), (3) Indian Culture in Afghanistan (Dr. U.N. Ghoshal), (4) Indian Influences on Burmese Literature (Pandit Giris Chandra Vidyabinode), (5 & 6) Indian Influences on Burmese Monastic Life Pandit (G.C. Vidyabinode) and (7 & 8) Indian Influences on Burmese Social Life (Pandit G.C. Vidyabinode). To all these gentlemen who have benefited the Society with their lectures the Committee offers its most grateful thanks,

PUBLICATIONS

"Two issues of the Journal of the Society (Vol. VI, Nos. I and 2) appeared in course of the year. The Committee notes with satisfaction that notwithstanding the outbreak of the European war contributions were not lacking from the pen of leading scholars both Indian and foreign. It has also to be mentioned that there was no falling off in the number and variety of books sent to the Journal for review as well as in the number of first-grade Journals on its exchange list. All the new accessions of the Society were made over, according to the existing arrangement, to the Calcutta University Library for being kept as a separate collection. Among the publications taken in hand by the Society, the printing of Prof. G. Tucci's *Travels of Tibetan Pilgrims in the Swat Valley* was all but completed, only the Tibetan Text being kept by the author for correction of proofs. Another work namely, the English translation of Prof. Krom's *Hindoe-Javaansche Geschiedenis,* after being revised by the author was sent to the translator for further improvement of the language. The Committee repeats the regret expressed in the preceding Annual Report that all the Bulletins of the Society except one continue to remain out of stock or very nearly so. The Committee earnestly trusts that the revised editions of these useful monographs for which there is a steady demand might be undertaken at no distant date.

CONGRESS AND CONFERENCE

"During the last year the Society was glad to accept the invitation from the authorities of the Tenth All-India Oriental Conference at Hyderabad for sending delegates to the Conference. But the Conference was unfortunately postponed owing to the international situation. At the third session of the Indian Historical Congress held at Calcutta in December last the Society was represented by a number of delegates including Dr. U.N. Ghoshal, Mr. J.N. Banerjea and Dr. Nihar-Ranjan Ray. All these gentlemen actively participated in the work of the Conference, Dr. U.N. Ghoshal serving as Secretary of one of the sections.

CONCLUSION

"In concluding this brief report on the working of the Society for the last year the Committee cannot but convey its heart-felt thanks to those esteemed patrons and well-wishers of the Society who have helped it in various ways. Grateful mention has already been made of the kind help of the authorities of the National Council of Education, Bengal, of Dr. Narendra Nath Law and of Mr. P. K. Sen. Mention has also been made of the valuable help given by the Editor of *The Modern Review* as regards advertisement of the Society's publications. The Committee, however, feels that funds are urgently needed for meeting some of the Society's immediate needs. Such specially is the need for housing the Society's growing collection of publications. Still greater is the need for young recruits for continuing the good work that the Society has started on such a modest scale. The Committee appeals to all lovers of Indian culture, Indian and foreign to take up this work and it earnestly trusts that its appeal will not go in vain."

CHAPTER 6

Progress of Greater Indian Research during the Last Twenty-five Years (1917-42)

U.N. GHOSHAL

AFGHANISTAN

The systematic investigation of the ancient sites in Afghanistan dates only from 1922, when, thanks to the initiative of Prof. A. Foucher, France acquired from the Afghan government a thirty-years' monopoly for archæological exploration in the country. The opportunity thus presented in a land, to which access had for some long time been barred with seven seals, was eagerly utilized by a brilliant band of French scholars who gave to the world the results of their wonderful discoveries in a series of magnificent volumes (in French) called *Memoirs of the French Archaeological Delegation in Afghanistan*. These works have revealed to us numerous traces of great schools of art—of sculptures in stucco and clay and of mural paintings—of the third-fourth to the seventh-eighth centuries, to which have been given as indicative of their complex composition, the designations of "Graeco-Buddhist" and "Irano-Buddhist" art. Fragmentary as they often are, these objects of art represent fresh and vigorous offshoots of the decadent school of Gandhāra and form in their turn, as has been well said, "an ante-chamber to the art of Central Asia" (René Grousset). For it was there that grew up those schools which were destined to attain their full development at Khotan, Kucha, Turfan and other famous Central Asian centres. We can only find time to describe in the present place some of the more important discoveries that have rewarded the labours of the French archaeologists. On the site of Haḍḍa (known as Hi-lo by the Chinese Buddhist pilgrims and reputed to contain a collar-bone and a tooth of Buddha), J.J. Barthoux discovered between 1925 and 1928 the remains of a vast ancient city with hundreds of *stūpas* and thousands of stucco sculptures. The results thus obtained were given out in two elaborate volumes (*Les Fouilles de Haḍḍa;* tome III, *Figures et figurines*, Paris, 1930; ibid., tome I, *Stūpas et sites*, Paris, 1933). The former contains reproductions with short descriptions of 478 sculptures, mainly all heads, in stucco representing figures of Buddhas demons and warriors, which were found among the ruins of the 531 *stūpas* excavated at Haḍḍa, while the latter gives a minute account of the methods of

Source: *Journal of the Greater India Society* (IX/2, 1942, 59–135).

constructing the *stūpas* and attached buildings as well as of the structures belonging to seven different areas. It is interesting to learn that the *stūpas* exhibit a development of the depressed forms of Bharhut and Sanchi towards more elevated, slender and graceful types, as they generally consist of "a double square basement supporting two cylindrical drums which in their turn are surmounted by a third low drum and a dome". The stucco figures, comprising those of Buddhas, of deities and demi-gods and of groups of human worshippers indicate a masterly execution far surpassing the conventional and effeminate products of the Gandhāra school. Another famous site which has been examined by the French scholars is the cliff of Bāmiyān renowned from early times for its colossal Buddhas and its innumerable decayed cave shrines and monasteries. Between 1922 and 1924 this famous group of monuments was thoroughly examined by A. Godard, Mme. Y. Godard and J. Hackin. In their great work called *Les antiquités bouddhiques de Bāmiyān* (Paris, 1928), they reproduced a number of frescoes which have been rightly described as the earliest extant Buddhist paintings after those of Ajantā (Caves IX and X) and Miran. These paintings of which the earliest go back to the fifth or sixth century AD exhibit a strange medley of Indian, Iranian and Chinese influences. In the above-named work the authors also described the famous colossal Buddhas and illustrated with adequate plans and designs the equally famous Buddhist caves. A new series of excavations undertaken at Bāmiyān by J. Hackin and J. Carl in 1930 led to the discovery of one of the oldest caves (dated *c.* third century AD) in the vicinity of one of the colossal Buddhas. Other discoveries consisted of Sanskrit Mss in birch-bark as well as an octagonal grotto in the adjoining cliff of Kakrak with decorative paintings indicating Iranian influences. These finds have been described with adequate illustrations in Hackin and Carl's work *Nouvelles recherches archéologiques à Bāmiyān* (Paris, 1933), where attention is drawn to the characteristic blending of Indian, Iranian and Hellenistic influences on this local art. The Iranian element, indeed assumed from the end of the fifth century such an important part as to justify the application of the epithet "Irano-Buddhist" to the later art of Bāmiyān. The Sanskrit Mss from Bāmiyān were edited (*JA*, 1932) by the late Prof. Sylvain Lévi, who identified them as comprising fragments of Abhidharma texts of Mahāyāna schools, of the Vinaya of the Mahāsaṁghikas and of a rare Abhidharma text of the Sarvāstivādins. While the French explorations at Haḍḍa and Bāmiyān have yielded the happiest results, discoveries of striking interest have also been made at less known sites. At the hill of Khair Khāneh, north-west of Kabul, J. Carl excavated in 1934 the remains of a most interesting temple recalling the construction of the Śivite temple of Gupta times at Bhumara in Central India. Another discovery was that of a unique Sūrya image in white marble showing distinct influences of Iranian art of the fourth century AD (see J. Hackin and J. Carl, *Recherches archéologiques au col de Khair Khaneh près de Kābul*, Paris, 1936; also J. Hackin, "Explorations of the neck of Khair Khaneh near Kābul," *JGIS*, vol. III, no. 1, January 1936). The excavations of J. Hackin on the ancient site of Begram (Kāpiśi of Sanskrit literature) in 1937 resulted in the discovery of a mass of ivories with designs recalling the Mathura art of the Kushan epoch and forming in fact the only surviving samples of Indian ivory-work of that early date. (For a description of the above illustrated with plates, see J. Hackin, *Recherches archéologiques à Begram*, tome I: Text, tome II: Plates, Paris, 1939.) The very interesting excavations of the French archaeologists at Fondukistan, east of Bāmiyān, in 1937, brought to light an old (seventh century) Buddhist sanctuary with its appendages. Among the most precious discoveries on this site are a number of clay modellings and mural paintings of predominantly Indian type recalling Gupta and Pala models. (See J. Hackin, "The Buddhist Monastery of Fondukistan", *JGIS*, vol. VII, nos. 1 & 2, January & July 1940.)

BURMA

By the ninth century of the Christian era Burma with its two great natural (Upper and Lower) divisions, bearing in the ancient indigenous records the names of Mrammadesa and Rāmaññadesa, was occupied by at least three distinct peoples all of whom were strongly influenced by Indian civilisation. In the north lay the Burmese kingdom (Mrammamaṇḍala) with its capital at Arimaddanapura (Pagan) found in AD 849. In the south was situated the kingdom of the Pyu with its capital at Śrīkṣetra (Old Prome identified with the modern village of Hmawza near Prome). To the south-east lay the kingdom of the Mons (or Talaings), kinsmen (at least by speech) of the Khasis and Mundas of India, whose capital was located at Thaton and who had an important settlement at Haṁsāvatī (Pegu) founded early in the ninth century. It is only by piecing together the evidence of the archaeological finds and stray Chinese literary references that the lost history of Burma in early times has been recently recovered, for notwithstanding the abundance of local chronicles the authentic history of the country dates only from 1057 AD, the memorable year of the conquest of Thaton and Pegu by the Burmese king Anawrata.

The systematic investigation of the art and archaeology of Burma begins only in the first decade of the present century, although the Archaeological Department was established in 1899 and a serious search for antiquities had been made by Major (afterwards Sir) Richard Temple in 1894. The explorations of a French archaeologist, General L. de Beylié, in 1905 and the following years for the first time drew public attention to the wealth of antiquities at Prome. The first Superintendent of the Archaeological Department, Taw Sein Ko, devoted his energies to the description of some of the famous monuments of the eleventh and twelfth centuries at Pagan including the Ānanda temple built by King Kyanzittha in 1090 (according to tradition) and the Mahābodhi temple built after the model of the Bodhgayā shrine by King Nandaungmya in AD 1198. He had, moreover, the good fortune of discovering at Hmawza funeral urns in earthern-ware and stone with inscriptions in the forgotten Pyu language, a stone inscription with extracts from the Pāli canon and a Buddhist votive *stūpa* with images of the last four Buddhas and inscriptions in Pyu and

Pāli languages. These inscriptions were published by C.O. Blagden (*Ep. Ind.* XII) and Louis Finot (*JA*, 1912). To Taw Sein Ko also belongs the credit of publishing six volumes of a Corpus of Burmese inscriptions. These are (I) *Inscriptions of Pagan, Pinya and Ava*, ed. T.S. Ko, 1892; (II) *Inscriptions Copied from Stones Collected by King Bodawpaya*, vol. I, ed. T.S. Ko, 1897, (III) *Inscriptions Copied from Stones Collected by King Bodawpaya*, vol. II, ed. T.S. Ko, 1897; (IV) *Inscriptions Collected in Upper Burma*, vol. I, ed. T.S. Ko, 1900; (V) *Inscriptions Collected in Upper Burma*, vol. II, ed. T.S. Ko, 1903; (VI) *Original Inscriptions Collected by King Bodawpaya . . .*, ed. Charles Duroiselle after copy prepared by T.S. Ko, 1913. Containing mere transcriptions in modern Burmese characters and neglecting the distinction between originals and copies, these volumes have been rightly condemned for their failure to satisfy the requirements of modern scholarship. During the first decade of this century Blagden published the first tentative reading of a Mon inscription (*JRAS*, 1909). This is the famous text on the Mon (or Talaing) face of the quadrilingual epigraph of Myazedi, "the Rosetta stone of Talaing epigraphy". In *JRAS*, 1911 the same scholar compared the Pyu version of the above record with the Pāli, Burmese and Mon versions. Afterwards he deciphered (*Journal of the Burma Research Society*, 1917) some of the Pyu inscriptions on the funeral urns discovered at Hmawza. Nevertheless it could justly be said by a competent scholar as late as 1913 that epigraphy in Burma was still to be founded (Charles Duroiselle, Preface to his edition of the *Original Inscriptions Collected by King Bodawpaya*, Amarapura, 1913). With the closing years of the second decade of the present century began a period of substantial progress. In the first volume (1919) of the newly started journal *Epigraphia Birmanica*, Blagden published his improved reading of the Mon version of the Myazedi inscription along with a glossary of Mon words and the text and translation of the Pyu version of the same record. A series of Mon inscriptions (including the Mon versions of the famous Kalyāṇīsīmā inscription of King Dhammacheti of Pegu), was edited by the same scholar in the following volumes (vols. II-IV) of the *Epigraphia Birmanica*. The soul of this recent progress in Burmese archaeology was Charles Duroiselle, who became the first editor of the *Journal of the Burma Research Society* in 1911 and who succeeded Taw Sein Ko as Archaeological Superintendent in 1912. He published (Rangoon, 1921) *A List of Inscriptions found in Burma, Part I. The List of the Inscriptions Arranged in the Order of Their Dates* with three Appendices listing Mon, Pyu, Siamese and Tamil inscriptions. Three Portfolios of *Inscriptions of Burma* (University of Burma Oriental Series Publications) consisting of accurate facsimiles of inscriptions from AD 1131 to 1237, those down to AD 1268 and those from AD 1268 to 1300, have since been published by Pe Maung Tin and G. Luce (Oxford, 1933 and London, 1939). The very valuable excavations of Duroiselle on the site of Hmawza in 1926-7 resulted in the discovery of an untouched relic-chamber of a Buddhist *stūpa* of the sixth-seventh century AD containing "a veritable wonder-house of archaeological treasures". The central object in the chamber was a gilt silver *stūpa* with Buddha figures in *repoussé* and a mixed Pāli-Pyu inscription. Among other objects was a MS of 20 gold-leaves in Pyu characters of the sixth century containing extracts from the Pāli canon. The characters of the inscription and the MS (like those of the gold-plate and the stone inscription at Hmawza discovered by Taw Sein Ko) bear affinities to those of the Kannaḍa-Telugu and Kadamba inscriptions of southern India at the same period. Other discoveries made at the same site consisted of terracotta votive tablets with figures of a Buddha flanked by Avalokiteśvara and Maitreya, a Bodhisattva with four arms and so forth and with the Buddhist creed inscribed in Pāli or Sanskrit in Nāgarī characters of the eighth-ninth centuries. Duroiselle's discoveries at Hmawza in the following year consisted of a gold-plate inscription in Pāli in the same south Indian characters, of a bronze Buddha image with Sanskrit inscriptions in Gupta characters on the pedestal, of a large stone image of the Buddha with a mixed Sanskrit and Pyu inscription in Gupta characters of the seventh-eighth centuries [for details, *see Ann. Rep. ASI*, 1926-7, 1927-8]. These discoveries have opened a new chapter in the history of India's old culture-contact with Burma. They have definitely proved that in the sixth and seventh centuries of the Christian era an Indian (or Indianised) dynasty with names of kings ending in *varman* and *vikrama* was reigning at Prome. During the same period Theravāda (or "Southern") Buddhism was the predominant religion in the kingdom, and the Pāli canon was known in its most abstruse aspects. The art-influence was derived both from the Northern Gupta tradition and the Southern Pallava style. The colonists came both from northern and southern India.

Next in importance to the archaeological discoveries at Hmawza are those made by Duroiselle at Pagan, the capital city of the Burmese kings, which during a space of nearly two centuries (1057-1286) was adorned by a succession of royal builders with innumerable *stūpas*, shrines and monasteries. On this memorable site Duroiselle brought to light hundreds of stone sculptures and terracotta votive tablets inscribed with the usual Buddhist creed in a variety of languages (Sanskrit, Pāli, Pyu, Talaing and Burmese). Some of these inscribed tablets written in Sanskrit in Nāgarī characters of the eleventh century bear the name of the great Burmese King Anawrata, the conqueror of Thaton, in the Indian form Mahārāja Śrī Anuruddhadeva (*Ann. Rep. ASI*, 1915, 1926-7).

One of the important signs of the remarkable progress of Burmese archaeology in recent times has been the steady growth of museums. Not to speak of the Palace Museum at Mandalay containing the relics of the last Burmese dynasty, the museums at Hmawza and Pagan have been greatly enriched with the finds of the recent explorations.

The dark corners of the religious history of the Irrawady Valley in the pre-Anawrata period have been illumined in recent times by the progress of research. In the middle of the second decade of this century because of the dearth of authentic documents it could still be said (Duroiselle in *Ann. Rep. ASI*, 1915-

16) that the religious history of Burma up to the eleventh century was practically a blank. A great, step forward was taken when Duroiselle identified the unique frescoes of a markedly erotic character from two old temples near Pagan as representing the Ari of the Burmese chronicles, whom he identified as a Mahāyānist Buddhist sect deeply tinctured with Tantrism and deriving its origin from Bengal (see Duroiselle's classical paper "The Ari of Burma and Tantric Buddhism" in *Ann. Rep. ASI*, 1915-16). This definitely proved the prevalence of Tantrik Buddhism among the Burmese before the absorption of Theravāda Buddhism by King Anawrata. To Duroiselle also belongs the credit of recognising traces of the Sanskrit (Sarvāstivādin) school in the Sanskrit records from Prome (*Ann. Rep. ASI*, 1913-14). In the last decade of this century an Indian scholar. Nihar-Ranjan Ray has contributed a series of valuable studies on the religious history of Burma. In his *Brahmanical Gods in Burma* (Calcutta, 1932) based on a critical study of the extant Brahmanical images and shrines in the country, he has brought together all the known facts about the remains of Brahmanism in Burma arranged in chronological order from the seventh to the fourteenth centuries AD. His next important work *Sanskrit Buddhism in Burma* (Calcutta, 1935), based on an equally thorough study of plastic remains and literary references, gives a comprehensive account of the fortunes of the Sarvāstivādin as well as the Mahāyāna and allied schools of Buddhism in the country from the earliest times. Among his main conclusions may be mentioned the fact that the Mūlasarvāstivādin canon was introduced into old Prome probably from East India some time before the seventh century AD. Down to the eighth and ninth centuries it flourished there side by side with the Theravāda school which had been introduced evidently from the Kannaḍa-Telugu country in the sixth century. In the eighth and ninth centuries Mahāyānism was introduced into Old Prome from East India. In Pagan it was known before the tenth century, having been probably introduced from Bengal at least in its Tantric form. Its most flourishing period coincided with the Golden Age of the Hīnayānist reformation at Pagan. Owing to the enlightened tolerance of the Burmese kings the two religions lived side by side, but Hīnayānism having the State support ultimately triumphed over its rival.

We may next mention two other publications by the last-named scholar ("Early Traces of Buddhism in Burma", *JGIS*, VI, January & July 1939; "Theravāda Buddhism in Burma", ibid., VIII, January 1941) forming the earlier chapters of a comprehensive History of Buddhism in Burma projected by himself. In the first paper the author has established by an elaborate examination of the literary and archaeological evidence that the famous tradition of Aśoka's sending (*c.* 250 BC) the mission of Soṇa and Uttara for the conversion of Suvaṇṇabhūmi has some claims to a historical basis, that the equally famous tradition of Buddhaghoṣa's infusing a new life into the Buddhism of Lower Burma (*c.* AD 400-50) has some probability in its favour, that the Pāli canonical texts evidently brought over by Indian colonists from the Kannaḍa-Telugu country were studied in their doctrinal and abstruse aspects in Old Prome (*c*. AD 400-50) and that Buddhism was in a very flourishing condition in that capital city (*c*. AD 550-950), that Brahmanical Hinduism along with Buddhism was prevalent in Pegu, and lastly that Theravāda Buddhism was exceedingly flourishing in the Talaing kingdom towards the middle of the eleventh century. In the second paper a good account has been given of the religious, artistic and literary activities of the Burmese people during the Golden Age of the Pagan dynasty (*c*. AD 1057-1286). How ennobling was the Buddhist influence on the minds of these alien rulers has been illustrated by the following quotation from an inscription of King Kyanzittha, the builder of the Ānanda temple:

> With loving kindness . . . shall King Kyanzittha wipe away the tears of those who are parted from their trusted friends . . . his people shall be unto him as a child to its mother's bosom . . . he shall soften the hearts of those who intend evil. With wisdom, which is even as the hand, shall King Kyanzittha draw open the bar of the Gate of Heaven, which is made or gold and wrought with gems.

The study of Burmese art, for which materials were almost completely lacking as late as the middle of the second decade of this century (cf. Duroiselle in *Ann. Rep. ASI*, 1913-14), has also shared in the general progress. It is true that a comprehensive history of this art involving the classification of types and schools and the analysis of their affinities down even to the end of the Pagan period has yet to be written. Nevertheless there has latterly been a good deal of preliminary studies in this direction. In his paper "Pictorial Representations of Jātakas in Burma" (*Ann. Rep. ASI*, 1912-13) Duroiselle gave a connected account of the sculptures and paintings illustrative of the Jātakas in Burmese temples from 1057 to 1820. Dealing with the style of these works of art, he declared that while the main influence came from Eastern India, the local artists in copying the Indian models created a Pagan school. In the same context he stated that everything in the Jātaka reliefs except the style of the houses was Indian. The stone sculptures illustrative of Buddha's life from the corridor of the famous Ānanda temple at Pagan were noticed by Duroiselle in another paper (*Ann. Rep. ASI*, 1913-14) where he held them to be the work of Indian artists. In a third paper on the frescoes of Pagan (*Ann. Rep. ASI*, 1921-2), he declared these paintings with some looseness of expression to be the work of Bengali and Nepalese artists of the Varendra school. The illustrious French scholar G. Çoedés has recently suggested (*Le Musée National de Bangkok*, Paris, 1928, p. 31) that the type of Buddha images of the early Pagan period in Burma and the early Tai period in Siam was directly derived from the Pala art of Bengal and Behar, a suggestion which has been confirmed by later research (Le May, *Buddhist Art in Siam*, pp. 99ff.). Quite recently Indian scholars have made weighty contributions to the study of religious art in Burma. Nihar-Ranjan Ray, in his papers on Burmese religious history above-mentioned, has distinguished various Brahmanical and Buddhist sculptures at Hmawza and Pagan as belonging to the late Gupta, Pallava or Pala styles. He has also pointed out that not only the *stūpas* but also the rectangular temples at Hmawza are indebted to the late Gupta and Pala art traditions. In his paper "Paintings in Pagan" (*JISOA*, VI, 1938) the same scholar has distinguished four stages of this art. At first the conception was mainly plastic, the decorations, dress and ornaments, types, colour-scheme and composition being imported from the East Indian tradition. When the process of Burmanisation began to work, the plastic conception was overtaken by the linear. In the third stage the linear conception superseded the plastic, the colour-scheme, etc., remaining purely Indian. In the fourth or Burmese stage the linear conception came to stay. More recently Sarasi Kumar Saraswati ("Temples of Pagan", *JGIS*, IX, I, January 1942) has shown that these temples divide themselves into three classes having their prototype in certain old shrines of Hmawza and that the Ānanda temple, in particular, while resembling the Paharpur shrine in exterior elevation, differs fundamentally in plan, conception and internal arrangement.

By the first decade of the present century the investigation of the literary history of Burma had made substantial progress. Important chronicles for which Burma is so famous like the Gandhavaṁsa and the Sāsanavaṁsa had been published before the close of the last century. These and other precious texts were utilised by Mabel Bode in her standard monograph *The Pāli Literature of Burma* (London, 1909), where she traced the development of Pāli literature and Pāli scholarship in Burma from the eleventh to the nineteenth centuries. Among the branches of study developed during this period are those quite familiar to students of Sanskrit literature, viz., astronomy and astrology, law, medicine, rhetoric and prosody, and above all, grammar.

The progress of scholarship in recent years has made possible the publication of an up to date general history of Burma superseding the earlier work of Sir Arthur Phayre. This is the *History of Burma from the Earliest Times to the 10th March 1824, the Beginning of the English Conquest* by G.E. Harvey (London, 1925). The author, while treating the early history of Burma in a very summary fashion, has sought to utilise all available materials including the highly valuable indigenous chronicles which, as he says, are without a parallel in the mainland of Indo-China.

SIAM

Siam, or as it is now called, Thailand, was ruled before the complete establishment of T'ai sovereignty in the thirteenth century by peoples of diverse stocks, the Mons in Central and Northern Siam, the Khmers in North-East Siam and the Śrīvijaya kings in the Peninsula. In a country so diversified it was no wonder that there arose different schools and styles of art, but all of these were directly or indirectly saturated with Indian influences.

The beginnings of the State organisation of archaeological research go back in Siam only to the third decade of this century, though the Vajirañāna National Library (so called after the name of the then reigning king before his accession) had been established at Bangkok as far back as 1905. It was in 1924 that King Rama VI founded the Archaeological Service. His successor King Prajadhipok established at Bangkok in 1926 the Royal Institute (*Rājapāṇḍityasabhā*) of Literature, Archaeology and Fine Arts. In the same year he formed the National Museum at Bangkok out of the collections of King Mongkut, King Chulalongkorn and Prince Damrong Mahānubhava. Other museums were started before or after this time at Lopburi, Ayudhya and other places.

To no single scholar is Siamese art as well as archaelogy more indebted than to the illustrious French savant George Çoedès. Appointed Librarian of the Vajirañāna National Library in 1917 and thereafter called to the office of General Secretary of the newly founded Royal Institute of Siam, he enriched almost every branch of Siamese antiquities by his illuminating researches extending over many years. His preliminary studies of the documents bearing on the Sukhodaya dynasty ("Documents sur le Dynastie de Sukhodaya", *BEFEO*, XVII, 1917) were followed by a more intensive investigation of the beginnings of the dynasty ("Les origines de le Dynastie de Sukhodaya", *JA*, 1920). Of the greatest value as a source-book of the history of Siam was his publication of the text and translation of the inscriptions extending from the Indo-Mon Kingdom of Dvāravatī down to the Tai kingdom of Sukhodaya (or *Suk'ōt'ai*). This work bearing the title *Recueil des Inscriptions du Siam* was published in two parts, Part I (Bangkok, 1924) dealing with the inscriptions (Pāli and Thai), of the Sukhodaya kingdom (thirteenth-sixteenth centuries), and Part II (Bangkok, 1929) dealing with the inscriptions (Pāli and Mon) of the Dvāravatī kingdom (seventh-eighth centuries), the inscriptions (Sanskrit and Khmer) of the Śrīvijaya kingdom (eighth-twelfth centuries), the inscriptions (Pāli and Mon) of the Haripuñjaya kingdom (twelfth-thirteenth centuries). It contained, among other things, a masterly summary of the archaeological evidence relating to the early history of Siam. Of equally fundamental importance was Çoedès's publication (with a French translation and a learned Introduction) of two Pāli chronicles from the MSS collection of the National Library of Bangkok "Documents sur l'Histoire Politique et Religieuse du Laos Occidental" (*BEFEO*, XXV, 1925). These works are the *Jinakālamālinī* (Garland of the times of the Buddha) of the monk Ratnapañña (dated about the beginning of the fifteenth century) and the *Chāmadevīvaṁsa* (Chronicles of Chāma Devī) of the monk Bodhiraśmi (written in AD 1516) and they rank as first-rate authorities for the history of Yonakaraṭṭha (Western or Siamese Laos) from the beginning down to their own times. To the above-mentioned work Çoedès has added a number of valuable Appendices including *A list of chronicles and other documents relating to the history of Simese Laos preserved in the National Library at Bangkok*, *A List of inscriptions found in the two provinces of Siamese Laos*, *the text and translation of the Mon Inscriptions of Lopburi and Lampun* and so forth.

The study of art and architecture in Siam has equally benefited by the scholarly activities of Çoedès. In *JSS*, XXI (1928), he identified certain bronze Buddha images excavated from the ancient site of Pong Tuk in the previous year as belonging to the Amarāvatī (second century) and Gupta (sixth century) styles. In his important work (in French) called "The Archaeological Collections of the National Museum at Bangkok" (*Ars Asiatica*, XII, 1928) containing 40 Plates illustrating the art of Siam, he distinguished four schools classified under the heads "Art of Dvāravatī", "Art of Śrīvijaya", "Art of Lopburi", and the Tai (or Siamese) Art subdivided into the schools of Xiensen, Sukhodaya, Utong and Ayudhya. Explaining the characteristics of these schools he pointed out that the art of Dvāravatī (Central Siam) was based on Gupta models and was the intermediary through which Indian art influenced the "primitive" or "pre-Khmer" art of Cambodia. He also held that the school of Lopburi represented a provincial Khmer art, while the school of Xiensen was derived from Pala art by way of Burma. In this connection he did a distinct service by discarding the title Græco-Khmer applied by some scholars to the art of Dvāravatī. At a later date Çoedés identified (*Études d'Orientalisme Linossier*, pp. 159-64) certain sculptures from the ancient city of Srideb as forming the link between Gupta and early Khmer art.

While the main credit for investigating the art and archaeology of Siam belongs to Çoedés, other scholars have made important contributions to their study during the last twenty years. To the Siamese scholar-prince Damrong we owe "A History of Siam prior to the Ayudhya Period", which was translated into English in *JSS,* XIII (Bangkok, 1920). In this work new light was sought to be thrown upon the history of the Early Tai kingdoms. Prince Damrong also wrote in Siamese "A History of Buddhist Stūpas in Siam" (Bangkok, 1926), while he published in the *Jubilee Volume of the Siam Society* (Bangkok, 1930) a paper on the "Evolution of Siamese Art" illustrated with forty Plates. About this time A. Salmony produced his work *The Sculpture of Siam* (London, 1925; French edn., Paris, 1925) which, written from an aesthetic standpoint, has been rightly condemned (cf. Finot and Goloubev's criticism in *BEFEO*, 1927) for its grievous errors of history and chronology. In *BEFEO*, XXXI (1931), J.Y. Claeys published an important paper (in French) called "The Archaeology of Siam" where he described a large number of monuments with critical remarks on the history and chronology, architecture and sculpture, of Siam. The art of Siam has also been discussed by Pierre Dupont in his paper "The Art of Dvāravatī and Khmer Art" (*RAA*, 1935) where he points out that the standing Buddha images of the Bayon period represent the survival of the Dvāravatī art of Siam and Laos. Coming to epigraphy, we may mention the publication with translation and notes by R. Halliday of a list of seven Mon inscriptions of Siam (*BEFEO*, XXX, 1930). In this connection reference may be made to E. Seidenfaden's paper (in French) called "Complement to the Inventory of the Monuments of Cambodia from the Four Provinces of East Siam" (*BEFEO*, XXIII, 1923) supplementing Lunet de Lajonquière's *Descriptive Inventory of the Monuments of Cambodia* (1902-12) to be described below.

Another scholar who has enriched the art and archaeology of Siam in recent times is Reginald Le May, for some time Economic Adviser to the Siamese government. In his work *The Coinage of Siam* (Bangkok, 1932), while describing the coin-types of the Ayudhya and other dynasties, he pointed out that the Tai were the first people in the Far East to introduce a standardised silver currency. The ceramic art of Siam which is indebted to the famous Sung pottery of China, was studied by him in his paper "The Ceramic wares of North-Central Siam" (*Burlington Magazine*, London, 1933). In his *Buddhist Art in Siam* (Cambridge, 1938), hc has published the first comprehensive account of the rise and development of sculpture and architecture in Siam from the earliest times to the sixteenth century. Based chiefly on the researches of Çoedés to whom the author freely acknowledges his indebtedness, this work distinguishes no less than nine different schools: (1) Pure Indian, up to the fifth century, (2) Mon-Indian (Gupta), fifth to tenth centuries, (3) Hindu-Javanese, seventh to twelfth centuries, (4) Khmer and Mon-Khmer transition, tenth to thirteenth centuries, (5) Tai (Chiengsen), eleventh to fourteenth centuries, (6) Tai (Suk'ot'ai), thirteenth to fourteenth centuries, (7) Khmer-Tai transition (U'kong), thirteenth to fourteenth centuries, (8) Tai (Lopburi), fifteenth to seventeenth centuries, (9) Tai (Ayudhya), fourteenth to seventeenth centuries. To these has to be added a tenth, viz., the school of Funan. The influences bearing on all these schools, however, have been, directly or indirectly, all Indian. Le May's views have been endorsed by Çoedés who points out (*JRAS*, 1939) that the former has rightly prolonged the Mon-Indian school to the eleventh century and has emphasised the influence of the Pala art upon the Chieng-sen school.

Among recent explorers of ancient sites in Siam we may mention H.G. Quaritch Wales. As early as 1931 he had published his work, *Siamese State Ceremonies*: *Their History and Function*, where he showed that these ceremonies were a curious blend of Brahmanical and Buddhist elements and might be traced back to India through literary sources. As leader of the first research expedition (1934) under the auspices of the newly-started *Greater India Research Committee* in London, he explored, with the aid of a generous grant of H.H. the Gaekwar of Baroda, the Siamese portion of the Malay Peninsula. His discoveries including those of Brahmanical images at Takuapa (Ptolemy's Takkola) on the west coast and at Caiya on the coast of the Bay of Bandon in the east led him to confirm R.C. Majumdar's view relating to location of seat of the Śailendra dynasty in Malay. What is more, he held Caiya to be the original capital of this dynasty. He further suggested as against Parmentier and Bosch, that the region around the Bay of Bandon deriving its original inspiration from Indian influences across Takuapa was the cradle of the Far Eastern civilisation (see H.G. Quaritch Wales "A Newly Explored Route of Ancient Indian Cultural Expansion", *IAL*, IX, 1935). In his second expedition (1935-6) the same intrepid explorer visited the ancient site of Pong Tuk excavated by the Archaeological Department of Siam in 1927, and he was rewarded with the discovery of a ruined brick *stūpa* and *vihāra* of the Dvāravatī period. He explored the ancient city of Srideb in southern Siam which had been discovered by Prince Damrong in 1905 and had produced a few sculptures identified by

Çoedés as belonging to the Gupta school. Quaritch Wales' discoveries at this site consisted of the plan of the deserted city recalling that of Ancient Indian towns, of a ruined brick tower on a pyramidical base resembling the Gupta brick temple at Bhitargaon in the Cawnpore district, of Vaiṣṇava sculptures recalling the figures on the Gupta temple at Bhumara and of stone inscriptions in south Indian characters of the early sixth century (see H.G. Quaritch Wales, "The Exploration of Śrī Deva", *ABIA*, vol. X).

A fresh field for exploration of Siamese sites has been opened by the enterprise of the French School of the Far East in our own times. A convention signed with the Siamese government in 1937 has given the School the right of archaeological exploration in the country for a minimum period of five years. The first expedition led by Pierre Dupont in 1939 succeeded in excavating on an ancient site near Nakon Pathom the remains of a *stūpa* recalling the most archaic models of south India and Ceylon along with other antiquities belonging to the art of Dvāravatī (seventh-eighth centuries). At Nakon Pathom were also discovered votive tablets with the Buddhist creed in Pallava characters analogous to those of the oldest Indo-Chinese inscriptions of the fifth century AD (see *BEFEO*, XXXIX, 1939 for a full account illustrated with plans).

In the field of general history we have to mention the important work of W.A.R. Wood, *A History of Siam from the Earliest Times to the Year A.D. 1781* (London, 1926). While it has the merit of giving the first connected account of the country based on first-hand sources, it unfortunately fails to do juistice to the period covered by the Hinduised pre-Tai states of Siam. It brings down the history of Siam to the date of accession of Rama I, the founder of the present dynasty.

From a general review of the above accounts it will appear that an enormous influence was exercised by Indian civilisation upon Siam (or Thailand) during the past centuries. Not to speak of the bronze Buddha images directly imported from Amarāvatī by Indian immigrants probably in the third century AD, the Mons who were the dominant people in Central Siam (*c.* AD 500-1000) with Dvāravatī as their centre were devout Buddhists of the Hīnayāna school. The Buddha images of this period have been shown to bear close affinities to those of Sarnath and the Ajanta caves. The Mons have left behind inscriptions not only in their own language, but also in Sanskrit and Pāli. At a later period North Siam with Haripuñjaya (Lampun) as its centre was colonised by the Mons or Mon-speaking races. These colonists also were fervent Buddhists and they covered their cities with beautiful temples and *stūpas*. In Siamese Malay under the rule of the Hinduised Śrīvijaya and Śailendra dynasties Caiya and Nagara Srithammarat (Ligor) on the east coast and Takuapa on the west coast were important centres of Indian culture. On these sites have been discovered Mahāyāna Buddhist bronzes derived from Pala art and Brahmanical stone sculptures apparently based on Pallava art. It seems that there was at this period a fresh wave of immigration from East India. Between the third and sixth centuries central Siam (with its centre at Lopburi) as well as north-east Siam was included in the kingdom of Funan. The kingdom of Cambodia extended its sovereignty over the same region between the tenth and the thirteenth centuries. During this long period Brahmanism as well as Buddhism was in high favour. The Gupta art (according to Çoedés) or the Pallava, Chālukya and Pāṇḍya art (according to Le May) furnished the model for the Funan images. Khmer sculpture forms a distinctive type which is found in its pure form in the north-east and is mingled with Mon elements in central Siam. From the thirteenth century onwards Siam has been ruled by the Tai, a Mongoloid people from the Chinese province of Yunnan. The various Tai dynasties which were in power with their capitals at Chiengmai, Chiengsen, U'kong, Ayudhya and Bangkok were from time to time in contact with the great Empire of China. Nevertheless the civilisation of the Tai from first to last is almost completely dominated by Indian and allied cultures. The oldest Tai (Chiengsen) school of Siam has been proved to derive its new type of Buddha image from Pala art through the intermediary of Pagan. With the Suk'ot'ai school began a new Buddha type based largely on Chiengsen, but also partaking for the first time of Sinhalese influence. From this time Sinhalese Buddhism began to exercise considerable influence upon the religion and art of Siam. Nevertheless we find that at the beginning of the Ayudhya period in the sixteenth century there was erected a considerable number of Brahmanical images testifying to the continuation of the Indian influence. [For references, see Reginald Le May, *Buddhist Art in Siam*, pp. 149-50.]

CAMBODIA

Cambodia, the land of the Khmers (kinsmen by language if not by race of the Mons of Burma and the Khasis and Mundas of north India), now forms a protectorate of French Indo-China. For nearly 900 years (*c.* AD 550-1450) it was ruled by a succession of Hindu (or Hinduised) dynasties under whom it not only became one of the leading powers of South-Eastern Asia, but also developed an advanced civilisation testified to by its legacy of magnificent works of art and of Sanskrit inscriptions of a high quality. And yet Kambujadeśa, to give it its Ancient Sanskrit name, was not the oldest Indian colony in that part of the country. It was itself established on the ruins of another Indian kingdom known to the Chinese writers as Funan. Traditionally said to have been founded (about the first century AD) by the Brahman Kauṇḍinya and completely Indianised by another person of the same name *c.* AD 400, this ancient kingdom witnessed a full blossoming of Hindu culture before its disappearance about the end of the sixth century.

By the middle of the second decade of the present century the foundations of Cambodian studies had been well and firmly laid by a band of French scholars. The decipherment of the first Sanskrit inscriptions from Cambodia in 1879 by the renowned Dutch scholar Hendrik Kern, the founder of Cambodian epigraphy, was followed by the publication of the text and translation of a large number of similar inscriptions by Auguste Barth and Abel Bergaigne. Their work called "Inscriptions Sanskrites du Cambodge et du Champa" was published in vol. XX, part I of the *Notices and Extracts of the MSS of the Bibliothèque Nationale and other Libraries* (Fasc. 1, Paris 1885, Fasc. 2, Paris, 1893). The foundation of the renowned *French School of the Far East* (at first called by the modest name of *Archaeological Mission of Indo-China*) in 1898 was the signal for a great outburst of scholarly activities. To the famous *Bulletin* of this School (started in 1901) its members have contributed numerous papers which have illuminated the dark corners of the art, archaeology and general history not only of French Indo-China, but also of adjoining lands. The activities of this School were directed at first towards a systematic survey of antiquities. In 1901 Lunet de Lajonquière produced his *Archaeological Atlas of Indo-China* (in French) tracing the monuments of Champa and Cambodia. Afterwards he published his great *Descriptive Inventory of the Monuments of Cambodia* (in French) forming the First Part of his projected *Archaeological Inventory of Indo-China*. This work consisted of three volumes (Paris, 1902, 1907, 1912) containing along with useful general introductions short notices of all monuments and inscriptions in the different provinces of Cambodia, Siam and Cochin-China. From 1907 when Siam ceded to France the provinces of Battambang and Siemrap, the School began to devote its energies to the exploration and conservation of the world-famed Angkor group of monuments included in the cession. Meanwhile E. Aymonier published his comprehensive work *Le Cambodge* in three volumes (Paris, 1900-4). The volumes, dealing successively with the present kingdom of Cambodia, the Siamese provinces and the Angkor group, contained a detailed description of the land and the people, the laws and institutions, the monuments and inscriptions and last but not the least, the geographical regions. With this may be mentioned the great Bibliography of the Indo-Chinese peninsula (*Bibliotheca Indo-Sinica*) of H. Cordier which was published by the French School of the Far East in four volumes (1912, 1913, 1914), volume I dealing with Burma, Assam, Siam and Laos, volume II with the Malay Peninsula, volumes III & IV with French Indo-China. [The Index of the whole work from the pen of M.A. Roland-Cabaton had to wait for publication till 1932.] Work of a different kind was done by Pelliot who pushed back the history of Hindu civilisation in French Indo-China by recovering from the invaluable Chinese literary references the forgotten record of the Kingdom of Funan (*BEFEO* III, 1903). In *BEFEO* XVI Parmentier published a series of six maps illustrating the sites of the stone inscriptions and the gradual expansion of the Khmer domination.

The remarkable advance that has been achieved in recent years in our knowledge of Cambodian history and antiquities is almost entirely due to the activities of the French School, and above all, of its illustrious Directors Louis Finot and George Çoedés and architect Henri Parmentier. To begin with archaeology, there appeared under the auspices of this School a volume (in

French) called *General Lists of Inscriptions and Monuments of Champa and Cambodia*, 2nd edn., 1923. The first part dealing with inscriptions was the work of Çoedés and the second describing the monuments was written by Parmentier. In *BEFEO*, XXV (1925), XXVIII (1928), and XXIX (1929) Finot published a number of important inscriptions (especially from Angkor) discovered since 1923. The school took the lead in carrying into effect a scheme of Corpus of Cambodian inscriptions first projected by Georges Maspero. Between 1926 and 1928 there appeared four volumes, vols. I-III, Paris, 1926-7, vol. IV, Paris, 1928, of *Inscriptions of Cambodia* containing the facsimiles of inscriptions not comprised in the work of Barth and Bergaigne or else occurring there without facsimiles. A fifth volume of the usual facsimiles of Sanskrit inscriptions was published by Finot in 1931. The sixth and last volume of the Corpus containing 44 Plates of new inscriptions discovered since 1929 was produced by Çoedés in 1937. To this last the author added the text and translation of the inscriptions concerned, under the title *Inscriptions du Cambodge*, vol. 1 (Hanoi, 1937). Meanwhile Çoedés had deciphered (*BEFEO*, XXXI, 1931) two inscriptions of Funan, one mentioning the installation of the footprints of God Viṣṇu by King Guṇavarman (first half of fifth century) and the other referring to kings Jayavarman and Rudravarman (first half of sixth century). The same scholar has since identified (*JGIS*, IV, 2 July 1937) a newly-discovered epigraph as referring to this Jayavarman who reigned at the end of the fifth century. The inscription which begins with invocation to Lord Viṣṇu records the foundation of a hermitage by Jayavarman's principal Queen called Kulaprabhāvatī.

Coming to monuments and works of art, it could be a matter of reproach as late as 1921 that while disproportionate attention had been given to the epigraphy and philology of Cambodia, its art and archaeology had never been methodically studied. [Cf. Groslier, *Arts et Archéologie Khmers*, I (1921-2), Fasc. I, Introduction, pp. 7ff.] During the last twenty years, however, the School has pursued a ceaseless and most successful campaign of archaeological exploration and research. To take a few examples, we may begin by referring to Henri Marchal's discovery at Roluoh (identified by Çoedés with Hariharālaya, a capital of Jayavarman II), of a temple belonging to the end of the ninth century. Other excavations have recently been carried out at Phnom Kulen, probably identical with Mahendraparvata, another capital of Jayavarman II (latter half of eighth century—AD 854). These discoveries have proved (Philippe Stern, "La transition de l'art preangkoréen à l'art angkoréen et Jayavarman II" in *Études d'Orientalisme Linossier*, pp. 507-24) the architectural style of Jayavarman II to be intermediary between the "primitive" and the "classical" Khmer art. In the Angkor group of monuments themselves Çoedés has recently discovered a pre-Angkor monument. Remains of three brick towers having been brought to light by Marchal in 1930, Çoedés was able to prove the identity of the central tower with the sanctuary of Kuṭīśvara of the reign of Jayavarman II mentioned in the inscriptions. At Bantay Srei (Īśvarapura), 12 miles north-east of Angkor, was discovered in 1914 a Śivite temple which has been proved (Çoedés, *BEFEO*, 1929) to have wholly belonged to the reign of Jayavarman V (tenth century). The temple, which consisted of three sanctuaries and two libraries adorned with exquisite reliefs representing Śaiva and Vaiṣṇava mythology, has formed the subject of a magnificent monograph called *Le Temple d'Īśvarapura* (*Bantay Srei*), Paris, 1926. In this volume which forms the first of the series of *Memoirs of the French School of the Far East* the monuments have been described by Parmentier, the images by Goloubev, the inscriptions and general history by Finot.

By far the most important and fruitful of these explorations and researches have centred around the wonderful group of monuments at Angkor which was the capital of the Cambodian kingdom for more than five centuries. To the assiduous care of Henri Marchal the conservator of the group of Angkor monuments since 1916 is due a good deal of valuable work in the way of exploration, conservation and popularisation of these monuments. The first complete photographic inventory of the great monument of Angkor Vat was published as the second Memoir of the French School of the Far-East in a series of magnificent volumes (in French) called *The Temple of Angkor Vat*. Part I of this monumental work bearing the title *The Architecture of the Monument* (2 vols., Paris & Brussels, 1929) was illustrated with 73 + 78 Plates and 2 Plans with a Preface by Finot tracing the history of the temple from its foundation to its restoration under French auspices in recent times. Part II called *The Ornamental Sculpture of the Temple* (2 vols., Paris & Brussels, 1930) was brought out with 436 Plates and 2 Plans with an Introduction by Goloubev. Part III called *The Gallery of Bas-reliefs* (3 vols., Paris, 1932) was illustrated with 64 + 146 + 112 Plates and 4 + 5 + 3 Plans with a Preface by Çoedés. Among the subjects of these world-famed bas-reliefs are legends of Viṣṇu and his two incarnations of Rāma and Kṛṣṇa, the Hindu Heavens and Hells and the like. Altogether these seven volumes form a worthy record of the imperishable temple which has been rightly reckoned among the greatest monuments of the world because of the amplitude of its architecture and the richness of its sculpture. Built as a Viṣṇuite temple between the years AD 1115 and 1180 by Sūryavarman II and his nephew and successor Dharanīndravarman II, Angkor Vat underwent strange vicissitudes of fortune, for it was appropriated by Jayavarman VII (1181-1201) to the cult of Mahāyāna Buddhism and was afterwards annexed to Hīnayāna Buddhism. Passing to the famous city of Angkor Thom (north of Angkor Vat) with its well-known group of monuments like the Bayon and the Baphuon, we may first mention that the Baphuon has been recently identified by Çoedés (*BEFEO*, XXXI) with Svarṇādri which the inscriptions record to have been built by Udayādityavarman II in the second half of the eleventh century. Of fundamental importance is the discovery due to the recent researches of Çoedés and Goloubev that the present city of Angkor Thom with its group of monuments was not built by Yaśovarman I at the close of the ninth century as was formerly supposed, nor by Sūryavarman I (1002-

49) as was later suggested by Philippe Stern (*Le Bayon d'Angkor et Revolution de l'art Khmer*, Paris, 1927), but was the work of Jayavarman VII at the close of the twelfth century AD. The excavations carried out during 1931-2 and 1933-4 under the guidance of Goloubev supplemented by aerial surveys of the site have since revealed the plan of the original city of Yaśovarma I, which was a rectangle like its successor but was larger in size. At the exact centre of the rectangle representing the older city stands the Śivite temple of Phnom Bakheng which Goloubev has shown to be identical with the Central Mount mentioned in Yaśovarma I's inscriptions to have been built by that monarch for housing the tutelary deity of the realm. (See Çoedés, *BEFEO*, XXVIII, Goloubev, *BEFEO*, XXXIII; ibid., XXXIV, *JA*, CCXXVI, 1935.) So far as the Bayon (formerly identified with the Central Mount is concerned), the excavations carried out in 1933-4 in the pit of the central tower revealed fragments of a stone statue which have since been restored to form a large-sized Buddha image seated on a pedestal beneath the canopy of a polycephalous Nāga. This statue, which has been reckoned among the finest sculptures of Cambodia found so far, has been identified by Çoedés as the image of Jayavarman VII deified as Buddha. To the same scholar is due the suggestion that the large number of four-faced stone towers for which the Bayon is so famous represent colossal portraits of the great Emperor in the guise of Avalokiteśvara, the All-merciful deity of the Mahāyānist pantheon. Quite recently Çoedés has suggested in the light of fresh excavations that the central block of the Bayon was built by Jayavarman VII as a central temple of his restored capital with his own statue in the form of a Buddha.

The important discoveries connected with Angkor Thom and its great monument! of the Bayon have resulted in a complete reconstruction of the chronology of Khmer art. The new chronology may be stated as follows: (1) pre-Angkor style, sixth-ninth centuries; (2) style of Lolei and Koh Ker, tenth century; (3) styles of Bantay Srei, Baphuon, Angkor Vat, eleventh-twelfth centuries; (4) style of Bayon, twelfth-thirteenth centuries.

We have described the remarkable progress that the French School has achieved in the way of archaeological exploration and research. This work has been accompanied by that of conservation of the monuments concerned, A new era was opened in this line by the journey of Marchal to Indonesia in 1930 with the object of studying the Dutch methods of reconstruction (Anastylose) which had been so successfully applied to Chaṇḍi Kalasan and other Javanese monuments. The happy results of Marchal's expedition were seen in his reconstruction on similar lines of the southern sanctuary of the temple at Bantay Srei belonging to the tenth century (for a popular account of this reconstruction, see *IAL*, vii, 1933).

The growth of Museums has kept pace with the march of archaeological exploration and research sketched above. Not to speak of the fine collections at the Louis Finot Museum at Hanoi, the Henri Parmentier Museum at Tourane, the Blanchard de la Brosse Museum at Saigon (created as late as 1929), we may mention the Albert Sarraut Museum at Phnom Penh (founded in 1919) which has been described as "the National Museum of Khmer art from the earliest to the most recent times". The important collections of these Museums have been made available for study and research by the publication of adequate catalogues enriched with Introductions describing classifications of styles. To confine ourselves to those dealing with Cambodian antiquities, we may mention the catalogues of the Phnom Penh Museum by Goloubev (*Ars Asiatica*, XVI, 1931) and of the Hanoi Museum by Marchal (Hanoi, 1939). Reference may also be made to the catalogue of Indo-Chinese collections at the Musee Guimet (Paris, 1934) by P. Dupont, and others.

Turning to the critical studies of Cambodian art and archaeology, we have to record continuous progress during the last twenty years. A great impetus was given to these studies by the appearance of the valuable Review *Arts et Archéologie Khmers* under the able editorship of George Groslier. The successive numbers of this journal for the years 1921-4 contain, along with fine illustrations of the monuments and their sculptures, weighty contributions on such topics as the temples of Ta Prohm and Prah Vihear, the Rāma legend on the temple of Angkor Vat, the bronzes and ceramics of Ancient Cambodia and the evolution of Cambodian art. In his work *La Sculpture Khmère ancienne* (Paris, 1925), Groslier propounded a new theory of the origin and evolution of Khmer art which, however, has failed to command acceptance. According to his view, Kambuja art began in the first-seventh centuries AD and its remnants are monuments of purely Indian character. Cambodian art properly so-called, which has no connection with the art of the first period, began only in the eighth-ninth centuries AD. The first adequate study of Khmer bronzes with reference to their date and origin, their iconography and comparison with Siamese, Javanese and Indian bronzes, was given by Çoedés in his finely illustrated work *Bronzes Khmers* (*Ars Asiatica*, vol. V, 1923). The specimens were selected from public and private collections at Bangkok as well as from the collections at the royal palace at Phnom Penh and the museums of Cambodia and the French School at Hanoi. In his German work called *Old-Javanese Bronzes from the Ethnographic Collection of the Natural History Museum at Vienna* (Wien, 1925), Heine-Geldern described the character and quality of the Javanese bronzes and their relation to the Indian and Wayang types. A brief account of Cambodian architecture and sculpture was given by A.K. Coomaraswamy in his well-known work *History of Indian and Indonesian Art* (London, 1927). By far the most important works on Khmer art that have appeared in recent times are those of Parmentier [*L'art Khmer primitif*, 2 vols., Paris, 1927; *Complément à l'Art Khmer primitif, BEFEO*, 1936; *L'art Khmer classique: Monuments du Quadrant Nord-Est;* 2 vols., vol. 1: Text, vol. II: Plates (architectural drawings), Paris, 1929]. In these works we get a masterly and well-illustrated account of all the known Khmer monuments together with general characteristics of their style and valuable discussions on the relations between Khmer art and the related arts of Champa, Java and India. In his article "The History of Khmer Architecture" (*Eastern Art*, III, 1931), Parmentier gave a detailed analysis of the imported Indian architecture of Funan, of the architecture, sculpture and minor arts of the Early Khmer period and of the architecture of the classical period. In the same context he distinguished three chronological divisions of Khmer architecture, viz., Early Khmer (sixth-eighth centuries), Classical (ninth-fifteenth centuries) with five subdivisions, and Modern (from the fifteenth century onwards). Intensive studies in the evolution of the Khmer pilaster and pediment as well as of the *makara* arch have been recently carried out by Mme. Gilberte de Coral Rémusat (*Annales d'Extrême-Orient*, Paris, 1935; *Revue des Arts Asiatiques*, ix, 1935; *BEFEO*, 1936). A type of temple called *nandika* said to have been built by Indravarman I (ninth century) in one of his recently discovered inscriptions has been identified and described in the light of references in the Indian *Śilpaśāstras* by U.N. Ghoshal (*JGIS*, VII, no. 2, July 1940).

A fundamental question discussed by Parmentier in recent times in connection with his studies on Khmer art is its relation to Indian art. In a paper on "The Common Origin of Hindu Architecture in India and the Far East" contributed originally in French to the *Etudes Asiatiques* (ibid., II, Paris, 1925) and afterwards translated into English in the *Rūpam* (Calcutta, 1929), Parmentier concluded from an exhaustive analysis that the origin of all forms pf Indian architecture is to be found in the lost model of the ancient Buddhist Saṅghārāma of wooden construction, a type, which spreading outwards with the progress of Buddhism, was developed independently in each country according to its local conditions. This conclusion was re-asserted by the author in his later works (cf. *L'art Khmer primitif*, vol. I, p. 349). In her paper on the common origin of the lintels of Pallava India and the pre-Angkorian Khmer lintels (*RAA*, viii, 1934), Mme. G. de Coral Rémusat has been driven to the same conclusion by an exhaustive comparison of Khmer and Pallava lintels. On the other hand, Reginald Le May (*Buddhist Art in Siam*, pp. 63-6) has recently drawn pointed attention to the close affinity between the early Khmer architecture and that of the early mediaeval temples of Kharod and Sirpur in the Central Provinces of India. Çoedès has similarly recalled (*JRAS*, 1939) the astonishing parallelism between the Bhitargaon temples of the Early Gupta period and certain temple-towers of the pre-Angkor period.

Another important question discussed in recent times, which is of great interest for the student of Indian culture is the symbolism of the Cambodian monuments. Referring to the Angkor group, Przyluski has suggested that the square design and the central temple characteristic of such monuments is the architectural representation of the universe according to Indian and Indo-Chinese ideas of town-planning. Regarding the other characteristics of these monuments P. Mus has held that the giants' bridges at Angkor, generally interpreted as illustrating the churning of the ocean, in reality stand for the rainbow which according to Indian traditions is a link between the world of man and the world of gods which is materialised on earth by the royal city, while the four-faced stone towers for which the Bayon is so famous are the four-faced images of the God Avalokiteśvara. According to the same scholar the Bayon is both a portrait of its builder Jayavarman VII and a literal realization in stone of the *Saddharmapuṇḍarīka*, "the Bible of Sanskrit Buddhism". The symbolism of Angkor Vat has been the subject of some remarkable controversy in recent times. While Przyluski (*Festschrift Winternitz*, pp. 326-32; *JISOA*, V, pp. 131-44) held that it was a funerary monument of its builder Jayavarman VII, Çoedés (*BEFEO*, XXXIII) has declared that it was neither a temple nor a tomb but a funerary temple, thus denying its unique character and bringing it into line with the general body of the Khmer monuments.

Coming to the general history of Cambodia and its civilisation, we have to mention the work of E. Aymonier (*Histoire de l'ancien Cambodge*) bringing up to date his comprehensive volumes (*Le Cambodge*) already mentioned. An ambitious work illustrating Cambodian life and culture from the first century of the Christian era onwards in the light of the extant monuments and other antiquities was published by E. Groslier (*Recherches sur les Cambodgiens*, Paris, 1921). It consists of two parts, Part I dealing with writing, habitations, commerce, dress and ornaments and the like, while Part II describes the monuments, with their sculptures. To an Indian scholar, Bijan Raj Chatterjee, we owe a popular monograph (*Indian Cultural Influences in Cambodia*, Calcutta, 1928) based on the researches of French scholars. It traces the political history of Cambodia from the earliest times and concludes with interesting notices of Indian influences upon its civilisation. A work of a different kind is the *Bibliographic de l'Indochine Française* (1913-26), Hanoi, 1929, and ibid. (1927-9), Hanoi, 1932 forming the Supplement to the *Bibliotheca Sinica* of Henri Cordier already mentioned.

In the above pages we have recorded the achievements of the French School in the way of recovery of the lost culture of Cambodia. The School has also sought to introduce something like a cultural renaissance in the lands under its jurisdiction. To its stimulus and continued support we owe the foundation and maintenance not only of the Buddhist Institute at Phnom Penh, but also of the Royal Libraries of Cambodia and Laos at their present capitals Phnom Penh and Luang Prabang. Most recently has been founded under its auspices the Pāli school at Phnom Penh, which by its publication of a series of canonical texts, has led to a renaissance of Pāli students among the people.

A general survey of pre-Khmer and Khmer culture such as we obtain from the above records reveals the immense hold exercised by Indian civilisation upon it during the whole course of its history. In the oldest times Funan with its capital at Vyādhapura had its Indian dynasty tracing descent from the Brahman Kauṇḍinya and including Guṇavarman (a patron of Vaiṣṇavism), Jayavarman and Rudravarman (probably a Buddhist). Śaivaism (including the worship of a perpetual *liṅga*) was the predominant religion. The Kambuja kings of the late sixth and the seventh centuries, who delivered Cambodia from the yoke of Funan claimed descent from the Ṛiṣi Kambu. How deeply rooted was the Hindu influence at this time will appear from the fact that the

Brahman Vidyāviśeṣa, a high official of King Īśānavarman is credited with a sound knowledge of Sāṅkhya, Vaiśeṣika, Nyāya and Buddhism. Jayavarman II who unified the country under his rule in the early part of the ninth century introduced a Tantrik form of Śaivaism centering around a liṅga (*Jagat ta Raja*) which became the tutelary deity of the kingdom. Yaśovarma I (AD 889-910), the builder of the first city of Angkor including the Śivite temple of Phnoṃ Bakheng, was the author of a number of Sanskrit inscriptions written in the native Cambodian alphabet of south Indian origin and in a north Indian script as well as of other Sanskrit inscriptions written in the same north Indian script which indicate an extensive knowledge of Sanskrit literature. Sūryavarman II (AD 1112-52), built the wonderful Viṣṇuite temple at Angkor Vat enshrining probably his own image in the guise of God Viṣṇu. Jayavarman VII, the last of the Grand Monarchs of Cambodia, has now been shown to have built the present city of Angkor Thom with its wonderful group of monuments including the Bayon. Throughout this period Sanskrit literature in all its branches, including above all grammar and *kāvya*, was studied assiduously, as is proved by the evidence of the inscriptions. Brahmanism including specially the worship of Śiva was the dominant religion. The *Mahābhārata*, the *Rāmāyaṇa* (of which there was a version in Cambodia) and the *Harivaṁśa* furnished the themes of numerous bas-reliefs of the Cambodian temples. Among the most frequently illustrated scenes are the churning of the ocean, the war between the Kauravas and the Pāṇḍavas, Kṛṣṇa holding aloft the mountain Govardhana, Viṣṇu reposing in slumber upon the serpent Ananta with Brahma seated on a lotus springing from his navel, and so forth.

CHAMPA

The country of Champa, corresponding to the Annam province of French Indo-China without its northern districts, was inhabited from ancient times by the Chams, a people of Malay-Polynesian stock. Ruled by Hindu dynasties for nearly twelve centuries from the second or third century onwards, it became a great centre of Sanskrit culture testified to at present by its numbers of Sanskrit inscriptions. During this time the chief cities (Champāpuri, Indrapura, Vijaya, etc.) of Champādeśa (as it was called in the inscriptions), were adorned with fine monuments dedicated to Brahmanism as well as Buddhism. And yet Champa could not vie with Cambodia or Java in the greatness of its monuments. Exposed to the attacks of its formidable adversaries (specially the Annamites in the north and the Cambodians in the west and south) who, ravaged their country more than once, the people lived an agitated and precarious life allowing little leisure for development of the arts of peace. The brick constructions of the shrines have not helped to preserve them to our own times.

It is characteristic of the difference between Champa and Cambodia that while the great advance in our knowledge of Cambodian art, archaeology and general history has taken place only during the last twenty years, the study of Champa antiquities was all but completed by the middle of the second decade of this century. To begin with archaeology, we have referred above to the publication of the text and translation of the Sanskrit inscriptions of Cambodia and Champa by Barth and Bergaigne in 1885 and 1893. An important collection of inscriptions in Champa was edited by Aymonier in *JA*, 1891. After the foundation of the *French School of the Far East*, a large number of new inscriptions of Champa was edited in its famous *Bulletin* by Finot (see specially ibid., II-IV) and by Huber (ibid., IX, XI & XIV). Valuable lists of inscriptions from Champa were published by Çoedés in the same journal (vol. VIII & vol. XV). In the early years of this century Parmentier carried out a series of important excavations on the sites of the Buddhist monastery at Dong Duong (Indrapura) and the Brahmanical shrines at Myson and Po-Nagar. In 1909 the same scholar published the first volume of his great Work on the Cham monuments (*Inoentaire descriptif des monuments Cams de l'Annam*) bearing the sub-title of "*Description of the monuments*". It contains an exhaustive account of all known Cham monuments within and outside the country with valuable preliminary notices of their geographical environment and general characteristics of their style. Meanwhile the valuable Chinese texts bearing on the history of Champa were brought to light by Pelliot, Maspero and Aurousseau (*BEFEO*, IV & XIV). The scattered references in the Chinese and Annamite records and the evidence of Cham and Cambodian inscriptions were pieced together by Maspero in his important monograph called *The Kingdom of Champa* (*Le Roydume du Champa*, 1914) tracing the history of this kingdom from the earliest times to the final conquest of the greater part of the country by the Annamites in AD 1471.

The work that has been done in the investigation of the ancient Cham history: and culture during the last twenty-five years has been mostly of a supplementary character. In 1918 Parmentier completed his masterly survey of Cham monuments by publishing the second volume of his great *Descriptive Inventory* bearing the sub-title of *A Study of Cham Art*. Besides giving an elaborate account of the details of Cham architecture and sculpture, it described the civilisation and state of religion revealed by the monuments, the genius of Cham art, its origin and successive periods, its aesthetics and so forth. The same scholar afterwards published (in French) his *Descriptive Catalogue of Cham Sculptures in the Tourane Museum* (*Ars Asiatica*, 1922). In 1923 Çoedés and Parmentier published their *General Lists of Inscriptions and Monuments in Champa and Cambodge* to which reference has been made above. Mention may be made in this connection of the important *Catalogue of Indo-Chinese* (*including Cham*) *Collections at the Musée Guimet* (in French) by Pierre Dupont and others (Paris ,1934). Meanwhile important excavations were carried out by the French School on the site of Tra-Kieu long before (*BEFEO*, XIV) identified by Aurousseau with the first capital of the Cham kingdom. The reliefs of the Tra-Kieu temple have since been identified by Çoedés (*BEFEO*, XXXII) as illustrating the story of Kṛṣṇa and Balarāma told in the *Harivaṁśa* and the Purāṇas. As regards conservation of monuments, one of the most interesting examples in recent times has been the reconstruction by J.Y. Claeys of the principal temple-tower of Po-Nagar built in AD 817. (For a popular account, see J.Y. Claeys, "Po-Nagar, Recent Work of Restoration by the École Française d'Extrême-Orient", *ABIA*, 1931.) Coming to general history, we have to mention R.C. Majumdar's publication of a comprehensive account of the history and culture of Champa (*Champa*: Greater India Society's publication no. I, Lahore, 1927), forming the first volume of a projected series called *Ancient Indian Colonies in the Far East*. This volume, while based principally upon the monumental *Le Royaume du Champa* of Maspero and *Inventaire descriptif des monuments Cams* of Parmentier, seeks to throw new light upon some of the problems of general history and the history of the art of Champa. Most interesting is the author's attempt to prove against the high authority of Parmentier his thesis that Cham architecture was derived from Chalukya and Pallava styles as illustrated by the temples of Badami, Conjeeveram and Mahabalipuram. The value of Majumdar's work has been enhanced by its including the first complete Corpus of inscriptions from Champa with his own translations and notes. More recently the problem of palaeography of the earliest Champa inscriptions, on which hinges the question of *provenance* of the first Indian colonists, has been discussed by R.C. Majumdar (*BEFEO*, 1932) and K.A. Nilakanta Sastri (*BEFEO*, 1935). In his paper "Date of the Earliest Sanskrit Inscription of Champa" (*JGIS*, VI, 1939), D.C. Sircar has suggested a late date, viz. the fourth century AD, for the famous Vo-chañh rock inscription.

The researches of an Annamite scholar of the French School, based on an exhaustive study of the Annamite and Chinese as well as European authorities, have recently disclosed the interesting history of the origin and progress of Buddhism in Ancient Annam. Buddhism, it appears, was probably introduced from India into Annam by the direct sea-route. Among its great missionary were this Indian monks Mārajīvaka and Kṣudra (AD 294) not to speak of the Soghdian monk Song-houei (*c.* AD 280) and the Indo-Scythian monk Kalyā. naruchi (AD 255 or 256) (see Tran van Giap, "Le Bouddhisme en Annam des origines au XIIIe siécle", *BEFEO*, 1932). Excavations recently carried out in Annam have resulted in the discoveries of sculptures suggesting to J.Y. Claeys the Indian origin of Annam's first civilisation.

MALAYASIA

The vast regions comprised in the modern Malay Peninsula and the Malay Archipelago (otherwise called Indonesia or Insulinde) were, inhabited from remote times by peoples of Austronesian speech. Known to Ancient Indian literature under the vague designations of Suvarṇabhūmi and Suvarṇadvīpa and to the ancient Greek, Chinese and Arab writers under equivalent terms, they were visited by Indian merchants at least as early as the first century AD and were afterwards colonised by Indian settlers. "Paloura" (or to give it its

Indian name Dantapura) in Kalinga was in the oldest times the great port of embarkation from India to the Far East. Especially in Java, Sumatra and Malay the Hindu civilisation took firm root, as is evidenced by the records of numerous Hindu (or Hinduised) kingdoms flourishing in those regions for at least a thousand years till they were engulfed by the advancing tide of Islam in the fifteenth and sixteenth centuries. Twice during this long period, under the great Śailendra dynasty and under the Indo-Javanese empire of Majapahit (called in Sanskrit *Vilvatikta*), the greater part of Suvarṇadvīpa was brought under one political control.

JAVA

Apparently the oldest references to the inland of Java are to be found in the *Rāmāyaṇa* under the name of Javadvīpa and in Ptolemy's *Geography* in the form of *Iavadiou* translated as "Barley Island". A king called Devavarman, as appears from a Chinese literary reference, ruled the country in the first part of the second century AD. In the beginning of the fifth century Fa Hian found Brahmanism flourishing in the island. The oldest Sanskrit inscriptions found in the island mention King Pūrṇavarman, son (?) of a Rājādhirāja and grandson of a Rājarṣi, who ruled over western Java in the fifth or sixth century AD. The oldest Sanskrit inscription from central Java written probably in the seventh century shows this region to have been equally saturated with Brahmanical culture. Under the succeeding dynasties, as is proved by the splendid remains of architecture and sculpture dating from the eighth century and the works of the Old Javanese literature practically dating from the eleventh century, an Indo-Javanese civilisation flourished exceedingly.

The early steps towards investigation of Javanese history and culture were marked by the foundation of the Batavia Society of Arts and Sciences (the oldest of the learned Societies of the East) in 1778, by the first scientific exploration of the Barabudur and Prambanan monuments during the British interregnum by order of the Lt. Governor Sir Stamford Raffles (the founder of archaeological research in Java), by the publication of Raffles's *History of Java* (1st edn., 1817) and lastly, by the issue of the first scientific study of Javanese art in 1824 by C.J.C. Reuvens, Director of the newly-founded Leyden Museum; The critical study of the extensive Indo-Javanese literature largely based upon the Sanskrit was begun by Friedrich's editions of the Vṛttasañcaya, the Arjunavivāha and the Bhomakāvya (1849-51) and his disquisitions on the Javanese Vedas, *Brahmāṇḍa Purāṇa*, *Mahābhārata* and so forth (*Proceedings of the Batavia Society*, 1849). In the seventh decade of the last century H. Kern initiated the critical study of Indonesian epigraphy by editing a number of Sanskrit inscriptions from Sumatra, Java and Borneo (*VG*, VI), while A.B. Cohen Stuart published (in Dutch) an important collection of Charters in the native Kawi language with Introduction, facsimile and transcript (Leyden 1875) and W.P. Groeneveldt wrote his valuable *Notes on the Malay Archipelago nd Malacca Compiled from Chinese Sources* (Batavia, 1877). In the following lecade local museums were started at Jogyakarta (afterwards transferred to 'rambanan) and at Dieng, in Central Java. The first catalogue of the archaeological ollection of the Museum of the Batavia Society was issued by Groeneveldt n 1887. As regards the study of Indo-Javanese literature, the *Kuṭāra-mānava* regarded formerly as the highest authority on law in east Java) was edited vith Introduction and Dutch translation by J.B.G. Jonker (Leyden, 1885), vhile H.H. Juynboll in 1893 published his Dutch translation of the Javanese *1ahābhārata* (Parvans XV-XVII) which ushered in a period of serious research n the subject. We may also refer to the important studies in the Indo-Javanese neatre by Brandes (*TBG*, 1889) and by G.A.J. Hazeu (Leyden, 1897). The rst decade of the present century witnessed, after many years of sad neglect, ne establishment in 1901 of *the Committee in Netherlands-India for the rchaeological Explorations in Java and Madura* (replaced by *The rchaeological Service of Netherlands-India* in 1913) with J.L.A. Brandes as s first Chairman. (For a scathing criticism of the archaeological policy of the)utch Colonial Government, see J.F. Scheltema, *Monumental Java*, London 912.) During the twelve years of its existence the Committee published a aluable series of Reports (*Rapporten*) noticing the chief antiquities of the sland year after year. The Committee also started a series of works (in Dutch) alled *Archaeological Explorations in Java and Madura*, of which the first vo volumes giving an exhaustive and well-illustrated account of the well-nown temples of Caṇḍi Jago and Chaṇḍi Singhasari were published by Brandes 1904 and 1909 respectively. To the credit of the Committee must also e mentioned the restoration of the great *stūpa* of Barabudur (1907-11) by ol. Th. van Erp. Another significant feature of this period was the growth of useums. The archaeological collection of the Prambanan Museum was listed y J. Knebel (*Archaeological Report*, 1902) and that of the Dieng Museum y E.A. Sell (*Archaeological Report*, 1912). Meanwhile Juynboll published is Catalogue of Javanese antiquities in the National Museum of Ethnography Leyden. A new museum was established at Mojokerto near Majapahit in astern Java out of the collection made over to the state by an enlightened vanese officer in 1913. The Sriwedari Museum was founded at Surakerta in ntral Java out of the private collection of a descendant of the Royal House f Mataran. The Museum of the "Royal Colonial Institute at Amsterdam" was unded in 1913. As for epigraphy, Brandes edited a valuable collection of ld-Javanese charters (*Oud-Javaanasche Oorkonden*) of which a revised ersion was brought out by Krom in 1913. As regards the interpretation of the onuments, C.M. Pleyte attempted, with the imperfect materials at his ommand, a complete identification of the bas-reliefs of the first gallery of arabudur with the *Lalitavistara* text illustrating Buddha's life. His work (in erman) bearing the title *The Buddha Legend in the Sculptures of the Temple Borobudur* was published from Amsterdam in 1901. The progress in the udy of Indo-Javanese literature was marked by Kern's studies on the Old-

Javanese *Rāmāyaṇa* (*Rāmāyaṇa, Oud-Javaansche Heldendicht*, 1900) and his translation of the first six cantos of the same work (*VG*, X), by Juynboll's edition of the Javanese *Ādiparva* (1906) and *Virāṭaparva* (1912), by J.G.H. Gunning's edition (1903) of the *Bhāratayuddha*, "the Iliad of the Javanese people". Meanwhile the rich stores of the Javanese and related literature were made accessible to scholars by the publication (in Dutch) of the *Catalogue of the Javanese and Madurese Mss. in the Leyden University Library* by Vreede (1892) and the *Catalogue of the Malay and Sundanese Mss* in the same library by Juynboll (1899). A Supplement to the Catalogue of Javanese and Madurese Mss of the Leyden University Library was published by Juynboll in two volumes (Leyden, 1907 & 1911), and a Supplement to the Catalogue of Sundanese as well as Balinese and Sasak MSS in the same library was issued by the same scholar in 1912. These catalogues brought to light a large number of Old-Javanese poems of the Kakawin (roughly corresponding to Sanskrit Kāvya) class, such as the *Indravijaya* (story of Vṛtra's triumph and his subsequent death at Indra's hands), the *Pārthayajña* (story of Arjuna's asceticism and acquisition of the Pāśupata weapon), the *Sumanasāntaka* (story of the death of Indumatī, Queen of Aja and mother of Daśaratha) and the *Harivaṁśa* (story of Rukmiṇī's abduction by Kṛṣṇa and Kṛṣṇa's war with Jarāsandha). Useful comparisons were made by Hazeu in his (Dutch) work called *The Old-Javanese Ādiparva and its Sanskrit Original* (*TBG*, 1901) and by Wulff in his (Danish) work called *The Old-Javanese Virāṭaparva and its Sanskrit Original* (1917). Valuable light was thrown upon the Javanese religion by Juynboll's publication of Sanskrit *mantras* (with Old-Javanese translations) for the worship of Viṣṇu and his incarnations as well as by J. Kats's edition with an accompanying Dutch translation (1910) of the *Sang Hyang Kamahāyānikan*, a fundamental work on Javanese Buddhism.

During the last twenty-five years a steady, though not uninterrupted, progress has been maintained in all branches of Javanese research. To begin with archaeological exploration and research, under the fostering care of F.D.K. Bosch and W.F. Stutterheim, two successive Directors of the Archaeological Service of Java, the scope of the Service was gradually widened so as to include prehistoric archaeology along with Balinese, Muslim, Christian and European antiquities. The activities of the Service were registered in successive numbers of its valuable *Archaeological Reports* (*Oudheidkundig Verslag*), vol. VI of this *Report* (1926) contains an excellent summary of Archaeological work in Netherlands-India from 1901 to 1926 from the pen of N.J. Krom. The publication of these Reports, however, was stopped in 1931, to be resumed only in 1936. Meanwhile Bosch initiated a new era in archaeological conservation by starting the complete reconstruction of the ruined monuments in place of the usual practice of restoring their fallen parts. This process (called by the technical title of *Anastylose*) was very successfully applied for the restoration of some of the subsidiary shrines of the great Buddhist temple complex of Chaṇḍi Sewu (ninth century), of the famous Buddhist shrine of

Chaṇḍi Kalasan (*c.* AD 778), of the Śivite temple of Chaṇḍi Singhasari, of the Nāga temple at Panataran and last but not the least; of the great Śiva-shrine of the Lara-Jongrang group (*c.* tenth century) at Prambanan. Among the important discoveries standing to the credit of the department in recent times may be mentioned that of the two earliest Hindu temples in Central Java on the site of the Changal inscription of AD 732, one of them probably being identical with the Brahmanical temple said to have been built by King Sañjaya in that inscription. Another significant discovery is that of the two oldest temples of Eastern Java, viz., the Śivite shrines of Badut and Besuki dating from the eighth or ninth century, which by their plan and decoration belong to a purely Central Javanese style. We may, lastly, mention the discovery of a group of terraced sanctuaries on Mt. Penanggungan in Eastern Java belonging to the final period of Hinduism in the island (AD 1400-1500). These have been supposed to combine the indigenous ancestor-worship with Hinduistic beliefs. In the field of epigraphy, as in that of archaeological exploration, the progress in recent times has not been uninterrupted. In 1930 the epigraphist who was to have taken up the long-announced and much deferred publication of a *Corpus Inscriptionum Javanicarum* was transferred to another post and the appointment was not renewed till 1939. On the other hand, Stutterheim, Goris, Naerssen and others have edited numbers of new inscriptions in the various learned periodicals. At the same time old inscriptions were re-edited and discussed, e.g. those of King Pūrṇavarman by Vogel (1925) and the Kalasan and Kelurak inscriptions by Bosch (*TBG*, 1928). Among Indian scholars who have taken part in this work may be mentioned N.P. Chakravarti, H.B. Sarkar and B.Ch. Chhabra. Among the most notable discoveries in this field in recent times is that of three stone *Yūpa* inscriptions of King Mūlavarman written in 'Pallava script' of the fourth or fifth century AD, as announced in the Year-Book of the *Batavia Society* for 1941.

Turning to the critical study of Javanese art, we have first to mention the comprehensive account of Indo-Javanese monuments from the earliest times furnished by N.J. Krom's Dutch work called *Introduction to Indo-Javanese Art* (2nd edn., vols. I-II Text, vol. III: Plates, 1923). In this monumental work the author, after giving preliminary accounts of the history of Javanese archaeological explorations and the origin and technique of Javanese art, presents for the first time a systematic and detailed description of the monuments and concludes with a rapid review of Javanese metal-work. In the course of his illuminating survey the author clearly and pointedly explains the general characteristics of the building and plastic styles, and he frequently discusses, as in connection with Brandes's theory of the Indian origin of the Buddhist images of the Chaṇḍi Jago temple, the question of Indian influence. In 1926 Krom published his work (in French) called *Javanese Art in the Museums of Holland and Java* in the *Ars Asiatica* Series. It contains 60 beautiful Plates illustrating specimens of Javanese plastic art in stone and metal together with an illuminating Introduction tracing the development of Javanese art as a whole during successive periods. Recently R.C. Majumdar (*Suvarṇadvīpa*, part II Calcutta, 1938) has presented an elaborate and well-illustrated description of Javanese architecture and sculpture based primarily upon Krom's great work but also incorporating the results of later research.

The all important question of the relation of Indian to Javanese art has been discussed by Bosch in a Dutch paper called "A Hypothesis as to the Origin of Indo-Javanese Art" (1921; Eng. tr. in *Rūpam*, 1924). While rejecting the comfortable view that the Hindu emigrants were the actual builders of the Middle-Javanese shrines, Bosch seeks to prove from an elaborate comparison between the Mānasāra and the existing remains of Javanese architecture and sculpture that the native Javanese actually knew and applied the written instructions, but the texts which in India remained mere academic projects were executed by them with the zeal of neophytes. "The Hindus were the bringers, the propagators and interpreters of technical texts, but the Javans themselves were the makers of the Central-Javanese shrines." Similar, if less definite, views have been expressed by Krom according to whom (cf. *Hindoe-Javaansche Geschiedenis*, 2nd edn., chap. IV) the creators of the art of the Dieng Plateau were neither Hindus nor Indonesians, but rather Hindu-Javans who had adopted the art-traditions of the Indian masters but had also involuntarily (introduced some of their Indonesian characteristics. In his *Archaeological Description of Barabudur* (vol. II, chap. XI) Krom similarly says that the art of Barabudur is not foreign, but is a product of Java, a fusion of Hindu and Javanese elements. With this we may compare the following statement of Stutterheim (*JAOS*, LI, no. I). "The Hindu-Javanese Chaṇḍi is neither a Hindu temple nor a truly Hinduistic building, though its shape and ornaments are Hindu in origin. It is a thoroughly Indonesian monument based on purely Indonesian conceptions." Bosch's theory has been criticised by O.C. Gangoly (*Rūpam*, 1924) and R.C. Majumdar (*Suvarṇadvīpa*, part II, concluding chapter). According to the last-named author Gupta art was the source of the architecture and sculpture of Malayasia which remained untouched by south Indian influences till the tenth or eleventh century AD.

No single monument has attracted the attention of scholars so much as the great *stūpa* at Barabudur which has gathered a vast literature around itself since its first scientific description by H.G. Cornelius in 1814. (See *The Bibliography of Barabudur*, 1814-1926 appended to the second volume of Krom's *Archaeological Description* which runs through 18 pages.) A magnificent *Description of Barabudur* (in Dutch) illustrated with a complete and sumptuous set of Plates was published by the *Royal Institute of Linguistics*, *Geography and Ethnography* of Netherlands-India in two parts. The first part of this great work bearing the title *Archaeological Description* was issued by Krom in two volumes (1920) (Chap. III of this work with appropriate plates was published by the same author simultaneously in Dutch and in English translation, 1926. The complete translation of the whole world was published later by the same author in 1927). Among the outstanding features of the *Archaeological*

Description are the author's complete and accurate identification of panels of the first gallery of the *stūpa* with the *Lalitavistara*, the *Jātakamālā* of Āryaśūra, the *Divyāvadāna* and other texts suggested before by C.M. Pleyte, S. d'Oldenburg and A. Foucher respectively. He also showed the panels of the second gallery to be illustrative of the *Gaṇḍavyūha* (a Mahāyānist Sūtra describing the wanderings of the youth Sudhana all over India in the quest for enlightenment) and those of the third and fourth galleries to be illustrations of as yet unidentified texts associated with the Bodhisattvas Maitreya and Samantabhadra respectively. To his credit must also be mentioned the identification of the Dhyānī-Buddhas of the upper terraces with the group of six Dhyānī-Buddhas with Vajrasattva as their chief known to Nepalese, Chinese and Tibetan Buddhism. The probable date of foundation of the famous monument was found by the author, from a number of short inscriptions at its base, to be the second half of the eighth century. Finally we have to mention Krom's conclusion that the Buddhism of Barabudur (like Javanese Buddhism in general from first to last) was a kind of Tāntrik Mahāyāna based on the Yogācāṛa. The next step in clearing the mystery of the monument was taken by Sylvain Lévi who discovered (*Recherches à Java et à Bali*, Leiden, 1929) the reliefs on the buried basement of Barabudur to be illustrative of a very popular Buddhist text on the working of Karma, viz., the Karmavibhāga. The Sanskrit text was published (Paris, 1932) by him with a French translation and the parallel Pāli, Chinese, Tibetan and Kuchean versions. This was accompanied by a comparative table of the different recensions of the text and the corresponding panels of the Barabudur. Well might the great French scholar exclaim, "The stūpa of Barabudur had revealed one of its last secrets." A detailed comparison of the *Karmavibhaṅga* text and the Barabudur reliefs was made by Krom (*Med. Kon. Ak. van Wet.*, LXXVI, Series B, no. 8). Nearly at the time of Lévi's discovery Bosch was able to prove from a close examination of the original Sanskrit MS in Paris that the panels of the third and fourth galleries illustrated the conclusion of the *Gaṇḍavyūha* representing 110 travels of Sudhana mentioned in the text. (See Bosch's Report in *Arch. Rep.*, 1929 and his Dutch work called *The Identification of Reliefs of the Third and Fourth Galleries of Barabudur*, 1929.) It has thus been clearly established that the *Gaṇḍavyūha* was the principal and the central text of the Barabudur.

We have now to refer to the second part of the monumental *Description of Barabudur* above-mentioned. It was published (in Dutch) by van Erp (1931) under the title *The Architectural Description*. Dealing exhaustively with the style, the technique and the ornaments of the monument, the author says that Barabudur is "a special Javanese form of the *stūpa*, though fitting in the general evolution of the Indian *stūpa*". The ornaments, according to him, are of purely Indian origin.

The question of symbolism of Barabudur has become, as has been well said, "an apple of discord among scholars". While Foucher, Parmentier and van Erp have offered what may be called "architectural interpretations" of its unique plan and structure, "religious interpretations" have been presented by Krom, Stutterheim and Poerbatjaraka. The whole question has been discussed in a very thorough fashion by P. Mus in his series of papers (in French) called "Barabudur, The Origins of the Stūpa and the Transmigration: Essay in Comparative Religious Archaeology", *BEFEO*, 1932-4. According to this scholar the entire monument is a close microcosm, its exterior envelopment corresponding to the cosmic *stūpa* while its interior corresponds to a *prāsāda*.

Of other monuments in Java forming the subject of independent study in recent times, we may refer only to the great Siva temple of the Lara-Jongrang group at Prambanan (Central Java) and the main shrine of the temple-complex at Panataran (Eastern Java). These temples are adorned with a series of reliefs depicting the story of the *Rāmāyaṇa* from the beginning to the expedition to Laṅkā. A comprehensive account of these reliefs accompanied with adequate illustrations is given by Stutterheim in his German Work called *Rāma-legends and Rāma-reliefs in Indonesia* (2 vols., München, 1925). The author mentions the curious fact that while the earlier (ninth century) reliefs at Prambanan are distinctly Indian in character but illustrate a non-Vālmīkian version of the Epic, the later (fourteenth century) Panataran series is typically Indonesian in style but is more closely based on Vālmīki's *Rāmāyaṇa*. A popular and illustrated account based on the above is presented by J. Kats in his Dutch work bearing the title *The Rāmāyaṇa* on *Javanese Temple-reliefs* (Batavia-Leiden, 1925).

The Javanese bronzes which are remarkable for their high artistic quality and unique iconographic interest have engaged the serious attention of scholars in recent times, though it has not been possible as yet to classify their styles. We have already referred to Krom's very valuable *Introduction to the Hindu-Javanese Art* as well as his other work called *Javanese Art in the Museums of Holland and Java*, both of which contain important notices of Javanese bronzes. The old Javanese bronzes in the Ethnographical collection of the National Museum at Vienna have been described by R. Heine-Geldern (Vienna, 1925), while those in the Royal Ethnographic Museum at Leiden have been catalogued by A.C. Tobi (*Archaeological Report*, 1930). The bronzes in the Batavia Museum have been described by Bosch (*Archaeological Report*, 1923). More recently A.J. Bernet Kempers has discussed (*The Bronzes of Nalanda and Hindu-Javanese Art*, Leiden, 1933) the mutual relation of Pala and Javanese bronzes. His conclusion is that the Hindu-Javanese bronzes in general have not developed from Pala art, but the Pala images have enriched the art of Java with a number of *motifs* and types. In recent times a good synoptic view of this branch of art has been given by R.C. Majumdar (*Suvarṇadvīpa*, Part II, Calcutta, 1938).

Much attention has been bestowed during recent times upon the origin of the Javanese dance and shadow-play (*Wayang*), those two fine flowers of Javanese culture. In his exhaustive work published simultaneously in Dutch and in French called *The Javanese Art of Dancing* (or *The Dance in the Javanese*

Theatre, 1931); Th. B. Vein Lelyveld has traced the Javanese dance to a distinctly Indian origin. As for the Wayang, its indigenous origin was long ago asserted by Brandes (*TBG*, 1889) and by Hazeu (Leiden, 1897). On the other hand, Krom (*Hindoe-Javaansche Geschiedenis*, 2nd edn., pp. 49ff) has strongly asserted its Indian origin; and his view has been endorsed by R.C. Majumdar (op. cit.).

During the last quarter of this century the steady growth of museums and learned societies to which reference was made above has been well maintained. We may refer to the publication of Bosch's Catalogue of the *Sriwedari Museum* at Surakarta (*Archaeological Report*, 1923) and the opening of the *Museum of the Java Institute* at Jogyakarta (1935). The *Batavia Society* which issued in 1929 a commemoration volume (*Feestbundel*) on the occasion of its 150th, year (1778-1928) has been regularly publishing its valuable journal (in Dutch) called *The Journal of Indian Linguistics, Geography and Ethnography*. (abbreviated as *TBG*). Since 1933 it has been issuing its *Year-Books* containing detailed notices of its aquisitions under the heads "Pre-historic", "Archaeological", "Historical", "Mss", "Ceramics" and "Ethnographic" collections. Other specialised journals (in Dutch) are *Djǎwǎ*, the journal of the Java Institute at Welteyreden and the *Contributions to the Linguistics, Geography and Ethnology of Netherlands-India* abbreviated as *BKI*, which is the organ of *The Royal Colonial Institute* at the Hague.

Within the last twenty years intensive studies have been carried out in the field of Old-Javanese religious beliefs and practices. We have referred above to Krom's great work *Archaeological Description of Barabudur* in course of which the author discusses the pantheon as well as the form of Buddhism at Barabudur. His view is that the Buddhism of Barabudur was a form of Tāntric Mahāyāna based on the Yogācāra. In *TBG*, 1924 Moens has described the last phase of Mahāyāna Buddhism in Sumatra and Java and has called particular attention to the Tāntric beliefs and practices of the Javanese king Kṛtanagara and the Sumatran king Ādityavarman in the thirteenth century. In the same year Pigeaud published a critical edition of a fundamental work on Brahmanism in Java called *Tantu Panggelaran* (World-Theatre?) It contains cosmogonic and mythological legends, descriptions of *maṇḍalas* (orders of religious ascetics) and *pakṣas* (religious sects) and so forth. A large number of Javanese sacred texts, mostly based upon Sanskrit originals and containing Sanskrit verses with Old-Javanese translations, have been analysed by R. Goris in his fundamental work (in Dutch) called *Old-Javanese* and *Balinese Theology* (1926). Among the texts utilised by Goris may be mentioned the *Sūryasevana*, the *Bhuvanakośa*, the *Bhuvanasaṅkṣepa*, the *Sang Hyang Mahājñāna* and the *Bṛhaspatitattva*. The last work has been proved by A. Zieseniss (*ZDMG*, XIII, no. 2) to belong to the literature of Āgamas which are the sources of the Śaivasiddhānta. The last-named author has since published in German a valuable paper called "Studies in the History of Śaivism and Śaivistic System in the Old-Javanese Literature" (*BKI*, 1939). In the *de luxe* volume called *Mythologie asiatique illustrée* (Paris, 1928) H. Marchal contributed a chapter on Indo-Chinese and Javanese mythology, two other important contributions being those of J. Hackin on the *Mythology of Lamaism* and the *Mythology of Buddhism in Central Asia*. The descriptions are accompanied with excellent illustrations. A summary of religious conditions in Java based on Dutch authorities is given by R.C. Majumdar (op. cit.). Reference may be made in this connection to F.M. Schnitger's article (in Dutch) called "Some Archaeological Remarks on Tāntrism in Java", *BKI*, vol. XC.

Turning to the study of Old-Javanese literature, we have to mention Juynboll's translation of the Javanese *Rāmāyaṇa* (Cantos VII-XXIII) in *BKI*; in continuation of Kern's translation of the same (Cantos I-VI). A new series called *Bibliotheca Javanica* has been started under the auspices of the venerable Royal Batavia Society for the publication of Old-Javanese and Middle-Javanese texts with their translations. Among works so far published in the series are the *Tantri Kāmandaka* (ed. G. Hooykas), the *Smaradahana* (ed. L. Poerbatjaraka), the *Nītiśāstra* (ed. Poerbatjaraka), the Old-Javanese *Brahmāṇḍapurāṇa* (ed. J. Gonda) and the Old-Javanese *Bhīṣmaparvan* (ed. Gonda). The first consists of three mediaeval Jevanese versions of stories and fables with parallel Siamese and Laotian versions, which bear the closest affinity to the Kanarese version of the *Pañcatantra* by Durgasiṁha, the second tells the story immortalised by Kālidāsa in his *Kumārasambhavam* about Kāma's being burnt to ashes by the wrath of Śiva; the third is a collection of wise sayings, moral precepts and so forth of the *Chāṇakyanīti* class, the fourth is the most important Javanese work of the Purāṇa class. Another work of the last-named category, the *Agastyaparva*, has been edited by Gonda (*BKI*, 1933). The Old-Javanese prose works of the *Mahābhārata* class that have recently been published include the *Koravāśrama* (ed. J.L. Swellengrebel) and the *Navaruchi* (ed. M. Prijohoetomo). In his paper "Hindu Literature in Java" (*IAL*, VI, 1932) C.C. Berg distinguished between three periods of this literature as also between its two court literatures and its popular religious literature. The study of this literature, however, according to the same scholar has to remain provisional at present, because of the paucity of critical editions of texts and of works on grammar and lexicography. A comprehensive account of Old-Javanese and Balinese literature in all its branches with special reference to its Indian affinities has been presented by Himansu Bhusan Sarkar in his work *Indian Influences on the Literature of Java and Bali* (Greater India Society's Publication, Calcutta, 1934). More recently R.C. Majumdar has given a good summary of the whole subject based on the Dutch authorities in his *Suvarṇadvīpa* (Part II).

The last quarter of this century has been very prolific in discussions of problems relating to the history and culture of Java. To take a few examples, the place of the sage Agastya in Javanese culture-history has been discussed by O.C. Gangoly ("The Cult of Agastya and the Origin of Indian Colonial Art", *Rūpam*, 1926), L. Poerbatjaraka (*Agastya in den Archipel*, Leiden, 1926), K.A.N. Sastri (*TBG*, 1936). The history and topography of Śrīvijaya and Kaṭāha has been discussed by Ir. J.L. Moens (*TBG*, 1937), K.A.N. Sastri (*JGIS*, 1938; *BEFEO*, 1940). Of more general character is the "Expansion of Indo-Aryan Culture during Pallava Rule as Evidenced by Inscriptions" of B. Ch. Chhabra (*JASB Letters*, vol. I, 1935). Of outstanding importance is the standard work of N.J. Krom called Hindu-Javanese History (*Hindoe-Javaansche Geschiedenis*, 1st edn., 1926, 2nd edn., 1931). Based on an exhaustive study of all the available data, it traces the history of Java from the earliest times to the ultimate triumph of Islam in the early sixteenth century. Accompanying the author's notices of political history are illuminating studies on the art and literature of the island during the successive centuries. This fundamental work has been utilised by R.C. Majumdar (*Suvarṇadvīpa*, part I), but the author has also sought to throw new light upon the numerous unsolved problems of Javanese history and culture. A bird's-eye view of India's cultural and other contacts with the Pacific lands (extending from Java, Sumatra and Indo-China to China, Japan, Hawaii and New Zealand) during Hindu times as also in the Prehistoric Age and in recent years is presented by Kalidas Nag in his well-documented work *India and the Pacific World* (Calcutta, 1941).

BALI

The small island of Bali lying immediately east of Java enjoys, as is well known, the unique distinction of maintaining its Hindu culture down to modern times. But unfortunately the materials are lacking for a connected account of its history, art and literature. The plausible identification by Pelliot (*BEFEO*, 1904) of the island of P'oli mentioned by the Chinese authorities of the sixth and seventh centuries AD with Bali had the result of throwing some light upon the obscure history of the island during those centuries. From these accounts we learn that kings bearing the family name of Kauṇḍinya and belonging to the kṣatriya caste ruled the country in those early times and that the Mūlasarvāstivāda Nikāya was almost universally prevalent there. In recent times the systematic search for antiquities has yielded a number of stone and copper-plate inscriptions in Sanskrit, Old-Balinese and Old-Javanese dating from the eighth century onwards. Transcripts of these inscriptions have been published by P. van Stein Callenfels in the *Epigraphia Balica* I (1926) and by Stutterheim in his Dutch work called *The Antiquities of Bali* (1929), while other inscriptions have been published by R. Goris (*Archaeological Report*, 1929). These records have disclosed the existence of a line of independent kings of the tenth century bearing Hindu names, viz., Ugrasena, Janasādhuvarmmadeva, Keśarivarma and so forth. In 1926 a Dutch architect P.A.J. Moojen published an ambitious work called the *Art of Bali: Introductory Studies on the Architecture*, which claimed to discuss the history and general characteristics of Balinese art, its religious and sociological basis, the rules and traditions of its building construction and so forth. The history, palaeography, topography, religion and art of Bali were discussed along with its inscriptions by Stutterheim in the work *The Antiquities of Bali* above-mentioned. The art of Bali was also discussed by the same scholar in his *Indian Influences in Old-Balinese Art* (India Society, London, 1935) which traces the history of religion and antiquities of the island from early times down to the fourteenth century AD. Distinguishing four successive periods of Balinese art, the author says that the art of the early period (eighth-tenth centuries) was dominated by Indian traditions, while during the Early and the Middle Indo- Balinese periods (eleventh-twelfth & thirteenth-fourteenth centuries) the Indian tradition was gradually modified by local as well as the imported Javanese elements. The Modern period dating from the fifteenth century does not call here for any special comment.

In his work *Sanskrit Texts from Bali* (GOS, LXVII, Baroda 1933) Sylvain Lévi has classified the Balinese works collected by him in 1928 under four heads (1) *Chaturveda*, (2) *Stotras*, (3) *Buddhaveda* (4) *Kārakasaṃgraha*, *Charitra Rāmāyaṇa*, *Naiṣṭhikajñāna*, *Daśaśila* and the exercises in translation from Sanskrit into Balinese. The first really consists of the three first sections of the *Nārāyaṇa Atharvaśiras-Upaniṣad*, the second consists of 39 short pieces, the third dealing with the daily ritual of a Buddhist priest consists of fragments of Tantras.

The history and culture of Bali have been investigated by Krom in his *Hindu-Javanese History* already mentioned, and more recently by R.C. Majumdar in his *Suvarṇadvīpa*, Parts I & II.

BORNEO AND CELEBES

The large island of Borneo called Tañjungpura and Bakulapura in the mediaeval Javanese records was colonised by Hindu settlers as early as the fourth century AD. The oldest Sanskrit inscriptions of the island belonging to that period, viz., the *Yūpa* inscriptions of King Mūlavarman, were discovered as far back as 1879 and being first published by Kern, were afterwards (1918) re-edited by Vogel. These records refer themselves to a line of Hindu (or Hinduised) kings ruling in East Borneo, of whom the last namely Mūlavarman performed the Bahusuvarṇaka sacrifice attended with splendid gifts to brāhmaṇs. Inscriptions with Buddhist formulas have since been found in West Borneo and these have been edited by B. Ch. Chhabra (*JASB*, *Letters*, 1935). An important expedition sent to Central and East Borneo in 1925 resulted in the discovery of a remarkable group of Brahmanical and Buddhist images concealed in a cave. Among these were stone images of Mahādeva, Nandī, Kārttikeya and Gaṇeśa. The Buddhist images were of a peculiar iconographic type. These precious sculptures along with some related images in the Batavia Museum were published by Bosch in the *Archaeological Report* (1925) and in the official report of the expedition (1927). Judging from the style of the images, Bosch held that they could be attributed neither to Indian nor Indo-Javanese colonists, but were probably the work of Indo-Javanese settlers long out of touch with the home-land or else of Hinduised Dyaks. Another important group of Hindu relics from Borneo has been discussed (*JGIS*, III, 1936) by O.C. Gangoly, who concludes that the question whether Borneo derived its Hindu culture directly from India or indirectly from Java must remain open. Recently R.C. Majumdar (*Suvarṇa-dvīpa*, part II) has suggested from a fresh examination of the Hindu images on the East coast of Borneo that the Hindu colonists developed an independent art somewhat influenced by Indo-Javanese traditions.

Passing from Borneo to the neighbouring island of Celebes we have to mention the large-sized bronze Buddha which was found there and is now preserved in the *Batavia Museum*. Judging from schematic folds of its drapery, Bosch has concluded (*TBG*, 1933) that it was imported directly from Amaravati.

The fragmentary records of Hindu culture in Borneo and Celebes have been pieced together by R.C. Majumdar in his work above-mentioned (*Suvarṇadvīpa*, parts I & II).

SUMATRA

By far the most important contribution that has been made in recent times to the general history of Sumatra and adjoining lands is the brilliant reconstruction of the rise and fall of the Hindu kingdom of Śrīvijaya by the French scholar Çoedés in 1918. In his epoch-making paper (in French) with the title "The Kingdom of Śrīvijaya" (*BEFEO*, XVIII) he traced with the help of the surviving archaeological remains and the scattered Chinese, Arab and south Indian references the fortunes of this kingdom from the latter part of the seventh to the thirteenth century. From the evidence of the Chinese pilgrim I-tsing it was already known that Śrīvijaya was the chief emporium of trade between China and India and was the centre of Buddhist learning in the islands of the Southern Seas. Çoedés's new hypothesis that Śrīvijaya city which he identified with Palembang was also the nucleus of the great Śailendra dynasty that ruled Malayasia for more than two centuries was developed by Krom and Vogel in their respective papers (in Dutch) bearing the titles "The Sumatran Period of Javanese History" (Leiden, 1919) and "The Kingdom of Śrīvijaya" (*BKI*, 1919) respectively. In these papers was emphasised the enormous influence exercised by Śrīvijaya kings in introducing Mahāyāna Buddhism into Java and in building the splendid monuments of Barabudur, Chaṇḍi Kalasan and the like. These results were incorporated by Ferrand in his connected account (in French) called "The Sumatran Empire of Śrīvijaya" (*JA*, 1922) tracing the history of Śrīvijaya (or Śailendra) Empire from the earliest times to the twelfth century AD and later. The history of Sumatra was treated on similar lines by Krom in his *Hindoe-Javaansche Geschiedenis* already mentioned. In 1927 Çoedés published a French article on the "Fall of the Śrīvijaya Kingdom" (*BKI*, vol. 83), tracing its decline from about AD 1178. In *BEFEO*, 1930 the same scholar wrote (in French) a paper called "The Malay Inscriptions of Śrīvijaya", where, while re-editing the four oldest inscriptions of this kingdom, he took the inscription of AD 683 to mean that Vajrayāna Buddhism already known to have prevailed in Bengal towards the middle of the seventh century was established in Sumatra towards the close of that century. The brilliant hypothesis of Çoedés to which reference has been made above has met with a considerable amount of criticism in later times. In his paper "A Javanese Period in Sumatran History" (Surakarta, 1929) Stutterheim sought completely to reverse Çoedés's position by asserting that the Śailendras originally belonged to Java and afterwards conquered Śrīvijaya. Recently R.C. Majumdar (*BEFEO*, 1933; *JGIS*, 1934; *Suvarṇadvīpa*, part I, Bk. 2, App.) has given good grounds for doubting on the one hand the identity of Śrīvijaya with the kingdom of the Śailendras and the Zabag and San-fo-tsi kingdoms of the Arab and Chinese writers and on the other hand for identifying the last three as synonymous terms and placing them in the northern part of the Malay Peninsula. Majumdar's view was subtantially accepted by Çoedés (*JGIS*, 1934). In another respect Çoedés's view has been modified by later research. Referring to the old Malay inscriptions of Śrīvijaya, Vallée Poussin has shown the slight part played therein by Tāntrism and has rehabilitated the evidence of I-tsing about the predominance of the Sarvāstivāda school in the Archipelago.

Sumatra is very poor in archaeological remains so much so that a connected history of its architecture and sculpture cannot be written. Nevertheless important finds of Buddhist sculptures in stone and metal along with other antiquities were made at Palembang after 1920. The Indian affinities of these sculptures were discussed by Bosch (*Archaeological Report*, 1930) and Krom (*ABIA*, 1931) as well as by K.A. Nilakanta Sastri (*JGIS*, III), R.C. Majumdar (*JISOA*, vol. 1, *Suvarṇadvīpa*, part II, pp. 322-6) and D.P. Ghosh (*JGIS*, vols. I & II). The first systematic excavations were carried out in Sumatra on a number of ancient sites by F.M. Schnitger in 1935 and 1936. The results were recorded by him in a series of well-illustrated monographs (in Dutch) called *Archaeological Finds in Padang Lawas* (*Central Tapanuli*), *Hindu Antiquities of Batang Hari* and *Archaeological Finds in Palembang* (Leiden, 1936). A detailed account of his discoveries in central, southern and western Sumatra with a large number of illustrations was given by the same author in his work *The Archaeology of Hindoo Sumatra* (Leiden, 1937). This work discloses a wealth of antiquities, viz., terracottas, stone and bronze sculptures of superb workmanship representing Śiva and Viṣṇu as well as Buddha, Lokeśvara and Maitreya besides architectural remains of *stūpas* and so forth. The sculptures have been held to belong to Amarāvatī, Gupta and Pala styles. Reference is also made to the evidences of Bhairava cult in vogue in the country in the late Hindu times. Some of Schintger's iconographical identifications have since been corrected by J.N. Banerjee in *JGIS* (IV, 1937). Quite recently Krom has brought forward in a Dutch paper called *The Sanctuaries of Palembang* (*Mededeelingen der Koninklijke Nederlandsche Akademie van Wetenschappen*, Deel I, no. 7) evidence to prove that Palembang was identical with Old Malayu and that the

Buddhist sanctuary on its western side reflected the south Indian style, while the Siddhayatra sanctuary on its eastern side which was Indonesian at first was Hinduised after the seventh century.

MALAY PENINSULA

The first detailed and authentic account of the Malay Peninsula, the Malayadvīpa and the Kaṭāhadvīpa of the Purāṇas, is given by Ptolemy in the second century AD, evidently in the light of the accurate knowledge acquired at that time by the Indians. In the mediaeval period Malay was sometimes included in great empires like those of Śrīvijaya and the Śailendras as well as the Indo-Javanese empire of Majapahit. At other times it was split up into a number of insignificant kingdoms. But no connected account of the peninsula is traceable from the scanty records. The survival of Hindu rule in different parts of the peninsula (Pahang or Indrapura, Kelantan and Malacca) may be traced to the second decade of the fifteenth century which ushered in the advent of Islam.

It was nearly a century ago that Lt. Col. James Low carried out some unsystematic excavations in the north-west part of British Malaya forming Province Wellesley and the Kedah State. He discovered a set of twelve Sanskrit inscriptions which were published by J.W. Laidlay (*JASB*, 1848-9) in a very imperfect fashion. These inscriptions have since been edited by competent scholars like Kern (*V.G.*, III) and B. Ch. Chhabra (*JASB*, *Letters*, 1935). They prove that colonists from northern and southern India were settled on the west coast of Malay by the fourth or fifth centuries AD and that they followed the Buddhist religion. Four of these inscriptions refer to a great sailor Buddhagupta, an inhabitant of Raktamṛttikā (identified with Rāṅgāmāṭi in modern Murshidabad district of Bengal). Another group of Sanskrit inscriptions of the same early period discovered at Ligor, Takuapa and Caiya in North Malaya was published with facsimile in the *Bulletin de la Commission Archéologique de l'Indo-Chine* (1910), but they still remain un-edited. The opening up of the states of Kedah and Perak to rubber plantation and tin mining in quite recent times has brought to light a number of antiquities, which were described by Ivor H.N. Evans Ethnographer to the Perak Museum (*Papers on the Ethnology and Archaeology of the Malay Peninsula*, Cambridge, 1927). They show that the Kedah region was occupied by Indian colonists professing Śaivism as well as Buddhism during the fourth-fifth centuries AD. According to the same evidence an Indian colony was settled at Perak by the fifth century AD. Among the objects discovered by Evans was a seal from Perak with the legend *Śrī Viṣnuvarmmaṇah* written in incorrect Sanskrit in Pallava Grantha characters [For discussion of this seal, see B. Ch. Chhabra, *JGIS*, II, 1935 giving full references]. Unfortunately no law was passed for the protection of ancient monuments, as had been done in India and Indonesia. "Hence sites of the utmost importance must have been destroyed by mining operations in Perak, while in Kedah many promising mounds were demolished to provide road material or merely levelled down as being useless obstructions" (Quaritch Wales, *ABIA*, 1937, p. 38). However, that may be, chance finds have been made recently from the tin mines at Perak, of three bronze Avalokiteśvara images in addition to those brought to light by Evans. [For a description of the whole group with full references and some illustrations, see H.G. Quaritch Wales, "Archaeological Researches on Ancient Indian Colonization" in *JRAS*, *MB*, XVIII, part I, February 1940.] The first systematic archaeological exploration of British Malaya was undertaken by H.G. Quaritch Wales under the auspices of the Greater India Research Committee in London and with the generous support of the Malay states concerned. Following closely upon his first two archaeological expeditions to Siamese territory (to which reference has been made above), Wales led his third expedition (1937-9) into the Malay states of Kedah, Perak and Johore. The valuable results of this expedition were published in a special number (vol. XVIII, pt. I, 1940) of the *Journal of the Malayan Branch of the Royal Asiatic Society*. Among the objects brought to light by the explorer may be mentioned basements of *stūpas* containing Sanskrit inscriptions in south Indian characters of the fourth-sixth centuries mentioning the Buddhist creed and Mahāyāna Buddhist verses, the remains of Brahmanical temples of the seventh-eighth centuries with fragments of Śivite images, and lastly, gold and silver discs with names of Bodhisattvas inscribed in Sanskrit in south Indian characters of the ninth century. Deriving his historical conclusions from the above data, the author postulated four successive waves of Hindu colonisation from the first century to *c*. AD 900. Again, while finding further support for his view that the Śailendra empire had its headquarters in the Malay Peninsula, he was led to locate Kaḍāram, the capital of the Śailendras, in the Kinta Valley in Perak, in modification of his previous hypothesis (strongly criticised by Çoedés, *JRASMB*, XIV, 1936), identifying the same with Caiya and Ligor. He also attempted the reconstruction of the later history of Kedah (from the close of the thirteenth century to the conversion to Islam in AD 1474) by means of a critical analysis of the Kedah Annals. One of the kings mentioned in these Annals, Raja Bersiong, according to him, was not only a historical personage but was addicted to the Bhairava cult of which the popularity is proved by the famous Bhairava statue representing the Sumatran king Ādityavarman in the thirteenth century.

As regards general history of the Malay Peninsula, the invaluable Chinese texts referring to the kingdoms of the Southern Seas in the early centuries of the Christian era have been studied and discussed by a number of scholars such as Groeneveldt, Schlegel, Pelliot and Ferrand ever since the seventh decade of the last century. But unfortunately the identifications of most of these kingdoms still remain matters of dispute. Provisionally, however, we may take these accounts to mean that a certain number of Hindu kingdoms existed in Malaya in the fifth-sixth centuries. Such are "Lang-yu-su" (Isthmus of Kra or of Ligor) "where the precious Sanskrit was generally known, Kan-to-li (Kadāra?) where Buddhism was held in the highest veneration and

Karmaranga or Charmaranga (Ligor) mentioned in the *Mañjuśrīmūlakalpa* and other Indian works. Regarding the later history of Malay we have already referred to the brilliant paper of Çoedés on "The Kingdom of Śrīvijaya" (*BEFEO*, 1918) pointing to a great Sumatran empire having its capital at Palembang and including within its limits Malaya and Java in the late eighth century. We have also noticed that R.C. Majumdar has on good grounds called in question Çoedés' identification of the Śrīvijaya kingdom with the Śailendra empire and placed the seat of the latter in north Malay. In this connection Majumdar stated that the Śailendras were probably immigrants from Kaliṅga who spread their sway over the Far East by way of Lower Burma and Malay. On the other hand Çoedés (*JGIS*, I, 1934) has suggested that the Śailendras were originally related to the kings of Fu-nan and after their expulsion from Indo-China resumed the old dynastic title and reasserted the old political and territorial claims. Other views have been put forward by Przyluski (*JGIS*, I) and K.A. Nilakanta Sastri (*TBG*, LXXV). As for the last phase of Hindu rule in Malay, not to speak of the Chinese texts studied and discussed by Groeneveldt and Schlegel, we may mention the indigenous traditions collected from the Malay chronicles and the early Portuguese accounts by Ferrand (*JA*, 1918). In *JRASMB*, 1935, R.O. Winstedt published a connected history of Malay from the earliest times to the nineteenth century. It contains a chapter on the Hindu period based on the researches of Çoedés and Krom. Recently R.C. Majumdar has given (*Suvarṇadvīpa*, parts I & II) a complete account of the history and culture of Malaya from the earliest times to the end of Hindu rule in the peninsula. Based on the researches of previous scholars, it attempts the solution of many of the unsolved problems of Ancient Malayan history.

CHAPTER 7

In Memoriam: Sylvain Lévi

RABINDRANATH TAGORE

Sylvain Lévi is dead. The penetrating mind that explored the obliterated paths of India's ancient history, difficult of access, has laid down its task. And for the intellectual service he has rendered to India, precious in its rareness and luminous in its sagacity, we can but offer our homage of praise to his memory. He has joined the past which is immortal and which it was his own life's work to bring to the recognition of the living present. The students from India who had the opportunity of receiving his unfailing kindness and untiring help will ever mourn his loss, the loss of a friend and a guide.

He has special claim of gratitude from me who represent Śāntiniketan, for he was the first of the European scholars who readily responded to my call and came to train our own students and scholars in the scientific technique of historical research, he has helped me to create in our *āśrama* the tradition of the international fellowship of culture which he could do to a perfection, not only because his scholarship was great, but also because he had the beautiful gift of friendliness and a genuine sympathy for students and patience for them even when their capacity was too elementary for the learning which he himself possessed.

CHAPTER 8

Obituary Notice Gabriel Ferrand

KALIDAS NAG

It is not an unusual sight to discover some first-rate scholars and technicians amongst the French group of administrators. Paul Claudel, the eminent poet, is an able ambassador of France and author of *La Connaissance de l'Est*. Paul Painlevé was a great mathematician. George Maspero, like his father Gaston Maspero, was an able officer and a zealous historian. So Gabriel Ferrand was a Ministre Plénipotentiaire in Persia before he won his fame as the leading authority on Oriental geography in France. When I reached Paris fifteen years ago, the illustrious Sinologist Edouard Chavannes was just dead, but his friend and colleague Sylvain Lévi was carrying on the glorious tradition of French orientalism through a series of brilliant studies. It was in his home that I had the privilege of being introduced to Mon. Ferrand, already retired from diplomatic services and concentrating on his scientific studies. As a pupil of Lévi, I was warmly invited to the apartments of Mon. Ferrand on the Rue Racini where I was surprised to find this ex-minister of the Republic crowding his rooms with rare books and documents over which he ever looked affectionately and wistfully. For the world war, as he said, interrupted the publication of so many scientific studies, periodicals, etc., and his manuscript pile was already heavy, crying for publication at an age when the nation could ill afford money for intellectual pursuits, faced as it was, with grim economic crisis and privations. I found that Mon. Ferrand was famous already as the author of *Relations de voyages et texte geographiques Arab Persons et Turko relatifs à l'Extrême-Orient*, published between 1913 and 1914. In 1918, Mon. George Çoedès opened a new chapter in Greater Indian Studies with his paper on the kingdom of Śrīvijaya ("Le royaume de Çrī-vijaya", *BEFEO*, 1918). That forgotten chapter of Hindu-Javanese history soon engaged the attention of eminent orientalists like Krom, Vogel and Blagden. A veteran geographer that he was, Mon. Ferrand started soon a thorough documentation on the historical, geographical and other references to the kingdom of Śrīvijaya and published a splendid monograph: "L'Empire Sumotranais de Çrīvijaya" (*JA*, July-October 1922). It brought in a handy volume all the pertinent texts in Chinese, Arabic, Persian, etc., as well as the inscriptions (with translations) in

Source: *Journal of the Greater India Society* (II/2, 1935, 169–70).

Malaya, Tamil and Sanskrit, not forgetting the famous tenth-century MS of Nepal, mentioning "Suvarṇapure Çrīvījayapure Lokanātha", the value of which was first pointed out by Alfred Foucher (vide *Ètude sur l'iconographie bouddhique de l'Inde*, Paris, 1900).

Mon. Ferrand was loved and admired by the world of Orientalists as he served very ably in the capacity of Honorary Secretary of the Société Asiatique of Paris which, over a century ago (1826), honoured Rājā Rāmmohun Roy, the first Indian savant, with the title of the Associate. We are also grateful to Mon. Ferrand for his valuable aid in procuring the rare books and periodicals on Indology that have found their place in the rich Library of our *Purodhā*, Rabindranath Tagore's Visva Bharati at Santiniketan.

CHAPTER 9

Obituary Notice
Louis Finot

KALIDAS NAG

In the death of Mon. Louis Finot the world of French scholarship has lost a brilliant representative and the family of Indologists a most fruitful and loyal collaborator.

The thorough discipline of the *Ècole des Chartres* of the University of Paris, combined with the initiation into Sanskrit at the hand of no less a master than Sylvain Lévi, made Finot a researcher of first-rate importance in the field of orientalism. The French Schools of Athens (1850), of Rome (1875) and of Cairo have already made the name of French archaeologists respected all over the world. In 1867 Renan projected the *Corpus Inscriptionum Semiticarum* and he was followed by James Darmesteter with his exhaustive studies on the *Avesta* which was introduced into Europe about a century earlier (1771) by the Pioneer Orientalist Anquetil-Duperron. During the last quarter of the nineteenth century when Louis Finot grew from his early college days into a mature scholar taking his Doctor's degree with a thesis on the Sanskrit text of *Ratnaparīkṣā*, Finot watched his beloved professor Sylvain Lévi working with two masters of French Indology Abel Bergaigne and Auguste Barth editing the *Sanskrit Inscriptions of Champā and Cambodge* and Emil Senart publishing his *Inscriptions of Piyadasi*.

In 1898 the great French archaeologist Michel Bréal joined hands with Auguste Barth and Emil Senart in developing the project of a French School of the Far East after the models of the French Schools of Athens, Rome and Cairo. Originally Chandernagore was selected, but it could not materialise owing to the financial problems, which were solved by Paul Doumer, the Governor-General of Indo-China, which thus came to possess that magnificent research-centre and library of Hanoi: *Ècole Française d'Extrême-Orient*.

As the first Director of the *Ècole*, Mon. Finot rendered services of the highest order. From the very first number of the now famous *Bulletin*, he had been contributing most valuable articles and studies. The Religion of Champā according to the monuments, Cambodian transcriptions, Indo-Chinese studies, Origin of Indian colonisation, Researches on Laotian literature; List of Khmér manuscripts, etc., are some of his contributions; while in the domain of Indo-

Source: *Journal of the Greater India Society* (11/2, 170–3).

Chinese epigraphy his able editing, transcriptions and translations will ever keep his name shining in that line of studies. I cherish with pride and gratitude his *Notes d'Epigraphie Indo-Chinoise* (1916) which he so kindly presented to me, when I had the privilege of enjoying the hospitality of this *Ècole* in Hanoi, which I visited on my return trip from China and Japan (1924). Not only his learned colleagues like Mon. Parmentier, Mon. Aurousseau, Mon. Demiéville and others, but he afforded me the greatest facilities in visiting the wonderful monuments of Hindu art in Champā and Cambodia: Nhatrang and Phanrang, Aṅgkor Ṭhom, Aṅgkor Vat and other historic sites.

When we had the honour of inaugurating the Greater India Society in 1926, Mon. Finot wrote a highly sympathetic note in the *Bulletin* (vide XXVII, pp. 504-7) and we got his help and encouragement whenever we approached him. This policy of collaboration has been continued by Mon. George Çoedès, the learned successor to Mon. Finot as the Director of the *Ècole*. When a member of our Academic Council, R.C. Majumdar of the Dacca University visited the *Ècole* in Hanoi, he was warmly received and his volume on the *Ancient Indian Colonies of the Far East, Champā*, vol. I, was reviewed and his learned article on the *Palaeography of the Inscriptions of Champā* was welcomed in the *Bulletin*.

A veteran Sanskrit as he was, Mon. Finot was a great lover of the Buddha and Buddhism. He translated many Buddhist texts and often contributed articles on Indo-Chinese History and on Buddhism to the pages of Indian journals like the *Indian Historical Quarterly* edited by our esteemed colleague N.N. Law.

One of his recent articles was published in the latest issue of the *Bulletin* on the former Governor-General of Indo-China, Paul Doumer, who was assassinated as the President of the Republic (May 1932). It was M. Doumer who by his Statute of 15 December 1898, brought the *Ècole Française d'Extrême-Orient* into existence and the tribute of gratitude from its first Director M. Finot was very appropriate.

As he was a facile writer in English, M. Finot wrote highly thoughtful and suggestive reviews of current literature on Indology published by Indian and non-Indian writers. Courteous by nature as he was, his courtesy never got the better of his critical spirit, and his co-workers in the field ever profited by his frank and creative criticisms.

M. Finot was a sincere well-wisher and an inspiring friend of the Greater India Society and we hope and pray that his soul would rest in peace. He lived a life which we can adequately describe only in his own words, which he applied to the late M. Emil Senart in his obituary notice: "Une grande âme consacreé sans réserve au service du vrai et du bien."

HISTORY, HISTORICAL SOURCES

CHAPTER 10

Relation Between Indian and Indonesian Culture

O.C. GANGOLY

The approximate date of the "colonisation" and the spread of Indian culture across the Indian Ocean has been the subject of keen debate amongst scholars. When the text of the *Arthaśāstra* was published, some scholars (Jacobi and others) suggested that a passage in that text distinctly recommended (as a piece of kingly obligation) the foundation of new places of habitation or colonies in already existing provinces by vomiting out inhabitants from one's own country in order to people new colonized tracts or by inviting the flow of foreigners into one's own countries (*bhūtapūrvaṃ-abhūtapūrvaṃ vā janapadaṃ paradeśāpavāhanena svadeśābhiṣyandavamanena vā niveśayet*, *Arthaśāstra*, Book II, Ch. I, I, Janapada-niveśa). Louis Finot in an adroitly argued paper[1] contested this suggestion, that the passage in question could be taken to offer a direct testimony to the commencement of Indian culture in the neighbouring peninsula.[2] Finot's paper has not unfortunately attracted the attention of Indian scholars. About twenty-eight years have elapsed since the matter was debated. Since then, a large volume of records has been unearthed bearing on the origin and history of Indian culture in Burma, Malaya, Siam, Cambodia, Campā, Java, Sumatra and Borneo. Quaritch Wales' recent explorations in Malaya have also brought forward some archaeological evidences to establish the fact that from very early times, Takkola (on the western coast of Malaya on the Bay of Bengal) and Tāmraliṅga (on the eastern coast of Malaya on the Bay of Bandon, later, the site of Nakon Śrī Thammarat) formed two important outposts through which

[1] "Les origines de la colonisation Indienne" par Louis Finot, *BEFEO*, tome XII, 1912, pp. 1-4

[2] Finot's views can be gathered from the following remarks: "That the Dekkhan was Brahmanised by this epoch (i.e. of Kauṭilya) one could admit; but Brahmanisation does not mean occupation, and it is to be believed that this country, all Brahmanised as it was, offered yet the vast spaces to interior colonisation. It is with that only, according to our opinion, that the *Arthasastra* occupies itself, because if it had in view establishments outside India, it could not omit to lay down particular rules for the solution of the many problems which were involved in the installation of a civilized minority in the midst of a barbarous population." (tr. by the present writer)

Source: *Journal of the Greater India Society* (VII/1, 1940, 51–69).

Indian culture radiated and spread over to Cambodia, Siam, Campā and other parts of South-Eastern Asia.[3] In an illuminating geographical study[4] contributed by Sylvain Lévi, that great *savant* of Indology has been able to establish on data extracted from the texts of the *Mahābhārata,* the *Rāmāyaṇa,* the *Mahā-Niddesa,* and the *Bṛhat-kathā* that Indian merchants, navigators, and adventurers were familiar with the products of Burma and the Malaya Peninsula from very early times and that some parts of the trans-Gangetic Peninsula [e.g. Suvarṇakuḍya, Suvannakūṭa, Subannabhūmi (some parts of Burma), Takkolam, Tāmlin (Tāmraliṅgaṃ), and Javam] were known to Indian authors from at least the first century of the Christian Era.[5] We may go a step further and claim that having regard to the fact that these Far Eastern ports and tracts bear Indian names, in fairly early texts, it may be reasonable to conclude that the "Indianization" of these tracts must have begun previous to the first century AD. But the point we are concerned with here, is not so much the ancient chronology of the Indianisation of the regions beyond the seas, as the nature of the relationship of the so-called "colonial" Indian culture with its parent stem. Generally speaking, it is usual to regard colonial cultures, as somewhat inferior to the parental culture in its place of origin,—on account of the fact that it is the second-rate men belonging to the surplus population that are usually sent abroad to people and develop distant colonies. And, as a rule, the colonised countries are scarcely regarded as strongholds, or significant points of expansion of parental culture on equal footing with the original sources.

To these general rules the expansion of Indian culture across the Indian Ocean offers a very significant exception. The pioneers who set out to plant the seeds of Indian culture, as well as those who permanently took up their abode in various cultural kingdoms of Greater India and developed Indian culture to a level of equal eminence with that of the mother-continent, were not worthless ne'er-do-wells, or second-rate men, who could be elbowed out of the Indian continent to eke out a fortune, or seek a chance success abroad. The representatives of various clans of learned brahmins (such as those of the Agastya *gotra*, or the Kauṇḍinya *gotra*) who carried the torch of Indian religious culture to distant countries were, undoubtedly, worthy and very distinguished representatives, the finest types of Indian intellectual and spiritual giants. The kṣatriya princes, probably some branch of the Pallava dynasty, who founded, built, and organised political kingdoms and culture-centres in various tracts of Cambodia (Fou-nan) were enterprising groups of typical Indian princes of

[3] H.G. Quartich Wales, "A Newly Explored Route of Ancient Indian Cultural Expansion", *Indian Art and Letters*, IX, no. 1, 1925. Ibid., *Towards Angkor*, 1938, Chap. X, pp. 147 ff.

[4] "Ptolémée, le Niddesa et la Bṛhatkathā", *Études Asiatiques* II, pp. 1-55.

[5] "Au lere siècle lère, il est presque certain qu'um auteur ecrivant dans l'Inde n'aurait pu dresser la liste des ports de'Extrême-Orient telle que nous la lisons dans le Niddesa."... "La date de cette liste, et par conséquent de l'ouvrage qui la contient, vient donc se placer entre la find du lere siècle et la fin du IIIe." Ibid., p. 51. From the above extracts it is clear that according to Sylvain Lévi, an author writing in India could not have prepared the list of the seaports of the Far East, such as we find in the *Niddesa*, before the first century AD.

remarkable talent, industry, and organising ability. The successive chains of brahmin ministers who advised the Cambodian kings (e.g. Śiva-Kaivalya, Rudrācārya, Hiraṇyaruci, Īśāna-mūrti, Sadā-śiva, Saṅkara-Paṇḍita, Divākara-Paṇḍita and a host of others) who advised and guided the polity, the military exploits, and the religious foundations of their *protégés*, were learned and wise men of remarkable talents and equipments. Likewise, the heroic types of Indian princes (probably some branch of the Cālukya dynasty as suggested by their characteristic *virudas*, "Uttuṅga deva") who founded and developed glorious kingdoms in Java were brilliant men of sterling qualities of head and heart and were justly deified as Devarājas or "Divine Kings" after their death. Similarly, the group of heroic Indian princes of the Śailodbhava or Śailendra dynasty who founded the great oversea Empire of Śrīvijaya were personalities of exceptional talent and brilliance.

That Sanskrit learning was kept up at a high pitch of excellence and was understood and cultivated by a large number of people in Cambodia, Sumatra and Java is proved by numerous inscriptions in Sanskrit, the high literary merit of which excels the continental compositions and deserves high praise. Some of these inscriptions offer valuable data for the history of Sanskrit literature. Yaśovarman, king of Cambodia, and the builder of Angkor Thom, is said to have written a commentary on the *Mahābhāṣya*.[6] Valuable and rich collections of books were maintained in the "Pustakāśramas" or the "Hermitages of Books" or libraries. Endowments were provided for regular or periodical recitations of the Purāṇas and the Epics. That some cities in the colonies were specialised centres of some phases of Indian culture of greater importance than the continental centres may be illustrated from the fact that Atīśa (Dīpaṅkara Śrījñāna), the great Buddhist Patriarch, had to reside for twelve years in Suvarṇadvīpa, then the headquarters of Mahāyāna Buddhism, in order to master the teachings of Ācārya Dharmakīrti, the High Priest of Suvarṇadvīpa. Some of the establishments in various parts of Greater India were important centres of Tantric cults, contributing new and original developments. The two separate and sectarian cults of Śiva and Buddha attained a happy fusion in the Śiva-Buddhist cult of Java. Burma[7] and Siam[8]

[6] *Nāgendra-vaktra-viṣa-duṣṭa-tayeva bhāṣyaṃ*
Mohapradaṃ pratipadaṇ kila Śābdikānāṃ ।
Vyākhyāmṛtena vadanendu-vinirggatena
Yasya prabodhakaram-eva punaḥ prayuktaṃ. ।।

[Śloka 13, (D) from the Stêle of Thnāl Baray, A. Bergaigne, *Inscriptions Sanscrites de Champa et du Cambodge* 2d fascicule, p. 305 (485).]

[7] Mabel Bode (*The Pāli Literature of Burma*, 1909) has indicated the outlines of the rich literature of Buddhism developed in Burma. The Theras of Sagaing (e.g. Tilokaguru) appear to have taken the lead in Abhidhamma studies. The famous Pāli work of Burma, *Saddanīti*, composed by Thera Uttarajīva, when taken to Ceylon, was received with enthusiastic admiration and declared superior to any work of the kind written by previous authors.

[8] G. Çoedès has given an interesting survey of the enormous output of Siamese Buddhist Literature in his learned article: "Note sur les ouvrages Palis composes en pays Thai", *BEFEO*, XV, 1915, pp. 39-46.

have made original and distinguished contributions to Pāli Buddhism and to Buddhist literature. In the spheres of architecture, sculpture, applied arts, and crafts, the Indian continent must have sent some of its greatest masters to the "colonies" in order to cater to the artistic needs and to carry out the architectural ambitions of the Indian princes in Indonesia and to fashion innumerable images of the highest sculptural merits, for the use of religious devotees.

Borobudur, of Java,—the "Parthenon of the East", and Angkor Vat, the *chef d'oeuvre* of Cambodia, to name only two of the supreme masterpieces, eclipse anything that has been achieved on the soil of India itself. The brilliant schools of sculpture in Java, in Siam, in Cambodia, and in Malaya likewise put to the shade the schools of Image-making in continental India. These evidences unquestionably point to the fact that the Indians of the continent assiduously kept up the values and standards of Indian culture in the so-called colonies at a high level of excellence, and in some phases (e.g. in Plastic Arts) outshone the achievements at their original birth-place. They did not look upon these distant centres of Indian culture across the seas—as mere inferior reflexions of Indian culture—derived second-hand from continental sources, but, in many instances as independent seats and sources, as they developed the oversea tracts (*dvīpāntara*) into the most important limbs and significant centres of the best phases of Indian culture. The so-called colonies were regarded as integral parts of the Great Indian Continent—so as to make India and Greater India—as one unified and uniform texture woven by the best Indian hands—whether living at home, or abroad. This view of the relationship of the continental and the so-called colonial culture receives credence if we consider some of the texts of the Purāṇas.

According to the geography of the Purāṇas, India Proper is designated as "Jambudvîpa", while the total extension and limits of "Bhāratavarṣa" include the *nine* additional territories (*nava bhedān*) across the Indian Ocean, "each in-accessible from the other" (*agamyāḥ parasparaṃ*) being "separated by the barriers of the seas" (*samudrāntaritā*). Thus in the *Mārkaṇḍeya Purāṇa*, Krauṣṭuki addresses Mārkaṇḍeya in the following words: "Lord! you have summarily described the Jambu-dvîpa. . . . Please describe to me in detail Bhārata with its distinguishing parts (*bhedā*) their situations and extensions, specifying the territories and the mountains." To this Mārkaṇḍeya replied: "Bhārata-varṣa, you should understand, consists of nine distinct territories, separated by the seas and each inaccessible from the other: Indra-dvîpa, Kaśerumān, Tāmra-varṇa (? Tāmraparṇî), Gabhastimān, Nāga-dvîpa? Saumya, Gāndharva, Vāruna (? Borneo)—these are the nine islands girt by the seas."[9]

[9] *Mārkaṇḍeya Purāṇa*, Chap. 57, *ślokas*, 5, 6, 7:
Bhāratasyāsyavarṣasya nava bhedān nibodha me ।
Samudrāntaritā jñeyāste tvagamyāḥ parasparaṃ ।। 5 ।।
Indra-dvīpaḥ, Kaśerumāṃs-Tāmravarṇo Gabhastimān ।
Nāga-dvīpastathā Saumyo Gāndharvo Vāruṇastathā ।। 6 ।।

Even if all the nine islands cannot be satisfactorily identified, the description of their being separated from each other by seas appears to suggest the picture of an "Island-India", the "Greater India" of our modern scholars. In the *Vāmana Purāṇa* (Ch. 13, 1-11), after describing the component territories of Jambudvîpa, nine territories of Bhāratavarṣa (Greater India) are likewise indicated. Here the names of nine islands are slightly different: Indradvîpa, Kaseruṇa, Tāmaraparṇa, Gabhastimān, Nāgadvîpa, Kaṭāha, Siṃhala, Vāruṇa and Kumāra.[10] In this list, apparently a later list, Saumya and Gāndharva have been substituted by two new territories those of Kaṭāha and Siṃhala, and Kumāra is a new addition. It is immaterial for our purpose, here, whether we could identify all these nine islands. Nāga-dvîpa may be Nicobar Island.[11] Vāruṇa may be Borneo (Vahriṇa).[12] Kaṭāha is apparently the Province of Ke(d)dah in the northern parts of the Malaya Peninsula, having its chief city of the same name (Kaṭāhanagara) with its neighbouring city known as Gaṅgānagara, both of which were besieged and destroyed by Rājendra Cola. As suggested by D.C. Sircar,[13] the name of Kaṭāha must have been introduced in the *Vāmana Purāṇa* "after Kaṭāha became famous under the Śailendra Emperors in the eighth century".

In the *Agni Purāṇa* (Chaps. 118, 119) a distinction is also made between India Proper (*Jambu-dvîpa*) and Island-India (*Dvîpāntara*)[14] consisting of nine

---

Ayamtu navamasteṣāṃ dvīpaḥ sāgara-saṃvṛtaḥ ।

It should be noted that actually eight islands are mentioned instead of nine demanded by the context.

The description given of the oversea tracts in the text of the *Vāyu Purāṇa* which is believed to be one of the earliest, is substantially the same as in the *Mārkaṇḍeya Purāṇa*—see *Vāyu Purāṇa*, Chap. 45, *ślokas* 78-80.

[10] *Indra-dvīpaḥ Kaśeruṇās-Tāmraparṇo Gabhastimān* ।
Nāga-dvīpaḥ Kaṭāhaśca Siṁhato Vāruṇastathā ।। 10 ।।
Ayamtu navamasteṣāṃ dvīpaḥ sāgasa-saṃvṛtaḥ ।
Kumārākhyaḥ parikhyāto dvīpo'yaṃ dakṣiṇottaraḥ ।। 11 ।।
Vāmana Purāṇa, Chap. 13, *ślokas* 10-11

[11] Jayaswal's identification of Nāga-dvîpa with Nicobar has been confirmed by a passage in the *Valāhassa-Jātaka* cited by V.S. Agrawala, *JBORS*, XXIII, pp. 133-7.

[12] 'Vāruṇa' may be a variation of "Vahriṇa" which I have sought to identify with Borneo on the basis of passages in the 48th section of the *Vāyu Purāṇa*. See my note published in *Rūpam*, 1926, nos. 27-8, p. 114, and my paper: "On Some Hindu Relics in Borneo", *JGIS*, January 1936, pp. 97ft.

[13] D.C. Sircar: "Unhistoricity of the Kaumudi-mahotsava", *JAHRS*, IX, 1, 2, p. 67.

[14] As regards the significance of the term *Dvīpāntaram*, we have interesting light thrown on the word from a very curious source. In a Sanskrit-Chinese Dictionary compiled in Central Asia between the seventh and eighth centuries, reference is made to the countries situated in the Southern Seas as *Jipāttala*, which Sylvain Lévi has restored to *Dvīpāntara* and which Lévi paraphrases as "another isle" or "another continent". According to Sylvain Lévi, this term properly designates the Indian Archipelago and the neighbouring countries" ("Le nom de l' archipel Indien en sanscrit", *Actes du XVIIIe Congrès International des Orientalistes*, Oxford, p. 131).

islands or territories (*nava-bhedā*) girt by the seas.[15] What we are seeking to establish is that the nine islands of Greater India were regarded as integral part of Bhāratavarṣa, and an equal sanctity attached to the component parts of Island-India, as strongholds of national Indian culture—where Indians lived, fought, traded and performed their religious duties (*yajña*, *tapas*, etc.) and they were looked upon as suitable areas for their cultural activity (*karma-bhūmi*) on an equal footing with any part of India Proper (*Jambu-dvîpa*). From this point of view, a passage in the *Vāmana Purāṇa* (Chap. 13, 13) is very significant: "The nine islands have been sanctified by the performance of sacrifices,[16] by warfare,[17] by trade,[18] and diverse other cultural activities" (*ijyā-yuddha-va nijyādyaiḥ karmma-bhiḥ kṛtapāvanāḥ*). Now, if we take one by one each of these items, which according to the *Vāmana Purāṇa*, imparts sanctity to the oversea tracts, we have actual illustration and proof of each item. Thus as regards *ijyā yajña* or sacrifices)—we find, this is corroborated by the Yūpa inscription of Mūlavarman discovered in Borneo which commemorates the performance of a *vahusuvarṇaka yajña*. As regards battles and warfare, this is attested by numerous battles at various places in Malaya and Indonesia including the severe conflicts of the Śailendras and the Colas. As regards trade and commercial activity—that a brisk trade and mercantile intercourse were carried on between India and Indonesia is borne out by numerous evidences in the *Rāmāyaṇa*, the *Mahābhārata*, the two Tamil Epics, *Manimekhalai* and *Śilappadikāram*, and in the *Kathāsaritsāgara* some of which we shall presently cite here.

Put into modern parlance, the canon of sanctity laid down in the *Vāmana Purāṇa* would mean—wherever the Indians have lived, whenever they have rendered their homage to the Divinity through sacrificial rites—there they have built-up a New India. This is, in short, the principle of Indian colonisation.

[15] *Indra-dvīpaḥ Kaseruśca Tāmravarṇo Gabhastimān* ।। 3 ।।
Nāga-dvīpastathā Saumyo Gāndharwastvatha Vāruṇaḥ ।
Ayamtu navamasteṣāṃ dvīpaḥ sāgara-saṃvṛtaḥ ।। 4 ।।
Yojanānāṃ sahasrāṇi dvīpo'yaṃ dakṣiṇottarāt ।
Nava bhedā Bhāratasya madhyabhede'tha pūrvvataḥ ।। 5 ।।

In describing the oversea territories of Bhāratavarṣa, the *Agni Purāṇa* (Chap. 119, *ślokas* 27 & 28) refers to a peak, as the boundary of a tract, under the name of Aṇḍa-Kaṭāha, of which the limit is said to be the peak in question. Could it be the peak of Keddaḥ in Upper Malaya?

Lokā-lokastataḥ śailo yojanāyutavistṛitaḥ ।। 27 ।।
Lokālokastu tamasāvṛto'thāṇḍa-Kaṭāhataḥ ।
Bhūmiḥ sāṇḍa-kaṭāheṅa pañcāśat-koṭi-vistarā ।। 28 ।।
Vaṅgavāsi Edition, p. 285

[16] This is corroborated by the Yūpa Inscription of Mūlavannan in Borneo, which commemorates the performance of a *vahu-suvarṇaka yajña*. See Vogel's article in *Bijdragen*, Deel XXIV, 1918.

[17] This is attested by numerous battles including the severe conflicts of the Śailendras and Colas.

[18] This is borne out by numerous evidences in the *Ramayana*, the *Mahābhārata*, the *Manimekhalai*, the *Śilappadikāram* and the *Kathāsaritsāgara*.

This canon of sanctity prescribed in the *Vāmana Parāṇa* appears to meet and fully answer Finot's objections—that the *Arthaśāstra* could not possibly recommend a colony of Indians to emigrate across the seas and establish themselves in tracts, densely populated by non-Aryan and aboriginal inhabitants as these tracts would be unsuitable venues or fields for Indian cultural expansion. By the time of the earliest Purāṇas these oversea tracts must have been thoroughly Indianised and adopted and sanctified as *karmabhūmis* or appropriate areas of Indian cultural activity. The point established is that the intervening seas did not prevent the distant territories in Island-India—being actually placed on the map of Indian culture. That Indians have throughout the centuries regarded oversea territories of Bhāratavarṣa as essential and integral parts of India of which Jambudvîpa was only another segment, may be, a big segment—is further corroborated by the testimony of Arab geographers. Thus Masūdī in his work *Meadows of Gold* (AD 943) thus indicates the geographical limits of India: "India is a vast country *extending over sea* and land and mountains. It borders on the country of Zābāg (i.e. Sumatra or Greater Java) which is the kingdom of the Mahārāja, the king of the islands (i.e. the Śailendra Emperor). Zābāg which separates India from China is comprised within the former country (i.e. India)".[19]

Further corroboration of this view is offered by a curious but a very significant *śloka* in the Fifth Act of the *Kaumudî-mahotsava*, the upper limit of the date of which has been accepted by scholars as the seventh century. The *śloka* describes the shady and amorous adventures of a fashionable rake, a gallant sensualist who has tasted the gay life of all the famous cities of India (Bhāratavarṣa), having visited women in the cities of Ayodhyā (Sāketa), Kāncîpura (Conjeeveram), Pampā (Bellary), Vidiśā (Besnagar), Kaṭāha-nagara (Keddah, in Malaya Peninsula) and in Kuṇḍina (probably a city in Vidarbha).[20]

[19] Quoted in R.C. Majumdar, *Suvarnadvīpa*, vol. I, pp. 162-3 from Ferrand, *Relations de Voyages et textes Geographiques Arabes, Persans et Turks relatifs à l'Extrême-Orient du VIIIe an XVIIIe siècles*, vol. I, p. 92.

[20] The *Kāmasūtra* of Vātsyāyana, and other cognate literature, the *Arthaśāstra*, and the Sanskrit *kāvyas* and the dramas offer abundant evidence of the establishments of gay women and *hetarae* in all cities as essential part of a cultured city life. Even in the *Rāmāyaṇa* we get a glimpse of the existence of gay women in Ayodhyā itself—and Daśaratha, realising that the retinues of exiled Rāma will find their life in banishment very forlorn and drab, without these amenities of city life—enjoins that the *hetarae* should be sent out from Ayodhyā to this place of banishment.

Rāghavasyānuyātrārthaṃ kṣipraṃ pratividhiyatām ।
Rūpājivāśca vādinyo vaṇijaśca mahādhanāḥ ।।।
Ayodhyā-Kaṇḍa, 36 Sarga, 2-3

Viṭa, as a gallant and fast young man who has acquired considerable experience of the ways of *hetarae* frequendy occurs in the Indian dramas (e.g. *Mṛcchakaṭika*). The earliest definition of a Viṭa is that given in the *Kāmasūtra* (Chap. IV, 46): "*Bhukta-vibbavastu guṇavān sakalatro veśe goṣṭhyāṁśca vahumatastadrūpajīvī ca viṭaḥ*. "An accomplished person who

Aye ! Ayaṃ purāṇa-viṭo Veśarakṣitaḥ । *Śāntanavamiva Śaratalpagataṃ veśabāṭa-makaraketu-mandirāvasannamenaṃ paśyāmi* । Kutaḥ:

Śākete kṛta-kautuko vikalitaḥ Kāncîpure kañcibhiḥ
Pampāyāmabhisāritaḥ parijanair-vijñāpito Vaidiśe ।
Gotreṣu skhalitaḥ Kaṭāhanagare, yaḥ Kuṇḍine muṇḍito
Veśa-strî-nikaṣopalaściratarạṃ bhūtvaiva niṣṭhāṃ gataḥ ॥3॥

Translation:

Hullo I Here comes the old sinner Veśarakṣita. I find him in a very much chastened mood, pretty exhausted by his visits to the temples of Eros.

And how?

'Having indulged in pranks in Śāketa,[21] exasperated by the girdles (of the gay girls) at Kāñcîpura, run after (by girls) in Pampā, fired by old flames at the city of Vidiśā, discomfited by addressing (new lovers) by wrong names (of old lovers' names) in the city of Kaṭāha and shaved (in disgrace) in Kuṇḍina, having served as the touch-stone of gay girls, (he) has now finally settled down to a pious life !'

Here, in this picture, of a Rake's Progress, the object is to mention all the great cities of India famous for their gay life, where gentlemen of pleasure could seek satisfaction. Of the six cities mentioned in the verse Śāketa, Kāñcîpura, Pampā, Vidiśā, Kaṭāha and Kuṇḍina the first four are very well known. Special significance attaches to the two last-named cities, Kuṇḍina and Kaṭāha. Kuṇḍina is a very little known city, and does not figure very much in ancient history. We can offer two alternative identifications. On two inscribed stèlès (coming from Prasat Komphus, and Prah Einkosei, in Cambodia) a place called Kaṇḍin (? Kuṇḍina) is mentioned where Divākara-bhaṭṭa, the royal chaplain of King Jayavarman V, built and endowed a sanctuary of Śiva in 894 Śaka (AD 972).[22] The place came also to be known under the name of Madhu-vana or Madhu-kānana, the "Bower of Bliss". The date of the *Kaumudî-mahotsava* could hardly be pulled down as late as the last part of the tenth or the beginning of the eleventh century, a chronology necessitated by the fact that Kaṇḍin does not leap into the pages of history before AD 972. Besides,

---

has spent through all his patrimony and who lives by associating with hetaraes and their lovers and club-men."

[21] If *akṛta-kautuka* is the correct reading, the passage should be rendered as "being baffled in his pranks in Sāketa". I am indebted to Kshetresh Chattopadhyaya of Allahabad University and P.V. Kane of Bombay for valuable and courteous assistance in translating the *śloka*. According to Kane, in the word *abhisārita*, the Lake of Pampā (*Pampā-sarit*, or *sarovara*) may have been suggested.

[22] The inscription of Prasat Kompus, partly in Sanskrit and partly in Khmèr, is edited, and translated by Çoedès (*Inscriptions du Cambodge*, Hanoi, 1937, pp. 160-86). The inscription from Prah Einkosei is discussed in *BEFEO*, XXX, p. 224.

however, intriguing the name, Madhu-vana was after all a small provincial town (perhaps a large village) and never appears to have achieved the status of a major city, such as would attract visitors from India Proper, in search of a gay life—in this far-off "Bower of Bliss". We have, therefore, to seek an alternative identification which the text of the *Kathāsaritsāgara* offers. "The Ocean of the Streams of Story" composed by Somadeva (*c.* AD 1073) thrice mentions the city of Kuṇḍina: (a) in the story of Nāgasvāmin, a brāmhaṇa from a city called Kuṇḍina,[23] (b) in the story of the seven Brāmhaṇas who devoured a cow in time of famine and (c) in the story of Kanakavarṣa and Madanasundarî.[24] In the last-named story, Kuṇḍina is referred to as a prosperous and wealthy city,[25] in the province of Vidarbha (*Vidarbha-viṣayā-viṣayā-śritaṃ*), and may well be the city of gaiety, suggested in the text of our drama.

As regards the city of Kaṭāha, mentioned in the verse, ever since Çoedès wrote his epoch-making article: "Le Royaume de Çrī-Vijaya"[26] identifying the city as one of the main seats of the Śailendra kings of the Empire of Śrīvijaya, which comprised the greater part of the Malaya Peninsula, several Indonesian islands including, Sumatra, Banka, and Java, quite a formidable literature has grown up over the problem of identifying the exact site of Kaṭāhanagara which in ancient Tamil literature is also known under the name of Kāḷagam and Kaḍāraṃ.[27]

It is very probable, that Kaṭāha (Kāḷagam, Kaḍāraṃ) was an important sea-port and a brisk centre of trade, at least from the third century AD, long before the rise of the Śailendras. According to Nilakanta Sastri, on the authority of the text of the *Paṭṭinappalāi* (one of the early Tamil Śangam works), "Kāḷagam (= Kaṭāha) stands for the name of a place in constant trade relation with Paṭṭinam, or Kāveripaṭnam, the celebrated port of the early Cola monarchs of the Śangam age. And the mention of Kāḷagam which must mean Kaḍāram or nothing, in this early poem of the second or third century AD is not without considerable significance to a study of the early history of the Hindu colonies

[23] Tawney's translation, II, p. 449. Durgaprasad and Parab's edition, p. 511: *Nāgasvāmiti nāmāham Kuṇḍinākhyāt-purāddvijḥ* ।।20।।.

[24] Tawney I, p. 241. Parab's edition, p. 120: *Kuṇḍinākhye pure pūrvamupādhyāyasya kasyacit* ।।109।।

[25] Tawney I, pp. 539, 541, 548. Parab's Edition, p. 278: *Viḍarbheṣvasti nagaram Srīmat-Kuṇḍina-saṁjñakaṃ* ।।56।। and p. 286.

[26] *BEFEO*, tome XVIII, 1918, pp. 51-6.

[27] J.L. Moens: "Çrīvijaya, Yāva en Kaṭāha", *Tijdschrift voor Indische Taal—Land en Volkendkunde*, LXXVII, 1937, pp. 317-486. J. Ph. Vogel: "Het Koninkrijk Çrīvijaya", *Bijdragen tot de Taal—Land en Volkenkunde*, Deel 75, 1919, pp. 626-37. Ferrand in reviewing Çoedès thesis suggests that Kaṭāha and Kaḍāra are two different sites, *JAs*, 1919, p. 186. Moens in his paper cited above seeks to place Kaṭāha in the old Province of Keḍu in Java.

Nilakanta Sastri in an able article "Kaṭāha", *JGIS*, V, 1938, pp. 128 ff., elucidates the problem of identifying this important city of the Śailendra Empire.

of the East" (*JGIS*, V, p. 129).[28] That other parts of India were also in frequent mercantile and adventurous communications with the city of Kaṭāha appears to be borne out by numerous references to that oversea city, in more than one stories of the *Kathāsaritsāgara*. These references appear to establish that Kaṭāha was not only a city where a brisk trade was carried on in the sale and purchase of jewels,[29] to which merchants from India frequently resorted in search of fortune, but it was also a "home of all manner of felicities" (*Ketanaṃ Sarva-sampadāṃ*) the amenities of which attracted young men from India seeking pleasure, as the verse under discussion suggests. The principal port of embarkation for northerners sailing to Kaṭāha—was the old port of Tāmralipti (Tamluk). Various passages of the text of *Kathāsaritsāgara* leave no doubt as regards the fact that the people of India thought nothing of making frequent voyages to Kaṭāha. Very well known is the story of the foolish merchant who went to the island of Kaṭāha to trade. Among his wares he had a great quantity of fragrant aloes-wood which he foolishly burnt and made into charcoal and sold at a cheap price.[30] More romantic is the story of Guhasena, a merchant of Tāmralipti, who went to the city of Kaṭāha for the purpose of trade, notwithstanding the jealousies of his wife Devasmitā who was apprehensive that her husband would be ensnared by some other lady in Kaṭāha.[31] Guhasena took a long time to complete his sales and purchases of jewels and other wares in Kaṭāha[32]—a delay which afforded opportunity to four young merchants of Kaṭāha to come to Tāmralipti to make an unsuccessful attempt to seduce Devasmitā—who subsequently sails to Kaṭāha and punishes the rascals and brings back her truant husband. In the story of the brāhmaṇa Candrasvāmin, it is related that the father makes several oversea journeys in search of his son and daughter. From a city named Jalapura on the shore of the sea, he embarked on a ship and went across to the isle of Nārikela and from there he went in a ship to the island of Kaṭāha.[33] Thereafter, he visited in turn the islands of

[28] Gerini has suggested (*Researches*, p. 570, n.) that Kaṭāha is referred to by Ptolemy under the form of Ko-tat, Kau-tek Kiu-te, or Kortatha. He also suggests that Kaṭāha was taken by Fan-man the gallant king of Fu-nan (Cambodge), who reigned between AD 200-30 as referred to by the Chinese History of the Liang Dynasty.

[29] The precious stones which were the chief articles of commerce of Kaṭāhanagara were probably derived from the neighbouring peak of Keḍah (Gunang Cherai). Colonel Low, cited by Gerini (*Researches on Ptolemy's Geography of Eastern Asia*, p. 485, n. 2) says "that large crystals of quartz, gold and tin are to be found there".

[30] *Jagāma sa vaṇijyāyai Kaṭāha-dvīpamekadā*—Śakti-yaśo-Lambaka 10, Text p. 315

[31] *Athāstam pitare prāpte prerito'bhūtsa bandhubhiḥ* ।
Kaṭāha-dvīpa-gamane Guhaseno yadṛcchayā ।।
Taccāsya gamanam bhāryā tadā nāṅgīcakāra sā ।
Serṣyā Devasmitā Kāmamanyastri-saṅga-śaṅkinī ।।75।। Text, p. 41

[32] *Guhaseno'pi tam prāpa Kaṭāha-dvīpamāśu saḥ* ।
Kartum pravavṛte cātra ratnānām kraya-vikrayau ।। 83 ।। Text p. 42

[33] *Potena gacchatā sākam Ka*।*ṭāha-dvīpa-mabhyagāt* ।। 60 ।।
Evam kramena Karpūra-suvarṇa-dvīpa-siṁhalān ।
Vaṇigbhiḥ saha gatvāpi tam prāpa vaṇijam na saḥ ।। 62 ।। Text, p. 285

Karpūra,[34] Suvarṇa (Sumatra ?) and Siṃhala (Ceylon) in the company of merchants, in search of his children. That frequent voyages were also made by merchants to the island of Suvarṇadvîpa (Sumatra ?) at one time part of the Śailendra Empire, is proved by the story of Samudra-sūra (the hero of the seas) apparently a courageous sailor-merchant from Harṣapura (the city belonging to King Harṣavarman), who was shipwrecked near the coast of Suvarṇadvîpa, went to the city of Kalasapura; and came back with a lot of money, and lived in affluence ever thereafter.[35]

Reverting to the text of the *Kaumudī-mahotsava*, we have cited enough references to establish that Kaṭāha-nagara as a very popular city was very well known to Indians who made frequent voyages to the city, which was thus linked up with India Proper in various ties of mercantile and social interest. That Kaṭāha-nagara, in far-off Malaya should be mentioned in the verse in the drama in the same breath with the other well-known cities of India Proper—appear to surprisingly corroborate the view we are seeking to establish, viz., that the territories beyond the Indian Ocean were regarded as integral parts of Indian culture-area—not mere "Colonies" of Provincial, Indianised, or Indianesque culture. In fact, they were the very limbs of India expanding themselves beyond the seas with all the characteristic and essential qualities of Indian life and culture growing and sustaining itself in new environments.

In the field of Epigraphy, the characters of the various Indian alphabets were adhered to in the oversea tracts and kingdoms, with very few modifications and developments, which were natural growths, and were, in no sense, degenerations or decadences from original Indian standards.

In the field of Architecture and the Plastic Arts—we also find a logical, a natural, and a continuous development of the ideals and principles of Indian art as formulated at the sources, carried out to their utmost perfections in the various culture-areas in Greater India. Undoubtedly, certain new forms and new types are achieved in sculptural representations (e.g. in the images of Viṣṇu and Lokeśvara in Cambodia), but with the exceptions of a few local ethnic types in physiognomy, they strictly adhere to the principles and conventions of Indian sculpture and the canons of Indian image-making evolved on the continent. In architecture, notwithstanding, some adoptions here and there, of local structural forms, the fundamental principles and physiognomy of Indian temples, shrines, *stūpas* and other structures are faithfully followed, and they grow and develop on the same roads to new developments under novel conditions, and under luxurious, congenial, and very favourable environments. As I have shown elsewhere, that with very few exceptions, there are no features in Indian architecture or sculpture in the "Colonies" which cannot be explained as the natural development of essentially Indian forms in

[34] Very probably, Karpūra-dvīpa (the Land of Camphor) was an earlier toponym for Ṭakkola, a word which is an equivalent of "Karpūra" (cf. Bhaṭṭasvāmin: *Kecit Karpūram-ity-āhus-ṭakkolam iti cāpare* । *Śrī-vāsakam tathā kecit kecil-lohita-candanam* ।।

[35] *Kathāsaritsāgara*, Bombay edn., p. 273.

a new environment. Indian art in Siam, Indo-China, Malaya and the Indian Archipelago is a continuation and logical development by Indian hands of the principles and symbols of Indian creation, applied and developed under "Colonial" conditions. The art, culture and civilisation of India beyond the seas formed an integral part of the art and civilisation of the Indian continent. The culture-areas that developed and bore rich fruits in the trans-Gangetic territories and in the Indian Archipelago, were so many outlying frontiers and logical expansions of the civilisation of a Greater India stretching itself to the shores beyond the "moving waves" (*calormmi*). On the basis of the new evidences set forth above it may be justly claimed that the theory of a group of scholars of the so-called "Indian Influences" in Greater India demands a serious modification. It is not a question of "Influences", it is a question of a wholesale transportation of the characteristic features and phases of Indian culture, bag and baggage,[36] in all its characteristic features, elements and textures, with all its social and religious polities, its trade-guilds, and industrial systems, its canons of architecture and sculpture. Indian culture in Indonesia is in fact a substantial part of the original context of Indian civilization[37] carried overseas by Indian emigrants—to a new culture-area—a new *karma-bhūmi* इज्या-युद्ध वाणिज्याद्यैः कर्म्मभिः कृतपावनाः ।

[36] A. Bergaigne (*Inscriptions Sanscrites de Campā et Cambodge*, I, p. 170) cites Burnell with approval to suggest that more or less wholesale emigrations flowed from India to the Indonesian Colonies: "Burnell etait porte à l'expliquer par des emigrations opérees plus ou moins en masse, a la suite de crises religieuses, ou il faisait intervenir tantot les invasions mussulmanes." The suggestion that the emigrations were necessitated by Mussalman invasions or Brahmanic persecutions is wholly gratuitous. Dr. Kern, in an article in Dutch on "Dravidian Folknames of Sumatra" (*Bijdragen*, Deel 55, 1903) has shown that there was a large colony of Tamil workers settled not only in Sumatra, but also in Java; the Hindu noblemen employed such labourers and workmen imported from India. Kempers who does not believe that Indian colonisers planted themselves in the colonies in any large numbers, nevertheless concedes that "their numbers were regularly reinforced by new-comers" ("Cultural Relations Between India and Java," *Calcutta University Lectures*, 1937, p. 6).

[37] A keen controversy has raged over the problem—as to who were the actual authors of the architectural and sculptural master-pieces in Siam, Cambodia, Campā, Malaya (Śrīvijaya), Sumatra and Java—a controversy to which two eminent scholars Dr. Bosch and M. Parmentier have richly contributed (see English translation of Parmentier's article: "Art of Campā" (*Rūpam*, nos. 15 and 16, pp. 41-8), and of Bosch's article "A Hypothesis as to the Origin of Hindu-Javanese Art" (*Rūpam*, no. 17, January 1924, pp. 6-39). Reference may also be made to the present writer's "Note on the Origin of Indo-Javanese Art" (*Rūpam*, no. 17, pp. 54-7).

CHAPTER 11

The Struggle between the Śailendras and the Cholas

R.C. MAJUMDAR

Throughout the eleventh century AD the outstanding fact in the history of the Śailendras is an unceasing struggle with the powerful Chola rulers of south India.

The Chola state was one of the three kingdoms in south India which flourished from a hoary antiquity. It extended along the Coromandel coast, and its traditional boundaries were the Pennar River in the north, the Southern Vellaru River on the south and up to the borders of Coorg on the west. The rise of the Pallavas within this area kept the Cholas in check for a long time. But the Cholas re-asserted their ascendancy from the commencement of the tenth century AD. With the accession of Parāntaka I in AD 907 the Cholas entered upon a career of aggressive imperialism. By a succession of great victories, Rājarāja the Great (AD 985-1012) made himself the lord paramount of southern India. His still more famous son Rājendra Chola (AD 1012-35) raised the Chola power to its climax and his conquests extended as far as Bengal in the north.

The Cholas were also a great naval power and this naturally brought them into contact with Indonesia. At first there existed a friendly relation between the Chola kings and the Śailendra rulers. An inscription written partly in Sanskrit (AD 1044) and partly in Tamil (AD 1046), the so-called Large Leyden Grant, tells us that in the 21st year of Rājarāja Rājakeśarivarman (i.e., Rājarāja the Great), Śrī Māravijayottuṅgavarman, king of Kaṭāha and Śrī Viṣaya, and belonging to Śailendra dynasty, granted a village to a Buddhist monastery at Nāgīpaṭṭana which was constructed by his father Cūlamanivarman and named after him as Cūlamaṇivarmavihāra. In the Tamil portion the Chola king endorses the grant,[1] referring to the royal donor as king of Kiḍāra and Kaḍāra.

This interesting record naturally recalls the Nālandā copper-plate of the time of Devapāla. In both cases a Śailendra king grants villages to a Buddhist

[1]The inscription was edited by Burgess in *Arch. Surv. South India*, vol. IV, p. 206. The Sanskrit portion is dated in 1044 and the Tamil portion in AD 1046. The Tamil portion gives "Sulamaṇipadma" in place of "Culamanivarman" as the name of the king and the vihāra.

Source: *Journal of the Greater India Society* (I/1, 1934, 71–9).

temple, erected in India, through the favour and courtesy of the Indian king. Both furnish us with names of Śailendra kings not known from indigenous sources.

Fortunately the present inscription can be precisely dated, for the 21st year of Rājarāja falls in AD 1005. We thus come to know that Śrī Māravijayottuṅga-varman, son of Cūḍāmaṇivarman was on the throne in AD 1005. To G. Coedès belongs the credit of tracing these two names in the Chinese Annals.[2] The History of the Sung dynasty gives us the following details about them.[3]

In the year 1003 the king Se-li-chu-la-wu-ni-fu-ma-tiau-hwa (Śrī Cūḍāmaṇivarmadeva) sent two envoys to bring tribute; they told that in their country a Buddhist temple had been erected in order to pray for the long life of the emperor.

In the year 1008 the king Se-ri-ma-la-p'i (Śrī-Māra-vijayottuṅgavarman) sent three envoys to present tribute.

Comparing the Chinese and Indian dates we can easily put the death of Cūḍāmaṇivarman and the accession of his son Śrī-Māra-vijayottuṅgavarman some time between AD 1003 and 1005. So the relations between the Chola and Śailendra kings were quite friendly at the commencement of the eleventh century AD. It is interesting to note that while the Sanskrit portion of the Leyden Grant refers to Śrī-Māra-vijayottuṅgavarman as king of Kaṭāha and Śrī-Viṣaya, the Tamil portion refers to him only as the king of Kaḍāra or Kiḍāra. In spite of Ferrand's criticism[4] there is much to be said in support of the view of G. Coedès, that Kaṭāha, Kaḍāra or Kiḍāra are all equivalents of Kedah in the western part of the Malay Peninsula.[5] It would then follow, that while the king Māravijayottuṅgavarmadeva ruled over both Śrīvijaya and Malay Peninsula, as is also testified to by the Arab writers, the Cholas regarded them rather as rulers of Malay Peninsula with suzerainty over Śrīvijaya.

There were also commercial relations between the two countries. An old Tamil poem refers to ships with merchandise coming from Kalāgam to Kāvirippūmpaddinam, the great port situated at the mouth of the Kaveri River.[6] Kalāgam, which a later commentator equates with Kaḍāram denotes in any case Kedah in Malay Peninsula which the Arabs designate as Kala.

The friendly relation between the Chola kings and the Śailendra rulers did not last long. In a few years hostilities broke out and Rājendra Chola sent a naval expedition against his mighty adversary beyond the sea. The details preserved in the Chola records leave no doubt that the expedition was crowned with brilliant success and various parts of the empire of the Śailendras were reduced by the mighty Chola emperor. The reason for the outbreak of hostility

[2]*BEFEO*, vol. XVIII, no. 6.

[3]Groeneveldt, *Notes*, p. 65, *JA*, II-XX (1922), p. 19.

[4]*JA*, II-XX (1922), pp. 50-1.

[5]Ibid., pp. 19 ff.

[6]Quoted by Kanaksabhai in *Madras Review* (August 1902). Also cf. K. Aiyangar's remarks in *Journ. of Ind. Hist.*, vol. II, p. 347.

and the different factors that contributed to the stupendous success of the most arduous undertaking of the Chola emperor are unknown to us. Fortunately we have a fair idea of the time when the expedition took place and we also know the name of the Śailendra king who was humbled by the Indian emperor. These and other details are furnished by the records of the Cholas, and a short reference to these is necessary for a proper understanding of the subject.

1. Several inscriptions at Malurpatna dated in the 23rd year of King Rājarāja, record that he was pleased to destroy the ships (at) Kandalur Salai . . . and twelve thousand ancient islands of the sea.[7]

   The 23rd year of Rājarāja corresponds to AD 1007. It is therefore reasonable to presume that the Cholas possessed a powerful navy, and started on a deliberate policy of making maritime conquests early in the eleventh century AD.

2. The Tiruvalangadu plates, dated in the 6th year of Rājendra Chola (AD 1017-18), contain the following verse:[8]

[7]Nos. 128, 130, 131, 132 of Channapatna Taluq, *Epigraphia Carnatica*, vol. IX, trans., pp. 159-61.

[8]*South Ind. Ins.*, vol. III, part III, pp. 383 ff. The inscription consists of 271 lines in Sanskrit and 524 lines in Tamil. Both the parts are expressly dated in the 6th year of Rājendra Chola. But the Sanskrit portion is usually regarded as being engraved at a later date. When the inscription was first noticed in the *Annual Report of the Archaeological Survey* (1903-4, pp. 234-5), the following remarks were made: "The Tamil portion of Tiruvalaṅgadu plates is dated in the 6th year of Rājendra Chola's reign (AD 1016-17) and the Sanskrit portion also refers to the grant having been made in the same year. But the conquest of Kaṭāha, which, as we know from other inscriptions of the king, took place in the 15th or 16th year of his reign, is mentioned in the Sanskrit portion. It has therefore to be concluded that, as in the Leyden Grant, the Sanskrit *Praśasti* of the Tiruvalaṅgadu plates was added subsequently to the Tamil portion which actually contains the king's order (issued in the 6th year of his reign)." This argument has, however, very little force, for, as we now know, there is no reason to place the expedition to Kaṭāha in the 15th or 16th year and, as we shall see later, an inscription of the 13th year of the king refers to these over-sea conquests in detail.

Hultzsch, while editing the inscription, expresses the same view in a modified manner. Referring to the conquests recorded in the Sanskrit portion he observes: "These conquests of Rājendra Chola are mostly recorded in the historical introductions to his Tamil inscriptions dated from and after the 13th year of his reign. It may here be noted that the Tamil introduction given in lines 131 to 142 below is naturally the shorter one, since it belongs to the sixth year of the king's reign; and since it does not include a list of all the conquests mentioned above it has been suggested that the Sanskrit portion of the grant which includes the conquests of the later years must be a subsequent addition." (*South Ind. Ins.*, vol. III, p. 389).

It must be observed, however, that none of the records of Rājendra Chola gives any specific date for any of his conquests, and we can only conclude that the conquests must have been made before the date of the inscription which records them. It is, therefore, too risky to assert that any particular conquest is of a later date.

On the other hand, a comparison of the records shows that they contain stereotyped

Having conquered Kaṭāha with (the help of) his valiant forces that had crossed the ocean, (and) having made all kings bow down (before him), this (king) (Rājendra Chola) protected the whole earth for a long time. (v. 123)

3. An inscription at the temple of Malur in the Bangalore district, dated in the 13th year of Rājendra Chola (AD 1024-5), gives a detailed account of his over-sea conquests.[9]
4. The same details are also given in the Tanjore inscription of Rājendra Chola dated in his 19th year (AD 1030-1) in the following words:[10] "and (who) (Rājendra Chola) having despatched many ships in the midst of the rolling sea and having caught Saṅgrāma-vijayottuṅgavarman, the king of Kaḍāram, along with (his) vehicles, (viz.) rutting elephants, (which were as impetuous as) the sea in fighting, (took) the large heap of treasures, which (that king) had rightfully accumulated; the (arch called) Vidyādhara-toraṇa at the "war-gate", of the extensive city of the enemy; the "Jewel-gate", adorned with great splendour; the "gate of large jewels", Vijayam, of great fame; Paṇṇai, watered by the river; the ancient Malaiyūr (with) a fort situated on a high hill; Māyirudiṅgam, surrounded by the deep sea (as) a moat; Ilangāśogam (i.e., Laṅkasuka), undaunted (in) fierce battles; Māppappāḷam, having abundant high waters as defence; Mevilimbaṅgam, having fine walls as defence; Valaippandūṛu, possessing (both) cultivated land (?) and jungle; Talaittakkolam, praised by great men (versed in) the sciences; Mādamāliṅgam, firm in great and fierce battles; Ilāmurideśam, whose fierce strength was subdued by a vehement (attack); Māṇakkavāram whose flower-gardens (resembled) the girdle (of the nymph) of the southern region; Kaḍāram, of fierce strength, which was protected by the neighbouring sea.

---

official list of conquests repeated in exactly the same words, with additions from time to time in records of later years. This, no doubt, is a strong argument in favour of the belief that the 'additional conquests' took place after the date of the last inscription which does not mention them.

Judging from the above the conquest of Kaṭāha in the sixth year of Rājendra Chola is doubtful, as it is not included in the list of conquests in inscriptions dated in the 9th and 13th years of his reign. As will be shown below, the conquest of Kaṭāha with a number of other states beyond the sea is mentioned in inscriptions dated in the 13th and 20th years of the reign.

If, however, the Sanskrit portion of the Tiruvalaṅgadu plates were composed after these conquests, it is very difficult to believe that the author who has devoted 40 verses to the conquests of Rājendra Chola, would have merely referred to these mighty exploits in only one verse.

On the whole, therefore, until more specific evidence is available, we accept the clear deduction from the inscription that a naval expedition was sent to Kaṭāha. For reasons given below, it has to be distinguished from the more elaborate and successful expeditions of the 13th year, referred to in Channapatna and Tanjore Inscriptions.

[9]No. 84 of Channapatna Taluq (*Ep. Cam.*, IX, pp. 148-50).

[10]*South Ind. Ins.*, vol. II, pp. 105 ff. (Some corrections were made later, in *Ep., Ind.*, vol. IX, pp. 231-2.)

5. These details are also repeated in several other inscriptions dated in the 19th, 22nd, 23rd and 27th years of Rājendra Choladeva.[11]
6. The preambles of two inscriptions dated in the 18th and 32nd years of Rājendra Chola refer to him as ruling over Gange (or Gangai), the East country and Kaḍāram.[12]
7. In an inscription at Mandikere, dated AD 1050, Rājendra Chola is said to have conquered Gangai in the north, Ilaṅgai in the south, Mahodai on the west and Kaḍāram on the east.[13]
8. The Kanyākumārī inscription (verse 72) of the 7th year of Vīra Rājendra contains the following statement about Rājendra Chola.
"With (the help) of his forces which crossed the seas . . . he (Rājendra Chola) burnt Kaṭāha that could not be set fire to by others."[14]

In the light of the above records, the long passage in the Tanjore inscription (no. 4) seems to indicate that Rājendra Chola defeated the king of Kaḍāra, took possession of various parts of his kingdom, and concluded his campaign by taking Kaḍāra itself. In other words, the various countries mentioned in the passage were not independent kingdoms, but merely the different subject-states of Saṅgrāma-Vijayottuṅgavarman, ruler of Kaḍāra and Śrīvijaya.[15]

We must, therefore, try to identify these geographical names, with a view to understand correctly the exact nature of Rājendra Chola's conquests, and, indirectly, also of the empire of Saṅgrāma-Vijayottuṅga.

It is needless now to refer to the various suggestions and theories in this respect that were made from time to time till the ingenious researches of Coedès put the whole matter in a clear light.[16] Although some of the conclusions of Coedès are not certainly beyond all doubt, his views are a great improvement on his predecessors and we cannot do better than accept his results, at least as a working hypothesis. We, therefore, sum up below the views put forward by Coedès with some modifications necessitated by later researches.[17]

PAṆṆAĪ. This country is probably identical with Pane which Nāgarakṛtāgama includes among the states of Sumatra, subordinate to Majapahit. Gerini places it at modern Pani or Panei on the eastern side of the island of Sumatra.[18]

[11] Nos. 82, 83 and 133 of Channapatna Taluq (*Ep. Cam.*, IX, 148-50, 161). Nos. 7a and 37 of Nelamaṅgala Taluq (ibid., pp. 30-5).

[12] No. 1 of Nelamaṅgala Taluq (ibid., p. 29); No. 142 of Hoskote Taluq (ibid., p. 107).

[13] No. 25 of Nelamaṅgala Taluq (ibid., p. 33).

[14] *Travancore Archæological Series*, vol. III, part I, p. 157. *Ep. Ind.*, vol. XVIII, pp. 45-6, 54.

[15] This view, originally propounded by Hultzach (op. cit.) is accepted by Venkayya (*Rep. Arch. Surv. Burma*, 1909-10, p. 14) and Coedès (*BEFEO.*, vol. XVIII, no. 6, pp. 5-6).

[16] *BEFEO*, vol. XVIII, no. 6. For previous theories cf. *South Ind. Ins.*, vols. II, p. 106; III, pp. 104-5; *Ann. Report. Arch. Sure.*, 1898-9, p. 17; 1907-8, p. 233; *Madras Review* 1902, p. 251; *Rep. Arch. Surv. Burma*, 1906-7, p. 19, 1909-10, p. 14, 1916-17, p. 25.

[17] These are indicated by references to later authorities in footnotes. Unless otherwise indicated, the statements in the text are based upon Coedés article (op. cit.).

[18] Gerini, *Researches*, p. 513.

MALAIYŪR. This is no doubt the same as the country known as *Malayu* which is sometimes written with a 'r' at the end (as in this instance and in some Arab texts) or sometimes without it. The identification of this place has formed a subject of keen and protracted discussion.[19] It has been located both in the eastern as well as in the western coast of Sumatra, and even in the southern part of Malay Peninsula. We learn from I-tsing that it was fifteen days' Journey by sea from Śrīvijaya[20] and was conquered by this state sometime between AD 672 and 705.

Dutch scholars, however, agree in identifying it with Jambi.[21]

MĀYIRUḌIṄGAM. Taking the first syllable *mā* as equivalent to Sanskrit *mahā*, *Yiruḍiṇgam* has been identified with *Je-le-ting* of Chau Ju-kua. Schlegel identified this place with *Jeluton* in the island of Bangka,[22] while Gerini proposed various identifications, viz., with (1) Jelutong at the south-west of Jambi, (2) Jelutong in Johore and (3) Jelutong in Selangor.[23] Coedès concludes from a passage of Chau Ju-kua's book that it must be looked for in the centre of the Peninsula, and belongs to the northernmost group of states (in the Malay Peninsula) which were subordinate to the Śailendra empire. Rouffaer, on the other hand, locates it in the extreme south-east of the Peninsula, near Cape Rumania.[24]

ILANGĀŚOGAM. M.G. Ferrand has identified the country with the *Ling-ya-sseu-kia* which Chau Ju-kua includes among the vassal states of San-fo-ts'i, and also with Leṅka-suka referred to as a tributary state of Majapahit in Nāgarakṛtāgama.[25] On the basis of a passage in the Hikayat Maron Mahāvaṃśa Coedès places it in the Kedah Peak (Gunong Jerai).[26] But Ferrand places it in the Isthmus of Ligor[27] while Rouffaer locates it in Johor.[28]

MĀ-PPAPPĀLAM. Venkayya was the first to point out that this country is mentioned in Mahāvaṃśa.[29] There it is referred to as a port in the country of Rammaññadesa. But as the authority of the king of Pagan extended far to the south, the location of this place in the western part of the Isthmus of Kra is not barred out.

Rouffaer identifies it with Great "Pahang".[30]

[19] Cf. Pelliot, *BEFEO*, IV, pp. 326 ff., Gerini, *Restarches*, pp. 528 ff.; Ferrand, *JA*, II-XI, (1918), pp. 391 ff. and II-XII (1918), pp. 51-154.

[20] Coedès says that according to l-tsing Malāyu was in the immediate neighbourhood (voisinage immediat) of Cheli-fo-che. This is hardly accurate.

[21] Rouffaer, *BKI*, vol. 77 (1921), pp. 11 ff.

[22] *T'oung Pao* (1901), p. 134.

[23] Gerini, *Researches*, pp. 627, 826.

[24] Rouffaer, *BKI*, vol. 77 (1921).

[25] Ferrand, *Textes*, p. 647, fn. 1.

[26] Gerini was the first to point it out (*JRAS*, 1905, pp. 495 ff.).

[27] *JA*, II-XII (1818), pp. 134 ff.

[28] *BKI*, 77 (1921), pp. 89 ff.

[29] *Ann. Rep*., 1898-9, p. 17, *Arch. Survey of Burma*, *Ann. Rep*., 1909-10, p. 14.

[30] *BKI*, vol. 77 (1921), p. 83.

MEVILIMBAṄGAM. M. Sylvain Lévi identifies it with Karmaraṅga, the Kāmalaṅkā of Hiuen Tsang and places it in the Isthmus of Ligor.[31]

VALAIPPANDŪṚU. Rouffaer identifies it with Pandurang or Phanrang[32] but its accuracy may be doubted.

TALAITTAKKOLAM. It is almost certain that the country is identical with Takkola of Milindapañho and Takola of Ptolemy, the word "Talai" in Tamil signifying "head" or "chief". It must be located in the Isthmus of Kra or a little to the south of it.[33]

MĀ-DAMĀLIṄGAM. A short inscription found in Jaiya refers to a country called Tāmbraliṅga—which is to be located on the eastern side of the Malay Peninsula, between the Bay of Bandon and Nagor Śrī Dharmarāj (Ligor). Damāliṅgam has been identified with Tāmbraliṅgam, mā being equivalent to *mahā*. It is evidently the same as Tan-ma-ling which Chau Ju-kua includes among the tributary states of San-fo-ts'i.

ILĀMURIDEŚAM. Leaving aside the initial *i* which is often prefixed in Tamil to foreign names, this can be easily identified with Lāmuri of the Arab geographers and Lambri of Marco Polo, situated in the northern part of Sumatra. This country, under the form Lan-wou-li, is included among the tributary states of *San-fo-ts'i* by Chau Ju-kua.

MĀ-NAKKAVĀRAM. Taking the first syllable as equivalent to *mahā* the place can be easily identified with Nikobar islands. The form Necuveran used by the Marco Polo closely resembles Nakkāvaram.

KAṬĀHA, KAḌĀRAM, KIḌĀRAM. M. Coedès has shown good grounds to prove that Kaṭāha is the same as Kie-tcha referred to by the Chinese as a port as early as seventh century AD. The same place is referred to in later times as Kie-t'o and Ki-t'o, which may be equated to Kaḍa and Kiḍo. As the change of a "lingual" to "liquid" was very common in those days, the same place may be identified with Kaḷaḥ or Kila of Arab geographers and also with Ko-lo which Kia Tan places on the northern side of the Straits of Malacca, and Sintang Chou places at the south-east of Pan-pan. All these different names thus correspond, both phonetically and geographically, to the modern Kedah. In a Tamil poem it is referred to as Kaḷagam.

It has been seen above that Ilaṅgāśogam is also to be placed in Kedah. But as Ilaṅgāśogam or Gunong Jerai is placed too far in the south of Kedah, Kedah is also mentioned separately. It may be mentioned that in Nāgarakṛtāgama both Kedah and Leṅkasuka are mentioned as vassal states of Majapahit.[34]

The detailed discussion clearly shows that Rājendra Chola's conquests extended practically over the whole of the eastern coast-region of Sumatra, and the central and southern part of Malay Peninsula, and included the two

[31] *JA*, vol. CCIII (1923).

[32] *BKI*, vol. 77 (1921), p. 82.

[33] There is a vast literature on "Takkola". In addition to the authorities cited by Coedès, I may refer to the views of S. Lévi (*Etudes 'Asiatique*, vol. II, pp. 3 ff.).

[34] Nāgarakṛtāgama, chap. 16, vv. 13, 14.

capital cities Kaṭāha and Śrīvijaya. That the story of this victory is not merely an imagination of the court-poets but based on facts, is proved beyond all doubt by the detailed references to the vassal states. It is interesting to note that many of these states are included in the Śailendra empire (San-fo-ts'i) by later Chinese authorities like Chau Ju-kua.[35]

The date of this decisive victory can be ascertained with tolerable certainty. The Ins. No. 3, quoted above, shows that it must have taken place not later than the 13th year of Rājendra Chola. Now, the Tirumalai inscription,[36] dated in the same year, gives an account of his inland conquests, but does not contain a word about his over-sea conquests. If, for example, one compares the Tanjore Ins. (no. 4 above) with the Tirumalai Ins., it would appear that the former repeats word for word the entire passage in the latter, describing the inland conquests of Rājendra Chola, and then adds the passage, quoted above, describing his over-sea conquests. It may, therefore, be reasonably presumed, that these over-sea conquests had not taken place at the time the Tirumalai inscription was recorded. As the Tirumalai inscription is dated in the 13th year, we may presume that these conquests took place during the short interval between the drafting of this record and that of the Inscription No. 3. In other words, the over-sea conquests of Rājendra Chola took place in the 13th year of his reign, i.e. AD 1024-5, possibly during the latter part. We may, therefore, provisionally accept AD 1025 as the date of the great catastrophe which befell the Śailendra empire.

But according to the plain interpretation of the Inscription No. 2, quoted above, the hostility broke out much earlier, and as early as AD 1017-18, or some time before it, a naval expedition was sent against Kaṭāha. There is nothing surprising in it, for the Inscription No. 1, quoted above, clearly shows that early as AD 1007, the Cholas had begun an aggressive imperialistic policy to obtain mastery of the seas.

Although it is impossible now to ascertain exactly the cause of either the outbreak of hostility or the complete collapse of the Śailendra power, reference may be made to at least some important factors which contributed to the one or the other. According to the Chola records, the conquest of Kaliṅga and the whole eastern coast up to the mouth of the Ganges was completed before the over-sea expedition was sent. Prof. S.K. Aiyangar concludes from a study of all the relevant records that the actual starting-point of the over-sea expedition was in the coast-region of Kaliṅga.[37] Prof. Aiyangar infers from this fact that the conquest of Kaliṅga was undertaken by Rājendra Chola as it "was particularly necessary in view of the over-seas expedition that must have become necessary for some reason or other". He holds further "that the Kaliṅgas

[35] Chau Jukua's account has been translated by Hirth and Rockhill.

[36] *Ep. Ind.*, vol. IX, pp. 229 ff.

[37] *Journal of Indian History*, vol. II, p. 345.

were possibly rivals in the over-seas empire in connection with which the overseas expedition was actually undertaken".

Now these two statements are somewhat vague, and perhaps, even contradictory. But it is quite clear that the conquest of Kaliṅga and the whole coastal region furnished the Chola emperor with ample resources for his over-sea expedition. The mastery over the ports of Kaliṅga and Bengal, gave him well-equipped ships and sailors accustomed to voyage in the very regions which he wanted to conquer. The naval resources of the whole of the eastern coast of India were thus concentrated in the hands of Rājendra Chola, and it was enough to tempt a man to get possession of the territory which served as the meeting ground of the trade and commerce between India and the Western countries on the one hand and the countries of the Far East on the other. The geographical position of the Śailendra empire enabled it to control almost the whole volume of maritime trade between Western and Eastern Asia and the dazzling prospect which its conquest offered to the future commercial supremacy of the Cholas seems to be the principal reason of the overseas expedition undertaken by Rājendra Chola. But it is the conquest of the eastern coastal regions of India that alone brought such a scheme within the range of practical politics.

Although for the time being, the success of the Cholas seems to be complete from the very nature of the case, it could not have possibly continued for long. The task of maintaining hold upon a distant country across the sea was too great to be borne by the successors of Rājendra Chola and they had too many difficulties at home to think of the empire abroad. Rājādhirāja, the eldest son of Rājendra succeeded him in AD 1035. His whole reign was a period of un-ceasing struggle with the neighbouring powers and he himself fell fighting with the Chālukyas at the battlefield of Koppam in AD 1052 or 1053. Vīrarājendra who ascended the throne ten years later no doubt inflicted a severe defeat upon the Chālukyas, but his death in AD 1070, followed by a disputed succession and civil war, seriously weakened the prestige and authority of the Cholas. To make matters worse, Kaliṅga freed itself from the yoke of the Cholas and this crippled the naval resources of that kingdom. The supremacy of the Cholas was revived to a considerable extent by Kulottuṅga Chola (1070-1119), the grandson (daughter's son) of the famous Rājendra Chola. He reconquered Kaliṅga, and established peace and prosperity over his extensive dominions during a long reign of 49 years.[38]

The relation between the Cholas and the Śailendras and of both to China, during the period of nearly a century (AD 1035-1120) of which a short historical sketch has been given above, is referred to in Chola inscriptions and Chinese documents. We give below a short summary of them before drawing any general conclusions.

[38]V.A. Smith, *Early History of India* (3rd edn.), pp. 467-8.

I. CHOLA INSCRIPTIONS

(a) The Perumber Ins. of Vīra Rājendradeva[39] dated in his 7th year (AD 1068-9) states:

> Having conquered (the country of) Kaḍāram, (he) was pleased to give (it) (back) to (its) king who worshipped (his) feet (which bore) ankle-rings.

(b) The small Tamil Leyden Grant[40] dated in the 20th year of Kulottuṅga Chola (AD 1089-90) says:

> At the request of the king of Kiḍāra communicated by his envoys Rājavidyādhara Sāmanta and Abhimānottunga Sāmanta, Kullottuṅga exempted from taxes the village granted to the Buddhist monastery called Śailendra-Cūḍāmaṇivarma-vihāra (i.e. the one established by king Cūlamaṇivarman as referred to in the large Leyden Grant).

II. CHINESE DOCUMENTS

The following account is given by Ma Twan Lin in respect of an embassy from Pagan in AD 1106:[41]

(a) "The Emperor at first issued orders to accord them the same reception and treat them in the same way as was done in the case of the ambassadors of the Cholas (Chu-lien). But the President of the Board of Rites observed as follows: The Chola is a vassal of San-fo-t'si. That is why in the year hi-ning (AD 1068-1077) it was thought good enough to write to the king of that country on a strong paper with an envelope of plain silk. The king of Pagan on the other hand is ruler of a grand kingdom."

The History of the Sung dynasty gives the following accounts of embassies from San-fo-t'si.

(b) In 1017 the king Ha-ch'i-su-wu-ch'a-p'u-mi sent envoys with a letter in golden characters and tribute. . . . When they went back, an edict was issued addressed to their king accompanied by various presents.[42]

(c) In 1028, the 8th month, the king Si-li-tieh-hwa (Śrī Deva?) sent envoys to carry tribute. The custom was that envoys from distant countries who brought tribute, got a girdle adorned with gold and silver, but this time girdles entirely of gold were given to them.[43]

(d) In 1067 an envoy, who was one of their high chiefs, called Ti-hwa-ka-la, arrived in China. The little of "Great General" who supports obedience

[39] *South Ind. Ins.*, vol. III, part II, p. 202.

[40] *Arch. Surv. of the South India*, vol. IV, pp. 226 ff.

[41] D'Hervey and Saint Denys, *Meridionaux*, p. 586 quoted by Coedès, *BEFEO*, XVIII, no. 6, p. 8 and Gerini *Researches*, pp. 624-5.

[42] Groeneveldt, *Notes*, p. 65. Ferrand restores the name of the king as "Haji Sumatrabhūmi"—the king of Sumatra (*JA*, II-XX, 1922, p. 19 and fn. 3.

[43] Groeneveldt, *Notes*, pp. 65-6. Both Groeneveldt and Ferrand (*JA*, II-XX, 1922, p. 20) restore the name as Śrī Deva.

and cherishes renovation was given to him and he was favoured with an imperial edict.[44]

(e) During the period Yüan-fung (1078-1085) envoys came from the country bringing silver, pearls. . . . The letter they brought was first forwarded to the court from Canton, where they waited until they were escorted to the capital. The Emperor remembered that they had come very far, he gave them liberal presents and then allowed them to return.

The next year he gave them 64,000 strings of cash, 15,000 taels of silver and favoured the two envoys who had come with honorary titles.[45]

(f) In 1082 three envoys came to have an audience from the emperor and brought golden lotus flowers, etc. They all received honorary titles according to their rank.[46]

(g) In 1083 three other envoys came, who all received honorary titles according to their rank.[47]

(h) In the period Shau-Sheng (1094-7) they made their appearance once again.[48]

CHOLA EMBASSIES TO CHINA

(i) According to Ma Twan Lin an embassy sent by Lo-cha-lo-cha king of Chu-lien reached China in AD 1015.[49] Gerini restores this name as Rājarāja (the Great).[50]

(j) According to the Sung-Shih, two kings of Chu-lien sent embassies with tribute to China, Shih-li-lo-cha-yin-to-lo-chu-lo in AD 1033 and Ti-wa-ka-lo,[51] in AD 1077. Prof. S.K. Aiyangar has restored the first name as Śrī-Rājendra Chola.[52]

Now the fact that some time before AD 1068-9 Vīra Rājendra conquered Kaḍāram (I-a) shows that the country had regained independence in the meanwhile. Even Rājādhirāja, the immediate successor of Rājendra Chola claimed conquest of Kaḍāram. It would thus appear that for nearly half a century since 1024-5 when Rājendra Chola first conquered the country, the struggle between the two continued with varying degrees of success.

Even the restoration of the king of Kaḍāra, after he had acknowledged the suzerainty of Vīra Rājendra, does not seem to have ended the struggle. On the

[44] Groeneveldt, *Notes*, p. 66. Both Groeneveldt and Ferrand (op. cit.) restore the name as "Deva Kala", Coedès suggests Divākara (*BEFEO*, XXIII, p. 470).

[45] Groeneveldt, *Notes*, p. 66.

[46] Ibid.

[47] Ibid.

[48] Ibid., p. 67.

[49] Harvey and Saint Denys, *Meridionaux*, p. 574.

[50] Gerini, *Researches*, p. 609, fn. 2.

[51] *JRAS*, 1896, p. 490 fn.

[52] *Journ. of Ind. Hist.*, vol. II, p. 353.

one hand Kulottuṅga Chola, the successor of Vīra Rājendra, claims to have destroyed Kaḍāram, on the other hand, the Chinese represent the Chola power to be subordinate to Śrīvijaya (II-a). This conflicting statement perhaps indicates the continuance of the struggle, with alternate success and reverse of both parties.

The embassy from Kaḍāra to the Chola king in AD 1089-90 (I-b) seems to mark the beginning of a new era of goodwill and friendship between the two states. But if the Chinese statement that "Chola is a vassal of San-fo-t'si" be true of the year 1106 when it was recorded, it would again indicate the resumption of a hostile relation between the two.

On the whole, it would be safe to assume that in spite of the arduous nature of the task, the Chola emperors tried to maintain their hold on the distant over-sea empire, at least for nearly a century. It would be too much to assume that they could hope to exercise a rigid control over the distant land. The utmost they could fairly expect was to have their suzerainty acknowledged by the king of Kaḍāra. The latter must have seized every possible opportunity to shake off even this amount of control. On the other hand, the Chola emperors were unwilling to give up altogether their pretensions of suzerainty, and able monarchs like Vīra Rājendra and Kulottuṅga would occasionally fit out a naval expedition to re-establish their authority beyond the sea.

In spite of the claims of the Cholas to have destroyed Kaḍāram, that kingdom never ceased to function as a separate state. This is proved by the regular despatch of embassies to the court of China throughout the eleventh century AD (II.b-h.).

The embassy of 1017 was sent by a king, whose Chinese name has been restored by Ferrand as Haji-Suvarṇabhūmi or king of Suvarṇabhūmi (II-b). It must be regarded as some what unusual that this general term is substituted for the proper name of the king which was used in case of the two immediately preceding embasies.

The next embassy was sent in AD 1028 by a king whose name seems to correspond to Śrī-Deva (II-c). The Chola emperor must have conquered Kaḍāra shortly before this date, and it may be presumed that this Śrī-Deva refers to him or to his viceroy. It is to be noted that the Chinese emperor showed unusual honours to the envoy. This is perhaps due to the mighty fame of Rājendra Chola, who himself sent an envoy to the Chinese court, five years later (II-i).

The envoy who visited the imperial court in AD 1067 is called Ti-hwa-ka-la (II-d) and is described as a high dignitary. It is interesting to note that the Chola king who sent an embassy to China 10 years later was also called *Ti-wa-ka-lo* (II-j). Now, this Chola king is undoubtedly Rājendra Deva Kulottuṅga, and the Chinese name was made up of its second and third parts (Deva-Kulo).[53]

[53] This identification was proposed by S.K. Aiyangar (*Journ. of Ind. Hist.*, II-353). I am also indebted to him for the information, based on Tamil inscriptions, that both Rājādhirāja and Kulottuṅga claimed conquest of Kaḍāram.

It is not impossible that this Kulottuṅga was also the envoy, a high dignitary, who visited the imperial court in AD 1067. The history of the early years of Kulottuṅga lends support to this view. He was the daughter's son of Rājendra Chola, and his father was the Viceroy of Veṅgi. But when his father died in *c.* AD 1061-2, he did not succeed him, and indeed his position about that period is a mystery. S.K. Aiyangar writes:

One would naturally expect this Rājendra (Kulottuṅga) to succeed his father, when he died in 1061-62 or the next year. In all the transactions about the appointment of Vijayāditya VII as Viceroy of Veṅgi we do not hear of the name of Kulottuṅga.[54]

Then, again, the early inscriptions of Kulottuṅga affirm that he "gently raised, without wearying (her) in the least, the lotus-like goddess of the earth residing in the region of the rising sun". S.K. Aiyangar, although unaware of the identity of the two names Ti-wa-ka-lo (the Chola king) and Ti-hwa-ka-la, the envoy of Śrīvijaya, remarked as follows on the above inscription.

This land of the rising sun cannot well be the country of Veṅgi and if the conquest of Burmah [*sic*] by Rājendra I is accepted, as it must now be, this would only mean that Rājendra Kulottuṅga distinguished himself as a prince in the eastern exploits of his grandfather, either during Rājendra Chola's reign or under Vīra Rājendra when he reconquered Kaḍāram.[55]

For "Burmah" in the above passage we must, of course, read Kaḍāram. Now, since Kulottuṅga ruled till AD 1119 it is impossible to believe that he was old enough in AD 1024-5 to accompany his grandfather Rājendra Chola. The reference is therefore possibly to the expedition of Vīra Rājendra which took place some time before AD 1068-9 (I-a). This fits in with the date of the embassy in AD 1067.

If this view be correct, we must hold that Vīra Rājendra's conquest has an effective one, and for some time at least the Cholas definitely occupied the kingdom of Kaḍāra. Kulottuṅga evidently held a very high position in the conquered province and possibly paid a visit to China as an ambassador from Kaḍāra with a view to establish a friendly relation with that power.

Kulottuṅga must have returned to India shortly after, as he ascended the Chola throne in AD 1070, and the Perumbar Ins. (I-a) indicates that before doing so, he re-installed the king of Kaḍāra after he had paid homage and fealty to the Chola emperor.[56]

Once back in his country Kulottuṅga was faced with a grave political crisis, as noted above. Evidently the king of Kaḍāra took advantage of this to free himself from the yoke of the Cholas. Possibly he came out successful in some engagement with the Cholas and pretended to have established his suzerainty

[54] *Ancient India*, p. 129.

[55] Ibid., pp. 130-1.

[56] In addition to what is contained in the following footnote about the grandson of Raja Suran (Chola) the stories of the Chola conquest of Malaya occur in other legends (cf. *Journal of the Malay Branch of the Royal Asiatic Society*, 1926, p. 413; 1932, pp. 1 ff.).

over the latter. The Chinese who got their information from San-fo-t'si were thus misled into the belief that Chola was a vassal of Śrīvijaya (II-a). Otherwise it is impossible to believe, in the absence of any positive evidence, that the king of Kaḍāra could have established any sort of claim over the empire of the Cholas.

The successive embassies in 1078, 1083 and 1094 indicate that after the storm of the Chola invasion had blown over, Kaḍāra resumed its normal relationship with the Chinese court.

The political supremacy of the Cholas in the Far East for a period extending over a century is perhaps echoed in the Malayan tradition about the mythical expedition of Raja Suran [Chola ?] down the peninsula.[57] In any case it is positively indicated by some records in Sumatra. A Tamil inscription has been discovered at Lobu Tua near Baros in Sumatra. It is dated in AD 1088 and refers to the organisation, activities and mythological beliefs of a corporation of Fifteen Hundred.[58] There is no doubt that this was a Tamil corporation of the type of Banañja, Nānādeśi, Valaṅgai, Idaṅgai, etc., whose activities as trade unions, are frequently referred to in south Indian records.[59] According to an inscription found at Baligami in the Mysore state, the members of these unions were "brave men, born to wander over many countries ever since the beginning of the Kṛta age, penetrating regions of the six continents by land and water-routes and dealing in various articles such as horses and elephants, precious stones, perfumes and drugs, either wholesale or in retail".[60] It may be noted here that a Vaiṣṇava Temple was built at Pagan by the Nānādesis (merchants dealing with various countries).[61]

Another inscription at Porlak Dolok in Padang Lawas, and dated probably in AD 1245, is partly written in Kavi Script and pertly in Indian, probably south-Indian alphabet.[62] A third inscription at Bandar Bapahat belonging to the Majapahit period, is written in Kavi and then reproduced in south-Indian Grantha character.[63]

In addition to these records, the intimate intercourse between south India and Sumatra is further indicated by some existing Sumatran clan-names, such as Choliya, Paṇḍiya, Meliyala, Pelawi, which may be easily identified with

[57] A grandson of Suran is also said to have founded Singapore. The story is given in full in *Sejarah Malayu*. Tales of friendly correspondence between Malayan and Indian kings may also be attributed to the relations of Cholas with Malayasia. This point was first noted by Blagden (*Journ. Str. Br. R.A.S.*, no. 81, p. 26).

[58] *Oudh. Versl.*, 1914, pp. 113. *Not. Bat. Gen.*, 1892, p. 80. The inscription has been translated into English by K.A.N. Sastri in *TBG*, vol. 72 (1932), pp. 314 ff.

[59] Cf. R.C. Majumdar, *Corporate Life in Ancient India*, 2nd edn., pp. 87-96.

[60] *Epigraphia Carnatica*, vol. VII, S. 118.

[61] *Epigraphia Indica*, vol. VII, p. 107.

[62] *Oudh. Versl.*, 1914, p. 112, 1920, p. 70.

[63] *Oudh. Versl.*, 1912, p. 46.

the Chola, Pāṇḍya, Malayālam and Pallava. Another name Tekang is probably derived from Tekkanam, the general Tamil term for south, i.e. south India.[64]

It is, of course, impossible to say when these south-Indian names were introduced into Sumatra. In view of the political and trade relations between the two countries in the eleventh century AD the large influx of south Indian people and the consequent introduction of these tribal names may be referred to that period. Of course, with the evidence available at present, it is difficult to determine whether the more peaceful trade-relations preceded or succeeded the political relations between the two countries. In the modern age we can easily quote examples of either. In many cases, the commercial intercourse has led to political interference, and in many others, political supremacy over a foreign land has led to an intense development of trade of the conquering country. Whether the traders and merchants of south India paved the way for the over-sea conquest of the Chola kings, or whether the process was just the reverse of this, the future historian alone will be able to tell.

[64] *TBG*, vol. 45 (1902), pp. 541-76; Kern, *VC*, vol. III (1915), pp. 67-72.

CHAPTER 12

The Voyage of Buddhist Missions to South-East Asia and the Far East

W. PACHOW

The portion of Central Asia that stretches from the north-western boundaries of China to the northern territories of ancient India (including modern Afghanistan) was considered as the life-line of international trade and cultural exchange. It was also known as the silk-route through which silk, spice and other commodities were offered for commercial exchange with countries in the West. We are not sure of the actual date when this international route first came to be used. The earliest historical record[1] written in Chinese indicates that as early as the second century BC textile and bamboo products manufactured in China were sold in the market of Bactriana in the Oxus Valley. This was personally seen by Chang Ch'ien, the envoy sent by Emperor Wu-ti of the Han Dynasty in 129 BC to negotiate with the Yüeh Chi rulers in Bactriana in order to form a military alliance. Further he was reported to have said that these commodities were brought to Bactriana via India. This presupposes the existence of this international route between China and Central Asian countries including India. Therefore it appears to be very natural that most of the Indian and Central Asian Buddhist teachers who proceeded to China followed the trail of this caravan route through Central Asia or modern Chinese Turkestan. This particular route served a useful purpose for over 1,000 years from the beginning of the third or the second century BC. In addition to the missionary zeal shown by the Indian teachers, the Chinese Buddhist pilgrims like Fa-hsien and Hsüan-tsang took the same route to go to India. It is from the records of these travellers we get the impression that the land route via Central Asia was chiefly responsible for the spread of Buddhism to China. Of course, we cannot deny the importance of this route. We wish, however, to add that the sea route, too, played an equally important role in the international commercial and cultural interchange. As this fact is not widely known, it may not be out of place here to bring to the notice to those who are interested in the development of Buddhism in China, and the introduction of the Buddhist teaching to some of the South-East Asian countries. Naturally, this would mean the important

[1] See the chapter on Ta-wan or Fergana in Ssu-ma-ch'ien's *Shih-chi*.

Source: *Journal of the Greater India Society* (XVII/1-2, 1958, 1–22).

events concerning the various Buddhist missionary activities in these regions.

The fact that Fa-hsien in the early fifth century AC returned to China by the sea route indicates that the sea communication between China and India was fairly popular at that time. It is beyond our knowledge to trace the date of the actual beginning of this route. Han-shu,[2] one of the earliest Chinese historical sources of the Han Dynasty (206 BC-25 AC) gives us a list of names of countries in South-East Asia and India. Most of the countries could not be identified except Huang-chih (Kāñcī or Conjeevaram). It appears that Conjeevaram was on friendly terms with the Chinese Imperial Court, for during the reign of Emperor P'ing-ti (1-5 AC) the powerful minister Wang-mang presented to the king of Conjeevaram valuable gifts with the request that the latter should despatch to China a live rhinoceros. Later the Annals of the Later Han Dynasty[3] (25-220 AC) say that several embassies were sent to China by India in 159 and 161 AC. It also mentions that an embassy was sent to China by King Antonius of Rome in 166 AC. This particular mission reached China through the outskirt districts called Jih-nan and Hsiao-wai in southern China. These are the clear bits of evidence that the sea communication between the Indian Ocean and the China Sea was established at least in the beginning of the first century AC. Moreover, this route was not used by India alone, but other countries like Rome and Parthia as well. This shows that the sea route to China has an early beginning, and it has been proved as popular as the land route via Central Asia.

It is the intention in this paper to trace and discuss the Buddhist missions which proceeded to the South Seas and the Far East through the sea route. It is also hoped to point out the extent of the contributions made by these missions towards the spread of Buddhism in these regions. Therefore, a study of the following Buddhist teachers regarding their mode of travel, missionary activities and their achievement and so forth is essential and necessary.

I. *AN-SHIH-KAO* (*PĀRTHAMAŚIRI*?)

One of the earliest Buddhist missions to China which has been accepted as trustworthy is the one led by An-shih-kao. It is said that before taking the Buddhist vow he was the crown prince of King Pakor of Parthia.[4] He reached China in the beginning of the reign of Emperor Huan-ti (146-67 AC) and from 148 to 168 AC he devoted himself to the task of translating more than 30 Buddhist texts which deal with the practice of meditation and other types of early Buddhist literature. His biographer does not state precisely whether he reached China by the land or the sea route.[5] However, there are certain

[2] See the chapter on Geography in the *Annals of the Former Han Dynasty*.

[3] See the chapter on India in the *Hou-han-shu*.

[4] Fung-ch'eng-chun: *Les moines Chinois et étrangers qui ont contribué a la formation du Tripiṭaka Chinois*, p. 4.

[5] *Kao-seng-chuan*, Ch. 1, Nanjio No. 1490.

indications that possibly he went there by sea. For instance, it is said in his biography that at the end of the reign of Emperor Ling-ti (168-89 AC), on account of disturbance of national uprising, he left Loyang and went to southern China, when he had completed the task of translating Buddhist works. This would mean that he spent most of his time (over 20 years) in northern China. The reason for his lengthy stay at Loyang was that it was the capital of the Han Dynasty. Thus he would get ample assistance from the government to facilitate his task of translation. However, there is a very significant episode presented in the form of a legend in his biography. The gist of the legend is, according to the statement made by An-shih-kao himself, that in his previous birth he had been a Buddhist monk of Parthia. Owing to the effect of *karma* he went to Canton in South China and was slain by a youth there. After his death his "consciousness returned to Parthia and he was born again as the crown-prince to the King of Parthia—and that was the present life of An shih-kao".[6]

The story itself may not carry much weight, but conjoining the places[7] in southern China with which he was closely associated, it would appear that he came to China by the sea route and Canton was probably the port where he disembarked. If we interpret the legend in this way, it would give us some meaning which is probably closer to the truth.

II. *K'ANG-SENG-HUI*

The spread of Buddhism to southern China along the lower Yangtse Valley in the early part of the third century AC chiefly depended on the enthusiasm shown by a few foreign missionaries who had close connection with Central Asia and Indo-China. Among them K'ang-seng-hui's endeavour was unique. His ancestors were of Sogdian origin, but for generations they had been residing in India. Later his father migrated from India to Tonkin in Indo-China (it was called Chiao-chih at that time) for the purpose of trade. During his childhood his parents died and he took the vow of a Buddhist monk in one of the monasteries there. This must have taken place many years before 247 AC (because he reached Nanking in the 10th year of Tz'u-wu, viz., 247 AC of the Wu Kingdom). No mention is made of his voyage from Indo-China to Nanking except for a sentence indicating the direction of his journey: "Taking his monk's staff he travelled towards the East."[8] We presume he took the sea route from Indo-China and reached Nanking via Canton. That is the most convenient and direct route through which one could easily reach South China. Moreover, Canton is in the eastern direction judging by the standpoint of Indo-China.

[6]Ibid.

[7]It is said he converted the deity of the Kung-ting Lake which is situated at the lower Yangtse Valley in modern Chiang-hsi province. Secondly he met the man who had killed him in his previous life at Canton and thirdly it is said, he died an accidental death at Kuei-chi in modern Che-chiang province.

[8]*Kao-seng-chuan*, Ch. 1.

There is the other alternative route via Yunnan, Szechwan, Hupeh and Chianghsi provinces to reach Nanking. This is certainly circuitous and full of obstructions along the route. For instance, during the reign of the second ruler, Hou-chu (223-63 AC) of the Shu Kingdom (in modern Szechwan province), Kung-ming, the prime minister of this kingdom waged war constantly against the native tribes of Yunnan.[9] Under such circumstances, we are not quite sure whether one could pass through Yunnan at that time. It is very unlikely that K'ang-seng-hui ventured himself to take this risky and round-about route instead of the safe and comfortable sea voyage to China.

His contribution to Buddhism in southern China consists of converting Sun-chüan, the founder of the Wu Kingdom (222-51 AC), causing the miraculous power of the relics of the Buddha to be exhibited, thereby he gained a large following, the building of the First Buddhist Monastery (Chien-t' zu-ssu) and stūpa and the establishment of the Buddha's Village (Fo-t'o-li). Hence forward Buddhism was firmly established on the soil of southern China and a large number of people became Buddhists. Comparing this with the early beginning of Buddhism in that area, the contrast is rather shocking. It is said that when he arrived at Nanking in 247 AC, the officials of the Wu Kingdom were suspicious of his strange appearance and the monk's costume. He was officially interrogated and put to inconvenience. The whole trouble lies in the fact that he was the first Buddhist *śramaṇa* to enter that territory in southern China. However, Buddhist works like the *Dhammapada* and *Vimalakīrtti-nirdeśa* were known to a section of the people of the Wu Kingdom at that time, through the effort of Chih-oh'ien, a lay disciple of Yüeh-chi origin. He might have exercised some influence on the intelligentsia, but the credit in showing Buddhism as a popular religion should go to K'ang-seng-hui. Besides, in the existing Chinese Tripiṭaka two works are ascribed to be the translation of K'ang-seng-hui. They are:

1. *Ṣatpāramitā-sannipāta-sūtra.* (Nanjio No. 143)
2. *Saṁyuktāvadāna-sūtra.* (Nanjio No. 1539)

III. DHARMAYAŚAS AND BUDDHABHADRA

A. DHARMAYAŚAS

Among the Kashmirian teachers, who went to China, Dharmayaśas and Buddhabhadra may be said to have set up a record in finding a circuitous way to reach that country. Dharmayaśas was a native of Kashmir and an expert on the Vibhāṣā vinaya of the Sarvāstivādin school. He arrived at Canton in southern China during the period of Lung-an (397-401 AC) of the Eastern Tsin Dynasty. Later he proceeded to Changan in northern China during the I-shü period (405-18 AC), and together with Dharmagupta he translated two works, namely:

[9] *San-kao-chih* or the *Record of the Three Kingdoms*, see the chapter on Shu Kingdom.

1. *Strīvivarta-vyākaraṇa-sūtra.* (Nanjio No. 215)
2. *Śāriputrābhidharma-śāstra.* (Nanjio No. 1268)

His biographer does not state the details of his journey but simply says: "He travelled many well-known countries and passed through a number of kingdoms and districts."[10] As he disembarked at Canton, we presume he must have, first of all, travelled from Kashmir to Bengal and embarked on a ship at Tāmralipti for the South Seas and thence to southern China. This assumption may not be too far from fact if the case of Fa-hsien could be cited. Fa-hsien sailed from Tāmralipti for Ceylon, Java and China sometime in 413 or 414 AC. If 12 years later, the voyage could be easily undertaken by Fa-hsien, it was also possible for Dharmayaśas to have travelled by the same route, it is mentioned in his biography that he returned to the Western Regions (India) during the Yüan-chia period (424-51 AC). This time we are at a loss as to how he returned to India.

B. BUDDHABHADRA

Another interesting route through which an Indian teacher found his way to China has been recorded in the life of Buddhabhadra.[11] This teacher originally belonged to Kapilavastu. Later he went to Kashmir to study *dhyāna* under the guidance of Buddhasena, a renowned *dhyāna* master of Kashmir. He was highly praised by his teacher (Buddhasena) for his mastery in meditation and *vinaya* observance. The arrival of Buddhabhadra in Kashmir must have taken place sometime before 401 AC. This is calculated on the basis that Chih-yen, one of the companions of Fa-hsien, started his journey from China for India in 399 AC. It took him two to three years to reach Kashmir (*c.* 401-02 AC). As Chih-yen was very keen on inviting a renowned teacher to go to China to teach *dhyāna* practices in the proper way, the burden fell on the shoulders of Buddhabhadra, though in the beginning he was rather hesitant to accept the offer. It is in this regard we see how he travelled to Chinaz:

> Having crossed over the Pamirs (Ts'ong-ling, the Onion Ranges), he passed through six countries. The rulers of these kingdoms were sympathetic towards his missionary zeal in going to distant lands. They provided him with abundant requisites. Having reached Chiao-chih (Tonkin), he boarded a ship . . . after sometime he reached the Tung-lai Prefecture of Ch'ing-chow.[12] When he learnt that Kumārajīva was staying at Changan, he immediately proceeded thither to meet him.[13]

If we examine his itinerary carefully, it gives us the impression that Buddhabhadra, who was accompanied by Chih-yen,[14] started his journey from

[10] *Kao-seng-chuan*, Ch. 1.

[11] Ibid., Ch. 2.

[12] Ch'ing-chow was one of the 9 divisions of China under Yu the great. It was situated in the eastern part of the present Shangtung province.

[13] *Kao-seng-chuan*, Ch. 2.

[14] Ibid., Ch. 3, see the "Life of Chih-yen".

Kashmir and followed the trails leading to the Pamirs. When he was on the tracks of Central Asia or Chinese Turkestan, he passed through six countries. The names of these countries are not given. It is quite likely that some of the important places like Kashgar, Yarkand, Khotan, Niya and so forth situated on the southern route leading to the Chinese frontier, should be the kingdoms which he passed through. Otherwise, if he took the northern route along which the ancient kingdoms such as Bharuka near Uch-Tutfan, Kucī (modern Kuchar), Karashar and Turfan[15] were situated, he would have easily reached the north-western frontiers of China, and would not have taken the sea route to reach the Shangtung province in northern China. If our presumption be correct, it poses the problem as to how he travelled from Chinese Turkestan to Chiao-chih (Tonkin) in Indo-China. We have never heard of any Buddhist missionary or pilgrim who had taken that unusual and circuitous route before. As his biographer does not say anything about the journey from Chinese Turkestan to Indo-China, we may suggest that his journey from Central Asia might have covered the territories of Tibet, Assam, Burma, Thailand and Indo-China. This possibility is seen from the fact that the 14th Dalai Lama, who ran away from Lhasa owing to political disturbance, reached Tezpur in Assam in 1959. In the fifth century AC there might have existed foot-paths in the above-mentioned areas which were used by caravans for trading purpose. If that be the case, the possibility of Buddhabhadra's travelling from Chinese Turkestan to Indo-China cannot be ruled out. We must admit, however, that the itinerary of Buddhabhadra is the most strange and unique among the Buddhist missionaries to the Far East.

While at Changan Buddhabhadra met Kumārajīva. The latter was glad to receive him, and on many an occasion consulted him on Buddhist doctrines. As Buddhabhadra devoted himself to the teaching and practice of meditation as well as the observance of the Vinaya rules, his way of life was quite different from that of Kumārajīva It is said that on account of a prophecy made by Buddhabhadra, the disciples of Kumārajīva took advantage of it and expelled him from living among other members of the Saṅgha at Changan.

During his stay in southern China, many Sanskrit texts were translated into Chinese by him. Amongst his translations the *Avataṃsaka-sūtra* (Nanjio No. 87) and the *Mahāsaṅghika-vinaya* (Nanjio No. 1119) are some of the important works which have influenced Buddhism in China to a large extent. He passed away in 429 AC at the age of 71.

IV. GUṆAVARMAN

Among the Kashmirian teachers who took the sea route to China, Guṇavarman achieved greater success as a Buddhist missionary than most of his contemporaries. His missionary zeal took him to propagate Buddhism in the

[15] P.C. Bagchi, *India and China*, pp. 12-14.

countries in South-East Asia and the Far East, although his original plan was not specifically directed towards China. If we accept the statement of his biographer, it appears that he belonged to the ruling family of Kashmir. As he was interested more in the study of Buddhist literature and the practice of meditation he scorned the idea of being made the ruler of Kashmir. To avoid further trouble, he decided to leave Kashmir, and in course of time he reached Ceylon (Siṃhala country). According to the verses composed by himself before his death, we are told that he attained the Sakadāgāmin Fruition at the Ka-po-li (Kapārā or Kāpiri)[16] village in Ceylon. It appears that he lived in Ceylon for a very long time, and his fame as a saint must have spread far and wide, because he said:

> Offerings heaped up in large piles, but I regard them as fire and poison. My mind was greatly distressed, and to get rid of this disturbance I embarked on a ship . . . I went to Java and Champa. Owing to the effect of *karma*, the wind sent me to the territories of the Sung Dynasty (420-479 AC) in China. And in these countries I propagated Buddhism according to my ability. . . .[17]

The few lines quoted above indicate to us the causes and circumstances under which he was forced to carry on his missionary activities. He was essentially a Dhyāna master of the Sarvāstivādin school which was still popular in Kashmir at that time. There is no record available to us now regarding his missionary activities in Ceylon and Champa, but fortunately we have details about his success in Java and China.

Before the arrival of Guṇavarman in Java, the religion in that country was chiefly Brahmanic and there was hardly any influence of Buddhism. This is clearly stated in the Travels of Fa-hsien. We know that Fa-hsien reached Java from Ceylon in 413 or 414 AC. He was of the opinion that the Buddhist religion there was not of sufficient importance worth mentioning. Therefore, it is very likely that Guṇavarman converted P'o-to-chia (Vadhaka?), the King of Java and his mother to Buddhism. In the beginning, both of them received the five precepts from him. However, the king went a step further expressing the wish to his ministers that he intended to renounce the throne and become a member of the Saṅgha. His subjects strongly objected to his intended departure, and entreated him to continue to be their ruler. Finally he yielded to their request, if they could agree to his following conditions:

1. That the people throughout his kingdom should show respect to the venerable Guṇavarman.
2. That all the subjects in his kingdom should completely stop the taking of life of living beings, and

[16] In the eighth century AC there was a Kapārā Parivena (next to the Twin Ponds) in Anuradhapura. See *Epigraphy Zeylanic*, vol. V (part 1). Of course, there is a village Kāpirigama now so called. I am indebted to D.T. Devindra for this piece of information.

[17] *Kao-seng-chuan*, Ch. 3.

3. That the accumulated wealth in the government treasury should be distributed among the sick and the poor.

It is needless to say that the people in Java willingly agreed to all the conditions and received the five precepts from Guṇavarman. Later the king erected a *vihāra* for him. It is said that the king carried timber personally for the construction of the monastery. This indicates the tremendous success of the spread of Buddhism in Java in the early part of the fifth century AC. Naturally the credit goes to Guṇavarman.

His journey from Java to China is also of unusual interest. The news of Guṇavarman's missionary activities in Java reached China sometime before 424 AC. In 424 AC the Chinese Buddhists in Nanking headed by Hui-kuan requested Emperor Wu-ti (424-52 AC) of the Sung Dynasty to write to Guṇavarman and the king of Java (Vadhaka), with the intention of inviting him (Guṇavarman) to China. Later, the Emperor sent Fa-chung and other Buddhist scholars to Java in order to extend the Emperor's invitation to him in person. However, before the arrival of these messengers in Java, Guṇavarman had already left Java by boat and was going to a small country. But fortunately the seasonal wind caused him to reach the shores of Canton in southern China. He stayed at a place called Shih-hsin for quite a long time. It was only in the 8th year of Yüan-chia (431 AC) that he reached Nanking at the repeated request of Emperor Wen-ti. His advice to the Emperor on benevolent government was greatly appreciated by the ruler. Among his propagation activities, he preached the *Saddharmapuṇḍarika-sūtra* and the *Daśabhūmi-sūtra* to a large audience and translated more than ten works of which the following five are still extant:

1. *Upāli-paripṛcchā-sūtra.*	(Nanjio No. 1109)
2. *Upāsaka-pañcaśīlarūpa-sūtra.*	(Do. No. 1114)
3. *Dharmagupta-bhikṣuṇī-karma.*	(Do. No. 1129)
4. *Śrāmaṇera-karmavāca.*	(Do. No. 1164)
5. *Nāgārjuna-bodhisattva-suhrillekha.*	(Do. No. 1464)

Another important contribution of Guṇavarman was the assistance given by him towards the conferment of higher ordination to the *bhikṣuṇīs* in China in accordance with the specifications of the Vinaya. The normal practice is that *bhikṣuṇīs* should receive their Upasampadā ordination from both the *bhikṣu* and the *bhikṣuṇī* Saṅghas. Otherwise it is incomplete. The institution of *bhikṣuṇīs* in China has an early beginning. The Chinese historical annals inform us that towards the end of the fourth century AC the rulers and members of the royal family showed great respect to both the Buddhist *bhikṣus* and *bhikṣuṇīs*. Take for instance, the Queen of Mu-ti (345-61 AC) who built the Yung-an-ssū Nunnery for Bhikṣuṇī Tan-pi,[18] and Emperor Hsiao-wu-ti (373-95 AC) who

[18] See *Pi-chiu-ni-chuan* or the *Biographies of Bhikṣuṇīs*, Nanjio No. 1497.

was a great patron of Bhikṣuṇī Miao-yin,[19] though the latter misused that privilege. This shows that by the middle of the fourth century AC there existed a large number of Buddhist nuns. However, the earliest translation of the Bhikṣuṇī-Prātimokṣa[20] was done by Fa-hsien and Buddhabhadra in 414 AC, and the formal proceeding for the *bhikṣuṇīs* (Dharmagupta Bhikṣuṇī Karman, Nanjio No. 1129) was translated by Guṇavarman himself in 431 AC. This being the case, it is very doubtful that the *bhikṣuṇīs* in China were properly ordained before the arrival of Guṇavarman in 431 AC. Therefore, there arose the necessity (and a request was made to him) that he should help the *bhikṣuṇīs* perform the rites for the higher ordination for the second time. At this juncture there came from Ceylon to the Capital of the Sung Dynasty at Nanking, a batch of eight Sinhalese *bhikṣuṇīs*, with the intention of conferring higher ordination to the Chinese nuns. As their number was less than ten, and some of them had not yet completed the required age after the Upasampadā ordination,[21] Guṇavarman helped them to invite a fresh batch of *bhikṣuṇīs* from Ceylon, the leader of this new delegation was Theri Triśaraṇa.[22] As Guṇavarman was in Ceylon for a long time, he was possibly the most suitable person to do it. He passed away in 432 AC at the age of 65. This sad event took place just before the arrival[23] of the second batch of *bhikṣuṇīs* from Ceylon. He left behind him a verse of 36 stanzas regarding his views on meditation, his attainment and his missionary career.

V. GUṆABHADRA

Guṇabhadra was known as the Mahāyāna in China. He belonged to a brahmin family in Central India. Before his coming to China, he, too, had spent some time in Ceylon and other countries in the South Seas. He reached Canton[24] in 435 AC and was accorded a warm welcome by Emperor Tai-tsu of the Sung Dynasty (420-479 AC) at Nanking. During the period of his voyage from Ceylon to China, he and his companions experienced great difficulty owing to the shortage of drinking water. Fortunately Nature came to their rescue, and they were lucky in getting a shower of rain. This was said to be the effect of his prayer to the merciful Avalokiteśvara Bodhisattva.

He stayed in southern China for 33 years and passed away in 468 AC at the age of 75. He translated more than 20 works pertaining to both the Hīnayānic

[19] Ibid., *The Life of Miao-yin; Tsin-shu*, or *The Annals of the Tsin Dynasty*, see the *Biography of Tao-tze*; also see *T'ang-yung-tung: Han-wei-liang-tsin-nan-pei-ts'ao-fu-chiao-shih*, pp. 349 and 453-4.

[20] See *Bhikṣuṇī-saṅghika-vinaya-prātimokṣa-sūtra*, Nanjio No. 1150.

[21] See *Mahāvagga*, 1, 31, 2-6.

[22] W. Pachow, "Ancient Cultural Relations between Ceylon and China", *University of Ceylon Review*, vol. XII, no. 3, 1954; *Kao-seng-chuan*, Ch. 3.

[23] See the "Life of Saṅghavarman", *Kau-seng-chuan*, Ch. 3.

[24] *Kao-seng-chuan*, Ch. 3.

and Mahāyānic forms of Buddhism. Among his translations the *Srīmālā-devī-Simha-nāda* (Nanjio No. 59) and *Saṁyuktāgama-sūtra* (Nanjio No. 544) are very popular.

VI. SAṄGHAPĀLA AND MANDRA

Both Saṅghapāla and Mandra (or Mandrasena) belonged to Fu-nan or modern Cambodia. They were probably the first Buddhist missionaries to go to China from that country and undertook the work of translation. Naturally they must have gone to China by sea, because it is said in the biography of Saṅghapāla that he reached the Capital (Nanking) of the Ch'i Dynasty (479-502 AC) by ship. While at Nanking he studied the Vaipulya Mahāyāna texts (under Guṇabhadra?).[25] From 506 AC onwards for over 15 years he translated 11 works including the Vimokṣamārga-śāstra (Nanjio No. 1293) which is supposed to be the counterpart of the *Visudhimagga*[26] of Buddhaghoṣa with slight variations. The rest of his works are concerning the Mahāyāna doctrines,[27] although it is stated in his biography[28] that earlier he specialized in the Abhidharmaśāstras. He passed away in 524 AC at the age of 65.

Mandra went to China at the beginning of the Liang Dynasty (502-57 AC). He worked jointly with Saṅghapāla in translating Buddhist texts such as the *Ratnamegha-sūtra* (Nanjio No. 152) *Saptaśatika-prajñāpāramitā* (Nanjio Nos. 23, 46) and so forth. This indicates that Fu-nan at that time was very familiar with Mahāyānic literature. However, his translations were not satisfactory because he did not possess a good knowledge of Chinese.[29]

VII. PARAMĀRTHA

Paramārtha or Guṇaratna was one of the well-known Indian teachers in China who contributed extensively towards the propagation of Mahāyāna Buddhism by translating many important Sanskrit texts into Chinese. However, the way of his going to China, and the several attempts made by him with the intention of returning to India, indicate that originally he had no idea of going to that country; and apparently he was not very happy there.

He belonged to Ujjayinī (Ujjain) of western India and was very enthusiastic in travelling to distant lands to propagate the teaching of the Buddha. It is not very clear as to how he went to Fu-nan (Cambodia) from India, but we know how he went to China from Fu-nan. While he was in Fu-nan, the Emperor Wu-ti of the Liang Dynasty sent Chang-fan, his envoy to Fu-nan, to pay a

[25] As Guṇabhadra died in 468 AC he could not have been able to meet him (Guṇabhadra) in 479 AC at Nanking. It may be that Saṅghapāla was his disciple earlier.

[26] P.V. Bapat, *Vimuttimagga and Visuddhimagga: A Comparative Study*, 1939.

[27] See Nanjio Nos. 22, 308, 353, 442 and 1103, etc.

[28] See *Su-kao-seng-chuan*, Ch. 1.

[29] Ibid.

return visit during the period of Ta-t'ung (535-45 AC). This Emperor also requested[30] the king of that country to collect Mahāyāna texts and invite eminent Buddhist teachers to go to China, so that his envoy would accompany them. Paramārtha was chosen by the king of Fu-nan, and 240 bundles of Buddhist texts were entrusted to him to be taken to China. He arrived at Nan-hai in southern China in 546 AC and two years later he reached Nanking in 548 AC. Owing to the political upheaval in the country, he could not settle down, and had hardly any time to devote himself to the task of translating the Buddhist works into Chinese. He had to move from place to place in the regions of Kianghsi, Nanking and Canton. This upset his plan. Therefore, he was rather disappointed and wanted to seek a more fertile soil for the spread of Buddhism in the South Seas—that is he had the intention of going to Lankasuka (now the northern part of Malaya Peninsula). This happened in 558 AC. However, he was earnestly requested by both the members of the Saṅgha and the laity to stay on in China. Again in 562 AC he embarked on an ocean-going ship at the port of Liangan intending to return to India. This time, he must have felt very happy that he was finally going back to his home land. But unfortunately, unfavourable wind brought his boat back to the port of Canton in southern China. Since then he thought it was useless in trying to escape the effect from one's *karma*, and decided to settle down in China for good. During his 23 years' stay (from 546 to 569 AC) in that country, he translated 64 works of which 29 are still extant.[31] Among his translations the *Madhyānta-vibhāga-śāstra*[32] (Nanjio No. 1248), *Mahāyāna-samparigraha-śāstra* (Nanjio No. 1183), *Mahāyāna-śraddhotpāda-śāstra* (Nanjio No. 1249) and so forth are very popular. It is obvious that most of the Śāstras translated by him formed a nucleus of the Yogācāra doctrine of Asaṅga and Vasubandhu in China, and on the foundation of this, we see the establishment of the Dharmalakṣaṇa school of Hsüan-tsang in seventh century AC.

He passed away in 569 AC at the age of 71.

VIII. PUṆYOPĀYA

Puṇyopāya was known in China as Nadi, the master of Tripiṭaka. He was comparatively less fortunate in his missionary endeavour in that country. He came from central India. Before his arrival in China in 655 AC he had been to the Lanka Mountain (The Adam's Peak) in Ceylon (the Siṁhala country), and visited the countries in the South Seas for the purpose of propagating the Buddhist teaching. While in these regions he heard of the name of China; therefore, he collected over 500 bundles of both Mahāyāna and Hīnayāna texts amounting to 1,500 works. Later, he brought these texts along with him to the capital (Changan) of the T'ang Dynasty. He stayed in the Tz'ū-en-ssū Monastery

[30] *Su-kao-seng-chuan*, Ch. 1.

[31] Ibid.

[32] See Nanjio's Catalogue of the Chinese Buddhist Tripiṭaka, Appendix II, p. 423.

where Hsüan-tsang was engaged in the task of translating Buddhist works at that time. As the glory and fame of Hsüan-tsang at this juncture reached dazzling heights, Puṇyopāya was put into shade. Moreover, they differed greatly in their learning. Hsüan-tsang laid emphasis on Dharmalakṣaṇa or the doctrine of Consciousness while Puṇyopāya followed the traditional teaching of Nāgārjuna and his accent was on Śūnyatā philosophy. To add fuel to this unhappy situation, he was requested by Emperor Kao-tsung in 656 AC to go to the Kunlun regions (or the Pulo Condore Island in the China Sea[33]) to gather some rare medicinal herbs for him. This mission took him seven years to go and return. In 663 AC when he returned to the monastery where he used to stay, he found to his dismay that all the Sanskrit manuscripts he had brought with him were taken by Hsüan-tsang, and at that time the latter was staying in the Yü-hua Palace. Naturally he was at a loss and could not translate any work of importance except some minor texts.[34] Sometime in 663 AC, the king of Chen-la (Cambodia) expressed the wish to the Chinese emperor that they would like to have Puṇyopāya, their old spiritual teacher, to be with them, and the request was duly granted. He went to Cambodia and never returned to China.[35]

IX. VAJRABODHI AND AMOGHAVAJRA

Vajrabodhi and his pupil Amoghavajra were chiefly responsible for the establishment of a separate Esoteric School of Buddhism in China in the early part of eighth century AC. The former belonged to a brahmin family of the Malay region in south India, and his father was the preceptor of the king of Conjeevaram. He studied at the Nālandā University as well as in western India. He was famed for his mastery in the Tripiṭaka and Tantric Buddhism. We have a distinct record of his itinerary. He started his journey from his home town in Malay heading towards the Lanka Mountain (The Adam's Peak) in Ceylon. Later, embarking on an ocean-going ship, he passed through the Nicobar Islands,[36] Śrīvijaya (Palembang) and other countries over 20 in number in the South Seas. Then he proceeded to China and reached Canton in 719 AC. Through his effort many religious performances used to take place, and Tantric Maṇḍalas were made in various regions in China. There are 11 works ascribed to him to be his translations as found in the Catalogue of Nanjio. These texts are chiefly pertaining to the Tantric Dhāraṇīs. He passed away in 732 AC at the age of 71.

Amoghavajra was possibly the most successful disciple of Vajrabodhi. Not only he succeeded him in putting Tantric Buddhism on a firm footing by popularizing it among the members of the royal family and the general public,

[33] Ibid., p. 438.
[34] See Nanjio Nos. 462 and 521.
[35] *Su-kao-seng-chuan*, Ch. 4.
[36] *Sung-kao-seng-chuam*, Ch, 1. Nanjio No. 1495.

but the large number of Tantric texts translated by him, and the mission undertaken by him in search of the Buddhist texts in India and Ceylon should be regarded as an important event in the history of Chinese Buddhism. According to his biographer,[37] he belonged to a brahmin family in northern India, but according to Yüan-chao, author of Chen-yüan-hsin-ting-shih-chiao-mu-lu or a Buddhist Catalogue of the Chen-yuan period (785-804 AC), it is said that his native country was Ceylon, the Simhala country in south India. Probably the former statement is more correct, because Ceylon has never been a part of India in the sense in which we understand the expression, up to the time with which we are dealing. It is stated in his biography that after the demise of his parents, Amoghavajra went to China with his uncle on a visit, and at the age of 15, he became a disciple of Vajrabodhi. This part of his biography is rather complicated. If he were really of a brahmin family, and had nothing to do with trade, what was the purpose of going so far on a tour to the Far East? Granted that was so, then why should he become a Buddhist novice at such an early age ? These are points yet to be answered.

To carry out the wishes of his late teacher, who instructed him to go to India and Ceylon in order to collect more Tantric works, he began his journey in 741 AC with the assistance of Chinese government officials. The route he followed was from Canton to Ceylon via Java (Ho-ling Kalinga), and then from Ceylon to India. On his way to Java, he and his companions encountered with a terrific storm at one stage, and their boat was tossed about in the mountain-like waves caused by a huge whale at another stage. They managed to escape from these dangers unharmed. While in Ceylon he was respected by King Śilāmegha to such an extent that the king himself bathed him with scented water everyday, during his stay in the king's palace.[38] Later, he requested the well-known Sinhalese Tantric master Samantabhadra (P'u-hsien) *ācārya* to perform the ceremony of the two *maṇḍalas*, viz., the Vajradhātu and Garbhadhātu, and initiate him as well as his Chinese disciples into the profound mystery of Tantrism. It is said that he collected over 500 volumes of Sūtras, Śāstras and Tantric texts in the Island of Ceylon. When he completed his work in that country, he proceeded to India, and in 746 AC he returned to China.[39] From that time onwards till his death in 774 AC he engaged himself in the performance of Tantric rites and ceremonies. He was the spiritual teacher to three emperors of the T'ang Dynasty, i.e. Hsüan-tsung, Shu-tsung and Tai-tsung. It was under his influence that the Tantric practices dealing with talismanic forms and the occasional exhibition of supernatural powers gained currency in China.

According to his own statement[40] made in 771 AC he translated 77 works consisting of over 120 fasciculi, but according to the Catalogue of Nanjio there

[37] Ibid.

[38] W. Pachow, "Ancient Cultural Relations between Ceylon and China", *University of Ceylon Review*, vol. XII, no. 3, pp. 184-5.

[39] Nothing has been mentioned about his return trip.

[40] *See Sung-kao-seng-chuan*, Ch. 1.

are 108 works ascribed to him, and they arc extant in most of the editions of the Chinese Tripiṭaka. His translations chiefly deal with Tantras and Dhāraṇīs.

X. PRĀJÑA

This teacher may be regarded as one of the unhappy travellers who went to China by the sea route. He was a native of Kapiśā. He studied the Hīnayāna, Mahāyāna and Tantric literature in northern and southern India and at Nālandā. While he was in south India he learnt that Mañjuśrī Bodhisattva had his abode in China, therefore he decided to embark on a ship sailing for that country. It is said that when he was almost in the vicinity of Canton, an unfavourable wind brought his boat to the east of Ceylon[41] (Simhala Kingdom). No clear indication is given with regard to the actual position of his boat. It may be very doubtful that his boat was close to the shores of Ceylon. It may be that his boat was somewhere close to Indo-China or Cambodia. This is strengthened by the fact that after some time he collected funds and built a large boat, and then he travelled extensively all the countries in the regions of the South Seas. Later, when he was not very far from Canton for the second time, we are told, there arose a sudden storm and his boat was capsized, though he managed to save himself from drowning and salvaged his Sanskrit texts. He reached the city of Canton in 780 AC, and six years later he arrived at Changan in 786 AC. In 792 AC he was under the patronage of Emperor Teh-tsung (779-804 AC) who asked many Chinese Buddhist scholars to help him in his task of translating Sanskrit works.

In Nanjio's Catalogue,[42] there are four translations ascribed to him, amongst which the *Mahāyānabuddhi-ṣatpāramitā-sūtra* is well known.

He passed away at Loyang sometime after 792 AC.

The foregoing passages show some of the more well-known cases of Indian, Central Asian and South-East Asian Buddhist teachers who undertook their journey by the sea route to the South Seas and the Far East, especially China, for the propagation of Buddhism. However, this chiefly deals with those teachers who were connected with translation. A few others like Bodhidharma, who was known as the founder of Zen Buddhism,[43] also went to China by the sea route in 480 AC. He, first of all, reached the territories of the earlier Sung Dynasty (421-79 AC) in southern China, and them proceeded to Loyang and other places in northern China. Similarly, Pan-la-mi-ti (Parāmiti), a teacher from central India went to China by the same route. He reached Canton sometime before 705 AC and stayed at the Chih-chih-ssu Monastery in order to translate the *Śūraṅgama-sūtra* (Nanjio No. 446) into Chinese. Later he

[41] Ibid., Ch. 2.

[42] See Appendix II, p. 447.

[43] W. Pachow, "Zen Buddhism and Bodhidharma," *The Indian Historical Quarterly*, vol. XXXII, 1956.

returned to India by boat. The cases here cover a period of over 600 years from about 150 AC to the end of the eighth century AC. We notice that the sea route leading to India has been very popular, so much so that more than 30 Chinese and Korean monks undertook their journey[44] by this route either to India, Siam or the South Seas. I-tsing tells us that he embarked on a Persian boat from Canton in 671 AC. He stayed for six months in Palembang for learning Sanskrit or the Śabdavidyā, then he passed through Malayu (Sumatra), Kedah, Nicobar Islands and finally reached Tāmralipti in eastern India. On his return journey, he stayed for sometime in Malayu in 689 AC.

All this shows that up to the middle of the eighth century AC, the sea communication between India and China was chiefly monopolised by the Persians or other foreign[45] nationals, and the regions of Malaya, Sumatra and other nearby places were to a large extent influenced by Indian culture through the Indian colonists. Otherwise, I-tsing would not be able to learn Sanskrit at Palembang.

Regarding Buddhism in Java, it was due to the effort of Guṇavarman who introduced the Hīnayānic form of Buddhism into that country in the early part of the fifth century AC. This School of Buddhism must have existed till the end of the seventh century AC. The observation[46] made by I-tsing in this regard is very valuable. He was of the opinion that most of the Islands including Java (Ho-lin), Malayu or Śrīvijaya and Borneo, etc., in the South Seas followed the Mūlasarvāstivādin and Sāṃmitīya Schools. There was not much of Mahāyāna Buddhism there except to a certain extent in Malayu (Sumatra).

However, I-tsing did not mention clearly what form of Buddhism existed in Fu-nan (Cambodia) at that time, as there were no monks in that country on account of the persecution carried out by the evil kings. From the fact that Saṅghapāla and Mandra went to China from Fu-nan in the beginning of the sixth century AC and translated many Mahāyāna texts into Chinese, and later in 546 AC when Paramārtha went to China from Fu-nan, he took with him 240 bundles of Mahāyāna works from that country, it shows that Fu-nan was a strong centre of Mahāyāna literature. Moreover, in 359 AC, the envoy from Fu-nan to the court of the Liang Dynasty (502-57 AC) told the Emperor that in their country there were hairs of the Buddha measuring 12 feet in length.[47]

[44] See I-tsing, *Eminent Buddhist Teachers of the T'ang Dynasty who sought the Dharma in the Western Regions*, Nanjio No. 1491.

[45] It is stated in the Life of Amoghavajra that in 741 AC before his departure for Ceylon, Liu-chu-lin, an important minister summoned I-hsi-pin (Ibrahim?), chief of the foreigners residing at Canton to give instruction to the Captain of the boat by which Amoghavajra was travelling that Amoghavajra should be well-looked after. This would indicate that a large number of foreign merchants and shipping agents, chiefly from Persia or Arab, were in the ports of China. See *Sung-kao-seng-chuan*, Ch. I.

[46] Cf. J. Takakusu, *A Record of the Buddhist Religion as Practised in India and Malaya Archipelago*, Ch. 1.

[47] See *Liang-shu*, or *The Annals of the Liang Dynasty*, the chapter on Fu-nan.

All this indicates that Buddhism in Fu-nan (Cambodia) in the early part of the sixth century AC was chiefly Mahāyānic and the Buddhist texts were in Sanskrit. Till then, the influence of Pāli Buddhism had not yet reached.

Thus, the voyage of Buddhist missions to South-East Asian countries and to China gives us valuable evidence of the historical development of Buddhism in those regions. Further, it provides us with specific instances of the cultural relations of these countries between China on the one hand, and India on the other.

CHAPTER 13

Indian Colonisation in Sumatra before the Seventh Century

J. PRZYLUSKI

"It is almost a current opinion" says Ferrand, "that Java has been the focus and centre of the expansion of Indian civilisation in Indonesia. It seems, on the contrary, that we should give the credit of this expansion to the Sumatran empire of Śrīvijaya."[1] As Ferrand[2] has suggested, we may distinguish in the history of Sumatra an early period anterior, to the progress of the kingdom of Śrīvijaya. This period extends from the beginning of the Christian era to the year 644, the date of the sending of the first embassy to the court of China from the Sumatran country of Malayu. It is with this ancient period that we are now concerned.

* * *

Before the seventh century, the interpretation of texts is impeded by the inaccuracy of geographic nomenclature.

The Chinese pilgrim Fa-hien, on his return from India, by way of Ceylon, arrived at a country which he calls *Ye-p'o-t'i*, that is to say Yavadvīpa. The *Rāmāyaṇa* also mentions Yavadvīpa of which Ptolemy makes *Iabadiu*. What is the value of this geographical name?

The majority of authors, Kern, Sylvain Lévi and others, admit that Yavadvīpa designates the island of Java. Ferrand makes the objection that the Yavadvīpa of Indian literature and the Iabadiu of Ptolemy have this common characteristic of being a country rich in gold, a characteristic of Sumatra, not of Java. Ferrand, therefore, concludes that Yavadvīpa designates Sumatra, not Java.[3]

Other authors are less positive. With regard to the *Ye-p'o-t'i* of Fa-hien, Beal gives the definition "Java or, perhaps, Sumatra". In AD 132, the king of a country which is called in Chinese *Ye-tiao* (ancient pronunciation **Yap-div*) sent an embassy to the court of China. M. Pelliot, who has recognised in **Yap-*

[1]G. Ferrand, *L'Empire sumatranais de Śrīvijaya*, p. 3, *Bibliographie*, pp. 1-2. The historical importance of the empire of Śrīvijaya has been discovered by Coedès; cf. "Le royaume de Śrīvijaya", *BEFEO*, t. XVIII, no. 6.

[2]Ibid., p. 145.

[3]Ibid., p. 153.

Source: *Journal of the Greater India Society* (I/2, 1934, 92–101).

div the name Yavadvīpa, nevertheless observes: "In proposing to find Yavadvīpa in *Ye-tiao*, I naturally do not wish to say that I feel obliged to see in it Java rather than Sumatra; for me it corresponds to the name given by Ptolemy and that is all."[4] This prudence is justified. The most ancient travellers did not make a clear distinction between the islands of Java and Sumatra. These two great islands formed the continent of Yava, either because the strait which separates them was for a long time ignored, or because no great importance was attached to it. For us, New Zealand is a whole although it is composed of two islands. We are not at liberty to affirm either with Kern that Yava is Java or with Ferrand that Yava is not Java but Sumatra. Probably for Ptolemy and for all the ancient geographers Yava is Java-Sumatra.

The persistence of this ancient notion explains the fact that during the Middle Ages, when Java and Sumatra were no longer confused, they were still given the same name. For Marco Polo and later geographers that which we call Java is Java Minor, while Sumatra is Java Major. The ancient Yava has become an archipelago.

* * *

In the accounts of Arabian travellers Šumutra or Sumutra designates a port, a kingdom or the island of Sumatra as a whole.[5] In a panegyric in Old Javanese with the date of AD 1365 entitled Nāgarakṛtāgama, the country which the Arabs called Sumutra and which is found on the north-east coast of the island, is called Samudra.[6] It seems at first sight that Sumatra, Sumutra may be corruptions of Samudra, a Sanskrit word which means "ocean", and this is the opinion of a certain number of authors. "That Samudra, Sumatra signifies the island of the ocean" says Rouffaer[7] "and is to be identified with the city of Samudra on the river of Pasei on the Eastern coast of Ačeh, is a fact which is accepted by almost everyone." But G. Ferrand has objected that it has not been proved that a definite island has been called **Samudradvīpa*, "island of the sea", nor has this strange toponym designated the whole island or the northern part of Sumatra.[8]

The question has been brought up again by Rouffaer with regard to a king of San-fo-ts'i, designated in Chinese by *Hia-teh'e Sou-wou-teh'a-p'ou-mi* (*Hağı Sumatrabhūmi). The Dutch scholar explains this title as follows: "a King of the country of *Samudra*, that is of the country of the *sea*, that is of the country of *Tasik* (in Malay "sea"), Tĕmasik, Tumasik (forms with an infix of Tasik), otherwise said of the island of Singapore."[9] But G. Ferrand has persisted in his objection:

[4]"Deux itinéraires de Chine en Inde à la fin da VIIIme siècle", *BEFEO*, t. IV, p. 258, n. 2.

[5]Ferrand, op. cit., pp. 80-1, 91-5.

[6]Canto 13, p. 50; cf. canto 41, p. 105 and canto 42, p. 107.

[7]Ferrand, op. cit., p. 19, n. 3.

[8]*Bijdragen t. T. L. en Volkenkunde v. Nederlansh-Indië*, deel 74, 1918, p. 138.

[9]*Bijdragen t. T. L. en* V. deel 77, p. 75.

"How can the island of Singapore" he asks, be called "country of the ocean" ? This toponym is as impossible as the preceding one: a definite island can no more be called "Ocean" than "Land of the ocean", especially when "ocean" is applied to the north-east of Sumatra and "Land of the ocean" to the island of Singapore.[10]

The objection of G. Ferrand is not perhaps decisive. The 213th and 463rd stories of the Pali *Jātaka* begin with these words: "Formerly King Bharu reigned in the kingdom of Bharu". Now *bharu* is a word which signifies "sea" and the same word is contained in the name of the city and of the region of Bharukaccha. It is then not impossible that an Indian word signifying "sea, ocean" may have been used to designate a city, a kingdom and by extension a large island. Upon a closer investigation, the conjecture appears more probable.

I have shown elsewhere that *bharu* is an Indian word of non-Aryan origin and that it should be connected with the Malay *baroh* "low ground, sea-coast, sea".[11] In the dialects of the Malay Peninsula we find *baruh* "plain, fiat country", *baruk, barok* "shore" and *bâruh* "sea". The same name is found frequently in the geographic nomenclature of the Malay country. We read in the "Journey of the Arab merchant Sulayman in India and in China", written in 851: "From Langabâlûs (Nicobar islands), the ships then sail to come to a place called Kalâh-bâr (the port of Krah on the Malay Peninsula). This same name *bar* is given to both a kingdom and a sea-coast."[12] It is then no exaggeration to seek in a form *bâruh*, *bâr* the equivalent of the Indian kingdom of Bharu.

We may now explain the mention in the *Nāgarakṛtāgama* of a country called Samudra situated on the north-east coast of Sumatra. Samudra is probably the Sanskrit translation of a local name signifying "sea". We suppose that this name may have been extended to the whole island and, as foreign names are often deformed when they pass from one language to another, Samudra might easily have been pronounced *Sumadra, Sumatra, Sumutra by the Chinese and Arabian navigators.

In short, Yavadīpa designed primarily Java-Sumatra. When they wished to distinguish between the two islands, they called the one where they first reached land by the name of one of its ports situated in the north "To go to Samudra" meant that they went to the larger island in opposition to the smaller one which alone kept the name of Java.

* * *

In the Chinese history of the Ming dynasty, the account of the San-fo-ts'i begins as follows:

[10] *L'empire sumatranaits de Śrīvijaya*, p. 19, n. 3.
[11] *Bulletin de la Société de Linguistique*, XXX, fasc. 2, pp. 197 seq.
[12] Tr. G. Ferrand, in *Les Claasiques de l'Orient*, p. 41.

San-fo-ts'i formerly called Kan-t'o-li, for the first time sent envoys with tribute in the reign of the emperor Hiao-Wou of the former Song dynasty (454-464); during the reign of the emperor Wou of the Liang dynasty (502-549) they came repeatedly and in the time of the second Song dynasty (960-1279) they brought tribute without interruption.[13]

The Chinese history of the Liang dynasty provides the following facts concerning the Sumatran country of *Kan-t'o-li*.[14]

The country of *Kan-t'o-li* is situated on an island in the southern sea; its customs and manners are about the same as those of Fou-nan and Lin-yi. It produces cloth of variegated colours, cotton and areca-nuts, these last being of excellent quality and better than those of any other country.

In the reign of the emperor Hiao-Wou of the Song dynasty (454-464), the king of the country, *Che-p'o-lo-na-lien-t'o* (Śrīvara-narendra) sent a high official of the name *Tchou Lieou-t'o* (Rudra, the Indian), to present valuable articles of gold and silver.

In the year 502, the king *K'iu-ian Sieou-po-t'o-lo* (Gautama Subhadra) dreamt on the eighth day of the fourth month that he saw a Buddhist priest who said to him: "China has now a holy ruler and after ten years more the law of Buddha will greatly increase; if you send messengers to carry tribute and show your reverence, your country will be prosperous and happy, and the foreign merchants will visit it in numbers increased a hundred-fold. If you do not believe what I say, your country will not enjoy peace." The Icing, at first, could not believe this, but some time afterwards he saw again the priest in a dream, saying to him: "As you do not believe me, I must bring you there and make you see the Emperor." He then went to China in his dream and had an audience with the emperor. When he awoke he was greatly astonished, and as he was a skilful painter, he made a picture of the emperor's face as he had seen it in his dream, adorning it with various colours. He then sent an envoy, accompanied by a painter, to carry a letter to the emperor and present precious stones and other things. When the envoys had arrived, they made a picture of the emperor which they took home to their country and, comparing it with the original drawing, it was found to be exactly the same. The king now mounted this picture on a precious frame and honoured it more and more every day.

Some time after the king died and his son *P'i-ye-po-mo* (Vijayavarman ?) came to the throne. In 519 he sent a high official, called Pi-yuan-po-mo (Vi . . . varman) to present a letter of the following contents: "To the ever victorious emperor. . . ."

In the year 520 the same king sent again an envoy to present as tribute products of his country.

This text reveals that in the middle of the sixth century that part of Sumatra which the History of the Liang calls *Kan-t'o-li*, was ruled by a king who bore a Sanskrit name. This fact alone proves clearly that the Indian civilisation had been implanted in this country.

As for the religion which was there in practice, an examination of proper names will give us some information. The name of the royal envoy *Tchou Lieou-t'o*, Rudra, the Indian, seems to show that the king favoured Śivaite religion, while the name of the king, his successor, Gautama Subhadra, is

[13] Cf. Groeneveldt, *Notes on the Malay Archipelago and Malacca*, p. 68; G. Ferrand, *Śrīvijaya*, p. 24.

[14] Cf. Groeneveldt, ibid., pp. 60 seq., corrected by Pelliot, *Deux itinéraires*, p. 187, n. 4 and p. 392 and by Ferrand, *Śrīvijaya*, pp. 264-5.

rather inspired by Buddhism. Buddhism then must have made great progress at the court of *Kan-t'o-li* towards the beginning of the sixth century.

This conclusion is confirmed by the History of the Liang which, in a story legendary but not without significance, shows us the king of *Kan-t'o-li* receiving in a dream the visit of a Buddhist monk. In the Chinese version, this legend was evidently intended to flatter and glorify the emperor of China and Ma Touan-lin himself was already aware of this purpose.[15] But this story is related to a series of other stories where we find a king being converted to Buddhism under similar conditions. According to an erroneous tradition which has been widely spread in China, Buddhism was introduced into that country by the emperor Ming of the second Han dynasty as the consequence of a dream where this sovereign beheld a supernatural apparition. The emperor then despatched an embassy charged to bring back some Buddhist monks.[16]

The biography of Guṇavarman contains a similar episode: "This religious man belonged to the royal family of Ki-pin (Cashmere). When he was thirty years old, the king of Cashmere having died without children, they wished to put him on the throne, but he refused and left for Ceylon, where he dwelt in a village called *Kie-po-li*. Then he went into the kingdom of *Chö-p'o*. The night before his arrival, the mother of the king saw in a dream a religious man who entered the kingdom upon a flying junk. In the morning Guṇavarman arrived, and the queen-mother, convinced by her dream, was converted to Buddhism. She exerted her influence over her son so that he should imitate her; she succeeded in persuading him. The kingdom having been invaded by enemies, the king asked Guṇavarman if it was not contrary to the law of religion to strive against them; Guṇavarman replied that it was a duty ro chastise brigands; the king, therefore, started off to fight and won a victory. Little by little Buddhism spread throughout the kingdom, and the king who wished to enter the religious life, would not renounce his project at the entreaties of his ministers, except upon the condition that throughout the whole kingdom no one should be put to death. The renown of Guṇavarman spread far and wide; in 424, Chinese monks requested the emperor to invite Guṇavarman to come to China; messengers for this purpose were sent to Guṇavarman and to the king of *Chö-p'o*, *p'o-to-kia*. At that moment Guṇavarman embarked or had embarked in order to go to Lin-yi (Champa) in the ship of the merchant. Tchou Nan-ti (Nandin the Indian); when the wind was favourable, he arrived at Canton. He reached Nankin in 431 and must have died a few months later, at the age, as the Chinese reckon, of 65 years.[17]

When the biographer of Guṇavarman speaks of Chö-p'o, it is impossible to know exactly what part of Yavadvīpa he has in mind. Let us only notice the analogy of these pious stories intended to explain retrospectively the introduction of Buddhism in China, in *Chö-p'o* and in *Kan-t'o-li*.

[15] Cf. *Wen hien t'ong k'ao*, tr. Hervey de Saint-Denys. *Méridionaux*, pp. 451-4.
[16] H. Maspero, "Le songe et l'ambassade de l'empereur Ming", *BEFEO*, 1910, p. 95.
[17] Pelliot, *Deux itinéraires*, pp. 264-5.

Without exaggerating the chronological accuracy of these stories, we may, thanks to them, follow the progress of Buddhism. In 413, Fa-hien finds in Yavadvīpa so few Buddhists "that it is not worth while to mention them".[18] A little later, Guṇavarman converts the queen-mother of the "kingdom of *Chö-p'o*". In the beginning of the sixth century, the king of *Kan-t'o-li* was converted. Finally when, in 671-2, the pilgrim Yi-tsing stops at Śrīvijaya, he is amazed at the number and at the learning of the Buddhist priests, studies the "science of sounds", and advises his compatriots who may wish to travel to India to make in Śrīvijaya a sojourn of a year or two, in order to prepare themselves there to read the original Buddhist texts.[19]

In short, it is probably between 414 and the first decades of the sixth century that Buddhism spread through the principal states of Indonesia. And it is at this same period that Buddhism made a decisive progress in China under the Wei and the Liang. The sixth century is a great period in the history of the expansion of Indian ideas and of the intercourse by sea between the peoples of Asia.

What is exactly the country that the History of the Liang calls *Kan-t'o-li?* The History of the Ming identifies this kingdom with that of Palembang, at the south-east of Sumatra. But this identification may not be accepted without proof.

Kan-t'o-li seems to be the Chinese transcription of an original **Kandarī* or **Kandali*. Now M. Ferrand has drawn our attention to a passage of the *Ḥāwiya* of Ibn Majīd, with the date of 1462, where the port of Šinkel on the north-east coast of Sumatra is called *Šinkil Kandārī*. According to M. Ferrand this expression must mean Sinkel of the country of Kandār, or Sinkel (of the country of) Kandārī, and Kandārī would designate the whole island of Sumatra.[20]

But as there is no proof that the large island was ever called by this name, we may be sceptical as to the possibility of reaching a final decision.

Let us consider *Kan-t'o-li* from another point of view. These three syllables may transcribe an original **Kandālī*. Now in Sanskrit *Kandalī* or *Kadalī* is the name of the banana tree. We know that in India, Indo-China and especially in Indonesia many names of places and of peoples have been borrowed from the local flora.[21] *Kandalī* might be a name in the same category as *malaka*, *madjapahit*, etc.

Let us not conclude too hastily that *Kandalī* is the Sanskrit translation of a Malay word such as *pisang*, "banana tree". I have shown elsewhere that *Kadalī*, *Kandalī* are not originally Aryan words, but have been borrowed from the

[18] Legge, *Fa-hien*, p. 113.

[19] Takakusu, *Record*, pp. XXXIV and XL-XLI.

[20] "Le K'ouen-louen", *JA*, 1919, pp. 266-7 of the reprint.

[21] Cf. Ferrand, "Malaka, le Malāyu el Malāyur", *JA*, 1918, p. 156 of the reprint; and cf. *Notes on Name of Places in the Island of Singapore and its Vicinity* (*Journal of the Straits Branch of the RAS*, n. 50. pp. 76-82).

non-Aryan languages of India.[22] Just as in the Malay Peninsula, we find beside the Malay *pisang*, the Sakai or Semang names of the banana tree, such as *kelui*, *kle*, *telui*, etc., so in the island of Sumatra, in the fifth century, the banana tree may have had a variety of names, and it is not impossible that the Chinese *kan-t'o-li* is the transcription of an indigenous word.

This conjecture has at least the advantage of explaining the rapid disappearance of the name that the Chinese chroniclers have written *Kan-t'o-li*. If *Kandalī* was originally the indigenous name of a great kingdom, it was doomed to disappear before a nobler form such as Śrīvijaya or Samudra.

[22] Cf. *Pre-Aryan and Pre-Dravidian in India*, pp. 4-5.

CHAPTER 14

The Terminal Stūpa of the Barabudur

J. PRZYLUSKI

Stutterheim's researches, continued by M. Mus, have brought to light the analogies which exist between the Barabudur, the mountain-temple of the Indian Cakravartin, and the Assyro-babylonian *ziqqurrat*. I have endeavoured recently to lend more precision to these analogies, and showed that all those monuments consist of three parts: the tower of Babylon had a subterranean base, seven stories, and a shrine on its top. Likewise, mount Meru, the prototype of the mountain-temple, has an invisible base surmounted by the mountain, which, in its turn, is crowned by the palace of the gods. Again, the Barabudur has a base concealed by a facing of masonry, seven terraces and a terminal *stūpa*.[1] The question which I would now like to examine is the following: which was the deity worshipped in the terminal stūpa of the Barabudur?

Theoretically, there is scarcely any doubt about the answer. On the summit of the cosmic mountain sits the king of the gods. The Cakravartin's palace is the image of the god's palace. The Barabudur, being both the cosmic and the royal mountain, the personage who sits on its top must be the summit of the religious and of the political hierarchy. Thus he must be at the same time the Cakravartin-Buddha, and the king Cakravartin. We shall see that these politico-religious ideas, having spread to the distant boundaries of the Buddhist world, were given in the empire of the Śailendras, a special character.

Several Buddhist *sūtras*, translated into Chinese, bear a title which corresponds to *Brahmajāla-sūtra*. Here is the full title of one of them: "Part ten of the *Brahmajāla-sūtra* where the Buddha Vairocana declares the *cittabhūmi* and the *śīla* of a Bodhisattva". This text belongs to the Vinaya category and has been partly edited and translated by De Groot in 1893.[2] We will call it by its Japanese tide: "*Bommōkyō*". It was profoundly venerated in Japan. In AD 753, the *Bommōkyō* was read in all the more important temples.

[1]"Lei sept terrasses du Barabudur", article in the press in *HJAS* (*Harvard Journal of Asiatic Studies*).

[2]De Groot, "Le Code du Mahāyāna en Chine", in the *Verhand. der Konink. Akad. van Wetentch.*, Amsterdam, 1893; James R. Ware, "Notes on the Fan Wang Ching", *HJAS*, I, 1, pp. 156-61; for a bibliography of the Japanese studies about this text, cf. S. Elisseeff, "The Bommōkyō and the Great Buddha of Tōdaiji", *HJAS*, I, 1, p. 84, n. 3.

Source: *Journal of the Greater India Society* (III/2, 1936, 158–69).

"*Bommōkyō* doctrines," writes S. Elisaeeff, "as well as Buddhist concepts in general profoundly influenced the political ideas of the Emperor Shōmu. This Japanese sovereign felt that the government should be organised in conformity with this Buddhist text, where it is said that Locana produces one thousand great Śākya, who are in their *nirmāṇa-kāya*; from each of these Śākyas come forth millions of small Śākyas, who simultaneously are preaching in all the millions of worlds. In this same way the Emperor occupies in Japan die supreme rank, corresponding to Locana Buddha; the Imperial will is transmitted to the thousand officials, who in the government organisation can be considered representatives of the Emperor, as the thousand great Śākyas are of Locana. The subjects are compared to the millions of small Śākyas. That the Emperor Shōmu identified himself with the central deity is revealed by the fact that after the *Śīla-samādāna* ceremony he took the Buddhist name Joman which is nothing other than the Chinese translation of the Sanskrit name Locana. It was this sovereign who erected the Great Buddha and thus represented in sculpture a passage from the *Bommōkyō*.

The casting of such a huge statue presented many technical difficulties and the statuaries succeeded in their work only after eight attempts. It was finished in 749, but was not yet gilded. The Japanese authorities were anxious to find the precious metal in Japan itself in order to gild this great statue with national gold. At the beginning of the year 749 gold had been discovered in northern Japan. The Emperor Shōmu was extremely glad of this event and in the fourth month went to Tōdaiji accompanied by his family and many officials. This same year the Emperor Shōmu abdicated in order to devote himself to Buddhism.

. . . The Great Buddha is the Great Enlightened; he is the essence of Buddha in the Dharmadhātu (world).

. . . The text of the Bommōkyō says: 'You, all Buddha's children, hear me attentively; think well (about my words) and make your conduct conform to it. I have practised already for hundreds of incomputable *kalpas* the qualities (of bodhisattvas) and the stages (of perfection), and taken them as my guide. At the beginning I abandoned the worldly (life) and attained *samyak-sambodhi*. I am called Locana. I dwell on the lotus throne which contains the worlds and oceans. [The grammar of this passage is obscure, but the Japanese engraver has understood it thus.] This throne is surrounded by one thousand petals. Each petal being a world, it makes one thousand worlds. I metamorphose myself producing one thousand Śākyas, conforming to the one thousand worlds. Further, on each petal which is a world there are a hundred million Sumerus, a hundred million suns and moons, a hundred million worlds each in four parts, a hundred million Jambudvīpas, a hundred million Bodhisattva-Śākyas, who are sitting under a hundred million *bodhi* trees, each of them preaching the qualities and stages of a Bodhisattva about which you have just inquired. Each Śākya of the remaining nine hundred and ninety-nine Śākyas produces thousands and hundreds of millions of Śākyas, who do the same. The Buddhas on the thousand petals are transformations of myself, and thousands and hundreds of millions of Śākyas are the transformations of these thousand Śākyas. I am their origin and my name is Locana Buddha.

This great Buddha in the Tōdaiji is represented sitting on a lotus throne. On each petal of the lotus flower is represented one of the thousand great Śākyas who are the emanations of Locana.

On the upper part of the petal is engraved the picture of the Great Śākya, who is sitting on a throne and preaching. Under his throne is represented the Grand Chiliocosm. The engraver has depicted the *arūpyadhātu*, the *rūpadhātu* and the *kāmadhātu*. In the lowest part of the petal is engraved the Sumeru world with mount Sumeru in the middle. This mountain has four terraces. On the bottom of the petal is engraved a sea. The statue of the Great Buddha was inspired by the passage translated above from the *Bommōkyō*, the details on the petals, inspired by other *sūtras* and *śāstras*, are there to show the relation of the whole world from here below up to the Great Enlightened Deity.[3]

The whole monument proves that an exact symmetry reigned between the state organisation and the religious cosmology in the Japanese Buddhism of the eighth century. The two organisations are correlative and this is why the emperor identifies himself with the central deity, taking the name of Locana.

In *Weltbild und Bauform Sudostasiens*, M. von. Heinegeldern has noted the application of similar principles in the Indo-Chinese and Indonesian kingdoms. The Burmese look upon the *prāsāda* which roofs the throne-room at Mandalay as the centre of the world. It is to imitate Indra that the Indonesian and Indo-Chinese kings had 32 vassals, and it is probably in view of an assimilation with Sudarśana, the city of the gods, that the capital of the kingdom was sometimes provided with 32 doors which corresponded to the 32 divisions of the kingdom. As a matter of fact, the *Glass Palace-Chronicle of the Kings of Burma* says that the city of Śrīkṣetra has been drawn by Indra after the model of Sudarśana.[4] In Burma, the king and his 32 vassals identify themselves with Indra, chief of the group of the 33 gods, just as in Japan the emperor, surrounded by his dignitaries, identifies himself with Locana in the middle of the 1.000 Great Śākyas.

The Chinese messenger Tcheou Ta-kouan, speaking of the Bayon which is in the centre of Angkor, the capital of the old Cambodia, said: "To mark the centre of the kingdom there is a gold tower, surrounded by more than twenty stone towers."[5] The Bayon, then, must have been, to use Heinegeldern's own expression, the magical centre of the kingdom." Erected in the centre of Angkor, this temple is made of some 50 towers, linked together by galleries. Each tower bears, looking towards each point of the compass, four big stone faces crowned by diadems. In the ground of the big tower, the idol which was worshipped in the centre of the Bayon, has been found: a Buddha 3 m high, in which M. Çoedés recognises the image of the Devarāja, that is to say, of the God-King. In the Śaivite sanctuaries, the Devarāja was the great *liṅga* of the kingdom; worshipped in the central temple of the capital, he personified both the king of the gods and the king of men. In the Bayon, the central temple of Angkor, the Devarāja is personified by the great statue of the Buddha, venerated in the

[3] S. Elisseeff, "The Bommōkyō and the Great Buddha of Tōdaiji", *HJAS*, I, 1, pp. 88-95.

[4] Pe Maung Tin and Luce, *Glass Palace Chronicle*, Oxford, 1932, pp. 14-15; Heine-Geldern, *Weltbild and Bauform*, pp. 45 ff. P. Mus, "Barabudur", *BEFEO*, 33, pp. 701ff.

[5] P. Pelliot, "Mémoire sur les coutumes da Cambodge", *BEFEO*, 2, p. 142.

great central tower. In this image, both the Great Enlightened and the sovereign of Cambodia are represented. As to the stone faces which adorn the 50 towers, epigraphy tells us that they stand for a whole pantheon of deities, Brahmanical as well as Buddhist: Viṣṇu, Śiva, Pārvatī, the Medicine Buddha, the Lion of the Śākyas.[6]

In a recent communication to the Academy of Inscriptions, M.P. Mus, having exposed those facts, proposed a clever explanation for them. "Four faces," says M. Mus, "resume space entirely because they mark the four principal directions…", "Brahmā does not possess four heads, his face is just one and it can be seen from everywhere. Four orients are the whole of space. Four faces are the symbol of a power which reigns over space." And M. Mus adds that the Great Buddhist Miracle proceeds in a large way from similar ideas. He quotes a part of the *Avataṃsaka-sūtra* where the Buddha of the Great Miracle is compared to Brahmā. "He is like the Great King Brahmā, who rests in his palace of the Brahma world, whilst everywhere, in the numberless thousands of worlds, bodies of Brahmā can yet be seen."[7]

M. Mus concludes that when the architect represented a four-faced personage on the Bayon towers, he wanted to figure "the royal power blessing the four orients of the country". But why, then, this multiplicity of gods who are worshipped in the Bayon towers? We know that Jayavarman VII, who built the temple,

> bore a special reverence to the Bodhisattva Lokeśvara, *alias* Avalokiteśvara. Now, the *Lotus of the Good Law*, a fundamental text, endows this personage with a faculty to assume all kinds of shapes, so that he may gather knowledge and save the creatures. He shall borrow, whenever it is useful, the features of a Buddha. But there is a particle of Truth, a primitive impulse towards Good in every cult, and Avalokiteśvara shall be, according to his will, either a great or a middle or a small Brahmanic god. . . . Appearing to each man under the exact shape of the god whom he worships and One, however, under this diversity, does not Lokeśvara deserve fully the name of *Samantamukha*, 'face everywhere', given to him by the book, and which is inspired by the power formerly ascribed to Brahmā?. . . It is because he has a part in the *dharmakāya* that Lokeśvara enjoys his transcendental powers. Jayavarman wants to associate with him. Together with Lokeśvara, in Lokeśvara, in every place where his subjects adore a god, at Vajrapura, at Chok Gargyar, the king is this god. In the whole universe, Lokeśvara—over entire Cambodia, Jayavarman—the Bodhisattva and the king are equally 'face everywhere'. And if the monument, by the disposition of its shrines, is like a positive map of the country, it is only to the scope of illustrating, and perhaps of contributing to assure magically, the penetration of the king's subtle essence all over the kingdom.[8]

These conclusions are illuminating. One point only is open to a slight criticism. If Lokeśvara assumes the shape of a Brahmanical god as well as

[6] G. Çoedès, "Notice archèologique du Bayon", in Dufour-Carpeaux, *Le Bayon d'Angkor-Thom*, Paris, 1914, t. II, p. 30.

[7] *Taissho Issaikyo*, no. 278, vol. IX, p. 618b.

[8] P. Mus, *Le symbolism à Angkor-Thom: le "Grand Miracle" da Bayon, in Compte rendu de l'Académie des Inscriptions et Belles Lettres*, sitting of 21 February 1936.

that of a Buddha, it is not because "there is a particle of truth" in the Brahmanic, religion as in the Buddhist, but rather because Indian gods are Brahmanic and Buddhist at the same time. In all periods, and more particularly in that of the Mahāyāna, Buddhism is a syncretism where the Brahmanic mythology comes in for an important part. This is why Lokeśvara, who has so many points in common with Śiva, is the king of the gods like him, or rather each god is just another shape of Śiva-Lokeśvara.

We are, now, in a much better position to understand the Buddhalogy of the Barabudur, because the religion which finds its expression in this monument, is also a syncretism where Śaivaism and Mahāyānistic Buddhism are mingled together. The three upper terraces of the Barabudur bear, as we have said, 72 small stūpas, with a 73rd and bigger stūpa in the middle. The identities of the personages carved in these stūpas have been much discussed. According to Krom, above the five Dhyānī-buddhas which are seen on the square terraces, it is their chief, Vajrasattva = Vajradhara, who was worshipped in the stūpa of the circular terraces. This opinion has been criticised by M. Mus. The latter objects that Vajrasattva, the chief of the five Dhyānī-buddhas, does not appear in the older layer of the redaction of the *Sang hyang Kamahāyānikan*. He comes in the more recent layer of this treatise only, and not, even then, as a sixth Dhyānī-buddha, but as a substitute for Akṣobhya.[9] Besides, M. Toganoo believes that the Buddha of the terminal *stūpa* of the Barabudur is Akṣobhya, and for him the *Buddhas* of the 72 small stūpas are Vairocana, and the symbols of the 72 tāntric *guṇas*.[10]

Does it seem possible to offer a solution which would comply with the suggestions and the criticisms of the three archaeologists? We must not forget that there is a close link between Akṣobhya and Vajrasattva: on the crown worn by the latter, there is a face of Akṣobhya. Vajrasattva is one of the shapes of Akṣobhya: he is Akṣobhya in his *saṃbhogakāya*.[11] It will no doubt be admitted that the Buddha of the terminal stūpa, like the Great Buddha of Tōdaiji, is the Great Enlightened, the essence of the Dharmadhātu, prefiguration of the Ādibuddha of Nepal. Under what name was he venerated at the Barabudur? He may have been known as Akṣobhya by some of the faithful. If the terminal stūpa contained Akṣobhya in his *dharmakāya*, the Buddha of the 72 smaller stūpas would be Akṣobhya in his *saṃbhogakāya*.

The names of the personages, however, are here of minor consequence. The main point is to admit that the Buddhas of the 72 small stūpas are the manifestations of the same essence which has its symbol in the Buddha of the terminal stūpa. And this brings us back to the symbolism of the Tōdaiji and of the Bayon, but at the Barabudur, the symbolism is more complex and announces already the Ādibuddha system of Nepal, for at Barabudur the essence of the *dharmadhātu* is shown under three hypostasis: the Buddha of the terminal

[9] Ibid., pp. 350-1.
[10] See Report by M. Demieville in *Bibliographie bouddhique* V, no. 450.
[11] P. Mus, op. cit., p. 351.

stūpa, the Buddha of the 72 small *stūpas* and those of the square terraces. These three hypostasis remind us not only of the three *kāyas* of the Buddha, but not the system of Nepal also: Ādibuddha, Dhyānī-buddha, Mānusi-buddha.

Before we proceed any further in our study of the similitudes between the several systems, it is necessary to examine an evident difference. At the Tōdaiji, the Great Śākyas which surround the central Buddha are 1,000 in number. In Burma, the number which defines the royal and divine court is 33 (1 + 32). At the Bayon, there are some 50 towers. At Barabudur, the symbolical number is 73 (1 + 72).

For Toganoo, this last number is explained by the fact that there are 72 tāntric *guṇas*. But this number may also have been suggested by iconography, or in regard to architectural symmetry. Two explanations offer themselves, not at all irreconcilable.

The three circular terraces of the Barabudur may be seen from four sides, as the basis of the monument is a pyramid. The terraces becoming smaller and smaller, the little stūpa that could be placed upon them had to get fewer in number: eight on the lower terrace, six on the middle one, four on the upper terrace, that is 8 + 6 + 4 = 18 for each side, and a total of 18 × 4 = 72. The reason of an architectural symmetry might then account for the number 72.

Besides, at the beginning of the *Saddharmapuṇḍarīka* a ray of light issues from the circle of hair which grew between the Bhagabat's eyebrows. This ray is directed! towards the 18,000 countries of the Buddha situated on the east.[12] 18,000 countries for one of the four orients make a total of 72,000 countries of the Buddha. The disposition, at the Barabudur; of the 72 small *stūpas* around the terminal *stūpa* is identical with that of the 72,000 countries of the universe around the centre of the world. It seems likely that the architect, not being able to represent the 72,000 buddhas who reside in the 72,000 countries, has satisfied himself by putting in 72 only, in order to suit both convenience and symmetry. Seventy-two and 72,000 are just conventional numbers, chosen to give an idea of the numberless manifestations of the Great Enlightened. Likewise, when the sculptures show Avalokiteśvara with 40 arms, when the texts call him Avalokiteśvara of the 1,000 arms, 40 and 1,000 are conventional numbers again, designed to mark the numerous activities of the god.[13]

Whether he has 33 shapes as in Burma, 50 shapes as at the Bayon, 73 as we see at the Barabudur or 1001 as at the Tōdaiji, the essence of the *dharmadhātu* is always the Great One and Only which fills up the universe. At Java, as in Indo-China, as in Japan, the sovereign identifies himself with him. That is why in the empire of the Śailendras, the name Śailendra belongs

[12] *Saddharmapuṇḍarīka*, f. 4b., cf. tr. by Burnouf, p. 4.

[13] About the statues of Avalokiteśvara, the 1,000 arms of which are customarily represented by 40, cf. Waley, *A Catalogue of Paintings Recovered from Tun huang by Sir A. Stein*, p. 31.

to both the king and the king of the gods. Śailendra then, could mean not only the dynasty, but Śiva-Buddha also, who was the highest entity in the Javanese religion. We know enough now to engage upon the study of an obscure question. Which was the statue contained in the terminal stūpa of the Barabudur?

The point is a strongly contested one. The first European visitors have not seen anything below the terminal stūpa, all blocked up by scattered fragments. In 1842, Resident Hartmann ordered excavations to be made, no authentical report of which has reached us, and an unfinished statue of Buddha would have been discovered then in the ruins. M. Foucher has proposed to recognise in this statue a reproduction of the famous one seen by Hiuan-tsang on the actual place of the Bodhi.[14] This statue, which showed Śākyamuni in the moment of the Māravijaya, was also an unfinished statue. On the contrary, Krom thinks that originally the *stūpa* contained no image whatever, and that some relics had only been put there. Stutterheim believes that the *stūpa* contained the unfinished statue of a supreme and bodiless Buddha. M. Mus does not see that the identification proposed by M. Foucher should be damaged radically by Krom's objection.[15]

In short, the authors hesitate between two hypotheses: (1) there was ho statue at all in the terminal stūpa, (2) there was an unfinished statue, the same which Krom describes as a "rough lump, thicker at one side than the other". Both hypotheses seem hardly likely. I wish to be allowed the suggestion of a third one.

According to Indian tradition, mount Meru is a mountain of gold. In the inscriptions of Cambodia the royal mount is of gold also. The central tower of the Bayon is called by Tcheou ta kouan, the gold tower. The ideas of gold and the cosmic mountain are closely bound together. As it was impossible to make a real gold mountain, would not the idea have arisen of replacing it by a lump of gold, placed at the centre of the world? Let us recall to mind the importance of the gold coating on the great statue of the Tōdaiji. The Japanese authorities were anxious to find the precious metal in Japan. National gold was necessary in order to realise the mystical union of the empire with the Great Enlightened. It was desirable, then, that there should be in the centre of the empire a statue of gold, or at least of gilded bronze, because it was the point wherefrom the power radiates which creates the cosmic and the social order.

This theory finds its confirmation in a Chinese text relative to the empire of San-fo-ts'i. It is extracted from the *Chu fan Chi* of Chau Ju-kua written in 1226.

> There is an idol (literally "a Buddha") which is called the idol of the Mountain of Gold and Silver. Its statue is cast in gold. Each king just before mounting the throne, causes his own image to be cast in gold to replace that statue. Vases and plates of gold are made and

[14] "The unfinished Buddha of the Boro-Budur", *BEFEO*, t. 3, pp. 76-80.

[15] Statement of the controversy in P. Mus, *Barabudur*, t. 32, pp. 344 ff.

solemn homage is paid to that image. The golden statue, the vases and plates, all of them bear inscriptions so that the future generations may not destroy them.[16]

The Mountain of Gold and Silver could only be the cosmic mountain, or its replica. The emperor being identified with the king of the gods must be enthroned on the cosmic mountain: that is why his golden statue is placed on the top of it and he is worshipped there. What Chau Ju-kua writes in 1226 about the king of San-fo-ts'i, alludes to politico-religious concepts which lie at the origin of the Barabudur. Then it is likely that the statue placed in the terminal stūpa was a gold statue, and this might suffice to account for its disappearance.

Besides, some narrations, the origins of which are not certain, accuse Resident Hartmann of having found a little gold statue in the stūpa, and of having stolen it: he would have put the big unfinished statue at the same place in order to divert suspicion.[17] This is not the place to judge Resident Hartmann for such an accusation. But it not infrequently happens that some such legend hundreds of years old is ascribed much later to a recent date. This explains how some old traditions relative to the theft of the statue may have been put down finally to the credit of the 1842 excavations.

In short the Barabudur is a reduction of the cosmic mountain surmounted by 73 stūpas. Consequently, it is difficult to look upon it as only a stūpa. At any rate it is widely different from the old Indian stūpa. It is an imperial construction designed, like the Great Buddha of Tōdaiji, to seal the mystical union of the empire and of the universe. The emperor, king of the mounts (Śailendra), identifies himself with the supreme deity in the central stūpa. This Devarāja is at the same time Akṣobhya, Bhaṭṭāra Buddha and Śiva-Buddha. Under which one of those names was he more generally adored? It is impossible to tell. But we must refrain from simplifying the Barabudur. The central deity must have been conceived in a different way by the initiated and by the humble subjects of the kingdom. It is permissible to suppose that different names corresponded to the different concepts.

[16] Bibliography and discussion relative to this quotation in *JGIS*, II, 1, pp. 35-6.

[17] Cf. P. Mus, *Barabudur*, t. 32, p. 346.

CHAPTER 15

Administrative System of the Kambuja Rulers

BAIJ NATH PURI

The Kambuja inscriptions adduce enough information to form a comprehensive view of the administrative system of that country in the time of the ancient Khmer rulers. It must be borne in mind that the extent of the empire coupled with the complexity of the population and its geographical position, encircled, as even at present, by the kingdoms of Annam or Champa, Tonkin and Siam entailed a complex administrative system so as to minimise the chances of external aggression and internal revolt. The matriarchal system of social structure and the absence of any regulated mode of succession had at times engulfed the country into disruption and disorder. But this state of affairs did not continue for long. The credit for retaining the independent existence of the country for well over seven hundred years is due to the system of country's administration which was borrowed from the homeland of the rulers in northern India, and the unshakeable faith of the people in the ruling sovereign in whom the sovereignty vested. The oath of allegiance on the part of the officials, their hereditary appointments, and the division of the country into provincial and local units had ensured efficiency, stability and room for progress. This had not ruled out democratic spirit which is clearly manifested in the reference to the Royal Assembly or *Rājya Sabhā*, the office of the *sabhāpati*, the chief of corporation and the part played by the village elders in local administration. In the light of the above observations we propose considering the system of administration under the following headings: the Position of the King, his powers, the Royal Assembly, Provincial Units, Vassal chiefs, High officials, Minor officials, Judiciary, Local administration, Sale transactions and transfer of title deeds, Military administration, Hereditary appointments and Oath of allegiance, Administration of Religious endowments, Administrative laws and uniformity of punishment.

POSITION OF THE KING

The reference to the *Arthaśāstra* and the *Dharmaśāstra*[1] in the inscriptions implies that the position of the king and his status was well defined. One of

[1] *tasya tau mantriṇāvastamsāmmatau kritāvedino.*
dharmaśāstrārtha śāstrājño dharmārthaviva rūpino.

Majumdar: Inscription no. 30, p. 39

Source: *Journal of the Greater India Society* (XV/1, 1956, 60–70).

the features of the cult of the Devarāja was the acceptance of the divine element in the king. One inscription[2] refers to King Jayavarman born as a portion of the God Śiva. He was the highest authority of the state in executive and judicial matters and was the fountain of law and its interpreter. He was also the head of the forces. He appointed the provincial chiefs,[3] and could interfere in all matters independently even at the head of the officials.[4] He was assisted by *mantrins*, and other officials.[5] An inscription refers to the *rājyasabhādhipati*,[6] but his relations with the king and his powers are nowhere defined. The personal safety of the ruler was a matter of vital concern[7] to the state, and there were special officials like inspector of bed chamber, special bodyguards (*nṛpāntaraṅga*) and *dvārādhyakṣa*.[8] The Chinese accounts have also referred to thousands of such bodyguards.[9] His position in the judicial set up would be considered when we take that aspect of administration into consideration. To what extent the king enjoyed the esteem of the people might be judged by the fact that the people were prepared to offer the merits of their austerities to the king.[10] The king sometimes had his own favourite.[11]

PROVINCIAL ADMINISTRATION

The vast Kambuja empire was divided into a number of provincial units, which, according to the Chinese accounts, were 30 in number. The inscription do mention a few provinces. They are Tatandrapura, Tāmrapura, Āḍhyapura,

---

In one inscription there is a reference to a favourite of the king who was *sarvopadhāsuddha* (no. 12, p. 18, v. 12. ibid. This might suggest that he had stood all temptations. The tests of such a nature are also mentioned in the *Arthaśāstra* (Book I, Chap 10).

[2]*yasya liṅga sahastrāram ...*
tadeśena = vatirṇena jitam Śri Jayavarmana.
No. 34, p. 45, vv 2-3

[3]Inscription No. 34 from Tan Kran suggests that a person was appointed to several junior posts before he was placed as the lord of district. Such appointments naturally were made by the king. The evidence furnished by the Chinese sources is very clear on this point, as it suggests that all appointments were made from the members of the Royal family, and in the absence of the male members even female members of the family were appointed (Remusat, *Nouv. Mel. As*., I, p. 109). We have considered this point in great detail.

[4]The Tuol Prasat inscription (Majumdar, no. 122) mentions the Chief Justice and other members of the tribunal reporting their decision to the king, and the Neak Ta Carek inscription refers to the king taking cognizance of an offence against an officer of the state who had done wrong to a private individual.

[5]It is difficult to suggest on the basis of these administrative terms the relation between the king and these officials, but it is evident he could interfere in all affairs. The powers of these officials are nowhere defined.

[6]Majumdar, *Inscription*, no. 33, p. 43.

[7]This is always the case where there is no regulated law of succession, and sometimes the close relations are disposed of.

[8]Majumdar, *Inscription*, no. 61, p. 82, v. 87; ibid., no. 34, p. 46, v. 16.

[9]*BEFEO*, vol. III, p. 264.

[10]Majumdar, *Inscriptions*, no. 139, p. 344; cf. no. 148, pp. 351 and 614.

[11]Ibid., no. 13 (*antaraṅgatvam āsthitah*).

Śreṣṭapura, Bhavapura, Dhruvapura, Dhanvipura, Jyeṣṭhapura, Vikramapura, Ugrapura and Iśānapura. The ruler of Āḍhyapura named Siṁhadatta was also the Royal Physician,[12] and that of Dharmapura was a brāhmaṇa.[13] The governors of the towns of Bhavapura and Jyeṣṭhapura are associated in a record[14] of dedication along with a few other donors. In a record[15] the ruler of Bhavapura named Samarādhipativarman is mentioned as the hereditary governor of Bhavapura. These heads were appointed by the king. Sometimes they were recruited from the services. One inscription mentions the appointment of the elder son of Dharmasvāmin who had held many royal offices, such as commander of the cavalry (*mahāśvapati*), lord of Śreṣṭapura, and lord of Dhruvapura, full of dense forests and ferocious men. The expression (*Punar = Dhruvapuram prāpya*) suggests that either he was a retired person, but that does not appear to be the case, or he was appointed at the post held by his father after he had shown his merit in other assignments. The contention also implies that the principle of hereditary appointment was accepted with reservations depending upon the capacity and talents of the succeeding incumbent. There is also a reference to vassal chief known as *rājñādhikṛta* and an inscription refers to the vassal chiefs of Tāmrapura who possessed in addition to the town of Cakrāṅkapura, Amoghapura and Bhīmapura.[16]

HIGH OFFICIALS

The Kambuja inscriptions mention a number of officials of a high status who were similar to their counterparts in India. These high officials included *kumāramantrin*,[17] *balādhyakṣa*,[18] *mantrins*,[19] *rājadhiṣaka*[20] and *rājakula-mahāmantrī*.[21] The *kumāra-mantrin* can very well be equated with the *kumārāmātya* of the northern Indian inscription[22] who were attached to the princes. The *balādhyakṣa* is also noticed in Indian inscriptions, and it may be taken as synonymous with *balādhikṛta* which term is noticed in many Indian inscriptions.[23] He was different from the *senāpati* who was actually in command

[12] Ibid., no. 30, p. 39.
[13] Ibid., no. 34, p. 45.
[14] Ibid., no. 42, p. 42.
[15] Ibid., no, 120, p. 310.
[16] Ibid., no. 25, p. 30.
[17] Ibid., no. 66, p. 127.
[18] Ibid., no. 71A, p. 149.
[19] Ibid., no. 66, p. 133.
[20] Ibid., no. 30, p. 39.
[21] Ibid., no. 100, p. 269.
[22] Bhandarkar's List, nos. 1270, 1271, 1272, etc.
[23] *Balādhikṛta* and *balādhaykṣa* appear to be synonymous terms and this official was probably different from the *senāpati* who led the forces on the battle front. *Balādhikṛta* or *balādhaykṣa*, on the other hand, seems to have been an adviser on army matters who remained in the secretariat (cf. *EI*, vol. 10, p. 85; vol. XIV, p. 182; also *Mahābhārata*, VII.189; *Harivaṃśa*, 15841).

of the forces on the front. The two officers are distinguished in the records in India, and so it may be suggested that the *balādhikṛta* was attached to the secretariat and he looked after the forces, and was not actually fighting on the front. The *mantrins* were certainly more than one, as in one inscription two names are mentioned. They were appointed by the king and were mostly from the blue blood. According to the Chinese account,[24] as noticed by Ma-touan-lin in his chapter on Chen-la, and translated by Abel Rẹmusat, in the first half of the seventh century, there were five classes of high officials who knelt before the king before they took their seats in a circle round the king to discuss the state affairs. The bas-reliefs of the first gallery at Angkorvat illustrate the court scene at Kambuja. It is possible to locate the officer and his name because the names and designations are inscribed. The ministers include the holy lord and master Vīrasiṁhavarman kneeling before the king and presenting a scroll, the chief Sri Vardhana, the lord and master Dhanañjaya, and the holy lord and master of the merits and defects, and the Chief Justice. Fortunately most of these titles and offices are mentioned in the records, and we shall refer to them later on.

The minor officials included *dvārādhyakṣa*,[25] *astrādhipati*,[26] *guṇadoṣa-parīkṣaka*[27] and a few others who were associated with the *vihāras*. The Prasat Komnap inscription[28] and associated ones mention a number of minor officials associated with the different sectarian *vihāras* established by the emperor Yaśovarman. These included *rājakuśipāla*, *pustakarakṣin*, and *lekhaka*. A host of others like torchbearers (*ulkaikadhāraka*), *śakādhihāraka*, *pāṇiyahāra*, *patrakāra*, *tāmbulika*, *tāṇḍulakariṣya* and *kṣuraka* had hardly any administrative status. The *lekhaka* or scribe could correspond to the *kāyastha* mentioned in many records, especially in the Damodarpura copper plate inscriptions,[29] and the *pustakarakṣin* might be the keeper of the records. The *rājakuṭipāla* probably kept royal seals. The association of these minor officers in the ecclesiastical establishments is not an uncommon factor. We find that the *rājahotṛs*[30] occupied a high position, and the interest taken by the Khmer rulers in setting up and managing such religious and humanitarian institutions could not nave been possible without administrative personnel being appointed for this specific purpose.

MILITARY ADMINISTRATION

The geographical position of Kambuja necessarily required both land and naval

[24] *Nouveaux Melanges Asiatique* (1829), pp. 85-6 quoted from Chatterji, *Indian Cultural Influence in Cambodia*, p. 61.

[25] *Journal Asiatique*, August-September 1883, pp. 199ff.

[26] Majumdar, *Inscriptions*, no. 61, p. 88.

[27] Ibid., no. 87, p. 176.

[28] Ibid., no. 125, 314.

[29] *EI*, vol. XV, pp. 131ff.

[30] Majumdar, *Inscriptions*, no. 71A, p. 148.

forces. The inscriptions mention officers connected with both. An inscription[31] refers to *mahānaubbhaka*, and *sāmantānauvāha*. The *sahastrāvargādhipati*[32] was in-charge of a force of a thousand men. The chief of cavalry was called *mahāśvapati*.[33] An idea of the Kambuja army and its structure can be had from a look at a scene from the Angkor bas-reliefs. It shows the march past of the generals with their escorts. Clad in armour one is seated on an elephant with a javelin on his shoulder and a shield in his left hand. He has an escort with umbrellas over his head. His pilots are four horsemen. There are also Sañjakas or bodyguards. It may be interesting to learn that the king had separate palace guards under a commander known as *narendraparicāraka*.[34] They had arms in their hands and wore helmets on their heads. The palace force under a tried (*sarvopadhāśuddha*) was a sheer necessity when succession to the throne was disputed and the chances of a *coup d'état* were not slender.

JUDICIAL ADMINISTRATION

There is enough information on this point in the Kambuja records. One inscription[35] mentions the chief judicial officer (*vyavahārādhikārī*), and the superintendent of the court of justice (*dharmādhikaraṇapāla*) who along with the other officers of the court, the inspector of the property of gods (*amṛtakadhana*), and the inspectors of the bailiffs who were working under the authority of Prithivīndra Paṇḍita, called in this record the inspector of qualities and defects (*guṇadoṣadarśī*). This person is mentioned in another record[36] as the Chief Justice, who along with the other judges of their tribunal reported their decision to the king at that time in the sacred town of Jayendranagarī. An inscription mentions a term *samyadhipa*,[37] supposed by Majumdar to be the head of the magistrates. Actually it was the king who was the highest judicial authority who could be approached even in the initial stage of the complaint. He was the highest court of appeal, and he could punish officials, if found guilty. In one case Mratāñ Kurun, the chief of the Vīrapura district, was found guilty of removing the boundary and reaping the corn of the field of the complainant and was fined ten ounces of gold, while his younger brother who abetted the crime was condemned to 102 stripes on the back (*pṛṣṭhādana*).[38] Another inscription records that Śrī Prithvīndra Paṇḍita, president of the civil tribunal of the first category conveyed a royal order of donation and the order was engraved on stone.[39] The procedure in a civil law

[31] Ibid., no. 34, p. 46, v. 18.

[32] Majumdar, *Kambuja Inscriptions*, no. 34, p. 46, v. 19.

[33] Ibid., v. 11.

[34] Ibid., v. 5.

[35] Ibid., no. 125, p. 314.

[36] Ibid., no. 122, p. 311; cf. no. 125.

[37] *Kambujadeśa*, p.

[38] Majumdar, *Kambuja Inscriptions*, no. 99, p. 269.

[39] Ibid., no. 146, p. 349.

suit is noticed in a Khmer inscription[40] which refers to the replacement of a slave who was ultimately handed over and placed in the service of god. We notice here the name of the judge, his two assistants and the witnesses. Similarly a legal judgement is recorded in the Tuol Prasat inscription[41] presided over by Śrī Prithvīndra Paṇḍita and assisted by some others whose names are also mentioned.

ALIENATION OF LAND AND SALE PROCEDURE

The Prasant Kok inscription[42] furnishes very interesting details of the procedure for the sale of lands, and its reference to a number of officials connected in the deal is very interesting. At the request of the purchaser for acquiring proprietary rights, there was a notification issued to the inspector of qualities and defects (*guṇadoṣadarśī*). This official was given full powers to the inspector who asked the assembly to summon the other party, naturally the vendor. The inspector on his part entrusted the execution of the royal order to the inspector of wages, the chief judicial officer (*vyavahārādhikārī*), the superintendent of the court of justice (*dharmādhikaraṇapāla*), the inspector of the property of the gods (*amṛtakādhana*) and the inspector of the bailiffs of the third class. The land called *ārāma* was delimited with the help of the nobles (*puruṣa-pradhāna*) the elders (*grāma-vṛddha*), and the dignitaries of the four regions in the neighbourhood. In the presence of these notable personages the boundaries were defined, and with the striking of the drum at the site the formalities were completed. The same inscription mentions a few other officials connected with the sale transactions. It mentions the chief *ācārya* and president of the court, the usual inspector of qualities and defects, the reciters of Dharmaśāstras, an inspector of boys of the country, and the inspector of the bailiffs of the third class, as usual. The sale transaction and the details connected with it can favourably be compared with the data from the Damodarpura Copper Plate Inscriptions.[43] It would appear that both the official and non-official elements were connected with such sale transactions in both the countries.

Another inscription[44] furnishes some additional details regarding the transference of land by royal order. In this case the leaders and noble persons from four neighbouring villages—four from each—came and fixed the boundaries of the land given by royal order. The elders included the person who fixed the auspicious moment, the chief of ten villages (*daśagrāma*), a notable and another chief of ten villages, the leader of the village (*grāmavṛddha*), a third chief of ten villages and several other persons who probably acted as

[40] Amonier, *Le Cambodge*, vol. I, pp. 247-47. Chatterji, Ref. cit., p. 149.
[41] Majumdar, *Kambuja Inscriptions*, p. 314.
[42] Ibid., no. 122, p. 314.
[43] Ref. cit.
[44] Ibid., no. 145, p. 347.

witnesses. Another inscription[45] refers to Vrāh Sabhā or the holy assembly fixing the boundaries of the land which was purchased from the contributions made by several officials and consecrated to god Jayakṣetra. This shows that there was little room for the acquisition of private property even for ecclesiastical purposes, and the private interest never suffered. The persons selling the land took solemn vows never to reclaim the land already sold.

LOCAL ADMINISTRATION

The democratic spirit was manifested in local administration. The villages, as usual, had a head whose title *grāmika* unfortunately is not noticed in any record, but there are references to heads of ten villages in the Khmer text of the Prasat Trapan inscription of Jayavarman.[46] It is therefore quite clear that there must have been the head of a village unit as well. Certain inscriptions[47] mention village elders (*grāmavṛiddha*) and notable persons (*puruṣapradhāna*) who assisted the officials in fixing the boundaries. Here their ripe experience and status were taken advantage of.

APPOINTMENTS AND OATH OF ALLEGIANCE

To ensure efficiency and smooth running of administration, it was necessary that all appointments should be made on certain considerations. Here it appears that efficiency was the first consideration, and next came the allegiance of the family. As these appointments were made by the king, he took these facts into consideration. Generally the son succeeded his father[48] provided he had shown his merit in other assignments. An inscription mentions a learned brahmin named Dharmasvāmin who was the chief of Dharmapura. His elder son held many royal offices such as "commander of the cavalry" (*mahāśvapati*), lord of Śreṣṭapura and lord of Dhruvapura. His younger brother was also a high official who held successively the post of the "commander of the palace guards" (*nṛpāntaraṅga*), some other office the name of which is not clear, "commander of navy" (*sāmantānauvāhana*), and a "commander of the thousand soldiers" (*sahasravargādhipati*).[49] It is also evident that transfers from one post to another were quite frequent. The allegiance of the family was taken into full consideration. In one inscription a family monopolised the office of "the bearer of the royal fan"—for thirteen successive kings beginning from Jayavarman II. According to certain Chinese accounts[50] the offices were mostly held by the members of the Royal family and when male members were not to be found, females were appointed. Actually we find Pranā, one of the wives of

[45] Ibid., no, 131, p. 333.
[46] Ibid.
[47] Ibid., no. 131, p. 333.
[48] Ref. cit., no. 34, p. 44.
[49] Ibid., no. 157, p. 400.
[50] Remusat; Ref. cit., p. 109; Chatterji, p. 165.

King Rājendravarman, who was distinguished by her lineage, conduct and talents, appointed on the death of Rājendravarman, the head of the private section secretaries of Jayavarman.[51]

The officers were expected to take the oath of allegiance, thereby solemnly offering their lives and devotion to the sovereign. This was taken in the presence of sacred fire, brāhmaṇas and *ācāryas*. They were asked not to honour any other king, never to be hostile to their king, not to be accomplices of any enemy, nor harm their king in any manner, show utmost devotion to him, fight on behalf of their sovereign in case of war to the best of their abilities, consecrate their lives to the service of the king even if it meant death, should not hesitate in discharging their duties minutely even if they were sent to remote place on king's business. Failure to do their duty entailed any corporal punishment which the king might inflict. In case they absconded, they were condemned to be born in the 32 hells so long as the Sun and the Moon endure. The king, on the other hand, was to provide for these people and their families, and the heavenly reward might follow for their devotion to duty.

THE INSTITUTION OF SAÑJAKAS

The Sañjakas were those people who owed special allegiance to the king and were always with him. They were actually proud of sacrificing their lives for the safety of their lord. The Bantay Chmar Inscription[52] mentions the situation when Bharata Rāhu treacherously rebelled against King Yaśovarmadeva and sacked his palace. All the troops of the capital fled. The prince fought, and the two Sañjakas fought to save him. In so doing they lost their lives, but Bharata Rāhu was defeated. Their images were set up by the king, and posthumous awards were conferred on them. The bas-reliefs at Angkor Vat also depict Sañjakas. These Sañjakas might be classed as personal bodyguards of the king.

LAWS AND PUNISHMENT

We have noticed certain cases of a civil nature which suggest that the rights of the individual were well protected, and even in cases where the state was a party in alienation the non-official element was always consulted for the delimitation of boundaries. In cases where the official element had misused his position, he was not immune from punishment. The state was certainly the owner of the property without any claimant. An inscription does refer to *mṛtakadhana*. People had to pay taxes. The king had the right to reduce the taxes. A Khmer inscription of Rolom Tim refers to the giving of a buffalo to the head of the collectors of the paddy tax in order to be exempted from the royal corvee.

[51] Majumdar, *Kambuja Inscriptions*, no. 163, p. 422, v. 24.
[52] Ibid., no. 183, p. 528.

We have, thus, visualised the administrative system of the Kambuja rulers on the basis of the inscriptions. It has been made very clear that the system was based on the *Artha* and the *Dharma Sastras*, and there were also reciters of the latter. It was just like the Indian administrative system. The divine origin of the king, his council of ministers, provincial chiefs, democratic spirit in local administration, the principle of hereditary appointments subject to efficiency were all akin to the Indian system. Only the institution of Sañjakas appears to be an indigenous one, though cases of faithful servants sacrificing their lives for the sake of their master could be traced everywhere and at all times. The oath of allegiance is also very interesting. On the whole the system seemed to be well planned, and there was hardly any change in the set up during the period of Kambuja history.

CHAPTER 16

Some Aspects of Social Life in Ancient Kambujadeśa

BAIJ NATH PURI

The Kambuja inscriptions mention a number of persons who from their names appear to be of Indian origin. Their presence in that country away from their motherland is an important factor suggesting their emigration from India. The reference to brahmins coming to this country from India, and the high esteem in which such emigrants were held by the local people is a clear indication of the encouragement given to this move, so that in course of time the country was Indianised, with its Indian rulers, and a social structure which was based on the Indian caste system. As the persons who came into Kambuja country were either brahmins or kṣatriyas, their impact with the local population resulted into a new social structure of which the flexibility of the caste and inter-caste marital relations were important features. The indigenous matriarchal society continued to exist, and it did influence the patriarchal system of the Indian immigrants. This resulted in people tracing their descent from the mother's side in a number of cases, and the absence of any regulated succession order. Some of the names seem to represent a combination of Sanskrit and Khmer endings. This complex social structure was, nevertheless, Indian, and we propose considering the subject under the following headings: Social divisions and creations of new castes, marital relations, dress and ornaments, food and utensils, position of women, pastime and recreations, slavery, and disposal of the dead.[1]

SOCIAL DIVISIONS

There are references to the four *varṇas* in the Kambuja records (*catvāro varṇas*), but primarily only the brahmins figure as very important persons who sometimes married in the royal family. This marital relations between the brahmins and the kṣatriyas had resulted in the emergence of a *brāhma-kṣatra*[2] class which

[1]Majumdar, *Inscriptions of Kambuja*, no. 179, p. 497, v. 19.

[2]Ibid., no. 52, p. 56; no. 95, p. 295, v. 10. The Prah Ko inscriptions mentions Pṛthvīndravarman belonging to Kṣatri family (no. 55, p. 62, v. 4).

The brahma-kṣatriyas are also noticed in the inscriptions from Champā, and also mean India *JRASB* (New Series), vol. V, 1909, p. 167.

Source: *Journal of the Greater India Society* (XV/2, 1956, 89–92).

term is also noticed in several records. There is not one reference to the vaiśyas[3] in the Kambuja records. The important position accorded to the brahmins is due to the traditional Kauṇḍinyas who established their rule in Kambujadeśa in different periods. They married the local queens and legalised their position as rulers of the country. According to a Khmer tradition,[4] the brahmins from Java came to the Kambuja country, and set-up a kingdom here. These brahmins were darker in complexion, kept long hair and were inhabitants of Vārāṇasī. According to a Chinese tradition,[5] there were more than 1,000 brahmins in Tuan Siuan, a principality under Fu-nan. The local people gave their daughters in marriage to them, and followed their tenets. The Kambuja records also mention a number of brahmins who came from India. A brahmin Hiraṇyadāma came from a *janapada* in India to teach Tāntric texts to Śivakaivalya, the royal priest.[6] After that a brahmin named Agastya came here and married a princess named Yaśomatī.[7] The brahmin Divākara of Vṛndāvana on the Kālindī married Indumatī, the daughter of Emperor Rajendravarm.[8] Hṛṣīkeśa of the Bhāradvāja *gotra* came to Kambujadeśa from Narapatideśa (Brahma) and was the Royal Purohit of Emperor Jayavarman VII. He married the daughter of a person at Brahmapura, and had by her four sons and two daughters. The elder of the two daughters became the queen of Jayavarman VIII.[9] The brahmins enjoyed special positions in the court. Śivakaivalya and his descendants occupied the status of royal *purohits* for well over 250 years. A brahmin named Vāmaśiva was the preceptor of Indravarman.[10] Thus, it appears that the brahmins enjoyed the highest and supreme position, and even princes of blue blood were also offered to them.

In the time of Sūryavarman, there was the division into castes[11] and Śivācārya was accorded the highest position in the social order. Caste, however, did not interfere in the choice of an avocation. An inscription[12] refers to the members of a brahmin family being elephant drivers, royal concubines, artisans and priests. Certain new castes were also created in the time of Jayavarman V.

[3]The vaiśyas and śūdras are not noticed even in the Champā records. In one inscription from Champā they are only casually mentioned (Majumdar; *Champā*, p. 214).

[4]Chatterji, *Indian Culture in Kambuja*, p. 8.

[5]Pelliot, *Fou-nan*, *BEFEO*, vol. III, p. 277.

[6]Majumdar, *Inscriptions of Kambuja*, no. 152, p. 362.

[7]Ibid., no. 60, p. 76, v. 5.

[8]Ibid., no. 111, p. 285.

[9]Ibid., no. 190, p. 541.

[10]Ibid., no. 158, p. 366.

[11]Majumdar, *Kambuja Inscriptions*, p. 353.

[12]Ibid., no. 158, p. 41; accordidg to the Smṛtis, a man could take to avocations other than the one prescribed for him in adverse circumstances (*Gautama*, Chap. 7; *Manu*. 10: 81; *Yājñavalkya* 3: 35). In early Mediaeval Indian inscriptions we also notice such instances, e.g. a kṣatri cultivator, a kṣatritailika (*EI*, vol. I, p. 149) and brahmin cultivators (Kaman Ins).

These were Khmuk and Karmāntara. The same inscription[13] also refers to the *ācāryas* of the seven castes (*saptavarṇa*). In this connection we might refer to the accounts of Arab historians, more particularly Ibn Khurdād[14] who, too, has referred to seven castes in Hindu society. According to the inscription from Kambuja, cited above, the king, after the performance of a grand sacrifice, asked the Guru to select, from among the religious men and *ācāryas* of the seven castes, 20 persons for each of the two new castes, Khmuk and Karmāntara, and they were the foundation members of the two new castes. It was also provided that they could be married to three superior castes, but not vice versa. The Emperor had given final sanction to the creation of these new castes. The Angkor Vat sculptures also depict people of different castes, as is evident from their dress.

Besides these castes, we also find references to offsprings from mixed marriages. An inscription[15] refers to the setting up of an image of Trailokyavijayagīśvara by Tribhuvanarāja whose sister was named Ten Vai and brother-in-law Somavajra. There are reference to names like Loñja Yudhiṣṭhira, Mritāñ Jayendrapaṇḍita Mritāñ Prithvīndrapaṇḍita. It is, thus, not unusual to find mixed names representing the offspings of marriages with the native population.

MARRIAGE

The brahmins seem to have enjoyed a privileged position, and they could marry any one they liked. The brahmin girls were also accepted in the kṣatriya group representing royal blood. Bhavavarman I's sister was married to a brahmin named Somaśarman and this lady is compared to Arundhatī because of her devotion to her lord.[16] Yaśovarman's mother Indradevī was a descendant of the family of Agastya who was well-versed and had come to Kambujadeśa from Āryadeśa.[17] Jayavarman II had married a brahmin girl named Bhāssvāminī, and Yogeśvara Paṇḍita was a descendant of that family.[18] Both the queens of Jayavarman VII were brahmins,[19] while the queen of Jayavarman VIII was the younger daughter of a brahmin from Narapatideśa, who had married a brahmin girl named Prabhā.[20] Yaśovarman had married his maternal uncle's daughter which custom is popular in southern India in certain families.[21] The marital

[13] Majumdar, *Kambuja Inscriptions*, no. 110A, p. 589.

[14] Elliot and Dowson, *History of India*, vol. I, pp. 16-17; 74-93. These are *Sabkufria*, *Brahma*, *Kataris*, *Sudaris*, *Basuria*, *Sandalia* and *Lāhud*.

[15] Majumdar, *Kambuja Inscriptions*, no. 113, p. 299.

[16] Ibid., no. 13, p. 19.

[17] Ibid., no. 182, p. 515.

[18] Ibid., no. 148, p. 351.

[19] Ref. no. 17.

[20] Ibid., no. p. 541.

[21] Chatterji, op. cit., p. 228.

relations were generally arranged by the parents, but one inscription[22] mentions a lady named Me Sok, granddaughter of Mritāñ Śrī Sarvādhikāra who herself approached the author of the record with the proposal of marriage and gave as dowry one horse and saddle and some other object. Polyandry seems to have been practised. In one inscription[23] there is a reference to 43 male slaves and their nine wives. This was probably common among the slaves and other lower castes. The Chinese history[24] of the Sui Dynasty notices certain social customs as existed in Kambujadeśa in the seventh century AD. The girl was given a handsome dress, and members of both the parties used to stay together for eight days. During this period the lamp used to burn the whole day and night. After marriage the boy used to live separately from his wife. There is also a reference to widow's remarriage.[25] Yuvarāja, the youngest of the three sons of Hiraṇyavarman died and his widow became successively the wife of his two elder brothers. It seems strange how a younger brother's widow could be married to an elder brother.

DRESS, ORNAMENTS AND TOILET

Information of this point is available from the Kambuja sculptures at Angkor Vat and certain Chinese accounts. In this respect the Indian *dhotī* was very prominent. People tied it round the waist and had a band. It is also corroborated by the Chinese historians. It is mentioned by Cheo-ta-kuen,[26] and the *dhotī* was worn with a scarf thrown round both the shoulders. A sculpture at Bayon depicts the king in this *dhotī* with a *hāra* round his neck. According to the Chinese accounts, the *dhotī* was of a very good stuff which was imported from the western seas. In one inscription[27] there is a reference to Chinese silk. According to the History of the Southern Tsi,[28] persons of high family dressed themselves in brocade. It appears from the account collected by Remusat that the demand for Bengal Muslin was high in the sixteenth century.[29] In the 'History of the Sui Dynasty', it is mentioned that the king was dressed in purple silk clothes which were embroidered.[30] In sculptures the brahmins wear earrings like the king, but the warriors have no ear-ornament though the lobes of their ears are bored for wearing them. An inscription[31] mentions golden ear ornaments, rings, bracelets, armlets along with utensils which formed part of the gift. The sacrificial fee (*dakṣiṇā*), wealth and other ornaments given by

[22] Ibid., no. 19A, p. 581.
[23] Ibid., no. 23, p. 29.
[24] Majumdar, *Kambujadeśa*, p. 65.
[25] Majumdar, *Kambuja Inscriptions*, no. 174, p. 456.
[26] Pelliot, *BEFEO*, vol. III, p. 296.
[27] Majumdar, *Kambuja Inscriptions*, no. 177, p. 466, v. 44.
[28] Chatterji, *Indian Influences in Kambujadeśa*, p. 229.
[29] Ibid.
[30] Pelliot, *BEFEO*, vol. III, p. 254.
[31] Majumdar, *Kambuja Inscriptions*, no. 152, p. 369.

King Śrī Udayādityavarmadeva included diadems (*mukuṭa*), ear-pendants (*kuṇḍala*) bracelets (*keyūra*), wristband (*kaṭaka*) and *mukuṭaveṇā*.[32] The best[33] evidence of the use of ornaments put on by the ladies is furnished by the famous dancer in the Turin Museum, who puts on ear pendant, diadems, bracelets, waistband, armlets and *hāra*.[34]

ITEMS OF FOOD AND UTENSILS

Rice formed the principal item of food. There are references to *taṇḍula* (*bhojana taṇḍulānam*[35]), which was boiled (*pākya taṇḍula*). *Bhakta* was any eatable grain boiled with water. There are also references to seasoning which included pepper and cardamom.[36] The Ta Prohm inscription[37] also mentions items of food *khārya*, *tila*, *mudga*, besides *ghṛta*, *dadhi*, *kṣīra*, *guḍa*, *madhu*, and *taila*.[38] Clarified butter is also mentioned in another inscription. The "History of the Sui Dynasty" and that of the "Tang Dynasty" also mention some items of food of ancient Kambuja people. According to the former work, food included a large quantity of butter, cream, sugar and millet in the form of cake or bread. Before meals the people took some morsels of meat with a little salt. The latter work has referred to drinking in private.[39] The utensils of the people consisted of pitcher (*ghaṭa*), kettle (*kaḍāha*), bronze pitcher (*kalaśa*), bronze plate (*śarāva*), large silver jars and caskets of gold and silver.

PASTIME AND RECREATIONS

In the social life there was room for pastime and recreations. The inscriptions mention dancing, music and theatrical performances. Dancing girls were well versed in vocal and instrumental music. They were skilful in playing on lyres and other instruments, and were well versed in pipes and *tāla*.[40] There is also a reference to beautiful and well-dressed men, skilful in dancing and other arts.[41] Such dancers were dedicated to the temples. One inscription refers to the dedication of seven dancing girls, 11 songstresses, four players on *vīṇā*, *kañjarī* and *lābu*.[42] The Prah Einkosi inscription[43] mentions a number of musical instuments, kettledrum (*paṭaha*) the Indian flute (*vīṇā*), bell (*ghaṇṭā*), a kind of drum (*mṛdaṅga*), cymbal (*paṇava*), a kettledrum (*bherī*), and *kahala*. There

[32] Ibid.
[33] Grousset, *Histoire de l'Extreme Orient*, vol, II, p. 570.
[34] Majumdar, *Kambuja Inscriptions*, no. 111, p. 290, v. 26.
[35] Ibid., no. 145, p. 348.
[36] Ibid., no. 177, p. 467, vv. 53ff.
[37] Ibid., no. 171, p. 587.
[38] Pelliot, *BEFEO*, vol. III.
[39] Majumdar, *Kambuja Inscriptions*, n. 66, p. 331.
[40] Ibid., no. 111, p. 288, v. 7.
[41] Ibid., no. 55, p. 64, v. 36.
[42] Ibid., p. 588. Supplement, no. 6.
[43] Ref. 39.

are families noted for their musical talents.[44] Dramatic performances were also arranged. One inscription refers to a dramatic performance by Jayavarman VII's sister-in-law who later on became his wife, and the plot of this drama was adopted from the Jātakas.[45] Yajñavarāha, the *guru* of Jayavarman V was a good story teller and a dramatist.[46] Beside these, there were several other items of recreation as well. One inscription refers to a wrestling bout.[47] Festivals were equally enjoyed. The spring festival lasted for a week, and detailed rules for its celebration are also given in an inscription.[48] In the time of Jayavarman one of his officers, the governor of Āḍhyapura installed a religious festival in honour of Śiva on the third day of the month of Mādhava (Caitra). There were dancing performances on such occasions.

FAMILY LIFE AND POSITION OF WOMEN

Women seem to have enjoyed a high and respectable position in society. This was due to the indigenous matriarchal system, in which the mother had an upper hand. In some inscriptions genealogy is traced from the mother's line. Generally it was the father who had an upper hand, and the son succeeded his father. One inscription[49] refers to the performance of *pitṛtarpaṇa* by the son with water. The old man had also an important position in the house. On a record there is a reference to the preservation of the tooth of an old man.[50] Pobably this custom had little meaning save that the wisdom of the old man might continue in the family. The ladies also created a number of endowments. Joint family was usually in force.

SLAVERY

This institution was flourishing in Kambujadeśa. The slaves were inherited, but sometimes they were also acquired from the conquered country. They were mostly attached to the temples. They established marital relations among themselves, probably in a legal form and with the consent of their lord. One inscription[51] mentions 42 male servants with their 9 wives. The number of children of slaves are also mentioned in another inscription.[52] The Prah Khan inscription[53] mentions 306 male and 372 female slaves from Champā, Yavana, Pukam (i.e. Pagan in Burma) and Rvan. The slaves were the exclusive property

[44] Majumdar, *Kambuja Inscriptions*, p. 503.
[45] Ibid., no. 182, p. 524.
[46] Ibid., no. 102, p. 274, v. 21.
[47] Ibid., no. 100f, p. 584.
[48] Ibid., no. 177, p. 470, vv. 83ff.
[49] Ibid., no. 30, p. 41, v. 23.
[50] Ibid., no. 49, p. 55.
[51] Ibid., no. 81, p. 166.
[52] Ibid., no. 51, p. 56.
[53] Ibid., no. 178, p. 477.

of the owner, and if any one fled and subsequently caught, the official cut-off his nose and ears.[54] One inscription refers to the division of the products of the land among the different chiefs of the slaves.[55]

FUNERARY RITES

The Chinese annals furnish some information on this point. According to the "History of the Liang Dynasty", there were four kinds of disposal of the dead bodies: burning the body, throwing it into the river, burying it in the ground, and leaving it in the field for being eaten up by the birds. In case of mourning there was also the custom of shaving the beard and the head. The "History of the Sui Dynasty" also mentions some interesting points. According to this work, the children of the deceased did not eat or shave for seven days, and uttered loud cries. The dead body was accompanied with priests and priestesses and with prayers and music, and it was burnt with all kinds of aromatic woods. The ashes were put in an urn of gold and silver and thrown in a big river. Sometimes the body was left to be devoured by the beasts.[56]

We have, thus, referred to the social life of Kambuja on the basis of epigraphic evidence and the accounts available from the Chinese annals as well as sculptural evidence. It would appear that the influence of Indian culture was perceptible in every sphere.

[54] Ibid., p. 582.
[55] Ibid., no. 81, p. 166.
[56] Pelliot, *BEFEO*, vol. III, op. cit.

CHAPTER 17

Glimpses into the Hindu-Javanese Society of Central Java
(*From the Middle of the Seventh to the Early Part of the Tenth Century* AD)

HIMANSU BHUSAN SARKAR

THE SOURCES

Inscriptions, works of art and references in the Chinese annals constitute our chief sources for reconstructing the social history of Central Java between the middle of the seventh and the second quarter of the tenth century AD when it was the leading political factor in the history of the island. But great caution is needed before we can make use of these materials. In the introductory portion of Prof. Krom's *Hindoe-Javaansche Geschiedenis* he has surveyed with a masterly hand the difficulties attending a correct understanding of these records. The transference of copper-plates from one place to another, the great uncertainty regarding the true import of Hindu-Javanese official titles, the obscurity of the Old-Javanese language, the demarcation of the exact boundary between real and fantastic reliefs depicting contemporary social life, are some of the outstanding difficulties besetting the path of the historian. Although great strides have been taken in recent years towards solving some of these problems, we must say that we have not yet reached finality regarding most of them. It is well to bear this in mind while studying the pre-Islamic Institutions of Java. In view of these difficulties we have to proceed on the basis of the greatest common unanimity among scholars. Starting from this standpoint we can draw an outline picture of social life in Central Java for several centuries.

THE CULTURAL BACKGROUND

The inscriptions and monuments of Central Java may be considered as the expression of a virile social life, and their sites would mark the zone where the life and culture of its people developed and flourished. If we draw a line from Pekalongan in the north to Baratengah in the south and from Semparang in the north to Wanagiri in the south, that would roughly represent the area

Source: *Journal of the Greater India Society* (VIII/2, 1941, 104–15).

where the people were most active in building up their complex Hindu-Javanese culture. Within this area, there are some hills and rivers, in whose vicinity are found most of the inscriptions and monuments of Central Java. We may recall in this connection the names of Dieng, Perot, Kali bĕbĕr, Pĕsindon, Gandasuli, Banjarnĕgara, Ngabĕan, Baratĕngah, Kĕmbang Arum, Canggal, Tuk mas, Tumbu, Pakis, Barabudur, Salatiga, Argapura, etc. The rivers were the earliest channels of communication with the interior, and the earliest wave of Hindu colonisation, both in Bornéo and in Java proceeded along their courses. Even the earliest records of Central Java, those of Tuk mas[1] and Canggal,[2] lie not far from Kali Ela, and if we proceed a little to the west, along the Kali Praga, this brings us to the vicinity of Dieng, the Old-Javanese Dihyang, where the earliest dated Old-Javanese inscription of Central Java has been discovered.[3] It is not, however, possible to determine whether this influx of Hindu culture into Java proceeded from the northern or the southern shore of the island. What is, however, observable in the Sanskrit charters is that their dates become gradually later as we proceed from north to south.

The early inscriptions of Central Java, those of Tuk mas (about AD 650) and Canggal (AD 732), bear resemblance to the Pallava script and are written in Sanskrit verse. It is therefore reasonable to hold that the colonists of this region at the beginning of its recorded history, came from the Coromandel coast of southern India or from the Hinduised tracts of Western Java where the Pallava script was in vogue several centuries back. Probably there were also some colonists from the Kaliṅga region of India, as the name Ho-ling, which is deemed to be a Chinese transcription of Kaliṅga and applicable to Central Java,[4] seems to testify. The use of Sanskrit language and metre and the elaborate representation of the Hindu religious tradition indicate that there was no dearth of Sanskrit scholars in Central Java from *c.* AD 650 onwards. The Chinese reference to a Javanese scholar from Ho-ling, Jñānabhadra,[5] whom the Chinese

[1]Kern, *VG*, VII (1917), pp. 199-204.

[2]Ibid., pp. 115-28.

[3]*OJO*, 11.

[4]Prof. Krom, *Geschiedenis*, p. 104, says that the term Ho-ling should signify no more than that the Chinese had round there a "Hindu"-land, because the term "Kaling" is used in a much broader sense than what is derived from Kaliṅga. Cf. the modern parlance in the Archipelago where every Indian, irrespective of the place of his origin, called a Kling. It is possible, continues the same scholar, that the Chinese, after meeting elsewhere the Kaliṅga-people as the representatives of the Hindu-element, also spoke of "Kaling" in connection with a similar culture in Java, without meaning that the Indians had actually come from Kaliṅga. Without denying the force of Prof. Krom's argument, it may be pointed out that it is not for the first time that the Chinese found a "Hindu-land" in Java, nor is there any proof that the term "Kaling for all Indians" was current in the period under review. If we admit that the culture of Central Java was similar to that of the Kaliṅga-people elsewhere, we indirectly admit the possibility of Kaliṅga-element and culture in the Hindu-Javanese society of Central Java.

[5]I-tsing, *Mémoire*, pp. 60 ff.

call Joh-na-poh-t'o-lo points to the same conclusion. It is stated of the Chinese pilgrim Hwui-ning that he visited Kaling in AD 664-5 and remained there for three years, translating in collaboration with Jñānabhadra the extracts about the *nirvāṇa* of Buddha from the Āgama-texts that belonged to the first class of Hīnayāna-sūtras. After the translation of Hwui-ning was completed, he despatched it to China through Yun-k'i, a youthful Chinese clergyman, who had received ordination under Jñānabhadra. It has been related of such Chinese scholars that they knew not only Sanskrit, but also the native tongue. It appears therefore that the native language, which the Chinese called K'ouen-louen, played a certain *rôle* in the literary Studies. We have said above that all the inscriptions of Central Java up to AD 782 (the chatters are dated respectively in *c.* AD 650, 732, 778, 782[6]) are written in Sanskrit, which was indifferently used for Hindu and Buddhist charters. We have also seen on Chinese evidence that the monk Jñānabhadra was well versed in Sanskrit. From these facts it follows that Sanskrit had found its way into the highest circles of society by the seventh and eighth centuries. Two phases are noticeable in the introduction of this Sanskrit culture into Central Java. The first phase is represented by the script of the Tuk mas and the Canggal inscriptions which are usually described as written in the Pallava script. We may then imagine that there were southern Indians in these places in *c.* AD 650 and 732. The second phase is represented by the "Pre-Nāgarī" script which is associated with the efflorescence of Mahāyāna Buddhism and the rise of the Buddhist Śailendra emperors of Central Java, and represented in the charters of Kalasan[7] (AD 778), Kĕlurak[8] (AD 782), Ratu Baka,[9] Plaosan[10] and Sajiwan.[11] These "Pre-Nāgarī" inscriptions sustain the traditions of the previous period, and prove the infusion of new blood from northern India; into the Hindu-Javanese society of Central Java. Krom holds[12] that those who introduced these Indian influences into Central Java were culture-bearers *par excellence*, and not political potentates, for this apolitical organisation of Central Java was much too "native" for this last development. We may recall in this connection that the preceptor of a Śailendra king came to Java in AD 782 from Bengal and he purified the head of the Śailendra monarch with the dust of his lotus-feet.[13] There must have been other missionaries who emulated the example of the Bengal preceptor, and moreover the journey from India to Java must have been more convenient and frequent at this period than in the days of Fa-hian. These circumstances, gave a great impetus to the propagation of Mahāyāna Buddhism in Central Java, which pushed Hīnayāna

[6] Inscriptions of Tuk mas, Canggal, Kalasan and Kĕlurak.
[7] The latest edition by Bosch in *TBG*, 68 (1928), pp. 57-62.
[8] Ibid., pp. 16-56.
[9] Ibid., p. 63.
[10] *OV*, 1915, pp. 89-91.
[11] *VBG*, 7 (1814), pp. 22-4.
[12] *Geschiedenis*, pp. 100-1.
[13] The Inscription of Kĕlurak.

Buddhism into the background. But whether this expansion of Indian culture was due to those culture-bearers *par excellence* or to the traders or to both, the fact remains that Sanskrit is used in all early records of Central Java, and the earliest literary work of that region the *Candakaraṇa*,[14] is an attempt to familiarise the Javanese population with Sanskrit. There were also other books of the same class, the *svaravyañjan* for example, which Juynboll describes in *BKI* 6: 8(1901), pp. 630-3 and which also attempt to teach Sanskrit. To the Indians coming from various parts of the Indian continent Sanskrit was perhaps something like a *lingua franca* from the very beginning of Indians' contact with Central Java, but Sanskrit could make an appeal only to the intellectual class of the Javanese and it could not be understood by the common people. This might have led to the development of the Old-Javanese language, which was probably a mixture of Old-Malay and Sanskrit with a couple of centuries of uninterrupted and independent development on the Javanese soil. I say a mixture of Old-Malay and Sanskrit, because when the Chinese pilgrims speak of K'ouen-louen as the native language of Java and Sumatra, Old-Malay was used in the inscriptions of Sumatra. This shows that Old-Malay is equivalent to K'ouen-louen. But Old-Malay is somewhat different from Old-Javanese, consequently we have to postulate an independent development of Old-Malay in Java under the circumstances mentioned above. The oldest of the Old-Javanese records is elated in AD 809. The specimens of the oldest literary Old-Javanese records are preserved in the above-mentioned *Candakaraṇa*, whose date is not certain, but Prof. Krom places it between AD 750 and 850.

Let us imagine that the formative period of Old-Javanese falls between *c.* 650 (date of the Tuk mas inscription and of the Chinese report about K'ouen-louen) and AD 809 (date of the Old-Javanese stone inscription at Dieng). This was perhaps a period of mutual understanding and penetrative social intercourse through the medium of corrupt Sanskrit and K'ouen-louen. This reminds us of the remark of Brandes, who mentions three stages in the appropriation of Sanskrit into Old-Javanese: first, when Sanskrit was learnt by hearing alone, then when it was learnt by study, and lastly, when it was known by ever debilitating memory alone. In the first period, Sanskrit words followed the peculiarity of the Javanese language, in the second period they were correctly given, in the third period Javanese pronunciation again triumphed. According to Krom, the *Amaramālā* (*Candakaraṇa*), which is placed by him between AD 750 and 850, belongs to the second stage. The first stage is therefore to be pushed back before *c.* AD 750, since when no non-Sanskritic records have reached our hands.

The influence of Indian culture on the upper strata of society was undoubtedly great, but how far did it penetrate among the masses? If we consult the inscriptions of Central Java, both Sanskrit and Javanese, it would appear that important personages sometimes bear Sanskrit names, but even then, it is not possible to determine whether they were Hindus or Hinduised Javans.

[14]*Med. Kon. Akad.* v. *Wet.* 58 (1924), pp. 203-6.

While discussing the name of Pūrṇavarman in the West-Javanese inscriptions, Prof. Vogel[15] has admirably summed up his views on this point, and his remark, quoted below, is equally applicable to the present instance:

> It would, perhaps, be equally risky to conclude from Pūrṇavarman's name, that he was of Indian birth or extraction. He may, no doubt, have been an immigrant from some part of the Indian continent, or a descendant of such an immigrant, but equally well he may have been an indigenous prince of Malay race who had adopted Hindu culture and religion and along with it had assumed an Indo-Aryan name. A Sanskritic name in itself would prove as little with regard to the nationality of the bearer as a name in Arabic, Hebrew, Greek or Latin. That Pūrṇavarman, if not a Hindu, was at any rate Hinduised, may be taken for granted.

The names of the common folk in the inscriptions are, on the other hand, mainly Javanese, but we should not fail to mention that some Puranic and Epic names also occur in Old-Javanese inscriptions. They first occur in the inscription of Kuburan Caṇḍi,[16] dated ŚE 753 where we come across the names of Narada (Nā°), Pāṇḍava (Pā°), Baruṇa, Nandi (°dī) and Ravan (Rāvana). The names of women are also given in the charters of Central Java with the further designation that they are the wives or mothers of such and such persons. We should, however, bear in mind that the significance of the "name" was, and still is, very peculiar in Java. The meanings of "name", "title" and "social status" are synonymous in Javanese; for example, the Javanese word jĕnĕg may mean anyone of these; it often happens that a Javanese changes his "name" on several occasions in a lifetime, e.g., on marriage, fatherhood, change of occupations or promotion, etc. We may recall in this connection the classical example of King Balitung (AD 898-910) who changed his name in AD 907 into Dharmmodaya Mahāśambhu on the occasion of his marriage.[17]

A general study of the inscriptions leaves, however, the impression that the social organisation was very little affected by Indian factors. But it may perhaps be admitted that many Indians, who had come over to Java for trading or other purposes, remained in the land and married Javanese maidens. This intermarriage accelerated the pace of Indianisation of Central Java and had the same result as Islamic intermarriages in the last days of Hindu supremacy in Java in the beginning of the sixteenth century, with this difference, that the Hindu intermarrying families did not probably exercise sovereign powers which the Islamic princes of the harbour-regions evidently did. This fusion of blood and culture led to the development of a composite society, which was neither Hindu nor Javanese, but Hindu-Javanese, a society containing elements from both the races. While this impact did not much affect the social and political organisation of Central Java, it revolutionised the religious ideals of the Javanese people to an unprecedented extent. Worships of forefathers and spirits continued, but the highest homage was paid to the gods of Hinduism and Buddhism, clear

[15] While editing the West-Java inscriptions in *Publ. Oudh Dienst*, I (1925), pp. 15-35.
[16] *TBG*, 70 (1930), pp. 157-70.
[17] The Kĕdu charter of ŚE 829 (*TBG*, 67, pp. 172-205).

traces of which are found in the inscriptions of Java. There are not only invocations to Hindu and Buddhistic deities, but there are also temples and images to glorify the blessings conferred by these imported gods. We may recall in this connection the august *caitya* of Barabudur and the temple-complex of Lero Jonggrang, which respectively bear eloquent tributes to Buddha and Śiva, the two highest gods of the Indian religious systems.

Against this cultural background, we may best try to understand the social life of the Hindu-Javanese population of Central Java. The people of villages were divided into various classes, such as *anak wanua*, *tuha wanua*, *rāma*, *samakaki*, etc., which terms we frequently come across in the inscriptions. At the village of Kalasan, there were *bhikṣus* in AD 778. We also read in the copper-plates of Panaraga[18] that noblemen and slaves, house-dwellers and *bhikṣus*, and even the four *varṇas* participated in the foundation of freehold in AD 901. The four *varṇas* are mentioned for the first time in the inscription of Kĕboan Pasar,[19] dated AD 873, but the authenticity of the charter is not beyond doubt, and moreover the charter is probably of East-Javanese origin. The four *varṇas* are again mentioned in a record of the time of King Dakṣa, who ruled in AD 915.[20] In the reliefs of Barabudur we find representations of the royal court where the king confers with his brahmin ministers, the first of the four *varṇas*. It is doubtful if there were pure brahmins of Indian extraction, nor is there any reason to suppose the three other *varṇas* as living in Central Java in strict aloofness from the Hindu-Javanese society. What is probable is that the Hindu-Javanese society of Central Java was artificially modelled upon the ancient society of Hindu India, but the similarity did not go beyond this class division. Besides these four *varṇas*, we have references to particular class divisions. In the stone inscriptions of Pereng,[21] dated AD 863 there is a passage referring to the *Kalangs* of the Hindu-Javanese society of Central Java. They have been supposed to be the descendants of war-prisoners, or the Ur-population or the lower folk with un-Javanese elements. The term *hulun haji*, a class of slaves, first occurs in the stone inscription of Diëng,[22] dated AD 809. Of classes of women we do not hear much. It is only in the New History of the T'ang dynasty[23] that we hear of a class of women—if we may use the term "class"—called *viṣakanyā*. The passage runs as follows: "In this country (Kaling) there are poisonous girls. When one has intercourse with them, he gets painful ulcers and dies, but his body does not decay." Whether we believe in the story or not, such "poisonous girls" are also known to us from Indian literature.[24]

[18] *OJO*, XXII.

[19] *OJO*, IX.

[20] *KO*, XVII.

[21] *Poerbatjaraka, Agastya*, pp. 45 ff.

[22] *OJO*, II.

[23] This dynasty ended in AD 906. The statement given above may refer to the last half of the ninth century.

[24] Cf. Penzer in Tawney's *Kathāsaritsāgara* (tr.) II (1924), pp. 311 ff.

Besides these class divisions there are also others known to the inscriptions of Central Java, but their import is either unknown or uncertain. The list of such terms will run into several dozens. It appears therefore that there were various classes of people and that there was gradation in the ranks of the villagers. The latter point is clearly illustrated in the inscription of Wanagiri,[25] dated AD 903, where reference is made to people of the lowest, mediocre and highest positions.

THE POSITION OF WOMEN

The position of women in the Central Javanese society was fairly high. The Chinese annals state[26] that in AD 674-5 the people of Ho-ling took as their ruler a woman of the name of Si-mo. Her rule was most excellent. In her time even things dropped on the way were not stolen. Although there are some untrustworthy elements in the story, the reference to a particular year invests the story with a halo of reality, and what is more important, the story refers to the choice or selection of the ruler by the people. A mutilated passage in the Canggal inscription, dated AD 732, has been deemed by some scholars[27] to refer to a joint sovereignty of a king and his sister.

In the inscriptions of Central Java prior to AD 929, we do not hear of any other ruling queen or princesses. But there are notices of other notable women who occupied high positions in society. The stone inscription of Karangtĕngah,[28] dated ŚE 769 (Brandes) or ŚE 719 (Juynboll and Goris), seems to refer to a land-grant by a certain Palar and his wife. This may indicate that the wife had some control over the property disposed of. An East-Javanese inscription[29] leaves no doubt about the matter, but some Central Javanese charters also furnish substantial evidence on this point. The copper-plates of Panaraga, dated ŚE 823 refer, for example, to the names of some women who were the owners of lands at Taji and who gladly gave them away for the temple of Devasabhā. In the inscriptions officers receive gifts of various kinds, but it is not until AD 884[30] that we hear of gifts being awarded to women, but even then the instance is not beyond doubt, because there is a mutilated passage round about. The first positive reference is found in AD 901[31] when Lady Dhetā, the wives

[25] *TBG*, 74 (1934), pp. 269-95.

[26] *Notes*, p. 14 and Pelliot, *Deux itnéraires*, p. 297.

[27] Vide Krom, *Geschiedenis*, pp. 123 ff.

But the interpretation of the passage by Vogel seems to me to be nearer the mark: "He the son of the sister of (the person) named Sannāha . . . is (now) ruling the kingdom with justice." If King Sañjaya ruled *with* his sister, the poet was bound to use the third case-ending for *svasṛ*. Secondly, the very next verse opens with '*yasmiñchā-sa*(*ti*), which can only signify that the king ruled alone.

[28] *OJO*, IV.

[29] *OJO*, XXXII.

[30] *OJO*, XVII.

[31] *OJO*, XXIII.

of the *patihs* and the *nayakas* receive gifts of various kinds. This distribution of gifts to women becomes almost a regular feature of central Javanese inscriptions from this date onwards. Women were also entrusted with other functions. For example, Lady Dhetā and her children are alone placed in charge of the temple of Devasabhā and its freehold, so that they may protect the sacred religious foundation. What is noteworthy is that Lady Dhetā was probably the *raka* of Śrī bharu (Lord of Śrī bharu), the latter possibly being a place-name. If my interpretation of the relevant passage is correct, it would furnish an additional proof of the rights of women over manors.

Early marriage was not unknown in Central Java. A proof is furnished by the inscription of Kembang Arum, AD 902,[32] where among the donees we come across the names of older matrons, mothers of young children and wives of youngsters. In some cases men were polygamous, and a presumptive evidence is furnished by the inscription of AD 908, published by Van Naerssen in *Aanw. Kol. Inst.*, 1934, where Ladies Sucintĕ, Kina, Waita and Sawitā appear to be the wives of *samgat* Kalangwungkal (Pl. II, re° 11-12), but a more conclusive evidence is furnished by the inscription of Pĕsindon,[33] dated AD 904, which states that "the spiritual teacher Siwita purified his body (and) went away with all (his) wives and two daughters". This very passage also indicates that women went to pilgrimages along with their husbands. But, far the most important record throwing light on the status of women is the so-called *jayapattra-Dieduksman*[34] which resembles charters of Central Java though its findspot is not known. According to Brandes, its date is ŚE 849, but Goris[35] and Stutterheim[36] read the date as 829. It records that a certain Tabwĕl was sued by *samĕgat* Pinapan, viz., Gawul and his wife Gallam for the repayment of money borrowed from *sang* Dharmma by Campa, the wife of Tabwĕl. As Campa died childless and the complainant did not arrive at court, the case was dismissed. It is also noteworthy that among the witnesses there was Guru woju, the wife of a former (?) *samĕgat* Pinapan. The inscription proves that there were women-judges, that women could borrow on their own account and that a women could also be a witness which last privilege is usually denied to women in Hindu Law. Women also participated in religious festivities celebrated on the occasion of founding freeholds, when there were feasts, music, dancing, jesting, recitals, boar-fights and cock-fights. We shall have occasion to describe this fully later on.

(*To be continued*)

[32] *JGIS*, 1938, no. 1.

[33] *TBG*, 25, pp. 464-5.

[34] *TBG*, 32 (1889), pp. 98-149.

[35] *OV* (1928), p. 64.

[36] *TBG*, 75, p. 421 n. 1 and 437 n. 4.

CHAPTER 18

Dvīpāntara

K.A. NILAKANTA SASTRI

About ten years ago Sylvain Lévi established the correct form of the word rendered into *Kouen-louen* in a Sanskrit-Chinese Lexicon compiled by a Central Asian monk, Li-yen, of the kingdom of Koutcha; the Sanskrit word is *dvīpāntara*.[1]

Considering the apparently very corrupt form in which the Sanskrit words are given in the lexicon, this must be considered in itself a great gain, and P.C. Bagchi, who knows more about the lexicon than any one else, has accepted the correctness of his master's restoration, and stated further[2]: "We may add that the tradition localising the *dvīpāntara* in Indonesia has persisted in India to this day. Even recently while speaking of the islands to which exiles are sent, people spoke not of the Andamans or of Tennasserim, but of *dvīpāntara*." This statement, I may say, holds good of south India as well.

But the use of the term in ancient times is decidedly of greater historical interest, and Sylvain Lévi himself, in the article cited above, discussed several passages, mostly drawn from the *Kathāsarit-sāgara*, in which the term *dvīpāntara* occurs. He also cited *Manu* III.158 and *Baudhāyana Dharmasūtra* 2.1.2.2. on prohibition of sea-voyages (*samudrayāyin* and *samudrasamyānam*) and the glosses of Kullūka and Govindasvāmī thereon where the term *dvīpāntara* occurs.

It is curious by the way to note how this prohibition against sea-voyages is a very old affair and how very systematically it has been disregarded in practice through the ages. Baudhāyana, for instance, places it at the head of *patanīyanī,* of sins which according to his annotator are only a little less heinous than *mahāpātakas,* and prescribes a three years' penance for it. Yet we have incontrovertible evidence from the epigraphy of Indonesia of orthodox brahmins having crossed the sea to perform the most meritorious Vedic sacrifices in the lands colonised by them long after the age of Baudhāyana. Are we to assume that these brahmins, having crossed the sea once, purified themselves by the prescribed penance in the new lands? Are we further to assume that there was no regular intercourse between the brahmins in India and their brethern abroad,

[1]*BKI*, vol. 88, pp. 621-7.

[2]*Deux Lexiques Sanskrit-Chinois*, tome ii (1937), p. 349, n. 28.

Source: *Journal of the Greater India Society* (IX/1, 1938, 24–30).

or that each voyage was followed by a penance? True we have no definite data before us, but he would be a bold man who would answer these questions in the affirmative without any hesitation.

Sylvain Lévi came to the conclusion that like *Kouen-louen* in Chinese, *dvīpāntara* in Sanskrit was applied to the Islands and the continent of the "Southern Seas" as the Chinese called them. Let us note also this. Among the citations discussed by Lévi, there are two which use *dvīpāntara* and *dvīpānta* in the plural, viz.,

(1) *tasya dvīpāntareṣvasti sarveṣu api gatāgatam.* "He goes to and fro among all the other islands" (Tawney);
(2) *nagarī tvadabhipretā dvīpānteṣu śruta punaḥ*— ". . . is situated in one of the distant islands". It seems possible that the plural in these instances is just in accordance with the ordinary rule of Sanskrit grammar that the names of the countries must be used in the plural, and if this is the correct view, *dvīpāntara* may be treated as more or less the proper name of the entire region specified. The name in that case would be one describing the lands concerned from the standpoint of India. India is one *dvīpa*—Jambudvīpa; Malaya is its sister—*dvīpāntara*—across the sea. It is of course well known that *dvīpa* in these contexts does not mean "island" exactly.

There are two passages, one in Sanskrit and the other in Tamil, in which the word *dvīpāntara* occurs and which both go far to confirm the correctness of Sylvain Lévi's surmise. The Sanskrit verse is so well known that it is a surprise that it has not been taken into account so far in the discussion; it occurs in the *Raghuvaṃśa* (VI.57) of Kālidāsa in Sunandā's description of the Kaliṅga king Hemāṅgada to Indumatī on the occasion of her *svayaṃvara*; among the amenities the princess could enjoy if she chose Hemāṅgada for her husband was this:

anena sārdhaṁ vihārāmburāśeḥ
tīreṣu tālivana-marmareṣu ।
dvīpāntarā-'nīta-lavaṅga-puṣpaiḥ
apākṛta-sveda-lavā marudbhiḥ ॥

The bride is told by her maid that if she chose the ruler of Kaliṅga for her husband, she could sport with him on the shore of the ocean in the midst of rustling palms, while the winds wafting the flowers of cloves from the *dvīpāntara* remove the sweat from her skin. It takes no effort to see that the land described as the home of the cloves, *lavaṅga*, is the Malay peninsula. It must be noted at the same time that all the commentators on this verse fail to exhibit the slightest inkling of this. But this is perhaps not surprising as Kālidāsa's political geography has baffled his commentators at many other points.

The other reference occurs in the life of Tirumangai Āḻvār as narrated in the *Guruparamparai, Āṛāyirappaḍi,* one of the earliest hagiologies of Tamil Vaiṣṇavism. The work may be taken to date from the twelfth or thirteenth century AD, Tirumangai was casting about for funds with which to complete the plans he had made for the renovation of the Raṅganātha temple at Śrīraṅgam. and he hit upon the idea of robbing the Buddhist *vihāra* at Negapatam of its Buddha image of solid gold. In this project, the information given by an old Vaiṣṇava lady residing at Negapatam was found very useful. It was to this effect: "The artisan who made this golden image and the Vimāna under which it is enshrined lives at present in *dvīpāntara*." This statement was enough to send Tirumangai to *dvīpāntara* where he had no great difficulty in identifying the house of the celebrated artist and getting him, by a ruse, to surrender the secret of the construction of the *vimāna* which enabled the *āḻvār* to enter the temple easily and remove the golden image according to plan.

Obviously in this story *dvīpāntara* is not any other island, or an indefinite distant island, as it is usually understood, but some specific country which needed no further description for its identity to be established; in short, *dvīpāntara* is a proper name. May we not suggest that this term was specifically applied to Malaya, Malayadvīpa, which was the "other island" across the sea to a person speaking from India? If this is correct, Chinese *Kouen-louen* must be taken to mean definitely the entire Indo-Chinese peninsula, if not merely Malaya.

We must, however, beware of pressing too far these suggestions derived from the Central Asian Chinese Lexicon and supported by the usages we have discussed above. The Chinese term in the equation, *Kouen-louen*, is used by other writers in other widely different applications as even a cursory glance through Ferrand's celebrated article on the subject in *Journal Asiatique* (1919) would show.[3] On the other side the Sanskrit term *dvīpāntara* does not get completely free of its grammatical origin *anyad dvīpam dvīpāntaram*, and develop into a full-fledged proper name, as the vacillation in usage between the singular and plural forms shows. Still there is enough before us to justify our recognising at least a pronounced tendency in Indian usage to localise *dvīpāntara* in the Malay peninsula with some of the larger islands in its neighbourhood.

[3] See also *Etudes Asiatiques*, II, pp. 261-3.

CHAPTER 19

Some Notes on the Kingdom of Dvāravatī

H.G. QUARITCH WALES

Our knowledge of the ancient Indianised kingdom of Dvāravatī, which attained its height during the sixth and seventh centuries AD and occupied the lower parts of the Mênâm and Méklong valleys of Central Siam, is at present based almost entirely on the results of M. Çoedès's important researches in this field. Finds made from time to time at Năk'on Păṭhŏm and elsewhere, and the excavations at P'ŏng Tŭ'k,[1] though they have yielded no records of events nor provided us with the names and dates of kings on which to base an outline of the history of the kingdom, have yet given us a tolerably clear idea of the culture of the people, at least during the period of their greatness. But the later centuries of the Dvāravatī period remain veiled in obscurity and a primary object of this article is to suggest a means by which that veil might some day be rent asunder.

Before I come to that, however, I should like to take the opportunity of expressing my views on the question as to whether or not this territory played an important *role* as a medium for the distribution of Indian cultural influences to the further east, either during the fourth and fifth centuries when it seems to have formed part of the Fu-nan empire, or after the middle of the sixth when it became the independent State of Dvāravatī. When speaking of the magnificent statues of Aṅkor Bórĕi, which are so closely related to the Gupta sculpture of India, M. Çoedès says: "It is not impossible that this Buddhist art arrived in Cambodia, or rather in Fu-nan, through the intermediary of Dvāravatī. . . . For the Buddhist art of Fu-nan, Dvāravatī has perhaps played the part of intermediary between Gupta India and the Mékong delta."[2]

The difficulty of accepting this view is that the statues found at Aṅkor Bórĕi are so manifestly nearer Indian Gupta models than are any of the numerous Buddhist images showing Gupta relationship that have been found in Central Siam, and they must be placed at least a century earlier in date. There is ample evidence that Indian influences reached the mouth of the Mékŏng *via* the all-sea route, and afterwards *via* the Tăkuapa-C'ăiya transpeninsular route, at a very early period. It is difficult therefore to resist the conclusion that these almost purely Indian sculptures from Aṅkor Bórĕi are the expression of

[1]G. Çoedès, "The Excavations at P'ong Tuk", *JSS*, vol. XXI, pt. 3, 1928.

[2]*Recueil des Inscriptions du Siam*, pt. ii, p. 4; also *Ars Asiatica*, vol. XII, p. 23.

Source: *Journal of the Greater India Society* (V/1, 1938, 24–30).

influences brought to Cambodia *via* one of the more direct colonial routes just mentioned.

On the other hand, the Dvāravatī sculptures of Central Siam are without exception definitely stylised, if not decadent. They must be looked upon as the final expression of a more northerly stream of Indian culture that had probably already passed through its period of active development in the Môn country of Lower Burma before, penetrating eastwards *via* the Three Pagoda and Papun routes, it exhausted itself on the rich plains of Central Siam. In the neighbourhood of the Prăchin Valley, towards the border between modern Siam and Cambodia, these two cultural streams must have established contact and no doubt cultural exchanges took place; but it is difficult to imagine that cultural influences that had travelled *via* Burma, the mountain passes, and finally the wide plains of Dvāravatī, so far from their original Indian homeland, could have retained vigour and purity of conception enough to produce the superb statuary of Aṅkor Bórĕi. But if the influence of Dvāravatī culture on the growing Khmèr civilisation was probably small, its importance for the future of Siam was great; and this brings me to the consideration of the obscure later centuries of the kingdom of Dvāravatī.

During the twelfth and thirteenth centuries the Khmèr empire extended its sway over the territory of Dvāravatī, and buildings of provincial Khmèr style were erected at almost all the cities of the Dvāravatī kingdom that had survived until that time. In the thirteenth century, with the break-up of the Khmèr empire, the Thai State of Sũkhot'ăi spread its power southward over all this region. But its suzerainty was short-lived, and in AD 1350 we find a large part of Central Siam dominated by a Prince of U T'ông, a city situated some 50 miles west of Ayŭth'ya on what was then the main Sŭp'ăn River but is now an insignificant tributary. H.R.H. Prince Damrong, who visited the place in 1904, placed on record[3] the legend that in AD 1350 the Prince of U T'ông, fleeing from an epidemic, deserted the city and marched westward to the Menam where he founded the city of Ayŭth'ya which was for more than four hundred years to be the capital of a united kingdom of Siam. Not only is the name Dvāravatī one of the titles by which Ayŭth'ya came to be known, but Prince Damrong was able to establish a definite connection between U T'ông and the Dvāravatī culture when he found statues and coins of exactly the same type that had previously been found at Năk'on Păṭhŏm. It seems very likely that U T'ông was one of the old cities of the Dvāravatī kingdom, which, on account of its remote situation, had retained much of its early Hīnayāna Buddhist culture at the expense of a nominal vassalage to the Khmèrs. Later, having got rid of its Khmèr, and finally of its Sŭkhot'ăi Thai overlords, it was able to re-establish its independence.

There is good reason for believing that the early civilisers of the Dvāravatī kingdom were Indianised Môn colonists from Lower Burma, but the fact that

[3] "The Foundation of Ayudhya", in *JSS*, vol. I, p. 7.

the Prince of U T'ông was himself a Thai need cause no surprise. The local legend maintains that his family had comparatively recently migrated from the North; and if that is so they were members of one of the later waves of Thai immigration. But recent researches[4] suggest that the Thai had become established in Central Siam at a much earlier period than had formerly been supposed and the Thai of U T'ông had no doubt absorbed their Môn civilisers centuries before this city was deserted. I have mentioned that the Buddhist images found at U T'ông by Prince Damrong were of the Dvāravatī style, and hence it is necessary to note M. Çoedés's explanation for denominating as "School of U T'ông" a number of sculptures found not actually at U T'ông, but at other cities in Central Siam, and showing mixed Dvāravatī, Khmèr and Sŭkhot'ăi characteristics. M. Çoedés justifies this classification on the grounds that many of these sculptures may well date from the early part of the fourteenth century, before Ayŭth'ya had been founded and when U T'ông dominated the region. U T'ông, indeed, during the later centuries of its existence, could scarcely be expected to have escaped the varied cultural influences that must have been brought to bear on what remained of the Dvāravatī kingdom, and this is certainly supported by the presence of several stone Hindu figures of rather mixed ancestry still to be seen in the neghbourhood of U T'ông.

Following the useful pointers extended by Prince Damrong and M. Çoedés I myself visited U T'ông early in 1936. While my visit was too short to do justice to the site, it had the effect of still further stimulating my interest. The city is a rectangular enclosure measuring about a mile from north to south and half that distance from east to west. It is bounded by a moat and mound and the area within is largely occupied by thin jungle broken by extensive bare patches where little vegetation seems able to grow. Outside the city are one or two brick *stūpas* the style of which indicates that they probably date from not much earlier than the thirteenth century. Within the enclosure there are the remains of only one monument, an old *stūpa* basement, situated at the centre of the city. This basement was itself constructed from large re-employed bricks, many of them ornamented with whorls, which must have once formed part of a much earlier structure. At a spirit shrine in the neighbouring Chinese village I was shown a stucco head, said to have been dug up near some *stūpa* in the neighbourhood. The features were of exactly the same type as those of many of the heads found at Năk'on Pățhŏm and believed to date from the sixth or seventh century.

There had been several thunderstorms at U T'ông at the time of my visit and the rain had washed out large quantities of small objects from the surface soil of the open spaces that occupied so much of the city enclosure. Besides household utensils and pottery we found the crucibles of metal workers often associated with lumps of base metal and a few specks of gold. Moreover agate,

[4]"Tai Pottery" by P'raya Nakon P'rah Ram in *JSS*, vol. XXIX, pt. i, 1936; also "Further Excavations at P'ong Tük", by H.G.Q. Wales in *Ind. Art and Letters*, vol. X, no. 1, 1936.

cornelian, crystal and garnet beads mainly of Indian type were found in great abundance and here and there were uncremated human bones. These objects were lying on the sites of the houses of the last inhabitants of U T'ông and, while it is true that beads often tend to work to the surface, the evidence seems to offer some support for the legend which tells us that the city had to be hastily abandoned as the result of an epidemic. A few more objects of interest were produced by the villagers who said they were accustomed to search over the city site whenever heavy rain had washed over the soil. Among these objects were several gold rings, a golden earring set with polished rubies and a large primitive bullet coin, stamped with lion, elephant and *cakra* marks, of the type designated "pre-Ayuthian" by Le May.[5]

I decided to dig two or three trial trenches at different points on these open spaces, in order to determine whether the place would be likely to repay complete excavation at some future date. The deposits proved to be very definitely stratified with several clearly differentiated occupation levels each marked by a refuse of fragments of fish and animal bones, shells, pottery fragments and layers of charcoal, the remains of ancient kitchen-middens. No human bones were found at these levels, and beads only rarely. The most interesting point, however, was that while a whole C'ălieng jar was found only a foot beneath the surface, fragments of this ware were found as much as 7 feet thereunder. Below this level fragments of coarse earthenware only were found, down to a depth of about 11 feet at which depth natural soil seemed nearly to have been reached. While absolute depth of finds is in itself of course no criterion, it is certainly remarkable that C'ălieng ware should have been found 7 feet down in a city the great age of which is suggested by the images of Dvāravatī style that have been found there. Until recently it was not supposed that glazed pottery was made in Siam much before the twelfth or thirteenth century, but the depth at which these C'ălieng fragments were found at U T'ông must now be considered in conjunction with the evidence adduced by P'răya Năk'on P'raḥ Ram to the effect that C'ălieng pottery was made from AD 500 to 1374.[6]

For the present it would obviously be premature to attempt to build further on our scant knowledge of the remains at U T'ông. But the fact that at more than one level ancient brick courses were encountered in my trial trenches suggests that thorough excavation might not only tell us much about the everyday domestic life of the people, but that the foundations of brick temples, perhaps with sculptures and even inscriptions, might very well be brought to light. Indeed, now that P'ong Tü'k seems to have been more or less exhausted, and most of the other known Dvāravatī sites are not available for excavation either by reason of their sanctity or their being modern centres of civilisation, the possibilities of U T'ông deserve careful attention, not only for the additional

[5]"The Coinage of Siam", in *JSS*, vol. XVIII, 1924, Pl. 1, 3.
[6]Loc. cit., p. 23.

light that the excavation of that city might throw on the heyday of Dvāravatī culture, but because it might serve to illumine the whole history of Central Siam, right from the beginning of the Dvāravatī kingdom until the end of those later obscure centuries at the close of which the torch was handed on to the new kingdom of Ayŭth'ya. To the careful investigator U T'ông should make a strong appeal by reason of the clearly stratified nature of its deposits which have not attracted, and are not likely to attract, the attention of the treasure-seekers who have harmed so many other sites in Siam. The complete excavation of U T'ông would be no small undertaking and should not be undertaken lightly; but it is probably one of the most important of the tasks that lie before the archaeologist of the future in Siam.

LITERATURE AND ARTS

CHAPTER 20

On the Source of the Old-Javanese Rāmāyaṇa Kakawin

MANOMOHAN GHOSH

While going through the *Indian Influences on the Literature of Java and Bāli*[1] I found the author drawing attention to a passage[2] in canto II of the *Kakawin*[3] of Yogīśvara which resembled very much a stanza in canto II of the *Bhaṭṭikāvya*. The passage of the *Kakawin*, as we learn from an English translation of the Dutch version of the same by Kern, runs as follows:

> There was no watery place which was without lotuses. There were no lotuses which were not full of bees, and the bees were buzzing. There were no bees which would allow their songs go unheard.

The passage in the *Bhaṭṭikāvya* is as follows:

Na taj-jalaṃ yan-na sucārupaṅkajaṃ
Na paṅkajaṃ tad-yad-alīnaṣatpadam ।
Na ṣatpado' sau na juguñja yaḥ kalaṃ
Na guñjitaṃ tan-na jahāra yan manaḥ ।।

The striking similarity between the two passages even after one of them had to pass through the media of two different languages convinced me that the similarity might not be quite accidental and Yogīśvara, the author of the *Kakawin*, was most probably acquainted with the *Bhaṭṭikāvya* itself. Sarkar, however, did not view the similarity between the two passages in this light probably because of Kern's remark that the author of the Old Javanese *Kakawin* did not know Sanskrit.[4] But as I found from the excellent summary of the first nineteen cantos of the *Kakawin* given in Sarkar's work, that the passages occurred as the 19th strophe in canto II of both the works I could no longer consider Kern's opinion about Yogīśvara's ignorance of Sanskrit as conclusive. I strongly suspected that Yogīśvara was not only acquainted with Sanskrit and the *Bhaṭṭikāvya* in the original but that his *Kakawin* might have been a translation

[1] Published by the Greater India Society, 1934.
[2] *Indian Influences*, p. 180.
[3] Placed by scholars sometime between AC 950 and 1300 Sarkar suggests (ibid., p. 175) AC 1094 as the likely date of composition of this work.
[4] *Indian Influences*, p. 174.
Source: *Journal of the Greater India Society* (III/1, 1936, 113–17).

of this *Kunst-epos* into the old Javanese language. This hypothesis led me to examine thoroughly the *Bhaṭṭikāvya* in the light of the excellent digest of the *Kakawin* (up to its 19th canto) given by Sarkar.[5] This examination has yielded the following results:

1. The plot of the subject matter of the first five cantos is, even in detail, in wonderful agreement with that of the first five cantos of the *Kakawin*. But for the fact that the number of stanzas or strophes in the corresponding cantos of the two works is not equal we might consider one work (up to its 4th canto) to be a sort of replica of the other. The number in the first four cantos of the two works is as follows:

			Bhaṭṭi	*Kakawin*
I	...	...	27	59
II	...	...	55	77
III	...	...	56	46
IV	...	...	45	above 58

2. The strophes in canto V of the *Kakawin* which describe the appearance of Rāvaṇa in the Pañcavaṭī in the guise of an ascetic contain expressions marvellously similar to those in the corresponding passages of the *Bhaṭṭikāvya*. Thus we have in the *Kakawin:*

> He resembled a pure and upright Śaiva monk, virtuous and holy; his head was smoothly shaved except for a little tuft of hair on the crown.
> His teeth were as white as crystal. He expected to get a garland of roses(?)[6] and a bowl of pumpkin to attach to his shoulder belt. His monkish robe was beautifully red and dyed with lac. He proceeded to ask for alms, by which pretext he could conceal his (base) design.
> While moving on, he mumbled his prayers and had pious words in his lips. His glance was gentle and loving—it was outwardly very friendly and captivating, as if nothing remained of his demoniac character. Without any interruption, he wended through the beautiful and solitary woodland.

The corresponding passages in the *Bhaṭṭi* are as follows:

Gate tasmin *jalaśuciḥ śuddhadan Rāvaṇaḥ śikhī* ।।
Jañjapūko' kṣamālāvān dhārayo mṛdalābunaḥ ।। (61)

Kamaṇḍalukapālena śirasā mṛjāvatā ।
Saṃvastrya lākṣike vastre mātrāḥ saṃbhāṇḍya daṇḍavān ।। (62)

Adhīyann-ātmavid vidyāṃ *dhārayan maskarivratam* ।
Vadan bahvaṅgulisphoṭaṃ bhrūkshepaṃ vilokayan ।। (63)

[5] Ibid., pp. 179-94.
[6] Either the Dutch translation or the English version seems to be wrong here.

Sandidarśayiṣuḥ sāma nijuhnūṣaḥ kṣapaṭatām ।
Caṃkramāvān samāgatya Sītām-ūce sukhā bhava ।। (64)

One can easily notice that expressions italicised in the *Bhaṭṭi* passages have been almost literally translated in the *Kakawin*, the author of which appears to have taken as much from the *Bhaṭṭi* as he could easily assimilate in his work. A literal versified translation is surely an almost impossible task. Thus it may be assumed that Yogīśvara while writing the *Kakawin* had the *Bhaṭṭikāvya* before him and adopted the theme of the latter in its details and, as often as possible, number of expressions as well.

There is yet another passage in canto V of the *Kakawin* which betrays a connection with the *Bhaṭṭikāvya*. It deals with the conversation between Sītā and Rāvaṇa and is as follows:

Moon's beauty cannot be compared with yours, because her charms pass off by the time of the day.

If the lotus-flowers of the pond . . . they cannot yet stand comparison with your beauty; because they close down and decline on the approach of the night.

The place where you live is really dangerous, impossible for men, a wilderness! Do you not fear the malicious snakes and wild elephants?. . .

You are so exceedingly soft and tender and really so charming; the wood has been, as it were, delighted by your presence. How fortunate is the man who had been acknowledged by you as your husband! He must deserve some praises for possessing you at the present moment.

I have travelled through other lands of this world, but I have never come across any one like you; so beautiful you are indeed! You appear to me at least the most perfect type of beauty, and my present life is not going to be useless now that I have known you.

With this should be compared the following stanzas from the *Bhaṭṭi*:

Sāyantanīṃ tithipraṇyaḥ paṅkajānāṃ divātanīm ।
Kāntiṃ kāntyā sadātanyā hrepayantī śucismitā ।। (65)

Kā tvam-ekākinī bhīru niranvayajane vane ।
Kṣudhyanto 'pyaghasan vyālās-tvām-apālāṃ kathaṃ na vā ।। (66)

Hṛdayaṅgama-mūrttis-tvaṃ subhagambhāvukaṃ vanam ।
Kurvāṇā bhīmam-apyetad vadā'bhyaiḥ kena hetunā ।। (67)

Sukṛtaṃ priyakārī tvaṃ kaṃ rahasy-upatiṣṭhase ।
Puṇyakṛc-cāṭukāras-te kiṃkaraḥ surateṣu kaḥ ।। (68)

Pari-paryudadhe rūpaṃ ādyulokāc-ca durlabham ।
Bhāvatkaṃ dṛṣṭavatsvetad-asmāsvadhi sujīvitam ।। (69)

Now the *Bhaṭṭi* strophes, quoted above, show beyond doubt that the author of the *Kakawin* has deliberately copied the contents of the *Bhaṭṭi* and at times made literal translation of some expressions. Due to the fact that Sanskrit strophes of *Bhaṭṭi* had sometimes to be expanded and sometimes original strophes were composed, the number of strophes in the *Kakawin* and the *Bhaṭṭi* is not identical. The former work contains 2,771 strophes[7] and the latter only 1,624.

3. An examination of cantos VI-XIX of the *Kakawin* reveals that unlike the first five ones their subject matter does not correspond canto by canto to that of the *Bhaṭṭi* and moreover the *Kakawin* has 26 cantos while the *Bhaṭṭi* has only 22.

Thus we can conclude finally that the old Javanese *Rāmāyaṇa* is partially a translation and partially an adaptation of the *Bhaṭṭikāvya* and has nothing to do with the *Rāmāyaṇa* of Vālmīki or its conjectured extinct translation in the old Javanese.[8]

[7]Poerbatjaraka thinks that some interpolations occur in the Kakawin. This may be one of the reasons for its greater bulk. See Indian Influences, p. 173.

[8]For conjectures about the origin of the Kakawin see Indian Influences, p. 174.

CHAPTER 21

Comment and Criticism

"The Study of Javanese Literature in India"

HIMANSU BHUSAN SARKAR

Under the above title Berg has published in the current number of the *Annual Bibliography of Indian Archaeology* some critical remarks on my *Indian Influences on the Literature of Java and Bali*. It is not the custom to reply to a book-reviewer, but as remarks have been made which are not warranted by facts, not to speak of misuse of the superlative degree, I apprehend that silence on my part may mean acquiescence and have therefore been forced to write this reply.

In judging my work Berg has completely ignored the fact that it is written from an Indian point of view. The works which do not betray Indian influences to a great extent, as for instance the *Calon Arang*, could not demand the same attention as the *Rāmāyaṇa*, the *Bhārata-yuddha*, or even the *Arjuna-vivāha*. The Javanese element in these works, though not unnecessary for understanding them as a whole, could not but appear to me as a side-issue, because my theme was not the Javanese elements themselves, but rather the Indian aspect of the Indonesian literature. Even then I did not neglect to point out as far as possible the Javanese element in these works. Reference may be made, for instance, to my studies on the *Rāmāyaṇa Kakawin*, the *Korawāśrama*, the *Agastyaparva*, the *Arjuna pralabda*, the *Tantri kāmandaka* and other works. Moreover, it should not be forgotten (as Berg seems to have done) that of hundreds of old-Javanese works, not more than thirty or thirty-five have been so far published. For the rest we have to rely mainly on the MSS catalogues. It is possible to ransack these thirty-five works for Javanese elements, but what about the rest? Any way, the Javanese elements have received the share of credit that is due to them in a work that principally deals with Indian influences on Indonesian literature. Berg has raised another point. He says, "It is inadmissible to treat Middle Java and Eastern Java and their respective literatures in exactly the same manner. . . . It is necessary to keep one's eye on the differences existing between the two in order to judge correctly the final results of the influence of India on the literature of Java." This remark is out of place, since so far from treating Javanese literature as one organic whole I have described each work separately, analysing the Indian (and when possible, the Javanese)

Source: *Journal of the Greater India Society* (III/2, 1936, 188–96).

influences on the same. Berg knows fully well that the place of origin of most of the old Javanese works is not known, and as few of these works have yet been published, a comparison between the literatures of Middle and East Java is, to say the least, premature. These circumstances are so obvious that Berg should at least have referred to them. Regarding Berg's theory, enunciated in the *Hoofdlijnen*, of "parallel literature" (which has yet to be generally accepted) I regret I could not even refer to this, as the booklet reached my hands too late. I may, however, here be permitted to record my views on the same. Historical traditions of Central and Eastern Java are bound to be different on account of the diverse political and social factors at work in these two regions. These factors make a good case for parallel traditions but not for parallel literature, because, to judge from extant works, old-Javanese was the common vehicle of literature in Java in the ancient period. And my book is principally concerned with the ancient period.

The plan of my work has led me to consider the chronology of old-Javanese literature, the more so as each book has been separately treated. If in determining the date of one work I have become involved with other works, it is not my fault. Berg may remember that Krom, whom he quotes more than once, has, while discussing the *Smaradahana* (*Geschiedenis*, pp. 298-9) felt it necessary to utilise the data from the *Vṛttasañcaya*, *Lubdhaka* and the *Rāmāyaṇa* to elucidate the date of the first-mentioned work.

So far regarding the plan of my work and Berg's objections thereto. I shall now refer to the specific charges made by him. Regarding the so-called Middle-Javanese literature, its position with reference to old and modem Javanese literature, and its chronology (between 1478 and 1682), I was guided by an article on Javanese literature published in the *Encyclopaedie van Nederlandsch oost-Indie*. Berg has adversely criticised this view, but in doing so he should not have ignored my further statement (*Indian Influences*, p. 11). "It must not be imagined . . . that this division of literary epochs is, absolute—it merely represents a rough classification of literary ideals and styles in three distinct diversified forms." Berg's remark regarding pp. 160 ff. of my work misrepresents my viewpoint, for I tried to show that the date of some figures on the list, that of Udayan for example, exactly tallies with what is derived from inscriptions. Berg could have easily answered that this agreement of dates was accidental.

The impression which the critic has derived from the first few chapters of my work, namely that the Indian colonists turned Java into a miniature replica of Bhāratavarṣa is not correct so far as the interior regions are concerned. The mighty architectural remains, the *Record* of I-tsing, the occurrence of Sanskrit inscriptions jointly indicate the great influence exerted by the colonists on the cultural life of Java, particularly on the colonised regions. I refer in this connection to the struggle of languages—Sanskrit and Javanese—which resulted in the birth of *Kawi*, the artificial compromise language. How again can Berg explain the fact that 70 per cent of the old Javanese words are of Sanskrit origin, that all the oldest inscriptions of Java are written in Sanskrit and the *Amaramālā*, the oldest datable work (*c.* 750-850), is an attempt to teach Sanskrit? In the place of the Kalasan inscription, *c.* AD 778, however, I should now read the stone of Dieng, AD 809. This does not, of course, invalidate my main contention that the old-Javanese language arose from the struggle of the two languages.

On the date of the old-Javanese *Rāmāyaṇa* there is no unanimity among competent scholars and it can hardly be expected that my view will be accepted by all. In studying this problem I have placed the data in a new light. This has probably led Berg to make some remarks which are indefinite, except that the introduction of the *Vṛttasañcaya* cannot be relied on for ascertaining the date of the old-Javanese *Rāmāyaṇa*. Any way, as this introduction has not been my mainstay, the acceptance or rejection of its evidence does not affect my conclusion. I wonder how one can reject without consideration the persistent and independent traditions tending to the same conclusion. While dealing with the *liṅga* of Krapjak in *TBG* 74, has not Stutterheim shown how a particular tradition can run on for a thousand years? Berg also forgets what I stated in my book, that my chronology explains the existing data on the problems of the *Rāmāyaṇa* better. If Berg can prove that the writers of the *Lubdhaka* and the *Vṛttasañcaya* are the same person, he will do a great service to Indo-Javanese scholarship.

It is not also true to say that I have "taken it for granted that the entire religious literature of the Hindus was trans-planted to Java". While winding up the discussion on the religious literature of Java (*Indian Influences*, p. 79) I have said just the reverse thing: "The Javanese people thus accepted the principles of the social hierarchy of India and borrowed her religious views, but a substantial portion of her literature bearing on the subject practically remained sealed to them." Similarly Berg's statement that "the possibility that the Vedas, together with the Brāhmaṇas, Upanishads, Śāstras (a vague term, H.B.S.) and Sūtras may have been of as little interest to the Javanese as the Indian drama and several other branches of Indian literature, has seemingly not struck the author, and so . . . . he has not asked . . . . what were the causes of this phenomenon" ignores what I wrote on p. 396 and implied on p. 79 of my work. Whether the absence of this literature has to be attributed to the want of interest of the Javanese or the loss of *lontar*-records which were not duplicated in later times or whether the first brāhmaṇas compelled by necessity to intermarry with the aboriginal inhabitants conscientiously forbade the Vedic literature to polluted posterity in spite of the interestedness of the Javanese—is a question which may not now be answered with certainty. The last two possibilities have been mentioned in the book. With reference to Berg's remarks on pp. 44-5 of the *Annual Bibliography* I have not admitted the fact that the Javanese shadow-plays have re-oriented or transformed many Indian epic stories. In judging the *Wayang*-stories we should take Indian epics as the standard, because the outline or the inspiration has been drawn from them. So, if by working up Indian myths into *lakons*, the Javanese redactors make Nārada a clown or present Ghaṭotkaca and Abhimanyu as fighting over women, is that no harm to the Indian characters? Whatever be the motive for this transformation it cannot but appear to an Indian viewing the problem from the Indian standpoint (*Indian Influences*., Introd., p. 1) that Indonesian presentation does scant justice to the original characters.

Berg finds my characterisation of the *Nāgarakṛtāgama* as "more of a history than a poetical composition" to be wrong. May I put the query, what was the occasion for his explaining the name as "the *history* of the growth and blossoming of the kingdom" (*Inleiding*, p. 61)? As the work was written in verses the author was bound to pay attention to the verse-technique. Berg quotes the authority of Krom, but the latter scholar, while discussing the sources of old-Javanese history, has not included the *Nāg*° under the heading of literature and has referred to it (*Geschiedenis*, p. 10) as one of "the couple of historical works". Elsewhere (ibid., p. 14) Krom also refers to invaluable particulars of the *Nāg*°. Does he not also say (ibid., p. 19). " . . . It continues to be the history of the ancestors of the king glorified in a panegyric . . ." and that "he (Prapañca) is in general perfectly reliable"? There are at least half a dozen explanations of the name of Barabudur. From the nature of the case, certainty cannot be reached on such a question but one can never shut his eyes to the possible alternatives. The theory about the Śaivite renaissance in AD 863 (misprinted in the *Bibliography* as 563) originally propounded by Goris in *Theologie* appeared acceptable to me when I wrote my book, but from my notes on the Pereng stone inscription to be published in this journal, it will appear that Goris's case is not so strong as I took it to be. Any way those who are acquainted with the influence of Śaṅkarācārya in India and the history of contact between India and Indonesia during this period, will not wonder if that were really so. Regarding Maduran literature, I should indeed delete the word "important" but in respect of the Wawekan Berg's remark is, to put it mildly, a travesty of truth. In *no* place of my work have I accepted the data of the *Wawatekan* excepting in the case of the *Rāmāyaṇa*, and that for special reasons. As to the *Brahmāṇḍa Purāṇa*, Gonda's edition reached me when a few chapters of my work were already printed. The alternatives, open to me, were either (*a*) to rely on Friederich, or (b) not to refer to the work at all. I preferred the former course. I now gladly recognise that my reasons for a supposed period of Vaiṣṇavism in Java were not adequate. If I remember correctly, I was here led by an Encyclopaedia-article. As to another point, when an Indian author writes from India, the island of Sumatra is little indeed, but it does not seem so to one writing from Holland or Great Britain. If from my work (p. 71) Berg gets the impression that the Museum of Mojokerto is more important than those of Batavia and Leiden, that is unfortunate because I have said (*Indian Influences*, Introduction) that the major number of MSS is not available outside Batavia and Leiden. Regarding the *Kuñjatrakaṇa*, I fear I have been a little misunderstood. What I said was that the work "*may be*" of Western Javanese origin and that the "*oldest MSS*" has been found from that region: When other sources do not help us much, the find-spot of the oldest MS offers provisional indication of its origin. Regarding the position of women in Indonesia I observed (p. 105), "The position of Indonesian women, though not very high, was at least similar to or a little better than, that of their Indian sisters." Berg retorts, "Any book dealing with *adats* of the Indian archipelago might have told him that the position of women in Java is on the whole more favourable than that of their sisters in India proper". Allowing for Berg's confusion of the present for the past, is not this a paraphrase of my statement? Regarding his remark on p. 114 of my work, I cannot do better than quote Krom (*Geschiedens*, p. 11), "The method whereby the data have come to us is of two kinds. . . . The authors especially those of the poems, have *frequently* offered, at the beginning or at the close of their works, diverse informations regarding themselves. . . ." (Italics mine). I am, however, thankful to Berg for pointing out that I should have considered the possibility of Indian origin for the so-called "small metres". His remarks on *jinn* and the *usadas* may be correct. In the following line Berg has misunderstood me. I have referred to the chronograms not as fixing the date of particular works, but merely as "a mode of expression". As a mode of expression, they are certainly a legion. Berg may refer to the *Nāg*°. The explanation of the name of the *Tontu Panggelaran* by Kern appears doubtful to me now, but Berg's elucidation of the linguistic characteristics of two different epochs present in the work will be appreciated by all. Hidding's *Nji Pohatji Sang-jang Sri* is not yet available to me.

The possibility of the old-Javanese *Rāmāyaṇa* being an independent creation is ruled out by the consideration that some portions of the old-Javanese text are an exact echo of the text of Vālmīki (*Indian Influences*, p. 402). While referring to 1200 early Javanese versions, I doubted its correctness, but the name of Kats, I thought, was a sufficient guarantee for the genuineness of the information I note what Berg says about the date of the *Uttarakāṇḍa* and the alternative explanation of "abilawa". The old-Javanese recension of the *Bhagavadgītā* has been discussed by Gonda only recently, and I could not therefore utilise it for my work. To an Indianist, the Sanskrit *ślokas* of the old-Javanese *Mahābhārata* are of great value for solving the problem of a complete recension of the Sanskrit text, and I have recognised their importance (ibid., p. 241). Before making the remark on Jaya-katwang, Berg should have noticed Krom, *Geschiedens* (p. 296), which I have followed in some respects. Berg has certainly seen that my remark on the source of the *suluk* was based upon that of Stutterheim. My remarks on the *lakon Mintaraga* and on Damar Wulan were based upon Juynboll's article in the *Encyclo. Ned. Ind.* IV. The title *Koravāśrama* has not been used on pp. 325-35 of my work and Berg might have misunderstood the bearing of my statement on p. 325. I note, however, that my reference to the Bal. translation of the *Bhomakāvya*, based on Juynboll, is not correct. Berg writes that Poerbatjaraka has "certainly never written anything on the subject of Panji romances". Poerbatjaraka has certainly written on the same and it may be seen in *TBG*, LVIII, pp. 461-89. I recognise the importance of Rasser's researches, but the results are so startling that we shall have to await further light from other sources (ethnology for instance). The last part of the history of Majapahit falls between 1378-1478, and 1278-1478 is a printing mistake. Regarding the last note on p. 402 of my work, Berg has misunderstood me, as the earlier opinion refers to that of Kern which is no longer acceptable. My work is principally based on Dutch sources. If Berg has noted the footnotes of my work, his remarks on my study of old and new Javanese languages would not have arisen at all. All books and articles concerning Indonesia do not reach India, but I have tried to make the best use of those available here. Berg recognises the importance of maintaining contact between the two poles of research. If Dutch and Indonesian scholars make it a point to present copies of their works to the Greater India Society, which centralises Indian intellectual curiosity on Greater India, the work of their Indian colleagues will be more fruitful and the task less arduous.

Unbiassed readers may now judge for themselves what is the nature of Berg's "critical remarks". I do not pretend that my book is free from all blemishes. In a pioneer work of this character small mistakes are inevitable, but they are not such as to provoke rancorous remarks from a sober scholar. Berg should remember that in old-Javanese matters there is always room for doubt and one should not misuse terms like "certainly", "unfortunately", "goes too far", etc.

CHAPTER 22

Notices of Books

Indian Influences in Old-Balinese Art*

O.C. GANGOLY

In this latest publication of the India Society, Stutterheim has put within a short compass of 42 pages the leading facts connected with the history and culture of Bali—one of the most beautiful and interesting islands in Indonesia, recently very much exploited by tourists. To Indians that mysterious little island, still a replica of Hindu India of early times, with its simple faith, primitive rites and native social customs and life, is of peculiar interest—as it visualises in a living form a typical image of Ancient India—which has passed away on the continent. Suniti Kumar Chatterjee wrote a series of letters to the Bengali monthly *Pravāsī*, in which he gave a graphic description of Balinese life with very intimate and picturesque details, and in which he showed how many old Hindu customs and ritual-practices still survived in Bali mostly in pristine forms and sometimes adapted to the old animistic beliefs of the old Balinese races. Chatterjee has shown by an analysis of numerous phases of Balinese life how Hinduism almost completely imbued the pre-Hinduistic culture of Bali. Stutterheim's book, apparently a *rechauffè* of his Dutch work *Oudheden van Bali* published by Bali Society for the scientific study of Balinese history and culture (*Kirtya Liefrinck—van der Tuuk, Singaradja, Bali*), is an excellent introduction to the history of the art and culture of the island and will undoubtedly provoke further studies. And all lovers of Indian culture are grateful to the author for offering in this book in a readable and accessible form the main outlines of Balinese culture—the material for which is buried in numerous archaeological reports and learned articles in antiquarian journals. The records of the antiquities of Bali are not as numerous as those of Java, and the available inscriptions and copper plates have not yet been fully studied. The author is therefore compelled to leave many spaces blank and to fill in some of them on the basis of analogy and probabilities. Before the advent of Hinduism, Bali, peopled by a branch of the Austronesian family (to which the Muṇḍas of India belong), had not much by way of a political organisation. Its simple life was divided into groups of village communities—governed by elders who performed the double function of priests and administrative heads,

* W.F. Stutterheim, 42 pp., 23 plates, The India Society, London, 1935.

Source: *Journal of the Greater India Society* (III/1, 1936, 118–28).

in a peculiar form of ancestor worship. "Daily life was directed by the souls of the departed ancestors who were supposed to be dwelling in the mountains. It was they who lived on at the hidden sources of the rivers, without whose waters no rice would grow. They were the founders of the village communities; they had established its customs and cared for its growth" (ibid., p. 2). The living elders of the community were charged with the duty of "getting into contact with the souls of the dead, to receive them temporarily into themselves in order to replenish the waning store of the community's life-power or to furnish it with extra strength" (ibid., p. 2). When the souls of the dead ancestors were invoked, they were believed "to provide the community with the absolutely necessary magic life-power; to further the growth of rice; to calm the devastating overflowing streams; to subdue epidemics afflicting the population" (ibid., p. 3). The sacred acts (*śrāddhas*) of invoking the spirits of the ancestors by offering oblations (*balis*, *naivedyas*) were performed in temples—which were enclosed spaces (not shrines in the sense of the Hindu *mandiras* of the cult-images) and were more or less like *yajña-śālās* of Vedic times and contained stones as seats for the souls of the ancestors—"upright stones for the male, and horizontal stones for the female souls" (ibid., p. 3). The outer wall was designated *mekhalā*, the closed gate with the roof was called *gopura*, and the structure for offerings *bale-nyāsa* (ibid., p. 20). The author interprets the word *bale* as the native word for small *maṇḍapas*. More probably *bale-nyāsa* is the incorrect Sanskrit for *bali* (offering) *nyāsa* (deposit)—the place where the offering has to be placed (*nyasta*). This evidently corresponds to the *vali-pīṭha* of southern Indian temples—a small pedestal on a Lotus cushion with a horizontal piece of stone—to hold the offerings to the deity. Stutterheim does not cite sufficient details, or any extracts from Balinese ritual texts to enable one to judge in what respect the Balinese form of ancestor-worship differs from the Hindu forms. In the surviving Hindu forms in India, the rituals of *śrāddha*, ancestor worship, consist in offering various forms of oblations (*piṇḍas*) and gifts preceded by *mantras* to keep out evil spirits (*bhūta-śuddhi*) by the preliminary offering of incense (*dhūpa*), lamp (*dīpa*), holy water (*tīrtha*) and flowers. Stutterheim, not giving due weight to the details of Hindu ancestor-worship, is led to remark that "the part played by Hinduistic priests was not always the most important". "True, fully adorned, they had to receive Śiva into themselves in order to transform the flower-speckled water into holy water (*toya-tīrtha*); also, through recitation of their *mantras* accompanied by the steady ringing of their bell (*ghaṇṭā*), burning incense (*dhūpa*) and strewing flowers, they had to consecrate different ritual objects and cleanse the temple court from evil influences. But the actual celebration, the most important part of the feast—the offering of the hundreds of colourful sacrificial gifts to the gods—was not performed by the brāhmaṇas, but by the folk-priest, the successor of the highest of the magic village-heads of olden times" (ibid., p. 21). Our author does not state whether this has been the custom from time immemorial, or if this has been the *current* state of things. Suniti Kumar Chatterjee during his investigation into the current religious rites of the Balinese found out that the old families of brahmin priests in Bali have become extinct for some time, and as no brahmins have been imported from India, the duties of the priests are being performed by a class of priests who are not brahmins by birth. The description that Chatterjee gives of the rites with "six kinds of accessories"—*dhūpa*, *dīpa*, *gandha*, *puṣpa*, *phala* and *toya*, corresponds exactly to the *pañcopacāra pūjā* still current in Hindu India. It is quite possible that owing to want of trained brahmin priests, many of the rites have degenerated and become corrupt, and have in consequence deviated from the original standards. It is quite possible, on the other hand, that in unimportant parts of the rites, some of the old local Polynesian rites may have been adopted and amalgamated and used as part of the religious ceremonies and practices. Chatterjee has noted in the Balinese rites, as now observed, many differences from the current Indian rites. He has remarked:

All their (Balinese) rites are not identical in all respects to the Hindu rites of our country (India). There are numerous variations in details which are unknown to us and also to our ritual texts in Sanskrit. But they are part of the Hinduistic rites of Bali, and they have very skilfully adopted these rites with the Sanskrit ritual *mantras* and the due performance of the Hinduistic rites current here. They are ignorant of the ten kinds of accessories' current in our *purāṇic* forms of worship; on the other hand, it is difficult for us to follow the 'ten kinds of accessories' used by them. At the same time, their form of worship and rites *entirely corresponds* to the same class of worship or *pūjā* with the help of accessories (*upacāra*) current in India. The rites that were current in India in primitive times, had evolved, outside the pale of the Vedic forms of *Yajñas*, in certain Brāhmaṇical rites, using numerous accessory objects and appear to have evolved in differing details in Island-India (Indonesia), perhaps due to contact with ancient Malayan rites and rituals. ("Dvīpamaya Bharat: Bali-dvīpe-Bāṅgālī, VI", *Pravāsī*, *Jyaiṣṭha*, 1337, pp. 271-2, one of a series of articles recording Chatterjee's impressions of Bali).

Chatterjee's impression has been that the rites and rituals of Bali, fundamentally and in their main outline, are essentially Hinduistic in a strictly Brāhmaṇical sense, and although in unimportant details Malayan or Polynesian rites may have crept in—the present points of difference from the standard Indian practices are due more to degeneration due to want of contact with Indian standards and original Sanskrit texts than anything else. Stutterheim has remarked, "In former times, however, where there was constant contact with visiting brāhmaṇas from India, the *mantras* must have been pure in wording and identical with those used by corresponding sects in India" (ibid., p. 21). Chatterjee was very much impressed by the survival of the practice of invoking the spirit of the divinity through the skilful use of *mudrās*—the intricate details of which the Balinese *Padandas* have retained in a manner and with a skill which is becoming rare in India itself. Unless the details of the current Hinduistic rites are examined by an expert ritualist from India and compared with the Indian, prototypes, it is impossible to say to what extent the native Polynesian rites have overgrown the ancient Indian practices. For this branch of research, the cooperation of Indian scholars is essential in order to interpret and re-construct the nature of the religious history of the Balinese and to ascertain to what extent, if any, the current Hinduistic practices in Bali have retained the pre-Hinduistic beliefs and rituals. It was at one time believed that the existing state of Balinese culture represents a true picture of Javanese culture—as it existed before the fall of Hindu culture in Java owing to the invasion of Islam, and that the section of the Javanese who did not accept Islamic culture, migrated to Bali, and is preserving the same state of things as existed in Java on the eve of the advent of Islam. But this supposition does not square with the data now furnished regarding the history of Hindu culture in Java. It is quite true that after the defeat of Bra Vijaya, the last king of Majapahit, in the hands of the Mahomedans in 1478, the members of the royal family fled to Bali. But the Hindu culture of Bali dates from very early times. Stutterheim seems to assume on rather meagre grounds that Bali received its Hindu culture not direct from India but from Java in the eight and ninth centuries—"Thus we may accept that the eighth and ninth centuries were a period of strong Javanization for Bali, which also meant secondhand Hinduization" (ibid., p. 13). Of course, no tangible monumental or epigraphic evidence of early Hindu culture in Bali (such as that of the Mūlavarman Inscription of Borneo) has yet come to light. The charters and foundations of the Balinese royal dynasty—that of the Varmadevas, do not date before the tenth century—and our inference as to the state of Hindu culture previous to that date must be somewhat conjectural. The author while he suggests (p. 21) "constant contact with visiting Brāhmaṇas from India" has some doubts as to the possibility of Bali having received its Hindu culture direct from India. "Should we nevertheless believe that at some time there were as well at work in Bali direct influences from India?" (ibid., p. 13). The scriptural texts (yet to be studied) and the religious rites and ceremonies (very imperfectly investigated uptil now) are our only data on this interesting problem. Two very significant evidences appear, to this writer, to throw some light on the subject. Over ten years ago—this writer was the first to suggest that the *Meru* style of temple architecture and ritual "poles"—so common in Bali came from India, and that they were the structural *agnates* to similar structures of "a pyramidal system of super-posed storeys" met with in Nepal. It was at one time believed that this form of *Meru* temples came to Nepal from China. But the testimony of a Chinese pilgrim has given the quietus to this theory. Somewhat similar slope-roofed temples have survived in Kerala—in the sanctuaries of Cochin and Travancore, which, by the way, preserve many early relics of ancient Indian culture which have disappeared from other parts of India. Moojen's excellent introduction to Balinese Architecture (*Kunst op Bali*, *Adi poestaka, 1926*) has not unfortunately led to further searches in the field. The prevalence of the *Meru* style of temples in Bali, easily leads one to believe that it is either a characteristic Balinese form, or the evidence of an early contact with India where the form prevailed in *pre-lithic* periods of Continental Indian Architecture. But the replicas on some Javanese stone reliefs—of *Meru* temples seem to prove that the style was once current in Java also, and it must have been a gift from India common to Java and Bali. In Java the development of stone architecture appears to have supplanted the earlier forms of wooden architecture, possibly of the *Meru* type—which has survived in Bali. Another significant item connected with the funeral rites current in Java appears to have a link with India proper: Our author refers (p. 23) to a Balinese custom of electing an effigy of a dead king over the ashes collected from the remains. "Sometime after this ceremony, which corresponded to the Indian *śrāddha*, it was customary to consecrate a special piece of ground, to dig a pit and bury therein the conserved part of the king's ashes . . . . when the pit was closed, they placed over it a stone image. This image represented the deity whose incarnation the dead king was supposed to have been during his lifetime. But certain deviations from the traditional representations of that god indicated that the figure was not intended to be an image of the god himself, but only one of his incarnations" (ibid., p. 23). In Bengal, we have a curious custom of erecting a wooden effigy (painted in different colours) in connection with the departed soul. This is carried in procession, with great *éclat*, to the accompaniment of music, and then implanted at a consecrated place where other like effigies of departed ancestors (?) have been set up. This effigy is known as the *vṛṣa-kāṣṭha* the "Bull-shaft". It is a crudely carved effigy with human faces and other decorations in the different parts of the "shaft". Its shape and primitive decorative patterns seem to correspond to the curved staffs with Malayo-Polynesian decorations of human effigies from the island of Sumatra (see Figs. 6 and 7, Plate XXV, C.M. Pleyte, *Indonesian Art*). Comparison may also be made with an effigy from Bali, reproduced in Juynboll's *Katalog des Ethnographischen Reichs Museums, Band* VII, *Bali und Lombok* (Plate XII, Fig. I, 1912). Stutterheim, does not give us sufficient details of the rituals connected with its installation as current in Bali and it is impossible to say to what extent this significant funeral ritual in Bali has preserved the details of the original Indian model. G. Krause in his *Bali* (Insel Bali, Band II, 1920) published some photographs of funeral processions (Plates 138 and 139) which remind one of similar funeral processions in Bengal. The effigy of the bull (*vṛṣa*) is evidently used in Balinese funerals (see Krause, *Bali*, Band II, Plates 154, 155). These painted effigies of Bulls are made of stucco on a bamboo, or wooden framework, and have very significant relation to the Indian prototypes. In a *śrāddha* ceremony, connected with the death of an important personage, it is usual to purchase and liberate a family of Bull with cows as its spouses—at a symbol of liberation; the liberation of the animals (*vṛṣa-mocana*) is intended to secure the liberation (*mocana*, *mokṣa*) of the soul of the deceased from the cycle of re-birth. It is usual to mark the body of the bull and its spouses with the symbol of the *triśūla*, in order to distinguish the liberated group from other domesticated cattle that may stray into the streets. Before they are marked, or rather branded with the symbol it is usual to tie up the Bull and the cows to several wooden posts (*yūpa-kāṣṭha*, also called the *vṛṣa-kāṣṭha*) one of which is the principal one, used for the Bull, the other being minor or subsidiary ones (*upa-yūpa*). In some of the *smṛti* texts (manuals for rituals), it is stated that where it is not possible to secure the liberation of a family of bulls, the rite may be performed through the use of stucco or straw effigies. In the *Garuḍa Purāṇa*, in its chapter on *Preta-Kalpa*, the expiration of the period of impurification (caused by the advent of Death) the Bull and four calves after being branded with the mark of the "trident" and the "circle" should be let off. In the absence of the bull, its substitute may be used. Thus it is enjoined: "If on the eleventh day the bull cannot be secured, the wise should liberate effigies made of straw (*kuśa*-grass) or of stucco." "If at the time prescribed for liberating the bull, the same is not available, the same can be liberated in effigies made of earth or grass." It appears, that owing to dearth of sufficient cattle for such funerary rites, it has been the custom in Bali to offer stucco effigies of bulls—instead of in flesh and blood.

But we are straying into topics which form one only of the many ritual and ceremonial phases of Indo-Balinese culture. Reserving fuller treatment of this topic for another occasion, we are happy to turn to the images, statuary, and temples of Bali. Our author does not deal very much with the Balinese temples, but cites and discusses some very interesting specimens of sculpture. Indeed, temples and images stand on a somewhat peculiar footing in Indo-Balinese culture. Temples with images installed in the *garbhagṛha*, such as we find in numerous examples in India, do not appear to have survived in Bali. It is quite possible that temples made of wood or other impermanent materials were constructed in the earlier periods and have not survived the ravages of time. One is inclined to postulate the existence of such temples with images in earlier times, otherwise it is impossible to explain the surviving specimens of images in stone, of which some very peculiar forms are illustrated in the volume. In the existing stone temples there is no *garbhagṛha* or any arrangement for installing an image, or an icon. The characteristic forms of worship in Bali, as we have noted, are the presentation of *balis* or offerings in an empty shrine—the inner part of the typical Balinese temples. The outer gates of these temples are imposing *gopurams* derived from, but not actually following, the Indian or the Javanese models. Except for the decorative *motifs* on the outer faces of the *gopurams*, there is no room for iconic sculpture for the current Balinese form of worship. Yet the specimens cited in the volume are icons in stone, which must have been worshipped inside some temples which have now ceased to exist. The examples cited by the author fall into three groups: (1) images proper, (2) deified images of saints, or kings, (3) decorative *motifs* for water-spouts. A seated image of Śiva (eighth-tenth century) illustrated on Plate I recalls related images in Java. It may have been imported from Java rather than executed locally by Balinese sculptors. For a distinctive local style is apparent in the series of deified images of seated and standing kings and queens of which six examples are cited. Based on finer Javanese models, they are crude in conception as well as in execution and lacking in a general sense of proportion and finish. The remarkable head (Plate IV) with a tall *jaṭā*, or *karaṇḍamukuṭa* bearing an effigy of *kīrttimukha*, with a so-called "Khmèr" smile, may represent either Śiva, or a Śaivaite Prince. The technique and conception closely follow the models of southern Indian bronze images. Our author writes: "The open eyes distinctly point to a representation of a king" (Pl. IV). There are numerous images of Śiva with "open eyes". The so-called lion's head on the *jaṭā-mukuṭa* is unquestionably an effigy of a *kīrttimukha*—the protruding tongue is mixed up with the strings of pearls schematised to represent "entrails" (vide similar treatment of *kīrttimukha* on a stone pillar, Subramanya Temple, Tanjore, and numerous temples in Mysore). But the most important examples of icons cited by the author are the types of a peculiar *catuṣ-kāya mūrti* of the Hindu Trinity never met within India. In most of the Indian images of the *trimūrti* the portion below the breast is never represented. In the Balinese examples, of which the finest example is reproduced on Plate XI, the whole body with elaborate garments with decorated scarves is represented. The treatment of the crown in graded stages, stimulating the form of an expanded lotus—reminds one of similar treatment in Cambodian and Chinese sculptures. We have four-faced images in Caumukha temples of the Jainas, but excepting the Karāchi Museum Brahmā in metal—we have nothing to offer in India to resemble this manner of treatment. It reminds one of the famous wooden composite image of Kwannon in the Metropolitan Museum of Art, New York. Of the spout-heads (*jala-tuṇḍa*), the most remarkable example is one representing the death of Hiraṇyakaśipu (Plate XVIII) which the author ascribes to the thirteenth or fourteenth century. It challenges comparison, with the Javanese Viṣṇu on Garuḍa (Erlanga as Viṣṇu) (Museum of Modjokerta), and in spite of its florid decorations leaning to the baroque, is a *tour de force* of remarkable quality. If it was made in Bali, Balinese stone-sculpture must have attained a fine level of excellence. Similar remarks apply to the beautiful *aṣṭa-mukha-liṅga* (Plate XIX) a conception familiar in the texts but rare in plastic examples. But to us the finest example of Balinese sculpture cited in the volume is the moving conception of the *amṛta-manthana* depicted on the face of a Holy water vessel in stone (Plate XVII) from Pedjeng. It has all the mystery, all the skill, all the entrancing beauty, all the epic quality of Classic Indian Art at its best. Another sculpture, a spout-head deserves special mention, It is the figure of a "Ṛṣi" (Plate XVI) with matted locks carrying the effigy of another figure. Most probably it represents Bhagīratha carrying the Ganges (Gaṅgā-devī). The treatment of the matted locks in flattened shape is peculiar but recalls similar treatment in Indian prototypes. The author ignores another type of Balinese sculpture, the indigenous polychrome wooden figures of the Malayo-Polynesian School. The famous Hanumān and numerous effigies of Viṣṇu riding on Garuḍa—lend to the primitive Balinese School a peculiar flavour which deserved a place in the volume. We are grateful to the author for all he has been able to give us, and we have no doubt his excellent presentation of the general features of Balinese culture will provoke further interest and study.

CHAPTER 23

Migration of Indian Decorative Motifs

DEVAPRASAD GHOSH

(1) *CAITYA*-WINDOW ARCH.

The romantic history of the typical Indian device (*gavākṣa*), illustrates the amazing process of transformation of a purely architectural motif into a decorative device of elegant beauty and rhythmic grace, having in the end but a remote resemblance with the original pattern. By constant association with the early Indian *caitya*-halls (both rock-cut and structural), the horse-shoe openings have derived their ordinarily accepted nomenclature as *caitya*-windows. The Lomas Ṛṣi cave in the Barabar Hills, Bihar, offers the earliest example of this type.[1] The original wooden prototype of this ogee arch, lined with purlins, can be clearly made out from this and later examples. From the third century BC, to the thirteenth century AD—for nearly two millenniums—the unbroken development of this motif throughout India proper is an indication of the wonderful unity and continuity of Indian art.[2]

We may now enquire whether any simultaneous development was going on in the neighbouring lands of Campā, Cambodia and Java. In Indo-China itself, the people of which revelled in the art of decoration, the utter simplicity and stagnation of this everchanging Indian ornament, is indeed disappointing.[3] The *gavākṣa* of Indo-China and early Java are unduly flat, extremely broad and monotonously plain without bead-mouldings, side wings and *kīrttimukha* finials. A welcome variety is sought to be created by breaking the inner line into double curves in Tjandi Bhima. It is difficult to trace any window pattern in the stupendous Borobudur at a superficial glance. However, a closer scrutiny will reveal that the miniature decorative ornaments embellishing the parapets of each tier, are nothing but the full-fledged Indian device, completely resolved into scrolls.[4] Its various elements which are clearly perceptible, resemble the ornament from the temple of Sobhalde at Saladdapur, Jaipur, to a surprising extent.

[1]A.K. Coomaraswamy, *History of Indian and Indonesian Art*, pl. IX, 28.

[2]This is treated in detail in my forthcoming work on "*Decorative Art of Orissa*".

[3]A very important article, relating to the later transformation of this motif in Cambodia, "Concerning some Indian influences in Khmer Art" by Countess Coral-Rémusat appears in *Indian Art & Letters*, 2nd issue for 1933, pp. 110-21.

[4]Krom, *Hindoe-Jawaantche Kunsi*, vol. III, pl. 29.

Source: *Journal of the Greater India Society* (II/1, 1935, 37–46).

But the ingenuity of the Javanese craftsmen lies in skilfully converting the *gavākṣas* into magnificent *toraṇas*. The portals and niches of Central Java monuments, e.g. Tjandi Kalasan and Borobudur, are crowned by fantastic *kīrttimukhas* and richly wrought jamb carvings, which descending from their mouths end in graceful sweeping *Makara* spouts (Fig. 2).

"The very *Kāla-Makara* ornament" says Vogel, "though undoubtedly derived from Indian Art is the outcome of an indigenous combination and development... both the decorative device and the gateway which it adorns are not Indian but Indo-Javanese and the same may be said with regard to the monument to which they belong."[5] We, however, contend that of the so-called *kāla-makara* motif, not only the elements, but the whole design itself, is purely Indian. In our opinion the peculiar combination of the *kāla* and *makara* motifs was not evolved by the indigenous followers of the Indian master-builders of Java, but was known to Indian art long before. In the centuries immediately following the Christian era, floral devices are noticed to issue out of the distended jaws of the gaping *makaras* in the Bharhut, Sāñcī and early Amarāvatī art. Even as early as the first century BC, *makaras* are placed at the springing of the semi-circular arch-bands in the Gaṇeśa Gumphā, Rāṇī Gumphā and Jayā-Vijayā caves on the Udayagiri Hill in Orissa.[6] Arch-bands are also frequently made to start from *makara* mouths in the interior side walls of the aisles of Cave XXVI at Ajantā.[7] The representation of the *makaras* and *kīrttimukha* head at the springing and crown, respectively, on the façade of the fifth-century monument (Cave XIX) at Ajantā is well known. Moreover, the entire window device seems to flow out of the grinning head of the *kīrttimukha* (Fig. 1) with the usual *makara* spouts projecting outwards from each side in the Vaitāl Deul temple in Bhuvaneśvara (*c.* eighth century AD).[8] To crown all, the beautiful *toraṇa* in front of the Mukteśvara temple, Bhuvaneśvara (*c.* AD 950) is decorated with two exquisitely carved *makara* heads, which project boldly outward from the springing of the arch.[9] Similarly, the trefoiled arches, forming the background of the *pārśva devatās* of the Liṅgarāja temple, Bhuvaneśvara, are capped by a *kīrttimukha* accompanied with *makara* projecting spouts at the usual place.

In the face of these facts, it is difficult for us to accept the theory of Vogel that it was left to the indigenous artists of Java to combine the *kīrttimukha* and the *makara* into an organic motif. On the contrary, it is our strong conviction that the combined motif, represented by the *caitya*-window niches, migrated to Java from Orissa itself. Recent researches tend to show a close dynastic connection between Kaliṅga and Indonesia. In fact, Coedès has lately accepted

[5] Vogel, "The Relation between the Art of India and Java", *Influences of Indian Art*, London, 1925, p. 62.

[6] Fergusson & Burgess, *Cave Temples of India*, pl. 1.

[7] E.B., Havell, *Ancient and Mediaeval Architecture of India*, pl. 46.

[8] R.D. Banerji, *History of Orissa*, Calcutta, 1931, vol. II, pl. facing p. 348.

[9] Ibid., pl. facing p. 24.

the view of myself and R.C. Majumdar that the Śailendras of Śrīvijaya originated from the Śailodbhavas of Orissa.[10]

Leaving aside for the moment Indonesia, where the recurrence of this favourite Indian decorative formula is not surprising, let us turn to the north to explore traces of its overland migration. Is it accidental that in China itself the *caitya*-arch motif is strongly recalled by the flat ogee arches supported by two polygonal pilasters ending in lotus capitals, at the entrance and inside the caves of Lung Shan in Shansi?[11] By strange coincidence, also, the pairs of phoenix birds or dragons at the springing of the arches are curiously reminiscent of their Indian prototypes, the *haṃsa* and the *makara* respectively. As we shall see presently, this complex design re-appeared in the art of the Yuan dynasty (Fig. 4). A simplified form of the arch is to be found over door-ways of the

Fig. 1. *Caitya*-window, Bhuvaneśvara, Orissa, India.

Fig. 2. *Caitya*-arch, Central Java.

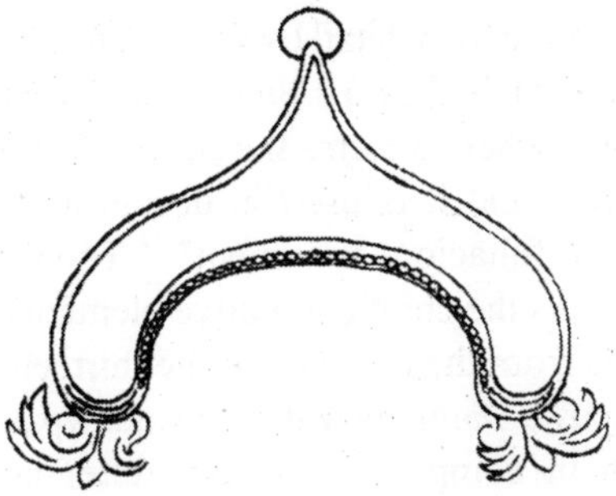

Fig. 3. *Caitya*-arch. T'ang dynasty, China.

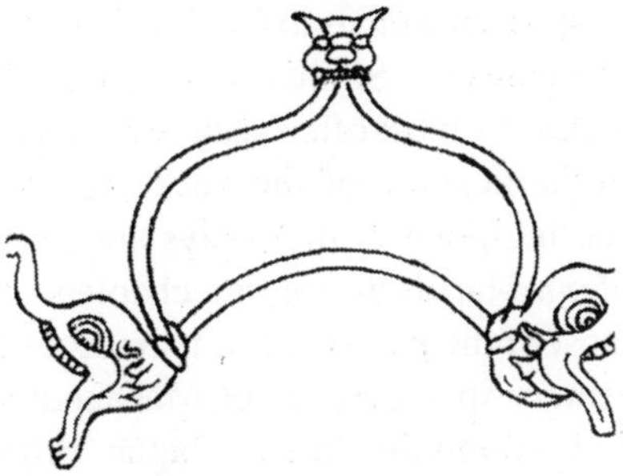

Fig. 4. *Caitya*-arch, Yuan dynasty, China.

Courtesy: JGIS, vol. II, no. 1, 1935, facing p. 2.174.

[10](a) G. Cœdès, "On the Origin of the Śailendras of Indonesia", *JGIS*, vol. 1, no. 2.

(b) D.P. Ghosh, "Relation between Buddha images of Orissa and Java", *Modern Review*, Calcutta, November 1933.

(c) R.C. Majumdar, "Les Rois Śailendra de Suvarṇadvīpa", *BEFEO*, tome, XXXIII, fasc. 1, p. 141.

[11]O. Siren, *Chinese Sculpture*, London, 1925, pls. 207, 208, etc.

T'ang period in Chili,[12] having a close affinity with early Mathurā types (Fig. 3).[13]

Turning from the Far East to the Near East, our attention is arrested by the presence of some curiously shaped ancient monolithic tombs in Lycia in south-western Asia Minor, among a series decidedly Hellenistic in character.[14] Archaeologists have long wondered as to their origin. However, the single rectangular cellas surmounted by barrel vaulted roofs, immediately recall to the mind some of the monolithic *rathas* at Mamallapuram[15] and the structural *caitya*-halls at Ter and Chezarla.[16] Is it possible that the arched gables of the sacrophagus tombs at Telmessus in Lycia, fringed with purlins, were inspired by Indian prototypes? It must be admitted that the Indian feeling has been emphasised by the introduction of a horned bull's head as the finial of such arch on the façade of a rock-cut tomb at Pinara, strikingly resembling the *caitya*-window arch with its horned *kīrttimukha* finial (Fig. 5).

2. *KĪRTTIMUKHA*

The *kīrttimukha* or the "glorious face" is another typical decorative symbol which penetrated all the lands where Indian art and culture travelled or left its impress. It is a fantastic lion face with spiralic horns, terrible goggle eyes, curling whiskers and a hideons grimace ejecting flames. As an auspicious symbol and protecting agent it always crowns the *caitya*-arches in architecture, decorative niches in sculpture and *prabhā-toraṇas* of the images, besides filling some minor offices in early mediaeval India.

It received a fresh and vigorous lease of life in the colonies. Some of the earliest specimens in Ceylon, have been referred to in detail by O.C. Gangoly.[17] In mediaeval Simhalese art, the full face detached of a *siṃha*, called *kibhi-muna*, "is most often seen in *makara-toraṇa*, where it forms the central feature in the position of the keystone of the arch; and it is used in design as the starting-point of the sprays and branches of foliacious ornament".[18] The row of ogre-heads disgorging chaplets of pearls, is the chief decorative element of most of the pagodas and temples of Burma from the eleventh to the thirteenth century AD, e.g. Seinnyet, Mahābodhi, Nanpayā, Dammayazaka, Gawadawpalin and Tilominlo—all at Pagan. Although in comparatively low relief and characterised by broad and stunted features, the earlier specimens are full of round and flowing lines. But the later reproductions, employed on the piers

[12] Ibid., pls. 535, 536.

[13] Coomaraswamy, "Early Indian Architecture", *Eastern Art*, vol. III, figs. 43, 66.

[14] J.C. Keene, "The Lycian Cities of the Xanthus River Valley", *Art and Archaeology*, Washington, May-June 1934, figs. 3, 4 and 11.

[15] Havell, op. cit., pl. XXIV.

[16] Coomaraswamy, *HIIA*, pl. XXXV, 147.

[17] Gangoly, "A note on Kīrttimukha: Being the Life History of an Indian Architectural Ornament", *Rūpam*, January 1920, pp. 12-13.

[18] Coomaraswamy, *Mediaeval Siṃhalese Art*, p. 86, fig. 23.

inside the Nanpayā temple, Myinpagan, are noted for the extremely floriated forms in low relief. The ornate character of the device is further augmented by the elongated and dangling ornamental foliages, inside the loops of pearl festoons,[19]

> Even in its conventionalised form as illustrated in the decoration of the Nanpayā temple (Fig. 17), it offers variations which cannot be said to be derived from successive copying of the patterns of India proper. So that, the examples of this decorative device met with outside India cannot be said to be derived by a direct line of descent from the patterns of the main land.[20]

We do not concur with this opinion. For so far as the design of the Nanpayā temple is concerned (Fig. 7), it is more than obvious that this particular combination was derived from Orissan monuments across the Bay of Bengal (Fig. 6).[21] However, the most astonishing factor in Burmese architecture is, that in spite of the universal application of the *makara-toraṇa*, the *kīrttimukha* is strongly absent from its traditional place at the top. Still we can discern from the images of Buddha, that in the domain of sculpture proper, it could not be dislodged from its hallowed position on the, finial of the *prabhā-toraṇa*.[22]

Next it is easy to detect strongly marked south Indian influences in the "glory face" depicted on a stone fragment from Prapatom in Siam.[23] Its representation in the Cham monuments, however, is extremely scarce, although it can be recognised in a highly stylised form, composed, of incoherent spirals, on the pedestal supporting a sitting Śiva, from the grand temple of Dong-doung.[24] This is almost similar to the types illustrated on some rectangular panels on the pedestals supporting figure sculpture in the *jagamohana* of the Sūrya temple at Konārak. It is more common in Cambodia, in the pre-Khmer and classical epochs alike. Elegantly chiselled broad and stunted faces, defined by graceful rhythmical curves, emitting festoons and surrounded by floral devices, decorate the mouldings of the Sambor-Preikuk group of the pre-Khmer period.[25] The classical examples, however, are different in character and more conventional. They are often noticed, on the door lintels in the centre of a rambling luxuriant foliage starting, as usual, from its gaping mouth. The head, unlike the Indian prototype, is circumscribed by a sharp trefoil outline, while the jaw set with pointed bristling fangs describes a shallow curve. Little ornamental horns grow from above the eyes.[26]

But, it is not until we reach Java, that the "glory face" is found to reach the climax of its glory and "the zenith of its artistic sensibility". The *kīrttimukha*

[19] Fergusson, *History of Indian and Eastern Architecture*, vol. II, pl. XXXV.
[20] Gangoly, op. cit., p. 18.
[21] W. Cohn, *Indische Plastik*, pl. 65.
[22] Duroiselle, "Excavation at Hmawza, Prome", *ASIAR*, 1911-12, pl. LXVIII, 5.
[23] Salmony, *Sculpture in Siam*, pl. 4, a.
[24] Parmentier, "Les Sculptures Chames", *An Asiatica*, vol. VI, pl. XXVIII.
[25] Parmentier, *L'Art Khmèr Primitif*, pl. XVI.
[26] *Arts et Archaeologies Khmers*, II, fasc. 3, 1929, pl. 32B.

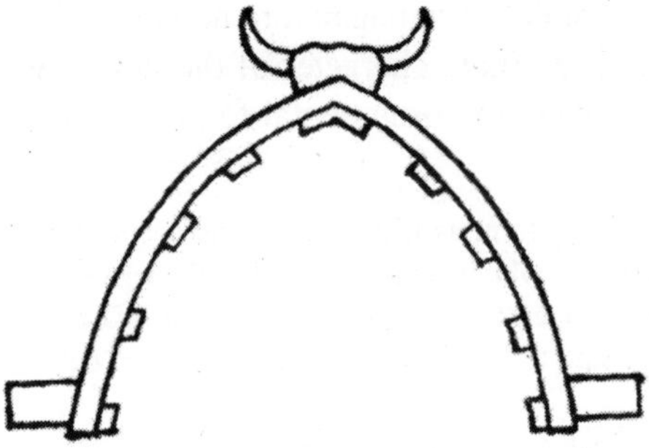

Fig. 5. *Caitya-arch*, Lycia, Asia Minor.

Fig. 6. *Kīrttimukha*, Konarak, India.

Fig. 7. *Kīrttimukha*, Pagan, Burma.

Fig. 8. *Kīrttimukha*, Lung-Men, China.

Courtesy: JGIS, vol. II, no. 1, 1935, facing p. 2.178.

(*kāla* or *banaspati* of the Dutch archaeologists) is the ornament "*par excellence* of Java, where it assumes a majestic form and a definite architectonic character". As an indispensible adjunct for the upper part of niches and arches it gradually develops into the arch itself, in which

the head forms the keystone and the two radiating necks terminating in '*makaras*' constitute the two abutments (Fig. 2). The most typical example of this novel use is here borrowed from Tjandi Kali Bening, near Kālasan. . . . It is not until its purely decorative and artistic feature, with all the exuberance of legendary or fanciful suggestion, combines with its structural or constructive function, that the *kīrttimukha* realises the supreme crowning moment of its life and may be said to have attained the apex of its career.[27]

Stutterheim in a searching article has recently tried to explain the origin, composition and underlying symbolism of this so-called *kāla-makara* ornament, from a novel and interesting angle.[28] A critical analysis will reveal that the gigantic central Javanese *kīrttimukha* pieces are greatly elongated horizontally. The ornamental folds over the oblique eyes are reminiscent of Calukyan types; but the tusks curve inwardly and the *makara* pairs are translated into *śārdalas*, emerging from the corner of the jaws. Frantastic horns, curly manes are denoted by fiery ornamental scrolls, growing upwards in fluttering agitation—the most striking element in the composition.[29] The upward urge of the vibrating spirals is admirably balanced by the broad sweep of undulating curve determining the distended jaw. Though elaborately treated, the superb modelling and ample breadth of composition are complemented by symmetrically disposed elegant and spreading curves. The *kāla* head, from Candi Singa-sāri, however, is more severely treated. It is less elaborate, more round in shape and notably gains in relief and volume. It appears to have a greater resemblance than anything else, with the archaic "glory face" of the Sārnath Gupta lintel.[30]

Regarding the "Tao-tieh" form of the early Chinese bronzes, Gangoly has already pointed out that "it has more than an accidental resemblance to the *kīrttimukha* both in its fundamental outline and its conventional representation in which the features of the original 'lion face' have' been skilfully dissembled". Further investigation has enabled us to discover a series of typical Indian *kīrttimukhas* in Chinese art beginning from the fifth century AD. This tangible evidence of Indian influence in the monuments of China, is a matter of no surprise, when we remember the brisk political and religious intercourse which commenced from the close of the fourth century between the two neighbouring lands.

The first instance of the crude lion masks in Chinese art can be traced in the round-eyed and tusked monsters which are employed to fasten the curtain framing the niche containing the Buddha image in Cave XXVI at Yun-Kang.[31] By the early part of the sixth century, the Chinese sculptor had thoroughly mastered the significant form of the Indian "glory face" as distinguished from the indigenous "Tao-tieh". In the decorative scheme of the Grotto of the Kuyangtung at Lungmen, the prominent features of the *kīrttimukha* are

[27] Gangoly, op. cit., p. 18, fig. 30.

[28] Stutterheim, "The Meaning of the *Kāla-Makara* ornament", *Indian Art and Letters*, vol. I, 1929, pp. 27-52.

[29] Krom, "L' Art Javanais", *Ars Asiatica*, vol. VIII, pl. 1.

[30] The survival of the *kīrttimukha* motif in Polynesia has been pointed out by Panchanan Mitra in an article on Indian and Polynesian art in *Journal of the Indian Society of Oriental Art,* December 1933, p. 114.

[31] Siren, op. cit., pl. 62.

portrayed in varying degrees of low relief. All the peculiar elements of a typical Gupta prototype[32] are present in the flying locks of hair, goggle eyes, ornamental horns and the terrible array of fangs flanked by a pair of small tusks (Fig. 8.). The unequivocal testimony of its Indian origin is furnished by the traditional festoons of pearls (here twisted), interspersed with ornamental buckles, which dangle from the grinning mouths and intersect one another.[33] That this typically Indian device did not meet with a premature end on the Chinese soil, is amply borne out by a votive *stele* from Shansi of the T'ang period, containing a niche of Śākyamuni Buddha, surmounted by symmetrically disposed tasseled pearl garlands issuing from a boldly carved "lion-face".[34]

It might be mentioned in this connection that Koop in his compendious volume on "The Early Chinese Bronzes" has all along characterised the "Tao-tieh" designs of the vessels of the First, Second and Han (or the Third) style-periods, as the *ogre or monster masks*, while the ornamental forms appearing in the T'ang (or the Fourth) style period, are distinguished as "*lion-masks*".[35] Thus he indirectly supports our assumption, that the fantastic decorative emblems, associated with the Buddhist remains only, are lineally descended from an extra-Chinese prototype, instead of the typically indigenous pattern. Further we find that festoons emanating from lion-heads, continued to be represented in Buddhist sculptures of the Sung period. But we are really amazed when we unexpectedly come across the combined *makara-kīrttimukha* design, in its Chinese version, in the Lung Hu ta pagoda at Sen T'ung ssee, constructed as late as the Yuan dynasty. The doorways of the square cella, are crowned with characteristic ogee arches, decorated at the finials by boldly projecting *kīrttimukha* heads and terminating in awful enormous gaping *makaras* in highly stylized forms.[36] They also enclose within their sweep other figure sculptures of exuberant richness, recalling the' inevitable components of the *caitya*-window arches of Indian and Indonesian art (Fig. 4.). It speaks not a little for the remarkable vitality and aggressiveness of the Indian motifs, that they could penetrate into and thrive on the Land of Pagodas, at the expense of the mighty all-pervading Dragon and the Phoenix bird.[37]

[32] Cohn, *Indische Plastik*, pl. 24 (Deogarh temple).

[33] Siren, op. cit., pl. 80.

[34] Ibid., pl. 509.

[35] Koop, *Early Chinete Bronzes*, pl. 96.

[36] Siren, op. cit., vol. III, pl. 617.

[37] For the migration of the *makara* motif to Greater India and China see my article "Makara in Indian Art" in *Calcutta Review*, October 1930 or "De Makara In De Indische Kunst", *Djawā*, 10 Jaargang No. 6, Einde, 1930, pp. 191-6.

CHAPTER 24

Sources of the Art of Śrīvijaya

DEVAPRASAD GHOSH

Recent explorations in Sumatra, generally held to be the seat of the ancient Indianised empire of Śrīvijaya, have yielded a surprising variety of antiquarian remains. They are naturally attracting the attention of scholars interested in Indonesian art and archaeology. Krom contributed a very interesting paper[1] on these finds and I tried to support and supplement his observations in this connection.[2] R.C. Majumdar has lately disagreed "with some of the most important conclusions arrived at in these papers".[3]

Majumdar, for instance, thinks it premature to conclude definitely that the enormous torso of a stone Buddha image discovered in Palembang belongs to the Amarāvatī school which was palpably influenced by the Hellenistic technique of Gandhāra, e.g. in the treatment of the drapery. Of course, our conclusion was mainly based on a study of the characteristic feature of the drapery "showing prominent folds". Majumdar is "tolerably certain that the art of Śrī-Vijaya was the product of Gupta art". "If we remember," he proceeds, "that the colossal copper statue of Buddha at Sultangunj in Bhagalpur district shows district folding lines of drapery,[4] we need have no difficulty in referring both the stone torso and the bronze images of Palembang to Gupta art."[5] But any one who compares the Palembang and Sultangunj buddhas, will, I feel sure, be convinced that it is difficult to conceive of two buddhas figures more unlike each other.

We admit that some of the sculptures of Bhārhut and Bodh-Gayā, why even some of the earlier sculptures too, have fold-lines on their drapery and "they are certainly not attributable to Gandhāra influence". Still we must distinguish between the folds of different schools of art. The Hellenistic folds of Gandhāra, whether natural or schematic, have a volume of their own which seeks to hide and obscure the body underneath, sometimes completely. Typical Indian folds, on the other hand, associated with the "wet drapery" treatment whether indicated

[1] N.J. Krom, "Antiquities of Palembang", *Ann. Bibl. of Ind. Arch.*, 1931, pp. 29-33.

[2] D.P. Ghosh, "Early Art of Śrī-Vijaya", *JGIS*, vol. I, no. 1, pp. 31-8.

[3] R.C. Majumdar, "Origin of the Art of Śrī-Vijaya", *Journal of the Indian Society of Oriental Art*, June 1935, pp. 75-8.

[4] A.K Coomaraswamy, *History of Indian and Indonesian Art*, fig. 160.

[5] Majumdar, op. cit., p. 76.

Source: *Journal of the Greater India Society* (III/1, 1936, 50–6).

by mere incised lines on a flat surface or by distinct ridges running in parallel curves, cling tightly to the flesh. So they allow ample scope for the tapering contour of the limbs to be fully revealed in all their soft rounded smoothness. The two different styles can be studied, side by side, in the early Mathurā sculptures. A mere glance at the Sultanganj Buddha folds will suffice to demonstrate that they are scarcely real folds at all in the Western sense of the term. They are nothing but few sweeping incised parallel curves lightly scratched on the transparent drapery which instead of covering the body emphasise the naked glory of a clearly accentuated form.

The Palembang Buddha[6] betrays the Amarāvatī technique in several unquestioning ways. If we scrutinise the treatment of the dress it will be found that broad heavy folds of the robe, covering both the shoulders, reach down to the feet in a regular succession of closely parallel semi-circular waves, each fold demarcated by a sharp edge or crest. The ultimate effect of the almost opaque sheet of drapery, with its prominently displayed fold lines, undoubtedly reminiscent of Gandhāra, is to obstruct a full visual appreciation of the delicate rendering of the details of the body. But the consideration of the folds is certainly not the only characteristic feature which led us to ascribe the image to the Amarāvatī school. It is also noteworthy that the broad heavy and almost flat rendering of the massive body, accompanied by a sense of rigidity and stiffness reflected in the erect frontal pose, vertically upraised hem and straight hanging pleats of the garment (note specially the sharp precise treatment of the back)[7] indicate the characteristic Amarāvatī style.[8] The presence of the above features as well as the absence of the peculiarly trough-like formation of the lower portion of the apparel of all the standing Gupta Buddhas of *Madhyadeśa*, created by the arms holding the *Sanghātī* a little away from the body, renders the question of the Palembang Buddha image ever being inspired by the classical Gupta art-ideals of Sārnāth or Mathurā extremely problematical. In this connection too, we cannot lightly brush aside the fact that the earliest sculptures representing Buddha figures, discovered in Burma, Siam, Campā, Fu-nan, Java and Celebes, all belong to the Amarāvatī school.[9] Is it not natural, then, to seek traces of artistic ideals of that particular centre on admittedly the earliest find of Śrīvijaya?

At this point we should like to make some observations on the theory recently put forward by Bachhofer in the pages of this journal. He is of opinion "that Northern, Western and Southern India represent the Buddha indifferent attitudes and differently clad" and that "from about 150 AD a free-standing Buddha in Southern India invariably has his right shoulder and arm bare, and carried his *Sanghātī* in the manner described above."[10] But we have reasons

[6] *Annual Bibliography*, 1931, pl. XI, a-b; *JGIS*, vol. I, no. 1, pl. I, a.
[7] *Annual Bibliography*, 1931, pl. XI, b.
[8] Coomaraswamy, op. cit., figs. 137, 141.
[9] *JGIS*, vol. II, no. 2, p. 123; *Calcutta Review*, February 1931, pp. 224-6.
[10] *JGIS*, ibid., p. 124.

to believe that this mode did not meet with "unchecked approval in Amarāvatī". Instances showing the Buddha with both shoulders covered are not rare in Amarāvatī in the second century AD.[11] Our stone Buddha image from Palembang also points to the contrary. Bachhofer's view that the Buddha continued to be presented only with covered shoulders and arms in northern India is also to be accepted with some reservation. For, there are some examples, at least, where the standing Buddha in northern India, is shown with the right shoulder and arm bare, the robe closely drawn to the right side of the body and hanging down loosely from the extended left fore-arm in the so-called western and south Indian fashion.[12]

Now we come to the bronze figures of Palembang. Here Majumdar seems to have misunderstood me. My argument for correlating some of these bronze figures to the Pāla art of eastern India is based upon the study of the sitting bronze image of Maitreya[13] and not of the bronze image of the standing Buddha, which has obvious Gupta affinities. It still appears to me that the characteristic features of the Maitreya, viz., the peculiar *jaṭāmukuṭa*, a marked advance in the ornamental aspect, the undulating lines of the *uttarīya* running across the breast, the fine *upavīta* dangling loosely along the left side of the torso, the nature of the jewellery and particularly the bowlike double curves of waistline are seldom found in "what we are accustomed to call the Gupta style in Sārnāth and other parts of Northern India prior to the seventh or eighth century AD."[14] That these elements are peculiar to post-Gupta art will be evident from a study of some of the bronze bodhisattva figures lately recovered from Kurkihar, Bihar belonging to the Pāla period.[15] Under the circumstances it is difficult to agree with the view of Majumdar and Bernet-Kempers that none of the bronze images from Palembang betrays any Pāla feature and that the art of Śrīvijaya was a product only of Gupta art. Even if we "get rid of the prevailing conception that Śrīvijaya and Java were closely connected by the political authority of the Śailendras" and admit the correctness of Majumdar's recent theory supported by Coedès "that there are no reasonable grounds to "affirm that before the 11th century the kings of Śrī-Vijaya belonged to the Śailendra dynasty or that they reigned at Śrī-Vijaya",[16] we see no insuperable difficulty in recognising the influence of Pāla art or of the magnificent Śailendra art of its powerful Javanese neighbour upon the art of Śrīvijaya.

Regarding the difference of opinion between Majumdar and myself about the little bronze Buddha head from Palembang,[17] I cannot but still adhere to the view that in the absence of better and more illuminating specimens, the

[11] Coomaraswamy, op. cit., figs. 137, 141.
[12] *JISOA*, December 1934, pl. XXIX, 1.
[13] *Annual Bibliography*, 1931, pl. X c; *JGIS*, II/2, pl. II, 4.
[14] *JISOA*, June 1935, p. 76.
[15] Ibid., December 1934, pls. XXXIV, 4, and XXVIII, 2.
[16] Ibid., June 1935, p. 76.
[17] *Annual Bibliography*, 1931, pl. X a and b; *JGIS*, loc. cit., pl. II, 2, 3.

bronze Buddha heads from Buddhapād near Bezwada, discovered by Sewell, offer the nearest clue to its origin. Its southern Indian kinship is suggested by a comparison with the head of the standing bronze Buddha from S. Djember, Java.

To Majumdar, my "view about the stone image of Avalokiteśvara[18] is also hardly convincing". He is inclined to see certain definite traits of Gupta art in it, too, although he has, unfortunately for us, failed to indicate those particular traits. In the absence, however, of any precise reference to the prototypes of this image which according to him "are met with in so distant localities as Kaliṅga and Kaṇheri",[19] it is difficult to share his views. If we take into account the severe treatment, flat summary modelling, omission of all minor details and smooth immobile mass of the figure of Avalokiteśvara, it seems to illustrate the Śrīvijaya interpretation of a Pallava icon, apparently modified by some Javanese intrusions as suggested by Krom.[20]

It is stated that Krom and Bosch hold the view "that Southern India exercised no influence of any importance on the art of Śrī-Vijaya".[21] It is, however, significant that the recent interesting finds, of three stone Śaiva images at Takuapa in the northern part of Malay Peninsula, "though evidently made in the Peninsula, are fairly close to the Pallava style of South India and appear to date from the 7th or 8th century". Quaritch Wales, who explored the region so admirably last year, rightly guesses that there is some resemblance of these sculptures to the Gaṅgādhara group at Trichinopoly.[22] Such evidence of predominance of Pallava art traditions in some of the earliest remains of the northern province of the Śrīvijaya empire (vide Ligor inscription of AD 775) may prove helpful in the reconstruction of the early art of Śrīvijaya.[23]

Only two definite periods may, according to Majumdar, be postulated in the Indo-Javanese and Indo-Sumatran art-traditions. "First, the earlier period during which the Gupta influence was dominant, and secondly, the later period, when as a result of intimate contact between the Śailendras and the Pālas, the Pāla traditions gradually made their influence felt."[24] My contention is that two other forces, besides the above, both connected with south India, should be reckoned in considering the formative stages of the evolution of Indonesian art, viz., (1) the Āndhra-Ikṣvāku element which certainly was the earliest to operate,[25] followed by (2) the Pallava-Cālukya factor whose action is perceptible

[18]Ibid., pl. XII, d; *JGIS*, loc. cit., pl. I, 1.

[19]*JISOA*, ibid., p. 77.

[20]*Annual Bibliography*, 1931, p. 33.

[21]*JISOA*, ibid., p. 77.

[22]H.G.Q. Wales, "A Newly Explored Route of Ancient Indian Cultural Expansion", in *Indian Arts and Letters*, vol. IX, no. I, p. 15, pl. IV, 2-4.

[23]To my mind the South Indian component is not negligible in the Javanese primitives too.

[24]*JISOA*, p. 76.

[25]Coomaraswamy, loc. cit., p. 157.

almost simultaneously with the Gupta idiom. Broadly speaking, Indo-Javanese and Indo-Sumatran art passed through the same phases as the art of *India as a whole* and not only of "*Eastern India*" as Majumdar would like to put it.[26]

It is not our intention to minimise, in any way, the influence of Gupta art upon the early art of Śrīvijaya. Its profound impression upon the aesthetic achievements of Indonesia and Further India is both indelible and undeniable. But in our opinion it was merely one of the outstanding forces and not the only or even the earliest one to mould the art of Śrīvijaya. Further discoveries are required to illuminate this complex but fascinating problem of Greater Indian studies.

[26] *JISOA*, p. 77.

HISTORICAL LINGUISTICS

CHAPTER 25

The Malay

R.C. MAJUMDAR

By philological researches Schmidt and other scholars have sought to establish a definite connection between the languages of some primitive tribes of India such as Muṇḍā and Khāsi with Mon-khmèr and allied languages including those of the Semang and the Sakai. They have presumed the existence of a linguistic family which is now called Austro-Asiatic.[1]

Schmidt believes that "the linguistic unity between these peoples which is now definitely established, points to an ethnic unity among them as well, though positive and satisfactory evidence on this point is lacking yet".[2]

"Schmidt has extended his studies even further and proposed to connect the Austro-Asiatic family with the Austro-nesian" to which, as stated above, the Malays belonged. Schmidt thus seeks to establish a "larger linguistic unity between Austro-Asiatic and Austro-nesian and calls the family thus constituted 'Austric'." Here, again, Schmidt indicates the possibility of an ethnic unity among the peoples whose linguistic affinity is thus definitely assured.

Schmidt thus regards the peoples of Indo-China and Indonesia[3] as belonging to the same stock as the Muṇḍā and allied tribes of central India and the Khāsis of north-eastern India. He regards India as the original home of all these peoples from which they gradually spread to the east and south-east. The following passage sums up his views in this respect:

> In the same way as I have presented here the results of my investigations on movements of peoples who, starting from India towards the east, at first spread themselves over the whole length of Indo-Chinese Peninsula, and then over all the islands of the Pacific Ocean up to its eastern extremity—my attention has for long been drawn to another current which, in my opinion, also started from India, but turned more directly towards the south and

[1] *Die Mon-Khmèr-Volker*, etc. (1906), pp. 35 ff. I have used the French translation in *BEFEO*, vol. VII (pp. 213-63), VIII (pp. 1-35). A good exposition of Schmidt's view, so far as the linguistic aspect is concerned, is given in the introductory chapter in *Pre-Aryan and Pre-Dravidian in India* by P.C. Bagchi (Calcutta University, 1929) from which I have freely quoted. (The page marks within bracket in the text refer to this book.)

[2] Schmidt, op. cit., cf. specially p. 233.

[3] The Muṇḍā group of language includes Kol, the more eastern Kherwari with Santali Muṇḍāri, Bhumij, Birhor, Koḍā, Ho, Turi, Asuri, and Korwa dialects, and the western Kurku; Khaṛiā, Juang; and the two mixed languages Savara and Gadaba (Bagchi, op. cit., p. vi).

Source: *Journal of the Greater India Society* (III/1, 1936, 86–96).

touching only the western fringe of the Pacific Ocean proceeded, perhaps by way of New Guinea towards the continent of Australia.[4]

Schmidt's views, must be regarded as only provisional.[5] But several other scholars have supported this view on entirely different grounds. Among them may be mentioned the names of S. Lévi, J. Przyluski and J. Bloch. The relevant articles on this subject by these eminent scholars have been published together in English version by P.C. Bagchi. The following summary is derived almost entirely from his book entitled "Pre-Aryan and Pre-Dravidian in India".

Thomsen first maintained that Muṇḍā influence can be traced in the formation of Indian vernaculars. Recent studies have tried to establish that this influence can be traced further back. Przyluski has tried to explain a certain number of words of the Sanskrit vocabulary as fairly ancient loans from the Austro-Asiatic family of languages. Jules Bloch has proved that the question of the Muṇḍā substratum in Indo-Aryan cannot be overlooked (pp. xi-xii).

But the problem has other aspects too, and it has been further proved that not only linguistic but certain cultural and political facts also of the ancient history of India can be explained by admitting an Austro-Asiatic element. In 1923 Prof. S. Lévi tried to show that some geographical names of ancient India like Kosala-Tosala, Aṅga-Vaṅga, Kaliṅga-Triliṅga, Utkala-Mekala, and Pulinda-Kulinda, ethnic names which go by pairs, can be explained by the morphological system of the Austro-Asiatic languages. In 1926 Prof. Przyluski tried to explain the name of an ancient people of the Punjab, the Udumbara, in a similar way and affiliate it to the Austro-Asiatic group. In another article, the same scholar discussed some names of Indian towns in the geography of Ptolemy and tried to explain them by Austro-Asiatic forms. (pp. xii-xiii)

In another series of articles, Prof. Przyluski is trying to prove a certain number of Indian myths by the Austro-Asiatic influence. He studied the Mahābhārata story of Matsyagandhā and some legends of the nāgī, in Indian literature, compared them with similar tales in the Austro-Asiatic domain and concluded that these stories and legends were conceived in societies living near the sea, societies of which the civilisation and social organisation were different from those of the neighbouring peoples, the Chinese and the Indo-Aryana. (p. xiii)

The bearing of all these interesting investigations on the question under discussion has thus been admirably expressed by S. Lévi:

We must know whether the legends, the religion and philosophical thought of India do not owe anything to this past. India has been too exclusively examined from the Indo-European standpoint. It ought to be remembered that India is a great maritime country open to a vast sea forming so exactly its Mediterranean, a Mediterranean of proportionate dimensions—which for a long time was believed to be closed on the south. The movement which carried the Indian colonisation towards the Far East, probably about the beginning of the Christian Era was far from inaugurating a new route, as Columbus did in navigating towards the west. Adventurers, traffickers and missionaries profited by the technical progress of

[4]Schmidt, op. cit., pp. 248-9. A critical summary of Schmidt's view is given by Blagden, "From Central India to Polynesia", *J. Str. Br. RAS*, no. 53, p. 63.

[5]Recently Schmidt's view has been challenged by W.F. de Hevesy, who denies the existence of the Austro-Asiatic family of languages (*JBORS*, vol. XX, pp. 251 ff.)

navigation, and followed under the best condition of comfort and efficiency the way traced from times immemorial by the mariners of another race whom the Aryan or Aryanised India despised as savages. (pp. 125-6)

In other words, the cumulative effect of all these researches is to push back the first phase of Indian colonisation in the Far East to a time prior to the Aryan or Dravidian conquest of India. It will not perhaps be rash to imagine that that colonisation was partly, at least, the result of Dravidian and Aryan settlements in India which dislodged the primitive settlers and forced them to find a new home across the seas.[6]

It may be noted, however, that conclusion of an almost opposite character has been arrived at by certain scholars. Krom, for example, believes that the Indonesians had colonised India in primitive times, and the later Aryan colonisation of the Far East was merely the reverse of that process.[7] This is in flagrant contradiction to the views of Schmidt and Lévi and seems to be based mainly on the theory of J. Hornell. In his Memoir on "the origins and ethnological significance of the Indian Boat Designs" Hornell

admits a strong Polynesian influence on the Pre-Dravidian population of the southern coast of India. He thinks that a wave of Malayan immigration must have arrived later, after the entrance of the Dravidians on the scene, and it was a Malayan people who brought from the Malay Archipelago the cultivation of the Coco-palm. (p. xvii)

Two other observations by different scholars probably lend colour to this view. In the first place, Das Gupta "has brought out the striking analogy between some sedentary games of India (specially of the Central Provinces, Bengal, Bihar, Orissa and the Punjab) and those of Sumatra" (p. xvii).

Secondly, we have the following remarks made by J.H. Hutton with reference to some pre-historic monoliths of Dimapur near Manipur.

The method of erection of these monoliths is very important, as it throws some light on the erection of pre-historic monoliths in other parts of the world. Assam and Madagascar are the only remaining parts of the world where the practice of erecting rough stones still continues. . . . The origin of this cult is uncertain, but it appears that it is to be mainly imputed to the Mon-Khmer intrusion from the east.

In his opinion these monoliths take the forms of the *lingam* and *yoni*, and he thinks that they possibly originated in Indonesia (pp. xvii-xviii).

In all these cases the similarity that undoubtedly exists may be explained by supposing either that India derived the practices from Indonesia or that Indonesia derived them from India. The recent discoveries at Mohenjo-daro,[8] however, prove the existence of the cult of *Liṅga* and *Yoni* in the Indus Valley at least in the beginning of the third millennium BC. Thus the migration of the

[6]Kern also held a similar view, cf. *VG*, vol. XV, p. 180. He held that they came from India, their ultimate home being Central Asia. This is not in conflict with his original view that the home-land of the Malayo Polynesians was the eastern coast of Further India.

[7]Krom, *Getchiedenis*, p. 38.

[8]Marshall, *The Indua Civilisation*, pp. 58 ff.

cult towards the east seems most probable. Considering the whole course of Indian History it seems more probable that the migration of the people and ideas was generally from India towards the east and no tangible evidence has yet been obtained that the process was just the reverse. On the whole, therefore, the views of Schmidt and Sylvain Lévi appear far more reasonable than those of Hornell and Hutton.

In view of a possible pre-historic connection between India and Malayasia it is necessary to examine in all its bearings the word Malaya which has given the name to the dominant race and the dominant language in Malayasia. It is a well-known fact that an Indian tribe called Mālava (*var.* Malava) or Mālaya (*var.* Malaya) is known from very ancient times. The common form, of course, is Mālava, but the form 'Mālaya' also occurs on their coins. In a discussion of these coins Douglas maintained that Mālaya is the older form of the tribal name. His conclusion rests chiefly on the Greek form of the name. "The Greeks" says he "called them the Malloi. Had the name Mālava been in common use at that time, I feel sure that the Greeks would have transliterated the word as the Malluoi. This seems to me to show that the commoner form of the tribal name at the time of the Greek invasions was Mālaya."[9]

Whatever we may think of this view, there is no doubt that both the forms were in common use. The form Malaya occurs in Mudrā-Rākṣasa[10] and Mālaya in an inscription found at Nasik.[11] The interchange of *y* and *v* is also attested by the alternative names of a Sātavāhana king as Pulumāyi and Pulumāvi.[12]

The antiquity of the Mālava-Mālaya tribe is proved by Pāṇini's reference to it as a clan living by the profession of arms (*āyudhajīvin*). There is no doubt also that the Mālavas were widely spread in different parts of India. Alexander met them in the Punjab, but their settlement in Rājpūtānā is proved by the discovery of thousands of their coins at Nagar in Jaipur State[13] and the reference in the Nasik inscription mentioned above.

The Indian literature also makes frequent references to the Mālavas. The *Mahābhārata* knows of various Mālava tribes in the west, north and south.[14] The *Rāmāyaṇa* and *Matsya Purāṇa* include the Mālavas among the eastern tribes[15] while various other texts refer to them, as a people in one or other parts of India.

The widespread of the Mālavas may also be guessed from Indian dialects or toponyms connected with them. Grierson has referred to a Malavia dialect

[9] *JASB*, N.S., vol. XIX (1924), Numismatic supplement no. XXXVII, p. 43.

[10] Act I, verse 20.

[11] Rapson, *Catalogue of the Coins of the Andhras*, etc., p. LVII.

[12] Ibid., fn. 1.

[13] V.A. Smith, *Catalogue of Coins in the Indien Museum*, pp. 161 ff., 170 ff.

[14] Cf. *Mahābhārata*, II-32, III-51, VI-87, 106.

[15] *Rāmāyaṇa*, IV.40, V.22. *Matsya Purāṇa*, Ch. 114, V.34.

extending from Ferozepur to Bhatinda in the Punjab and we have also the well-known Malayalam language of southern India. The well-known Indian provinces of Mālava in northern India and Malayabar or Malabar in southern India still testify to the influence of that tribal name. The Malaya mountain, the source of Sandalwood, is referred to in the Purāṇas and other ancient literature as one of the seven *kulaparvatas* or boundary mountains in India. Lastly the famous era, beginning in 58 BC, has been associated with the Mālavas from the earliest times.

The Buddhist literature also refers to Malaya country. The famous *Laṅkāvatāra Sūtra* is said to have been delivered by the Buddha in the city of Laṅkā on the summit of the Malaya mountain on the border of the sea. The Buddhist reference to Malaya has been regarded by some as purely imaginary but the existence of a Malaya mountain in Ceylon is proved by Ptolemy and Mahāvaṁsa. That of a Malaya country and a Malaya mountain in the south of India also rests on definite grounds. The great Buddhist Vajrabodhi who came to China in AD 719 is described as a native of the Malaya country adjoining Mount Potalaka his father being preceptor of the king of Kāñcī. Hiuen Tsang places the country of Malakūṭa, 3,000 li. south of Kāñci and refers to its mountains Malaya and Potalaka. Alberuni also places Malaya 40 farsakhs (about 160 miles) south of Kāñcī. Thus we have both a Mālava country and a Malaya mountain in the extreme south of the Indian Peninsula.[16] There is no doubt that this name is preserved in modem Malabar which the Arab Geographers call either Malaya-bar or simply Malay.[17]

While the Mālava and Mālaya can thus be traced as tribal or geographical names all over India, up to its north-western, eastern and southern extremities, the spread of this name across the sea is no less conspicuous. On the east, the famous Malays of Malayasia, the place names Malay and Malacca in the Peninsula, Malayu in Sumatra,[18] Mālā or Mālava for Laos and perhaps even Molucca islands in the eastern extremity of the Archipelago, and on the west Maldives (Māladvīpa), and Malay the ancient name of Madagascar[19] testify to the spread or the name in Indo-China and along the whole range of the southern ocean.

Now Ferrand has drawn our attention to the fact that the Indonesian language, mixed with Sanskrit vocabulary, was current in Madagascar. Combining this

[16]S. Lévi in *JA*, CCVI, pp. 65 ff. Watters, *On Yuan Chwang*, vol. II, pp. 229-31. Ptolemy, (M'cCrindle), p. 249. Geiger, *Mahāvaṃsa*, p. 60. Sachau, *Alberani*, vol. I, p. 200, cf. also *BEFEO*, vol. IV, p. 359.

[17]Ferrand, *Textes*, p. 38, fn. 5, pp. 204, 340.

[18]"The name Malayu is very common in Sumatra. There are a mountain and a river of that name; there are five villages called Malayu and a tribe of that name. *T'oung Pao*, series II, vol. II, p. 115.

[19]Ferrand, *Textes*, pp. 389, 396.

fact with other traditional evidences he has come to the conclusion that Madagascar was colonised in ancient times by Hinduised Indonesians.[20] It is not necessary for the present to discuss the further implications of this theory as enunciated by Ferrand, and I must rest content by pointing out the bearing of the account of Mālava-Mālaya, as given above, on this as well as several other theories.

Now the theories of Schmidt, Lévi, Hornell and Huttoh (as modified by the discoveries at Mohenjo-daro) referred to above all presuppose or are at least satisfactorily explained by a stream of migration of Indian peoples towards the east and south-east, to Assam, Burma, Indo-China and Malay-Archipelago, both by land and sea. The migrations of the Mālava tribe, so far as we can judge from the occurrence of geographical names, follow, as we have seen above, exactly this course, as we can trace them from the Punjab to Assam on the one side and to Malabar on the other.

From Malabar we can trace the name, in the east through Ceylon (Mālaba mountain in Laṅkā) and Sumatra (Malyu) to Malaya Peninsula, perhaps even to Moluccos. On the west we can trace it from Malabar to Maldives and Madagascar. It is no doubt more reasonable to explain the linguistic facts observed by Ferrand in Madagascar by supposing a common centre in India from which the streams of colonisation proceeded both towards the east as well as towards the west, than by supposing that Hindu colonists first settled in Malayasia and then turned back to colonise Madagascar. The people of Madagascar have a tradition that their ancestors came from Mangalore.[21] This place is located by Ferrand in the south of Malay Peninsula, but it should not be forgotten that Mangalore is the name of a well-known place in Malabar Coast, and is referred to by Arab writers as one of the most celebrated towns of Malabar.[22]

I do not wish to be dogmatic and do not altogether reject the views of Ferrand. But the known facts about the Mālava-Mālaya tribe in India seem to me to offer quite a satisfactory explanation not only of the problem of colonisation of Madagascar but also of the racial, linguistic and cultural phenomena observed by Schmidt, Hutton and Hornell. It is interesting to note in this connection that various words inscribed on the coins of the Mālavas which have been provisionally explained as names of tribal leaders, are non-Sanskritic. Thus we have Bhapamyana, Majupa, Mapojaya, Mapaya, Magajaśa, Magaja, Magojava, Gojara, Masapa, Mapaka, Paccha, Magacche, Gajava,

[20] *JA*, II-XII (1918), pp. 121 ff. *JA*, II-XIV (1919), pp. 62 ff., 201 ff. Krom, however, thinks that the Indonesian people colonised Madagascar before they came into contact with the Hindus. He attributes the Indian element in the language of Madagascar to later intercourse (*Geschiedenis*, pp. 38-9).

[21] *JA*, XIV (1919), p. 64.

[22] Ferrand, *Textes*, p. 204.

Jāmaka, Jamapaya, Paya. Whatever the language may be, it shows one peculiar Austronesian characteristic, which has been traced by Sylvain Lévi in certain geographical nomenclatures of ancient India, viz., the existence of a certain number of words constituting almost identical pairs, differentiated between themselves only by the nature of their initial consonants. Among the terms on the Mālava coins noted above we may easily select two series of this type:

1. Paya, Ma-paya, Ja-ma-paya.
2. Gajava, Magojava.

The tribe Mālava-Mālaya has played a great part in the history of India. Its name is associated with an old language, the most ancient era and two important provinces of India. The Mālaya tribe has played an equally dominant part in the Indian seas. It has been the dominant race in the Indian Archipelago and its name and language are spread over a wide region extending almost from Australia to African coast. I have shown enough grounds above for the presumption—and it must not be regarded as anything more than a mere presumption—that the Mālava of India may be looked upon as the parent stock of the Mālayas who played such a leading part in the Malayasia. It may be interesting to note here that Przyluski has shown from linguistic data that Udumbara or Odumbara was the name of an Austro-Asiatic people of the Punjab and also designated their country.[23] The Odumbaras were neighbours of the Mālavas and the coins of the two peoples belong approximately to the same period.[24] Thus, *prima facie* there is nothing inherently objectionable in the assumption that the Mālava-Mālaya may also be the name of an Austro-Asiatic people.

If the presumption be held a reasonable one, we may refer to Ptolemy's account as an evidence that the Mālayas had spread to the Far East before his time. Ptolemy refers to mountain Malaya in Ceylon and cape Maleou Kolon in the Golden Khersonesus. Regarding the latter, McCrindle remarks as follows: "Mr. Crawford has noticed the singular circumstance that this name is pure Javanese signifying 'Western Malays'. Whether the name Malay can be so old is a question; but I observe that in Bastian's Siamese extracts the foundation of Takkhala is ascribed to the Malays." Thus indications are not wanting that various branches of the Malay tribe had settled in Malayasia before the second century AD. There is a general tradition among the Malays of Minankaban that their parent-stock came from India and settled in the western coast of Sumatra.[25]

Thus while it is impossible to arrive at any definite conclusion in this matter,

[23] P.C. Bagchi, *Pre-Aryan and Pre-Dravidian in India*, pp. 149-60.
[24] V.A. Smith, op. cit., pp. 160 ff., 166.
[25] Cf. Ferrand in *JA*, XII, p. 77.

pre-historic migrations of Austronesian tribes from India to Malayasia appear very probable, and if this view be correct, we may regard the Indian Mālaya-Mālava people as one of these tribes.[26]

[26]Although I have arrived at the theory of the Indian origin of the Malaya quite independently, it is only fair to note that Gerini made the same suggestion in his *Researches on Ptolemy's Geography of Eastern Asia* (pp. 101 ff.). I have not referred to his views as they are mixed up with a great deal of extraneous matter and some amount of fanciful etymological derivations. So far as I can see his view rests primarily on the resemblances of geographical names.

Gerini explains Maleou-Kolon as referring to two prominent Indian tribal names—Malay and Kola (Cola) of south India, and he traces many other south Indian tribal names to the Malay Peninsula (cf. pp. 102-3). He holds that Malacca was either a modification of Malaykolam or Malayaka (meaning the country of the Malays) or identical with Mālaka, the name of a southern Indian tribe mentioned in the *Mahābhārata* (p. 105). I have tentatively adopted this view in respect of both Malacca and Moluccos. With the exception of this and the statement that Laos is referred to as Mālava (p. 117) I have not borrowed from Gerini any views or statements recorded in this chapter.

I must also state that it is usually held, though without sufficient reason, that the term Malaya as designating the Malay Peninsula came into use only in the seventeenth century AD (*J. Mal. Br. RAS*, 1930, p. 85), presumably in consequence of the migration of a large number of Malays from Sumatra, in the fifteenth century AD (*Bull. Com. Arch. Indo-Chine*, 1909, p. 184). Blagden refers to I-tsing's Malayu and infers; that Malaya country, *par excellence* was in Central Sumatra, a fact agreeing very well with native Malay tradition on the subject which derives the origin of many of the Malays of the Peninsula from the old Central Sumatran State of Menangkabau (*J. Str. Br. RAS*, no. 32, pp. 211-13). This view admits the possibility of the name Malaya being applied to the Peninsula at an earlier date. Cf. Crawfurd, *Dictionary*, pp. 250-2.

CHAPTER 26

Miscellany

Date of the Earliest Sanskrit Inscription of Campā

DINES CHANDRA SIRCAR

The famous Vo-chañh Rock inscription was edited by Bergaigne[1] and commented upon by Finot.[2] It has been re-edited by R.C. Majumdar in his *Champā*.[3] It has been pointed out that several lines at the beginning of the record are lost; that the inscription, composed in Sanskrit, may be referred, on palaeographic grounds, to the second or third century AD; and that there are two verses in *Vasantatilakā* metre in the record the rest of which is in prose.[4]

It seems to me that palaeography has misled scholars in determining the date of the Vo-chañh inscription. The language, style and the metre used in the record prove, in my opinion, that the inscription is later—at least not earlier than the fourth century AD.

It is known to all students of Indian epigraphy that almost all Indian records (both of kings and private persons), earlier than the first century AD, are written in Prakrit. Sanskrit was not in general use even in the second century AD. This century, however, offers us a number of inscriptions written in Prakrit mixed with Sanskrit, and also a few records like the Junagadh Sanskrit record of Rudradāman (*c.* AD 130-50) which points to the victory of Sanskrit over the inscriptional Prakrit in some quarters of western and north-western India. Generally speaking, Sanskrit began to gradually oust Prakrit from the field of epigraphy in that part of India about the second century AD; but the victory was not complete before the fourth century. Prakrit lost the field in south Indian epigraphy only about the middle of the fourth century AD. These points have been fully discussed in my paper, "Inscriptional Evidences relating to the Development of Classical Sanskrit".[5]

Now, which part of India was responsible for introducing the fashion of composing records in an Indian language in Far Eastern countries like Campā?

[1] *Notices et Extraits de Manuscripts de la Bibliothéque Nationale*, etc., tome 27, rere partie fascicule 2e, no. 20, p. 191.

[2] *BEFEO*, XV, no. 2, p. 3.

[3] R.C. Majumdar, *Anc. Ind. Colonies in the Far East*, I, Lahore, 1927, Book III, pp. 1 ff.

[4] Ibid., p. 1.

[5] *IHQ*, December 1938.

Source: *Journal of the Greater India Society* (VI/2, 1939, 538–5).

Even if we believe that the colonists belonged to the western and north-western parts of India, we must admit that the Vo-chañh inscription is considerably later than the middle of the second century AD, because its diction cannot be compared with any Indian inscription in Sanskrit earlier than the Junagadh inscription (AD 150) of Rudradāman. If the colonists belonged to eastern India, the date of our record should be later, as there is no proof that Sanskrit became popular in that part of the country before the rise of the Guptas (AD 320). If, however, it is believed that the colonists went from near the mouths of the Kṛṣṇā and the Godāvarī, the Vo-chañh record can hardly be earlier than the closing years of the fourth century AD, because Prakrit was the language of inscriptions in that part of India as late as the middle of the fourth century.[6]

Again, when were classical metres, like *Vasantatilakā*, extensively used in Indian epigraphs? Inscriptions prove that such metres were certainly not popular or in general use in India before the rise of the Guptas.[7] The Vo-chañh inscription which contains at least two verses in *Vasantatilakā* metre, can therefore be hardly assigned to a period earlier than first half of the fourth century AD. It may be later; but certainly not much earlier.

[6]D.C. Sircar, *Successors of the Sātavāhanas in Lower Deccan*, Calcutta University, 1939, pp. 166 ff. It must be noted that the Cho Diñha Rock inscription which is palaeographically assigned to *c.* AD 400 (Majumdar, op. cit., p. 3) refers to king Bhadravarman as *Dharma-mahārāja*. This is a typical south Indian style (Sircar, op. cit., p. 171 n.). Possibly the Cho Diñh record too should be placed several decades later.

[7]For the date of Patañjali who gives examples of classical metres in the *Mahābhāṣya*, see my paper in *Ind. Hist. Quart.*, December 1938.

CHAPTER 27

The Copper-plate of Barabudur, 828 Śaka

HIMANSU BHUSAN SARKAR

This copper-plate was dug out from the neighbourhood of Barabudur. Through the intermediary of Leydie Melville, Bosch received this plate for inspection and he has offered us a transcription of the same.[1] The date of the inscription was variously read as 828 and 848, but the former date appears now to be generally accepted.[2]

The inscription records a difference of opinion between the *rāmantas* of Palĕpangan and the *nāyaka*, viz., *bhagawanta* Jyotiṣa, regarding some *sawaḥ*-fields. It was maintained by the latter that these fields measured *lamwit* 4 and for each *tampaḥ* the *rāmantas* were charged to pay silver 6 *dharaṇa*. When the *rāmantas* made representation to the *rakryān mapatiḥ i Hino*, viz., *Pu Dakṣottama bāhubajrapratipakṣakṣaya*, a re-measurement took place and it was found that the fields measured much less. For each *tampaḥ* of these re-measured lands, the *rāmantas* were charged to pay silver 6 *dharaṇa*.

This explanation of the inscription differs, however, from that of Bosch who remarked in the *Oudheidkundige Verslag* for 1917 that the inscription records a difference of opinion regarding some principles of Astronomy. I consider this interpretation of the text to be doubtful, because Jyotiṣa is a proper name with the honourable title of *bhagawanta*. This title also occurs in other inscriptions, e.g. in the Sukabhumi inscription of AD 784, *OJO* nos. XCVII, XCIX, etc. Besides, the contents of other portions of this inscription run counter to the view of Bosch.

If my interpretation of the text is correct, it would appear that there were either different standards of measuring lands in different parts of Java (as in medieval Bengal) or there were abuses in land-measurements. As the *rāmas* of Palĕpangan did not agree with *sang nāyaka bhagawanta* Jyotiṣa about the measurement of their *sawaḥ*-fields, it seems that the *bhagawanta* could also be connected with land-measurements, and were not simply spiritual personages, as seems to be suggested by Krom in *Geschiednis* (p. 161) in his remark on the *bhagawantas* of Culanggi. It also appears that the institution of the *bhagawantas* was not exclusively confined to the region of Dieng. It is also

[1] *OV*, 1917, p. 88.

[2] For references, see *BKI*, 75 (1919), pp. 8 ff; *OV*, 1920, pp. 98 ff.; 1922, p. 85; 1923, p. 105; Krom, *Geschiedenis*, p. 186.

Source: *Journal of the Greater India Society* (VI/2, 1939, 124–9).

noteworthy that in the dispute between the *rāmas* and the *nāyaka-bhagawanta*, the appeal directly lay to the *rākrayan mapatih i hino*, who was at this time *Dakṣottama bāhubajrapratipakṣakṣaya*. There were also different names for denoting lands of various sizes, such as *blaḥ*, *suku*, *tampaḥ*, *lamwit*, etc. The *tampaḥ haji* appears to be the royal standard of measuring lands; the inscription itself says that 1 *tampaḥ haji* = 100 *ḍpa sihwax* 30 *ḍpa sihwa*. Reference has also been made to lands devoted to the service of deities. It is probably the same deities to whom tributes were brought for worship in the month of Māgha. It is instructive to recall in this connection that the inscription refers at least to one *vihāra*, that of Pahai, in I.12.

TEXT

1. ||O|| *swasti śakawarṣātita*[3] *828 . . . māsa tithi aṣṭami*[4] *śukla-pakṣa; ha; wa; śu; wāra irikā diwasa rāmanta i palĕpangan makabehan i*
2. *nanugrahān wineḥ makmitana prasasti*[5] *de rakryān mapatiḥ i hino pu dakṣottama bāhubajra pratipakṣakṣaya samwandhanya sangkā i tan patūt nikanang*
3. *rāma lawan sang nayaka bhagawanta jyotiṣa ikanang sawaḥnya sinanggu . h lamwit 4 kinon ta ya modhāra pirak dhā 6 i satampaḥ satampaḥ kunang sangkā ri*
4. *hötnya tan wnang modhāra samangkana yata matang yan panamwaḥ rāmanta i rakryan mapatiḥ kinonakan sawaḥnya ukuran*[6]*ing tampaḥ haji sinangguḥ*
5. *tampaḥ haji sātus ḍpa sihwā pañjangnya singkrĕnya tlung puluḥ ḍpa sihwā kinon mangukura wadwa rakryan i hino sang brahma muang rowang samgat pring sakañcur*
6. *mijilakanya lamwit 1 tampaḥ 7 blaḥ 1 ikana samangkana yata kinon modhāra pirak dhā 6 i satampaḥ jari rāmanta matahil pirak dhā*
7. *6 i satampaḥ satampaḥ piṇḍa pirak patahil rāmanta rikanang sawaḥ lamwit 1 tampaḥ 7 blaḥ 1 pirak kā 5 dhā 5 len sangkā ri pilih mas muang kaṭik prāṇa*
8. *8 mara i bhaṭāra prāna*[7] *4 i sang nayaka prāna*[7] *4 piṇḍa sawaḥ ni kaṭik lamwit 1 tampaḥ 1 suku 1 kina-behanya sawaḥ rāmanta lamwit 1 blaḥ 1 katuha la*
9. *wan tampaḥ 4 kapkanan tampaḥ 1 nāhan pratyeka ning sawaḥ rāmanta sampunyan inukur i tampaḥ haji len sumangkā rika hana ta sawaḥ bhaṭāra kmitan rā*

[3]Read: °*tīta*.
[4]Read: °*mī*.
[5]Read: °*Śasti*.
[6]Bosch reads *uturan* which appears to be a mis-reading for the above.
[7]Read: °*ṇa*.

10. *manta lamwit 1 dmak ni pajamūla lamwit 1 tan inukur ika āpan hinanyan swabhāwanya muang lañjān pirak dhā 14 patutan pirak dhā 4; panurat pira*
11. *k mā 4 umijil ri māgha winawa sang umikul wali bhaṭāra pawḍus pirak mā 8 umijil ri watangan nāhan anugraha rakryān mapatiḥ i rāmanta i palĕpa*
12. *ngan sapasug banuā tatra saksī*[8] *samgat pring ḍapunta udāra anak wanua i srāngan pumpunan*[9] *ni bihāra ing pahai amasangakan i rakryan mapatiḥ . . .*
13. *na anak wanua i syutan watĕk tiru raṇu tuha kala*[10] *rikang kāla pu baru na pu palinī tuha banua pu kmir pu gamana pu gambir gusti pu karṇa pu aruṇa pu*
14. *wari guru pu tarañjal pu pradhāna mangrangkpi pu kudhut winkas pu sādhā tuha banua i lampahan pu gammar wariga pu bur huler pu bay nā*
15. *han kweḥ nira mangagam kon kumayatnākan uja(r) rakryan mapatiḥ i hino likhita pātra citralekha samgat pring.*

TRANSLATION

1. ııOıı Hail! The Śaka year expired, 828, the month of … eighth day of the bright half of the month, *haryang*,[11] *wage*,[12] Friday. On this day, all the *rāmantas* of Palĕpangan
2. were favoured with privileges and were given the protection of an edict by the *rakryān mapatiḥ* of *Hino* (viz.) *Pu Dakṣottama bāhubajraprati-pakṣakṣaya*. The occasion thereof arose from the fact that the *rāmas* did not agree
3. with *sang nayaka* (viz.) *bhagawanta* Jyotiṣa[13] that their *sawaḥ*-fields measured *lamwit* 4. They were also charged to pay[14] silver 6 *dharaṇa* per *tampaḥ*. Moreover, on account of their
4. absence (?),[15] they were not in a position to pay such (charges). That is the

[8] The correct Skt. form is: °*kṣī*.

[9] Read: *punpu*°.

[10] This appears to be a mistake for: *Kalang*.

[11] A Mal-Polynesian day of the six-day week.

[12] A Mal-Polynesian day of the five-day week.

[13] While editing this inscription in 1917, Bosch remarked that the inscription refers to a difference of opinion regarding some principles of astrology. I consider this to be doubtful, as Jyotiṣa is a proper name with the honourable title of *bhagawanta*. This title also occurs in other inscriptions. Besides, the contents of other portions of this inscription run counter to the view of Bosch.

[14] The text has *modhāra*, whereof the root appears to be *u* (*d*) *dhara*. The term therefore appears to have the same significance as *soddhara* in *soddbara haji* (=*drawya haji*).

[15] *Höt* literally means "conceal", but the context makes this interpretation less acceptable.

reason why the *rāmantas* paid respects to the *rakryan mapatiḥ*, requesting him that their *sawaḥ*-fields may be measured by *tampaḥ haji.*[16]

5. The *tampaḥ haji* (contained) one hundred *ḍpa sihwā* in length, (while) its breadth was thirty *ḍpa sihwā*. (Accordingly), the *wadwā*-s of the *rakryan* of *Hino* (viz.) *sang* Brahmā and the assistant (*rowang*) *samgat* Pring,[17] (and) *sa*(*ng*) Kañcur, were charged to take the measurement.
6. (Ultimately) their (measurement) appeared to be *lamwit* 1 *tampaḥ* 7 *blaḥ* 1. For all these, they were charged to pay silver 6 *dharaṇa* per *tampaḥ*. Now the *rāmanta*-s paid (their) dues (viz.) silver 6 *dharaṇa*
7. per *tampaḥ*; the total amount of silver as dues against the *rāmantas* in respect of the *sawaḥ*-fields (measuring) *lamwit* 1 *tampaḥ* 7 *blaḥ* 1 was silver 5 *kati* 5 *dharaṇa*. Moreover, outside these (stipulations they shall give) some gold and 8 living animals(?).[18] (Hereof)
8. 4 animals shall come to the deity (*bhaṭāra*) and 4 animals to *sang nayaka*. The total amount of *sawaḥ*-fields for (the grazing of?) the living animals (?) shall *be lamwit* 1 *tampaḥ* 1 *suku* 1,[19] all together. The *sawaḥ*-fields of the *rāmanta*-s shall be *lamwit* 1 *blaḥ*[20] 1, of the united body of the *tuha*-s
9. also 4 *tampaḥ*-s, of the united body of the *apakan*-s 1 *tampaḥ*. Such are the specifications of the *sawaḥ*-fields of the *rāmanta*-s: henceforward they are measured by *tampaḥ haji*. Moreover, outside these (specifications), there are the *sawaḥ*-fields of the deity (*bhaṭāra*) to be protected by the
10. *rāmanta*-s: (they are) *lamwit* 1. The gift to the cause of worship[21](?) is *lamwit* 1. These were not measured on account of their position and their (religious) character. Moreover, the *lañjān*(*s*)[22] shall bring silver 14 *dharaṇa*, the *patutan*(s)[23] silver 4 *dharaṇa* (and) the *panurat*(*s*)[24] silver
11. 4 *māṣa*, as tribute in the month of Māgha. *Wali*-offerings for the deity (*bhaṭāra*) consisting of goat(s) and silver 8 *māṣa*, are to be brought by bearers as tribute at the audience-hall (of the deity). Such is the favour of the *rakryān mapatiḥ* to the *rāmanta*-s of Palĕpangan,
12. of the whole extent of the village. Witnesses thereof are: *samgat* Pring

[16]Lit. royal *tampaḥ*. This measure was probably adopted to avoid possible abuses in survey.

[17]He appears in the *rôle* of a scribe towards the close of the inscription.

[18]Horses? See the remark of Stutterheim on *kaṭik prāṇa* in *TBG*, 65, p. 241 fn. 61.

[19]The remarks of Stuttcrheim on this word in ibid., p. 242 fn. 63 may not be correct.

[20] It has been stated that the re-survey of fields measured *lamwit* 1 *tampaḥ* 7 *blaḥ* 1. Here we notice the omission of *tampaḥ* 7 from the share of the *rāmanta*-s. It appears therefore that this portion was distributed for other purposes. Cf. ll. 8-10.

[21]*Paja* may be a mistake for *pu*° (Skt. Pūjā).

[22]Apparently a class of people of unknown functions.

[23]They may refer to "followers".

[24]The scribe (s).

(viz.) *ḍapunta* Udāra (who is) resident of Srāngan in subservience to the *vihāra* at Pahai; the *amasangakan*[25] of the *rakryan mapatiḥ*

13. resident of Syutan under Tiru raṇu; the *tuha kala*(*ng*)-s of the time (viz.) *Pu* Baruṇa, *Pa* Palinī; the *tuha banua*-s (viz.) *Pu* Kmir, *Pu* Gamana, *Pu* Gambir; the *gusti-s* (viz.) *Pu* Karṇa, *Pu* Aruṇa, *Pu*
14. Wari ; the *gurus*[26] (viz.) *Pu* Tarañjal, Pu Pradhāna, the *mangrangkpi* (viz.) *Pu* Kudhut; the *winkas* (viz.) *Pu* Sādhā; the *tuha banua* of Lampahan (viz.) *Pu* Gammar; the *wariga* (viz.) *Pu* Bur; the *huler* (viz.) *Pu* Bay.
15. Now all of them having powers to pass orders[27] took care of the words of the *rakryan mapatiḥ* of *Hino*. The writer is the *citralekha* (viz.) *samgat* Pring.

[25] Slave.

[26] Lit. *Guru* = Teacher. If we consider that *guru* forms a part of the name of Wari (thus becoming Warigum), the following two names should then be included under the *gusti*-s.

[27] i.e., executive functions.

CHAPTER 28

Comment & Criticism

Siddhayātrā

K.A. NILAKANTA SASTRI

The expression *Siddhayātrā* occurs in five inscriptions from Indonesia and has given rise to not a little discussion. We may note the contexts in which this expression occurs before proceeding to discuss the different interpretations of its significance.

1. In the inscription of Nhan-bièu the phrase occurs twice in verses 8 and 11 which we read as follows:

   VIII. *Yavadvīpapuram bhūpānujñāto' nūtakarmmaṇi*
   gatvā yaḥ pratipattisthaḥ siddhayātrām samāgamat
   Ato vibhavasampadam adhigatavān iti

   XI. *Yavadvīpapuram bhūyaḥ kṣitipānujñayā ——*
   dvivāram api yo gatvā siddhayātrām upāgamat
   Ato yasmiṃś ca śrī Bhadravarmmāvanibhujo . . . kṣamāyās Sudāṅ Kumuvel kṣetrāṇi yo' dhigatavān iti[1]

2. In the well-known inscription of Mahānāvika Buddhagupta from the Wellesley Province of the Malaya Peninsula, we have the following line as read by B. Ch. Chhabra:

   Sarvveṇa prakāreṇa sarvvasmin sarvvathā
   Sarvva . . . siddhayātrāḥ santu.[2]

3. In the inscription of Kedukan Bukit (Palembang) we have the expression *maṅalap siddhayātrā* and *Śrī Vijaya-jayasiddhayātrā subhikṣa*.
4. In the fragmentary inscription from Koṭakapūr (Baṅgka)[3] we have only the letters *Jayasiddha*.
5. Lastly in a number of inscribed loose stones discovered by F.M. Schnitger in 1935 at Telaga Baṭu (Palembang) we have the expression *Jayasiddhayātrā sarva-satva*.

[1] *BEFEO*, 1911, p. 303.

[2] "Expansion of Indo-Aryan culture during Pallava rule as Evidenced from Inscriptions", *JASB, Letters*, vol. I, 1935.

[3] *BEFEO*, 1930, p. 59.

Source: *Journal of the Greater India Society* (IV/2, 1937, 1–4).

Hüber in editing the Nhan-bièu inscription translated the expression *siddhayātrām upāgamat* by "acquired the science of magic" (acquérir la science magique). Majumdar[4] considered this translation "far-fetched" and offered the translation 'obtained credit by the success of his undertaking'. Çoedès in his edition of the Keḍukan Bukit inscription adopted Hüber's view and translated *siddhayātrā* by "puissance magique", and put forward a tentative suggestion that it was a magical ritual accompanying a declaration of political independence and compared it with the phrase *apāsta bali bandhana* of the inscription, of Jayavarman II of Kaṃbuja.[5] He also said:

> *siddhayātra*, more correctly *siddhiyātra*,[6] designates a voyage or pilgrimage from which one returns endowed with supernatural powers. It is this sense which the word has in the inscription of Nhan-bièu and also in the inscription of Keḍukan Bukit according to which the king embarked on a boat for acquiring magical power in a place which unfortunately the text does not specify.[7]

Krom in his *Hindoe-Javaansche Geschiedenis*[8] also accepted the interpretation that the *siddhayātrā* of the king of Śrīvijaya was the journey (in a boat) for obtaining magical power, and he suggested that this *siddhayātrā* related to the foundation of the kingdom of Śrīvijaya, that in any case it commemorated a fact of the utmost importance to the State. Chhabra considers the interpretation of Hüber, accepted by Çoedès and Krom, and as we shall see presently, by Stutterheim also, as exceedingly improbable, and prefers Majumdar's interpretation. But the value of his discussion lies in his having drawn attention to two passages from the *Pañcatantra* and the *Jātakamālā* where this expression occurs. Even before the publication of Chhabra's thesis Çoedès had occasion to discuss the views put forward in it.[9] He expressed himself as quite willing to believe that the expression *siddha-yātrā* might well mean "successful in voyage" in most of the contexts under reference including the literary texts cited by Chhabra, but he felt a difficulty in accepting so weak an interpretation for the phrase in the Keḍukan Bukit inscription where it occurs twice, once in the beginning and again at the end of very significant contexts. He said:

> Que dans le textes Sanskrits cités dans l'inscription de Buddhagupta et même dans celle de Nhan-bièu, le mot *siddhayātrā* n'ait que le sens assex banal que lui attribue M. Shastri, je le crois volontiers. Mais dans l'inscription de Palembang, le sens doit etre beaucoup plus fort. On notera en effet que le mot *siddhayātra*, y apparaît deux fois, au début et à la fin. Sil ne s'agit pas de magie, . . . et je ne tiens pas beaucoup à cette interpretation qui n'est

[4]R.C. Majumdar, *Ancient Indian Colonies in the Far East*, vol. I, *Campā*, Bk. III, *Inscriptions of Campā*, p. 134, n. 3.

[5]*BEFEO*, 1930, p. 35 n. 1 and, p. 53 n. 1.

[6]This distinction between *siddha* and *siddhi* which Çoedès makes following Monier-Williams' *Dictionary* appears unnecessary, because both the forms are correctly employed in the same sense according to Pāṇini, 3.3.1.14.

[7]*BEFEO*, 1930, p. 58.

[8]p. 121

[9]*BEFEO*, tome. XXXIII, pp. 1003-4.

pas très satisfaisante . . . , il doit s'agir de la réussite d'une entreprise, peut-être aventureuse, en tout cas assez importante pour mériter d'être exactment datée et commémorée par une inscription sur pierre.

Lastly Stutterheim in discussing the inscribed stones discovered by Schnitger writes a very interesting note on the expression *siddhayātrā*:[10]

On the significance of this expression opinion is divided. In my opinion these different points of view can be reconciled by the translation 'pilgrimage of victory', that is to say, a pilgrimage on which one sets out to obtain the magic power necessary for a victory, though it is possible that in using this expression men did not realise any more the magic character of the word *siddha* [read *siddhi*]. The expression *siddhayātrā* or *siddhiyātrā* designates according to lexicons a pilgrimage undertaken for obtaining something which is produced by supernatural means. I do not think, as Çoedès does, that such a thing should necessarily be magical power, for there is some difference between seeking *barakat* (as I would compare this with Javanese usages) and the acquisition of magical power as it is practised at Bali by means of tantric treatises. The prefixing of the word *Jaya*, 'victory', makes it probable that it is a case of princes proceeding to a particular holy place in search of a blessing needed for a victory (or 'success', for *Jaya* need not always stand for victory in war). The expression '*Śrī-Vijaya-jayasiddhayātra*' of the inscription of Keḍukan Bukit may then signify that the prince in question had completed in the place where the charter is found (Palembang), a pilgrimage needed for victory over Śrī-Vijaya. If this interpretation is correct, it becomes self-evident that there can be no question of foundation of the kingdom of Śrīvijaya as some have thought. Çoedès has already raised a well-founded doubt on this point.

Commenting on this note of Stutterheim, Çoedès has observed[11] that this explanation of *siddhayātrā* as a pilgrimage to a holy place in search of *barakat* is new, and it is possible that it brings us very near to the solution of the problem posed by the enigmatic text of the Keḍukan Bukit inscription. Çoedès also observes very properly that it is necessary to prove otherwise than by simple affirmation that the object of the pilgrimage was to obtain a victory over Śrīvijaya. "May not *Śrīvijaya-jaya*", he asks, "signify also a victory of Śrīvijaya?" and adds, rightly, that this question is important, On this last question raised by Çoedès, one may at once say that until Stutterheim proves the new identification of Śrīvijaya that he has tentatively put forward, we shall be inclined to answer Çoedès' question in the affirmative, and treat the Keḍukan Bukit inscription as a record commemorating the beginning of an expansionist policy in the history of the kingdom of Śrīvijaya.

Except for a passing doubt in the mind of Çoedés after he read the thesis of Chhabra, there has been remarkable unanimity among the epigraphists working at first hand on the inscriptions of Indonesia that *siddhayātrā* is a reference to something mystical or magical in character. Çoedés himself has once more gone back to his original position after reading Stutterheim's note on the inscribed stones of Telaga Baṭu.

[10] *Qudhiedkundige Vondsten in Palembang* door F.M. Schnitger, *Bijlaga A*, Vertlag over de gevonden incriptie's door W.F. Stutterheim.

[11] *BEFEO*, 1935, p. 380.

We may now proceed to consider if the literary texts mentioned by Chhabra render this meaning either far-fetched or difficult of acceptance. The texts are from the *Pañcatantra* and the *Jātakamālā* of Āryaśūra, both works most probably anterior to the earliest of the inscriptions from Indonesia mentioning *siddhayātrā*.[12] In the *Pañcatantra* the expression occurs in the second tale of Book V. This is a tale of four treasure-seekers, a fact which seems to have led Chhabra to interpret the sentence *vayam siddhayātrikāḥ* in a rather summary fashion into "We are fortune-hunters".[13] But as he himself recognises "a *yogin* does play a rôle in the story and there is mention of a sort of occultism too". He does not explain how he gets the meaning "fortune-hunters" out of the phrase *siddhayātrikāḥ*. His own statements on this phrase at p. 19 do not seem to warrant this interpretation. He is right when he says that there is "hardly any ground for changing the term *siddhayātrikāḥ* into *siddhiyātrikāḥ* as the lexicographers have evidently done", but that is because there is really no difference between *siddha* and *siddhi* in the context. The rôle of the *yogī* and occultism in the story of the four treasure-seekers will be seen to be very much greater, in fact to be of the essence of the story, when one reads it in the original. Four poor brahmins, very friendly to one another, got disgusted with their poverty, held a discussion as to the best means of quickly becoming rich, and having rejected a number of secular means of obtaining wealth, finally decide upon seeking their fortune in foreign lands. After reaching the land of Avanti they bathe in the Siprā River, worship Mahākāla, and as they come out of the temple a *yogī* Bhairavānanda meets them. He takes them to his *maṭha* and then asks them where they were going and for what purpose. The original is this:

Kuto bhavantaḥ । *kva vā yāsyatha*
kiṃ prayojanaṃ । *tatas-tair-abhihitaṃ-*
vayam siddhayātrikāḥ । *tatra yāsyāmaḥ*
yatra dhanatṛptir mṛtyur vā bhaviṣyati.

The facts that they describe themselves as *siddhayātrikāḥ* after they meet the *yogī*, and that they meet the *yogī* only after worshipping Mahākāla, must be firmly grasped. Then they ask the *yogī* for means of getting wealthy and they do so in the following terms:

tat kathyatām asmākaṃ kaścit dravyopāyaḥ ।
vivarapraveśaḥ । *śākinīsādhanaṃ* । *śmaśānasevā* ।
mahāmāṃsa-vikraya-prabhṛtir-vā । *tvaṃ ca adbhuta-*
siddhiḥ śrūyase । *vayam ca atisāhasikāḥ* ।

[12] See Keith, *History of Sanskrit Literature*, pp. 68 and 248 for the probable dates of Āryaśūra and the *Pañcatantra*.

[13] Op. cit., p. 20. It is perhaps worthwhile noting that the sentence occurs at page 264 of Hertel's edition of the *Pañcatantra*, not 204 as Chhabra's note 3 on p. 19 has it.

i.e.,

Tell us some means of getting money, entering a cave, gaining the grace of Śākinī, practice at crematoria, sale of human flesh, and what not. You are reputed to be a person of wonderful *siddhi*, and we are dare-devils.

Now, one wonders if this is not seeking magical power for attaining one's ends, what *is* it? And the rest of the story is that the *yogī* gives to each of the *śiṣyas*, as they are called hereafter, a *siddhavarti*, which they are to carry and walk along in a northerly direction in the lands beyond the Himālayas. The fall of the *siddhavarti* on the earth will be an indication to each of the place containing the treasure he seeks.

In the *Jātakamālā* the reference is to the Supāraga Jātaka. Here again a study of the original narrative makes it clear that it is not success in any secular sense that is commemorated in the name Supāraga, but success due to possession of mystic power. It should be noted that it is a bodhisattva who is the *nausārathi* whose navigation was so successful that he was named Supāraga, The text is:

tasya parāma siddha yātratvāt-
supāraga ityeva nāma babhūva:

but as if to make it clear that this power was not a power of the body or mere technical skill, but that it was something occult and mystic in character, we read a few sentences later that even in his old age the sea-traders longing for a prosperous voyage applied to him who was well known to be an auspicious person; and the conversation between the aged Supāraga and the sea-traders leaves no room for doubt that the aid they sought from Supāraga was mystical in character:

So it once happened that merchants who trafficked with Goldland, coming from Bharukaccha, longing for a prosperous voyage, touched at the town of Supāraga and requested that Great Being to embark with them. He answered them:

What kind of assistance do you think to find in me ? Old age, having got power over me, makes my eyesight diminish: in consequence of the many toils I have endured, my attentiveness has grown weak, and even in my bodily occupations I feel my strength almost gone.

The merchants said: 'We are well acquainted with the bodily state of Your Hononr. But this being so, and taking into account your inability for labour, we will not cause hardship to you nor give any task unto your charge, but we want you for some other reason.

'The dust touched and hallowed by your lotus-like feet will be auspicious to our ship and procure her a happy course over yonder sea, even if assailed by great danger. With this in mind we have applied to you.'[14]

It seems clear therefore that *siddhayātrā* in the Indonesian inscriptions is a technical phrase with unmistakable reference to the acquisition of magic power

[14] Āryaśūra, *The Jātakamālā* or *Garland of Birth-stories*, tr. from Sanskrit by J.S. Speyer, pp. 125-6.

of some sort or other. Even in the Mahānāvika inscription there should be no difficulty in applying the same sense considering that the Suparaga Jātaka furnishes a conspicuous instance in literature of merchants seeking magic means to ensure success for their enterprises.

It may not be without interest to note, finally, that in Indian Purāṇic literature, a number of *kṣetras* (sacred spots) are mentioned as *siddha-* or *siddhi-kṣetras*, where human endeavour is easily crowned with success. Thus we read in the *Mahābhārata*[15]

Yatra gaṅgā mahārāja sa deśastat-tapovanam ।
siddhikṣetraṃ ca iaj-jñeyaṃ gaṅgā-tīrasamarvitam ।।

and this verse appears in the *Matsya Purāṇa* (I.10.12) with the variations: *mahābhāga* for *mahārāja*, *tapodhanam* for *tapovanam*—clearly a mistake, and *siddhakṣetram* for *siddhi-kṣeiram*. Again a *siddhakṣetram* is mentioned in the *Vāyu Purāṇa* (ch. 23) as located on the top of the Himālaya:

Himavacchikhare caiva mahātuṅge mahālaye
Siddhakṣetraṃ mahāpuṇyam bhaviṣyati mahālayam (v. 175)

siddhakṣetre mahāpuṇye devadānavapūjite
himavac-chikhare puṇye (v. 182).

Lastly, in the *Brahmāṇḍa Purāṇa* we read of a *siddhikṣetra* in Amarakaṇṭaka, where, it is said,

alpena tapasā siddhiṃ gamiṣyanti na saṃsayaḥ[16]

It is possible that a pilgrimage to some *kṣetra* like this to ensure success in any undertaking came to be called *siddhiyātrā* or *siddhayātrā*.

[15] III.83.97 Kumbakonam edition. Also a *siddhikṣetra* on the Sarasvatī in IX.40.16. See Sörensen s.v.—Siddh(a)ikṣetraṃ.

[16] III.13.13-15.

CHAPTER 29

The National Language of Indonesia

SUNITI KUMAR CHATTERJI

Mr. President, Esteemed Colleagues, and Sisters and Brothers of Indonesia:

First of all I have to apologise to you for my inability to address you in the official language of the Congress, the *Bahasa Indonesia*, and for my being forced to speak to you in a language which is neither yours nor mine. In India as in other parts of Asia we have not taken much interest so far in each other's affairs, and we are now feeling the need, for the sake of Asian solidarity and mutual understanding, to know each other's languages, histories and cultures. I do hope that when next a linguistic expert from India comes to Indonesia, he will be able to address you in your own language.

I have also to thank the organisers of this Congress for doing great honour to my country by requesting our Education Ministry to send a suitable person to participate in the Congress; and I also feel grateful to you, Mr. President, and to your Colleagues, for asking me to speak to you this evening.

I bring to you on this memorable occasion, when you are taking far-reaching decisions to improve and develop the language you have accepted as the National Language of the Indonesian People, the warmest good wishes of the People and the Government of India. We rejoice with you in your success in solving the initial problems connected with the setting up of the *Bahasa Indonesia* as the basic plank in the platform of your national unity. And we now wish you the best of luck in making this language a potent and a flexible instrument, to give the fullest expression to the modern culture that is evolving among your people, and to its hopes and aspirations and successes and achievements, through both informative and creative literature.

We wish sometimes that in the matter of language our problems were as simple as yours. You have taken courage in both hands, and are making a rapid advance. We are sure, as I personally believe, to profit by your experiences; and that, for myself, is one of the main reasons for my participation in this Congress.

* Speech delivered on 30 October 1954, by Suniti Kumar Chatterji, Chairman, West Bengal Legislative Council, Calcutta; Emeritus Professor of Comparative Philology and Dean of the Faculty of Fine Arts and Music in the University of Calcutta; and President, Asiatic Society, Bengal; Representative of the Government of India Ministry of Education at the *Konggres Bahasa Indonesia* held under the auspices of the Government of Indonesia at Medan, 28 October-2 November 1954.

Source: *Journal of the Greater India Society* (XIV/1, 1955, 1–12).

Personally I am not a new-comer to your country. Twenty-seven years ago, as a member of Rabindranath Tagore's party, I visited the land of Indonesia, having first landed at Belawan and spent the day at Medan on 16 August 1927; and then we spent a full month and a half in travelling all over Java and Bali. We could, with the poet's great humanism and sympathy and love for his fellow-men as our background, feel a little of the throb of the life of Indonesia. It was already a nation in the making, and its birth-pangs had started, so to say. On that occasion I had the privilege of knowing your President, who, as a young nationalist worker of 27, had come to see Tagore at Bandung on 27 September 1927; and no one could at that time prophesy that the handsome and intelligent young man would be the hero to usher in freedom to 75 millions of people and to be one of the foremost leaders of men in Asia.

The bonds of union between our two countries, India and Indonesia, are not on the surface only—they go deep down into the bases of our racial origins. We are not merely neighbours and friendly nations of Asia; we have a certain racial affinity and inherent racial sympathy with each other. As Indonesians, you are members of the Austronesian branch of great Austric people, and peoples of the other branch of this great race, viz., the Austro-Asiatic, formed one of the basic races of India. The Indian people of the present day are a mixed people, in the formation of which the Niṣādas or Austrics, the Dramiḍas or Dravidians, the Kirātas or Mongoloids and the Āryas or Indo-Aryans have contributed—in fact, men of all these races, each forming a distinct ethno-linguistic or language-culture group, have supplied elements to bring about the birth or evolution of the Indian Man. The same racio-linguistic texture as yours is partly in our national composition too. The Aryan language after the Vedic period had its own special evolution in India in an atmosphere of non-Aryan life and culture, and in the formation of Classical Sanskrit (as distinct from the Vedic), of the Prakrits and of the New Indo-Aryan *bhāṣās* or Modern Languages, the Dravidians and Austrics as well as the Sino-Tibetan speaking Mongoloid groups played a leading part. In the formation of Sanskrit in India, the Austric *Niṣāda* peoples, who were our ancestors too, and were brothers in blood and language of your Austronesian ancestors, had a hand. An Austric substratum, like a Dravidian substratum, is gradually being unearthed: and it is seen that in the syntactical development of Sanskrit and the Prakrits, as well as in their ever-extending vocabularies, Austric elements were operative. The Austric substrata in Sanskrit, related in their roots and terminations to the oldest forms of Indonesian, have been brilliantly brought to our notice for the first time by a band of eminent French scholars, like Jean Przyluski, Sylvain Lévi and Jules Bloch. Their initial investigations, revealing a new bond between the world of Sanskrit and the world of Indonesian, which may be described as "prehistoric" because no record has been preserved of it, were taken up by investigators in other lands—India and Holland; and we have to mention in this connection the recent work of F.B.J. Kuiper of Leyden his important contribution on fresh Austric material in Sanskrit, in addition to what has been suggested by Lévi, Przyluski and Bloch, and P.C. Bagchi and S.K. Chatterji from India.

I need not enter into this historico-linguistic study, which is hardly *à propos* to our present objective, viz., the study of the problems of the representative speech of Indonesia with the aim of making it one of the great modern languages of the world. I would therefore pass on from language and race connections between Indonesia and India to the consideration of the Indonesian speech *par excellence*, the *Bahasa Mĕlayu* which has become the *Bahasa Indonesia*.

A decade ago, Indonesia was not in the map of the world. With the advent of your freedom, a new nation has come into existence: and now, with this new nation, its national language, current among over 75 millions of people, has now become established before the eyes of men. Where was the *Bahasa Indonesia* all this time? People are asking themselves. When we get up in the morning, and find in the field in front of our house a tiny blade of grass growing, we seldom take notice of it—we often fail to see it. But if we find in the morning that overnight when we were asleep a great banyan or *waringin* tree has come into existence, filling the spaces of both land and sky, we are astounded, and rub our eyes in bewilderment. So, too, in the present world set-up for different languages which are now coming into prominence with the prominence, as members of a free world, their speakers are attaining. People who know anything of India also know of Hindi, as a great language of the country, but no one could dream of the position Hindi might be attaining to, as the official language of the second great state of the world from the point of numbers. Malay was known as a very useful *lingua franca* in the islands of the Indian archipelago and Malaya. But, as the national language of 75 millions of a very highly gifted race which is getting its deserved place as one of the great speeches of the world, the Malay language under its new name *Bahasa Indonesia* has to be accorded a place of honour as the Eighth Great Language of the world. Chinese, or rather Northern Chinese, is current over more than two-thirds of the great country of China, and is perhaps spoken by near about 350 millions of people, besides being, as *Gwo-yeu*, the national language of the People's Republic of China; and Northern Chinese thus in point of numbers has to be given the first place among the present-day speeches of the world. Yet Chinese is not so important outside of China, and although colloquially it is easy to acquire, written Chinese becomes a hopeless task for ordinary people, and this detracts very largely from the world-popularity of this great language. After Chinese comes English, the home language of possibly 180 millions, and the language of administration, of political life, of higher education and culture of some 500 millions more: and in addition to that, English has attained to a position unique among the languages of the world—it has become the completest exponent of World Culture, and is easily now the most important and most advanced languages of the world. After English we shall have to reckon Hindi, which has its home in the north-western tracts of India, but is now the accepted language of public life, education and literature of some 140 millions of human beings within India and in some places outside India; and, besides, Hindi is the most natural common language for some 260 millions of Aryan-speakers in India, and is the language most widely learned by the speakers of Dravidian and other non-Aryan speeches; and as such, it has been raised to the status of the official language of India (side by side with English, for the time being), a country of 360 millions of inhabitants. The Urdu Style of the Hindi language is also one of the national languages of the State of Pakistan, with its population of 73 millions. Then we have to mention in descending order, Spanish with its 120 millions, Russian with 110, German with more than 80, and Japanese with 78. Indonesian is now looked upon as the 8th in this order, but it is likely that with Indonesian speakers in the Southern Philippines and Malaya, its numbers would exceed those for Japanese. After Indonesian comes Bengali, another Indian and Pakistani language, with over 63 millions—the language of Rabindranath Tagore, with one of the most progressive literatures in the world. French and Arabic are to be enumerated after the above.

The problem with you now is to make your language a suitable vehicle for your highest education in the arts and sciences, and for your administration. The language is refreshingly simple in its grammar, and only in its vocabulary it is to be made supple and all-inclusive. You have in all seriousness started to exploit all the resources of the grammar of the language in its prefixes and suffixes.

As I said before, herein you have some advantage over us. Although your Indonesian speech is fairly old—the oldest specimens of Malay and Javanese, from Srivijaya times, going back to the eighth century AD, in inscriptions—and although there is a fair amount of literature early and modern in both, the Malay language which is being transformed into the *Bahasa Indonesia* has shown itself to be a speech on which the burden of tradition sits but lightly. The speakers of Javanese and Sundanese built-up a great culture, and with it a strong literary tradition which was bound up with Sanskrit and its literary conventions, and Javanese is largely within the orbit of this tradition. But the Old Malay speakers of Palembang who created the Srivijaya empire and its civilisation have left a language which ministered to the needs of a simple folk given to both agriculture and sea-faring, and this speech developed quite a cosmopolitan spirit in its tendency to absorb whatever was useful for expressiveness. This realistic approach to the problem of language as a means of conveying ideas I am glad to find has not worked itself out, and is showing itself once again in the creation of the scientific and technical terms for the modern *Bahasa Indonesia*.

I am very glad to find one thing which you have done in your educational system in connection with the higher study and teaching of the *Bahasa Indonesia*. You have retained old Javanese as a compulsory subject in your university courses in *Bahasa Indonesia*, side by side with Sanskrit and Arabic. You have built-up a great literary expression of your ancient and medieval

Indonesian civilisation through the medium of Old & Middle Javanese. This is a precious heritage, from which your new National Language can draw fresh material for its own enrichment whenever necessary. It should be like what Old Church Slavic is for the Modern Slavic Languages, and like what Sanskrit is for modern Indian languages. Sanskrit, a language which has never been so foreign to you—as a language which on the soil of India grew partly in an Austro-Asiatic or Austric background—will be helpful to understand your ancient and medieval culture, and will form a link with India and Indo-China, with Ceylon, Siam and Burma, and the value of Arabic for a Muslim Indonesia everybody appreciates. So your study of the *Bahasa Indonesia* will continue to profit by its living contact with three Classical Languages, Old Javanese, Sanskrit and Arabic.

From recent literature in various subjects in the *Bahasa Indonesia* which have come to my hands, I am glad to find that in the matter of your scientific and technical terms, you are quite eclectic or cosmopolitan. You have, to start with, your own native Indonesian elements; and then you have the rich heritage of Sanskrit in ancient and early mediaeval times, which has been particularly in vogue in Javanese, and this you are putting to modern employment to the fullest. Then there is the Arabic element; and here religious sentiment of at least some of the leaders of the great mass of Indonesians would like to extend this element to the point of saturation in the language. Finally, there is your reaction to impact of Europe with its scientific and literary, philosophical and cultural pre-eminence. And in this reaction you have, as far as I can see, shown the same spirit of realism and adaptiveness which has always characterised your national history. The spirit of exclusiveness is not at all in evidence. Your old and naturalised Sanskritic vocabulary is now sharing the privilege of citizenship with the more recent non-Indonesian elements; and with European science and the arts of European origin, European words (in their Dutch forms owing to your long association with the Hollanders) are being welcomed, for the simple reason that they are understood generally, and are precise and correct for the purpose.

This kind of linguistic mosaic would not be approved where there is a high and old tradition, or where there is recent (and sometimes unreasoning) revivalism. In India, we find that we cannot easily rid ourselves of this traditionalism, at least in the formal side of language which is generally the language of books, if not in our informal and colloquial everyday speech untrammelled by the ghost of tradition. Sanskrit has ever been the universally acknowledged source and background of our languages, and the greatness and prestige of Sanskrit have for over 2,500 years surrounded all forms of Indian speech as a ring or halo which they could never transgress. In fact, it has to be universally acknowledged that Sanskrit has been one of the greatest cultural forces in the world, both within India and outside India, particularly in Central and South-East Asia; and only three other languages as enshrining the highest achievements of Man in the realm of creative thought and culture during ancient and mediaeval times can be mentioned with Sanskrit, viz., Greek, Chinese and Arabic. It is no wonder that Sanskrit should have such pre-eminence in India—except in the case of the Urdu form of the great Hindi speech of north India, which for a number of political and other reasons affiliated itself during the last two centuries to Persian and Arabic particularly. We have been, whenever necessary, borrowing words from Sanskrit, as inevitably as the Romanic (and even Germanic and Slavic) languages of Europe have been doing so from Latin. The Sanskrit tradition is a living one over the greater part of India; and where it was languishing, it has been to a large extent revived during the last hundred years. Hence there is a strong general feeling that our Indian languages, including the official language Hindi, which have largely become "borrowing languages" like English, taking their words ready-made from some other speech ancient or modern, and have virtually ceased to be "building languages" creating new words with their existing materials of roots or other words and affixes, should as a nationalistic measure confine their borrowings to Sanskrit alone. With a few of our language-makers in Hindi, it has become an inviolable principle leading to a total eschewing of all foreign elements. But this form of "Don't-touchism" in language is also recognised in other (and I should say, intellectually more progressive) quarters as impracticable; and the official policy of the Government of India in the matter of enriching the vocabulary of Hindi has been to follow a *via media*, to take words of international application in their English forms wherever in wide use or found to be suitable, to retain words of foreign origin when universally understood, and to coin new words with existing materials maintaining all the while a basic connexion with Sanskrit and giving it the first preference when words are already found in Sanskrit or cannot conveniently be taken over from a foreign (European) language.

Our official language Hindi has not been given the same status that you have given to *Babasa Indonesia*. We have our regional languages of which each has had its independent literary life for ten centuries and more, and Hindi by virtue of its wide use and understandability could only be given the position of a *prima inter pares*, a first among equals. Hindi is to be used for inter-state or inter-provincial purposes only; and the regional languages like Assamese, Bengali, Gujarati, Kannada, Kashmiri, Malayalam, Marathi, Oriya, Panjabi, Tamil, Telugu, are not to be suppressed by Hindi. These are to remain the vehicles of state business, and of education up to the highest standards in the university (if English is to be replaced at all), and, of course, for literature, in their proper areas. The numbers of people speaking these regional languages (e.g. Bengali, current among over 25 millions within India, with nearly about 38 millions more in East Bengal within Pakistan; Tamil, over 22 millions, Telugu over 33 millions, etc.), and the pride and affection with which their speakers regard these great literary languages, could not but make the linguistic policy of the Indian state as it now is. The regional languages are to remain the queens in their respective areas; and boys and girls in India have now the right to get the highest training in the university, as soon as that can be arranged, in their mother tongue (or the language accepted in the place of the mother tongue), if it is one of the recognised state or regional languages of India.

Our Central Educational Ministry has started a Department for the Development of Hindi, and its various Technical Terms Committees, in collaboration with scholars from the regional languages areas, are now preparing terms not only for the Sciences and Arts for school and college use, but also for the various departments of administration. This is proving to be a rather slow and a difficult task, but considerable progress has already been made; and Hindi terms are generally taken over or built-up from Sanskrit, and in a good number of cases the existing terms from Persian and Arabic and from English are being retained; and in Science and other matters foreign languages are not neglected.

The weight of tradition not being so heavy on the *Bahasa Indonesia*, you are enabled to be more truly international in this matter. In the matter of script, our government has declared the Indian script the Devanagari to be the proper or official script for Hindi, and has not given any official support to the Roman script. Nevertheless, there is a strong group, which, however, is not very active now but which has the tacit support of many scientific scholars, particularly in Bengal and sporadically in other parts of India too, which is in favour of a general acceptance of the Roman script for all Indian languages. I myself am connected with a *Romaka Lipi Samiti*, a "Roman Letters Society" in Calcutta, as its President. We find that the flood-tide of national sentiment is in favour of the national Indian script, which in the arrangement or order of its letters is the most scientifically conceived alphabet in the world. This national sentiment will not at the present moment take the question of changing to the Roman script seriously, and will rather oppose it for educational and other reasons. I can only feel glad that the Indonesian people have accepted the Roman script for the *Bahasa Indonesia*. There are certain matters to which I would like to draw the attention of this Congress in connection with the Roman orthography as adopted for the *Bahasa Indonesia*. I am happy you have eschewed dotted and capped letters—characters with diacritical marks; the simplicity of the phonetic system of the *Bahasa Indonesia* ensures that. It is a good thing you have adopted the simple "u" for the Dutch digraph "oe". But I would like the special letter (*ĕ*) to be retained for the *pĕpet*, which is such a distinctive sound in Indonesian. And for the digraphs "tj, dj", you could use the single letters "c" and "j"; these are widely accepted for scientific work in Oriental and African languages, for the palatal affricates, and their adoption would create a wider field for Indonesians to participate in. As English will be more and more studied in Indonesia, the English value of "j" = "dj" will perhaps be better; and the semi-vowel "j" as in Dutch and German may be indicated by adopting "y" for this purpose. For the other digraphs, "sj, ng, ny or nj", the advantages of "s′, n· and n′"—ordinary Roman letters followed by the accent-mark or by a dot, as moveable *indicators*, may be thought of. But I am not going to discuss at length this question just now.

I have during these few days spent in this corner of Indonesia noticed great changes. There is a most refreshing literary activity which has just started. My Indian friends here tell me that they are noting among the people a very eager desire to read and learn. The spirit of adaptiveness, of taking from foreign cultures what will be helpful and assimilable, which is a sign of life in any people, is still strong with you. You have kept your racial bases and your racial spirit strong and effective in the creation of a special or distinctive Indonesian culture which has its own place in the assemblage of the living cultures of the world, by assimilating from pre-historic times various civilisations which came in touch with the basic Indonesian people and its native culture—the Dongson culture from north Indo-China, the composite Hindu culture of India, the homogeneous culture of China, the spiritual and social aspects of Islamic culture from India, Persia, and Arabia, and the mighty waves of Europeanism from the West brought by the Dutch. I feel that you have still the strength to be objective in your attitude to the world—an attitude which the great Prophet of Islam has prayed for to his God in a *hadith* or traditional saying which every man of culture will whole-heartedly support—"Ila′hi′, ari-na′; haqa′iqa-l-as′ya′i kama hiya" (My God, show to us the exact nature of things as they are).

I feel also that you are following, even in your language-building endeavours, the great principles of the *Pantja-Sila*—the Five Guides to Conduct—accepting the lead of your President—*Bung Karno* or "Brother Sukarna", as he has been affectionately and democratically named. There is the principle of Faith in your own People, in *Kebangsaan*, without which no nation can be led to freedom and advancement. There is Faith in Social Justice—*Keadilan*, without which a true democracy cannot be built up. There is the very essential Desire for Freedom, and ardent and active Faith in Freedom— *Kemerdekaan*. There is the spirit of a broad Humanism, a Faith in Man, a Universal Humanity—*Kemanusiaan*, which can alone make for the tolerance of all, and the acceptance of the best that mankind as a single entity can offer to any individual nation—a Sense of Universal Humanity, which is one of the most fundamental things in civilised life; it is in this spirit that you have sought international cooperation in what would be strictly a national or domestic affair, by asking scholars and delegates from Holland, France, India, Malaya and the Philippines to come and to be present; this *Kemanusiaan* will enable your *Bahasa Indonesia* to be human, and universal in accepting what would be necessary for you for your full self-expression through speech. And finally, it is this *Kemanusiaan* which leads you inevitably to a Faith in the God of All Mankind, the great principle enunciated in your Constitution, which you call in your own Indonesian *Ketuhanan*. And in that Faith, which is Indonesia's, and India's too, as well of the rest of the world, I close with a prayer in: both Arabic and Sanskrit for the success of your endeavours to give to your own people and to the world at large a fine and a potent means of expression which will most clearly mirror the ideals and aspirations, the experiences and achievements of the Indonesian Man—

"ihdi-na´-: s-: sira´: ta-l-mustaqi´m" (Lead us along the right path) and "asato´ ma´ sad gamaya" (From the unreal, lead me to the Real).

CHAPTER 30

Pūrvavideha

BUDDHA PRAKASH

According to the Buddhist geographical conception Mount Sineru (Sumeru) is situated at the centre of the world. In its east is the continent called Pubbavideha, in its west is that named Aparagodāna or Aparagoyāna, in its north is Uttarakuru and in its south is Jambudvīpa. From the aforesaid adjoining continents people came and colonised Jambudvīpa. The settlers from Pūrvavideha christened the eastern part of Jambudvīpa as Videha; the immigrants from Aparagodāna named the regions where they came as Aparānta; the colonisers from Uttarakuru called their new habitat Kurudeśa.[1] In this connection it is significant that according to the Pseudo-Hindu geography of Indo-China the region of Yunnan was known as Videharāj, pronounced as Videhayit, and its capital bore the name of Meittila (Sanskrit Mithilā). This Videharāj seems to correspond to Yunnan, and Meittila to Yunnansen.[2] This is an instance of the transference of Indian geographical nomenclature to foreign countries following the waves of colonisation and cultural influence. The location of Eastern Videha in Yunnan in the kingdom of Nan-tchao shows that India had close connections with this region in ancient times. If the Pubbavideha or Pūrvavideha of the Buddhist accounts is identical with Videharāj or the region of Yunnan, the tradition of the migration of people from it to the province called Videha in India under king Māndhātṛ may be equated with the theory of Parker[3] that the Nan-tchao kingdom expanded westwards up to Magadha and embraced Assam and the valley of the Ganges. Pelliot[4] does not subscribe to this theory, devoid as it is of sound historical evidence, but he admits that the Thai people occupied the regions of the upper Irawaddy and penetrated up to Manipur and Assam in ancient times. Whatever may be the worth of these traditions, they point to the contacts of the people of eastern India and Yunnan and show that they date from fairly early times. As Buddhism was born in eastern India it preserved these traditions and gave prominence to Pūrvavideha, a region of seven thousand

[1] *Papañcasūdanī*, I, p. 434; *Dhammapadaaṭṭhakathā* (Sinhalese edition), II, p. 482. G.P. Malalasekera, *Dictionary of Pali Proper Names*, vol. II, p. 236.

[2] Sri J. Scott, *Gazetteer of Upper Burma and the Shan states*, I, i, p. 219.

[3] Parker, *China Review*, XIX, p. 73.

[4] Paul Pelliot, *Deux Itinéraires de Chine en Inde à la fin du hutiême* siècle, Bulletin de l'ecole Française d'Extrême Orient, vol. IV (1904), p. 160.

Source: *Journal of the Greater India Society* (XV/2, 1456, 93–110).

leagues and the home of Acacia (Sirīśa), as the first continent to be visited by a *cakkavatti*, when on tour.

Though Pūrvavideha is not mentioned in the geography of the Purāṇas and the Epics, there are some references to the highlands of Yunnan in them which suggest their acquaintance with the same. Directing his envoys to traverse the regions of the east in search of Sītā, Sugrīva exhorts them to trace her in the regions of rivers, forests and mountain-fastnesses and to go to the Bhāgirathī, Sarayū, Kauśikī, Kālindī, Yamunā, Sarasvatī, Sindhu, Śoṇa and reach the great mountain (Mahāgiri) called Yāmuna.[5] In the *Saddharma-smṛtyupasthāna-sūtra* translated into Chinese by Gautama Prajñāruci in the sixth century AD the geographical account of which is based on the same source from which the information of lands and peoples of the Kiṣkindhākāṇḍa of the *Rāmāyaṇa* is derived, the reading for Yāmuna is Anūna.[6] Both these variants Yāmuna and Anūna seem to have been based on some such word as Yunnan and appear to refer to the mountainous regions of this country. There is no other name among the mountains of the east (Pūrvadik) which may correspond to Yāmuna or Anūna. The reading in the *Rāmāyaṇa* is manifestly corrupt and has no relation to the river Yāmuna for this river has not lent its name to any eastern mountain in Indian literature.

In the *Bṛhatsaṃhitā* of Varāhamihira there is a reference to a tribe named Tāla among the peoples of the north-west.[7] Ordinarily we do not come across this name in other Indian geographical accounts. Pelliot has drawn our attention to the fact that the Burmese call the Chinese *Tarop* (*Tarok*) or *Taret* even up to the present times. This name is based upon the expression Ta-li-kouo meaning the kingdom of Ta-li.[8] The valley of Ta-li was the cradle of the Nan-tchao empire and when it was divided into two parts it was this very region, dominated by the Touan, which maintained its relations with Upper Burma. Hence the Burmese generalised the name of Ta-li to designate the whole of China. The Indian word *tāla* which is the same as *Ta-li* or *Tārop-Taret* signifies the people of Ta-li, and Yunnan seems to refer to the Chinese people as a whole. It was probably through Burma that this name came to India and found a place in the geographical list of Varāhamihira. It is significant that in the verse cited

[5] *Rāmāyaṇa*, Kiṣkindhākānda, Ch. 40, verses 19-21:
अधिगच्छ दिशं पूर्वां सशैलवनकाननाम्
तत्र सीतां च वैदेहीं निलयं रावणस्य च।।
मार्गध्वं गिरिदुर्गेषु वनेषु च नदीषु च।
नदीं भागीरथीं रम्यां सरयूं कौशिकीं तथा।।
कालिन्दीं यमुनां रम्यां यामुनं च महागिरिम्।
सरस्वतीं च सिन्धुं च शोणं मणिनिभोदकम्।

[6] Sylvain Lévi, "Pour l'Histoire du Rāmāyaṇa", *Journal Asiatique* (1918), p. 16.

[7] *Bṛhatsṃhitā* of Varāhamihira XIV, 22 (Bib. Ind. Edition), vol. I, p. 288.
दिशि पश्चिमोत्तरस्यां माण्डव्यतुषारतालहलमद्राः।
अश्मककुलतहलडाः स्त्रीराज्यनृसिंहबनखस्थाः।।

[8] Paul Pelliot, "Deux Itinéraires de Chine en Inde", *BEFEO*, IV, p. 161, fn. 1.

above *cīna* is conspicuous by absence. Here *tāla* replaces *cīna* of the usual catalogues of the countries of the north particularly that of the *Mahābhārata* where the Gandhāras and Cīnas are bracketed together in an enumeration of the peoples of the north-west.[9]

The kingdom of Ta-li had close connections with India in ancient times. In the *Tien-k'ien ki yeou* of Tch'en Ting and the *Yun-nan-t'ong-tche-kao* the valley of Ta-li is called "the kingdom of the good perfume of India".[10] In this description a connection is sought to be established between Ta-li and *gandha*, the Indian word for perfume. This word provides the etymology of the name *gandharva* in Chinese texts. In the epithet of Ta-li it stands for the word *gandhāra* which was also a name of this region. Here *gandhāra* and *gandharva* seem to have been confused by Chinese writers. We learn from the *Jāmi-ut-Tawārikh* of Faḍlullāḥ Rashiduddin Abul Khair that this region was known as Kandar or Kandahar (Gandhāra) in ancient times. Elliot has translated his remarks as follows:

> Another large country is called Kandahar which the Moghuls call Karājang. These people spring from Khitai and Hind. In the time of Kúbilá ká-án it was subdued by the Moghuls. One of its borders adjoins Tibet, another adjoins Khita and another adjoins Hind.... Philosophers have said that these are three countries celebrated for certain peculiarities; Hind is celebrated for its armies, Kandahar for its elephants and the Turks for their horses.[11]

Rashiduddin also notes that the country to the south-west of Cathay was called Dai-liou or "great kingdom" by the Chinese and that it was identical with the Karajang of the Mongols, the Kandar of Hindu writers and Kandahar mentioned by him. Dai-liou mentioned by this historian is the same as Ta-li of Chinese accounts, both *dai* and *ta* meaning "great". As for Karajang or "black Jang", Pelliot is inclined to treat it as a Mongol transcription of the name of the Ts'ouan. The ancient Ts'ouan was divided by the Chinese into two groups of barbarians, the black and the white. The people of Nan-tchao had mixed with them. Hence the Mongols called all the peoples subject to Nan-tchao—those of Yunnansen and Ta-li—by the name Karajang. But in a narrower sense this name was applied to the people, of Ta-li.[12] The fact that this region was called Gandhāra is manifest from the remark that its boundaries touched China and Tibet and that it formed a part of the empire of Qubilai Khan. In Rashiduddin's treatise on the life and teachings of Buddha which he owes to the Kashmirian Buddhist Kamalaśrī, the population of (Qandahār)

[9] *Mahābhārata*, XII, 65, 13-15.
यवनाः किराता गान्धाराश्चीनाः शबरबर्बराः।
शकास्तुषाराः कङ्काश्च पह्लवाश्चान्ध्रमद्रकाः।।
कंथ धर्मांश्चरिष्यन्ति सर्वे विषयवासिनः।
मद्विधैश्च कथं स्थाप्याः सर्वे ते दस्युजीविनः।।

[10] Paul Pelliot, "Deux Itinéraires de Chine en Inde", *BEFEO*, IV, p. 161.

[11] H.M. Elliot, *History of India as Told by Its Own Historians*, vol. I, p. 73.

[12] Paul Pelliot, "Deux Itinéraires de Chine en Inde", *BEFEO*, vol. IV, p. 161.

Gandhāra is described as Chinese-looking having pierced ears (*burīda gosh*).[13] These data leave no room for doubt that Qandahār or Gandhāra represented the region of Ta-li and Rashiduddin's association of elephants with it is due to the confusion of this Gandhāra with the region of this name in the north-west of India.[14]

According to the legends of the eleventh century the king Anoyat's (Anuruddha) went to the country of Gandhārarāj (Gandhālayit) in search of a tooth of Buddha.[15] It is stated in the *Sāsanavamsa* that this Kaśmīragandhāra was not at first included in Cīnaraṭṭha (the empire of China) but was subsequently incorporated in it.[16] These references clearly relate to the region of Ta-li which was known as Gandhāra. Some Hinduised peoples of Indo-China and Indonesia had a tendency to transfer the geographical names of their parent country to their new habitat and thus create around them a sort of New India. Sometimes they, Sanskritised indigenous names so as to suit Indian designations and sometimes they imposed Hindu names on foreign lands and suppressed their original toponyms. Yunnan was situated to the north of Indo-China just as Gandhāra was to the north of India, it was flanked by mountain ranges which ran parallel to the big rivers of Indo-China as its Indian counterpart was surrounded by mountains. Thus the physical features as well as the geographical location warranted the christening of Yunnan and Tali as Gandhāra. It appears that these regions were formerly called Pūrvavideha and later named as Gandhāra. It is likely, as we shall see later, that these two designations are symbolic of two waves and traditions of colonisation.

Paul Pelliot has held that the region of Yunnan and Ta-li was in contact with India from the third century BC or even earlier and it was along the routes passing through them that India entered into cultural and commercial relationship with China.[17] When the Chinese traveller Tchang K'ien discovered the Central Asiatic routes during the reign of Emperor Wou-ti (140-87 BC) he was astonished to find Chinese bamboos and fabrics being sold in Bactria and to learn that they reached there through the caravans which traversed northern India (Shen-tou) and brought them from south China to Afghanistan. Tchang K'ien's report is as follows:

[13] Karl Jahn, "Kamalashrī-Rashid-al-Din's Life and Teachings of Buddha", *Central Asiatic Journal*, vol. II, no. 2 (1956), p. 90.

[14] Henry Yule, "An Endeavour to elucidate Rashiduddin's Geographical Notices of India", *Journal of the Royal Asiatic Society* (1870), new series, vol. IV, pp. 355-6.

[15] Alexander Phayre, *History of Burma*, p. 35.

[16] *Sāsanavamsa* (Pali Text Society edition), ed Mss. Bode, p. 8. The reading Kaśmīra-gandhāra was corrupted as Kośāmbi-gandhāra in Burmese traditions, Ko-rham-prañ (Ko-shan-pyi), the new Shan country, is based on the word Kośāmbi, which was a corruption of Kaśmīra.

[17] Pelliot's view has been accepted and followed by A. Herrmann [*Atlas of China*, maps 23, 27, 28,] O. Fratike [*Geschichte des chinesischen Rciches*, pp. 340, 410] and G. Coédés [*Les états hindouisés d'Indochine et Indonésie*, p. 108].

When your servant was in Ta Hsia he saw large bamboos and cloth of Shu (Szechuan). When he asked the people of Ta Hsia how they obtained these things they told him that their merchants bought them in Shen Tu (India) which is a country several hundred li south-east of Ta Hsia and is a sedentary nation like Ta Hsia. Both Ta Hsia and Ta Yuan are tributary to An Hsi (Parthia). So far as your servant could judge Ta Hsia is 12,000 li (4,000 miles) from China. As it is north-east of Shen Tu,[18] this kingdom cannot be so far from China.

Pelliot holds that the goods of Yunnan and Szechuan were brought into India by the Burma Road, which passed through Yung-tch'ang and Wan-ting. But Walter Liebenthal thinks that this commerce passed along the route which led from Shu (Szechuan) to Lhasa and Assam.[19] He holds that the track via Tibet was rarely used because of hostilities. Before 751 this route must have been difficult by reason of the complete absence of traffic organisation. Only a well-equipped expedition could have survived of which no trace is available. Hence pilgrims tried to bypass Tibet in the south and sometimes succeeded in reaching their destinations but this Tsang-K'o route never became a trade route. The route from Szechuan to Assam is mentioned in the *Glossary* of Hui-lin. Leaving Szechuan it passed through the towns of Yü-yao, Yüeh-hsi, Pu-wei and Yung-ch'ang inhabited by the tribes called Ngai-lao which were named as *Shen-tu*[20] after the fall of the Han dynasty. Then moving in a western direction the route entered the southern frontier area of Tibet and crossing rivers and valleys and scaling mountain tanges and peaks it descended into the south-eastern part of T'ien-chu in the region of Kāmarūpa. This mountain path though short was very difficult and dangerous. This route is also mentioned by Hiuen Tsang and is referred to in the second itinerary of Kia Tan. Liebenthal holds that the twenty Chinese monks, mentioned by I-Tsing, who arrived in India during the reign of Śrīgupta, who constructed a temple for them called Chinese Temple (Chih-na-ssu) 40 *yojanas* to the cast of the famous Mahābodhi Temple at Nālandā,[21] came by this Tsang-K'o route. According to Pelliot these pilgrims came by the Burma route.

Besides the evidence of Tchang K'ien, Pelliot's theory of the existence of the Burma road in the first two centuries before Christ is based on some other facts which are challenged by Liebenthal. The mention of a route from Ta-tsin to China through Yung-ch'ang in the *Wei-liu* has been interpreted by Liebenthal to mean that a route led from Szechuan to the province of Yung-ch'ang and reached modern Hanoi from where a sea route was available. Pelliot's reference

[18] C.P. Fitzgerald, *China: A Short Cultural History*, pp. 181-2.

[19] Walter Liebenthal, "The Ancient Burma Road: A Legend?", *Journal of the Greater India Society*, vol. XV.

[20] Yueh-hsi is a town in Hsi-k'ang on the road from West Szechuan to Kunming and Pu-wei is identical with Yung-ch'ang. The fact that these places were inhabited by the people bearing the name Shen-tu (Indian *Sindhu*) shows that they were colonised by the Indians.

[21] Edouard Chavannes, *Mémoires sur les religiemx éminents qui allérent chercher la loi dans les Pays d'Occident*, p. 82.

to the reign of Yung-yu-tiao in the country of Shan who received a kind of imperial investiture in 91 and sent the musicians and jugglers from Ta-ts'in to the Chinese court in AD 120 and sent an embassy there in AD 132 is also dismissed by Liebenthal on the ground that a Shan kingdom did not exist in Burma in AD 120 and that Shan kingdoms existed in the lower valley of the lower Mekong and Central Annam which were organised into the kingdom of Lin-i in the second century. The tradition of Kāśyapa Mātanga and Chu Fa-lan, the first Buddhist missionaries to China, reaching there through the route of the upper Irawaddy and Yunnan, to which Pelliot looks for some element of possibility, is taken by Liebenthal to be based on the arrival of the Buddhist Patriarch Mahākāśyapa in Yunnan about AD 1000.[22] Pelliot adduces some linguistic evidence also to show that the rulers of Nan-tchao bore names and titles derived from Burmese words. Siun-ko-k'iuan son of Yi-meou-siun, who ascended the throne in 808, assumed the title of *pīao-sin*. After the death of this king this title continued to be adopted by the rulers of this region and we come across it repeatedly in the eleventh century. In Chinese the character *p'iao* represented the Burmese *pyū* and the title P'iao-sin corresponded to the Burmese honorific Pyū-shin (written as prū-rhang) meaning the prince of the Pyū. Among these rulers there was also a tendency to prefix the last syllable of the name of the father to that of the son which is noticeable in the royal genealogies of Burma. Pelliot draws our attention to the fact also that the legend of Kieou-long found in the *Heou-han-shou* a fifth century work recording the data of 25-220 was later engrafted on the Buddhist tradition of the colonisation of the countries of Eastern Asia by the sons of Aśoka which has some significant Burmese features. The legend relates to a woman Sha-yi who was struck against a floating wood and thereby conceived and gave birth to ten sons. The wood soon appeared as a dragon and claimed the sons as his own. Nine of them fled for fear but the tenth sat on his back and became the king of those regions. This legend was later incorporated in the Buddhist story of A-yu (Aśoka) king of Magadha becoming the progenitor of the kings of the eastern countries. According to this story Aśoka's third son P'iao-tsiu-ti had a son named Ti-mong-tsiu by his wife K'ieu-mong-k'ouei, who had nine sons who became ancestors of the Tibetans, Chinese, Annamites, Singhalese, Nan-tchao, Pa-yi, etc. The fifth son Mong-tsiu-tou once sank and became a tree and gave birth to Kieou-long as in the aforesaid legend. The names P'iao-tsiu-ti and Ti-mong-tsiu resemble those of Pyū-so-t'i and his son T'i-min-yi who are said to have ruled from the second to the fourth century in Burma according to the genealogical lists. It is noteworthy that the Burmese kings from Pyū-so-t'i called themselves the descendants of Mariya (Mauroa). Liebenthal's objection to these data is that the Burmese chronicles date from the fifteenth century whereas these traditions were current in Nan-tchao around 900 which

[22] Walter Liebenthal, "Sanskrit Inscriptions from Yunnan", *Sino-Indian Studies*, vol. V, part I, pp. 46-70.

shows that the legends in question passed from Yunnan to Burma rather than the other way round. Besides this, the term P'iao was used to designate a kingdom lying beyond the southern frontiers of Nan-tchao perhaps in modern Laos. Pelliot emphasises the fact that the Hinduisation of Ta-li was accomplished through the instrumentality of the Burmese as is manifest from the royal titles of the rulers of Nan-tchao. In AD 752 the ruler of Tibet sent a message of friendship to Ko-lo-feng, king of Nan-tchao with a seal on which he was entitled "emperor of the east" (tung-ti) or Udayarāja. In 754 his successor I-mu-hsin adopted the title of "King of the east of the sun" (Sūryodayarāja). The title *tung* is the same as Sanskrit *udaya* which forms part of the titles of the Burmese kings as Udi-(Udi bliva). Here Liebenthal objects that these titles are of modern date and do not presuppose any ancient relationship. The aforesaid arguments of Pelliot and Liebenthal relate only to the overland route by which Sino-Indian cultural contacts were first inaugurated. Pelliot favours the Burma route which started from Ta-li, traversed Yong-t'chang, passed through Kao li-kong-shan to the west of the Salwin, bifurcated there, one branch leading directly to the west and the principal route directly joining the Irawaddy region in the south-west, whereas Liebenthal argues for the Tibetan tracks or the *tsang-k'o* route mentioned above. Both of them, however, agree that the overland route joined eastern India and southern China for the first time in history. Let us study the data of Indian texts relating to this question.

It is well known that in the *Mahābhārata* the Cīnas appear with the Kirātas among the armies of king Bhagadatta of Prāgjyotiṣa or Assam. In the Sabhāparvan this king is described as surrounded by the Kirātas and the Cīnas.[23] In the Bhīṣmaparvan the corps of Bhagadatta consisting of the Kirātas and the Cīnas of yellow colour appeared like a forest of *karṇikāras*.[24] It is significant that the Kirātas represented all the peoples living to the east of India in the estimation of the geographers of the Purāṇas.[25] Even the dwellers of the islands of the Eastern Archipelago were treated as Kirātas in the Epics.[26] The reference

[23] *Mahābhārata*, Sabhāparvan, 26, 9:
स किरातैश्च चीनैश्च वृतः प्राग्ज्योतिषोऽभवत्।
अन्यैश्च बहुभिर्योधैः सागरानूपवासिभिः।।
[24] *Mahābhārata*, Bhīṣmaparvan, V, 584:
भगदत्तो महीपालः सेनामक्षौहिणीं ददौ।
तस्य चीनैः फिरातैश्च काञ्चनैरिव संवृतम्।।
बभौ बलमनाधृष्यं कर्णिकारवनं यथा।
[25] *Mārkaṇḍeya Purāṇa*, 57, 5-7 Pargiters' translation, pp. 283-314:
पूर्वे किराता यस्यान्ते पश्चिमे यवनास्तथा।
ब्राह्मणाः क्षत्रिया वैश्याः शूद्राश्चान्तः स्थिता द्विजाः।
[26] *Rāmāyaṇa*, Kiṣkindhākaṇḍa, 40.27-28:
अक्षया बलवन्तश्च तथैव पुरुषादकाः।
किरातास्तीक्ष्णचूडाश्च हेमाभाः प्रियदर्शनाः।
आममीनाशनाश्चापि किराता द्वीपवासिनः।
अन्तर्जलचरा घोरा नरव्याघ्रा इति स्मृताः।।

to their wealth of gold, silver, gems, sandal, aloewood, textiles and fabrics clearly demonstrates their association with the regions included in Suvarṇadvīpa.[27] Thus the connection of the Kirātas and the Cīnas is a sure indication of the fact that the Indians came to know of the Chinese through the eastern routes and considered them as an Eastern people having affinities to the Kirātas, who were the Indo-Mongoloids inhabiting the Tibeto-Burman regions and the Himalayan and East Indian territories, the word *kirāta* being a derivation from *kirānti* or *kirati*, the name of a group of peoples in eastern Nepal.[28]

In early Indian literature China is invariably shown to be connected with India by a land route across the country of the Kirātas in the mountainous regions of the north. In the Vanaparvan of the *Mahābhārata* the Paṇḍava brothers are said to have crossed the country of the Cīnas in course of their trek through the Himalayan territory north of Badri and reached the realm of the Kirāta king Subāhu.[29] The Cīnas are brought into intimate relationship with the Himalayan peoples (Haimavatas) in the Sabhāparvan also. The land of the Haimavatas is undoubtedly the Himavantappadesa of the Pali texts,[30] which has been identified with Tibet or Nepal. In the *Sāsanavaṁsa* this region is stated to be Cīnaraṭṭha.[31] Thus it is clear that China was known to the Indians as lying across the Himalayas and was accordingly included in the Himalayan territories. In the Nāgārjunikoṇḍa inscription of Vīrapuruṣadatta, China (Cīna) is said to be lying in the Himalayas beyond Cilāta or Kirāta.[32] These references to the proximity of China to the Himalayan regions inhabited by the Kirātas show that there were regular routes through the Tibeto-Burman territories

[27] *Mahābhārata*, Sabhāparvan, 30, 26-28:
वसु तेभ्य उपादाय लौहित्यमगमद्बली।
स सर्वान् म्लेच्छनृपतीन् सागरानूपवासिनः।।
करमाहारयामास रत्नानि विविधानि च।
चन्दनागरुवस्त्राणि मणिमौक्तिककम्बलम्।।
काश्चनं रजतं चैव विद्रुमं च महाबलम्।

[28] Suniti Kumar Chatterji, "Kirāta-jana-kṛti", *Journal of the Royal Asiatic Society of Benagl* (*Letters*), vol. XVI (1953), p. 169.

[29] *Mahābhārata*, Vanaparvan, Ch. 177, verses 11, 12, 13:
नगोत्तमं प्रस्त्रवणैरुपेतं दिशां गजैः किन्नरपक्षिभिश्च।
सुखं निवासं जहतां हि तेषां न प्रीतिरासीद्भरतर्षभाणम्।।
ततः कमेणोपययुर्नृवीरा यथागतेनैव पथा समग्राः।
विहृत्य मासं सुखिनो बदर्यां किरातराज्ञो विषयं सुबाहोः।।
चीनाँस्तुषारान् दरदाँश्च सर्वान् देशान् कुलिन्दस्य च भूमिरत्नान्।
अतीत्य दुर्गं हिमवत्प्रदेशं पुरं सुबाहोर्ददृशुर्नृवीराः।।
Mahābhārata, Sabhāparvan, Ch. 47, verse 19:
चीनान्हूणाञ्छकानोडान्पर्वतान्तरवासिनः।
वार्ष्णेयान्हारहूणाँश्च कृणांन्हैमवतांस्ततथा।।

[30] *Mahāvaṁsa*, XII, 6 (Hindi tr. of Anand Kausalyāyana), p. 64.

[31] *Sasanavaṁsa*, op. cit., p. 13.

[32] B.C. Law, *Historical Geography of Ancient India*, p. 73.

along which the Indians could reach China. Some such land route is implied in the remark of the *Harṣacarita* of Bāṇabhatta that Arjuna conquered the Hemakūṭa region after passing through Cīna.[33] Of course, the route across Central Asia is perhaps alluded to in the itinerary of Cārudatta from the Indus Delta to China across the country of the Hūṇas and the Khaśas described in the *Vāsudevahiṇḍi*[34] and there is probably a reference to the sea route passing through Vanga, Takkola and Suvarṇabhūmi in the *Milindapañho*.[35] But there is no doubt that in a large number of ancient Indian texts China is mentioned near the Eastern Himalayan regions through which regular routes connecting this country with India passed from fairly early times. It was along these routes that India came into contact with China for the first time and developed commercial relations with her that are referred to by Chang K'ien in the second century BC. Liebenthal holds that the Tibetan routes were more ancient than the Burma Road. But it is certain that the southern parts of China notably Yunnan and Ta-li were known to the Indians in quite remote times. Thus the early existence of the Burma route is not an impossibility though the Tibetan route was also known to the Indians. Liebenthal himself observes, "I do not doubt that people went there (Burma) before that date (858 AD) but I know of no documentary evidence."[36]

It is clear from the above discussion that the eastern land routes brought India and China into cultural and commercial contact for the first time. The itinerary of Chang K'ien shows that the Central Asiatic route was opened long after the discovery and use of the eastern routes and that the articles brought from southern China through them to India were taken to Bactria before his arrival there in 128 BC. As for the sea route it was also popularised long after the eastern land routes. K.A. Nilakanta Sastri has quoted a passage from the *T'sin Han shou* of Pan K'ou, a Chinese writer of the first century AD, to show that the sea route from China to southern India was known in the second century BC and men and materials began to reach China in along it in that century.[37] The route described in this text started from Je-nan, Siu-wen and Ho-p'ou and passing through the kingdoms of Tou-Yuan and Yi-lou-mo reached Chen-li. From there a land route led to Fou-kan-tou-lou (Pagan) and from that place the sea route again started by which a boat could reach Houang-tche in more than two months. It is stated that from the time of Emperor Wou (140-86 BC) the kingdom of Houang-tche had been sending tribute to the Chinese

[33] *Harṣacarita*, ed. P.V. Kane, p. 59:
पाण्डवः सव्यसाची चीनविषयमतिकम्य राजसूयसम्पदेकुध्यद्रन्धर्वधनुषकोटिटंकारकूजितकुञ्जं हेमकूटपर्वतं पराजैष्ट

[34] *Vāsudevahiṇḍi* (Gr. tr. of Bhogilal Sandesra), pp. 191-2.

[35] *Milindapañho*, ed. Trenckner, p. 359. At p. 327 of this work Cīna is coupled with Vitālā which is a variant of Kirāta.

[36] W. Liebenthal, "The Ancient Burma Road: A Legend?", *JGIS*, vol. XV (1956), p. 6.

[37] K.A. Nilakanta Sastri, "The Beginnings of Intercourse between India and China", *Indian Historical Quarterly* (1938), Winternitz Memorial Volume, p. 380.

court and the traders and mariners of China used to frequent it for purchasing pearls, glass, rare stones and strange products in exchange for gold and silks. This route is said to have been infested with pirates and beset with tempests. A safe journey is, however, reported to take many years to go and return. It is also remarked that in the period of Yuan-che (AD 1-6) the revolutionary emperor Wang Mang sent rich presents to Houang-the and requested its ruler to send an embassy with a live rhinoceros. Nilakanta Sastri identifies Houang-tche with Kāncī following the view of G. Ferrand. But Herrmann locates this region in Abyssinia and Berthold Laufer in Malaya. We know that the current of Indian colonisation in the Eastern Archipelago started about the beginning of the Christian era in the wake of the improvement of the technique of navigation in the Indian Ocean.[38] Thus the aforesaid reference to the sea-route can be dated in the latter half of the second century or the first century BC at the earliest if the identification of Houang-tche with Kāncī is taken to be correct. The discovery of the Chinese coin at Candravalli in Mysore, out of the various dates, 138 BC, AD 502 and AD 886 suggested for which, the earliest falls in the period noted above leads to a similar inference.[39] Yet there are some indications of the still higher antiquity of the eastern land routes which brought China into contact with northern India.

We have seen above that the Cīnas figure in the retinue of the Assamese king Bhagadatta in association with the Kirātas. No early Indian text associates the Chinese with southern India. Hence it is unlikely that the first acquaintance of the Indians with the people of China was made in the south. Pelliot has drawn our attention to the fact that in the fourth century BC the Chinese knew the lion, which is not found in their country, by an Indian name.[40] Later on in the first century AD they came to know of the lion through Persia and adopted the Iranian name for this animal in their nomenclature. This evidence of the contact of the Chinese with the Indians in the fourth century BC is strengthened by Indian and Greek notions which dominated the scientific and philosophical thought in China in that century and gave it a new tone and orientation.[41] These contacts resulted from the intercourse of the peoples of these countries which proceeded along the eastern land route since the sea route was quite unknown in that age.

A significant evidence of the antiquity of the eastern land route is afforded by the prevalence of the word *Cīna* as a name for China in India. I have shown elsewhere that in India the country called Cīna was invariably associated with the Ts'in dynasty and its great emperor Ts'in Shih Huang Ti up to the time of Hiuan Ts'ang.[42] Berthold Laufer objected to the derivation of the name Cīna

[38] Buddhaprakash, *Kauṭilya Studies III*, Poona Orientalist, 1957.

[39] *Mysore Archaeological Reports* (1910), p. 44. For the view of the Japanese scholar Takasaki vide M.G. Dikshit, "A Chinese Coin from Sirpur", *Journal of the Numismatic Society of India* (1956), vol. XVIII, p. 66, fn. 1.

[40] Paul Pelliot, *La Haute Asie*, p. 8.

[41] Ibid., pp. 7, 8, 9.

[42] Buddhaprakash, *Kauṭilya Studies* II, Poona Orientist (1956), pp. 25-35.

from Ts'in on the ground that the Chinese did not call themselves by this name. He rather suggested that Cīna has been the ancient, perhaps Malayan, name adhering to the coast of Kuang-tung province and the coastline further to the south, in times anterior to the settlement of the Chinese in those regions. This name distinctly pointing to the coastal regions of southern China spread along the maritime route of the Indian Ocean to the west and became the basis of *Thinaī* of the *Periplus Maris Erythraei*, *Sinai* of Ptolemy, *Tzinitza* of Kosmos Indikopleustes and Marcianus of Heraclea and *China* of modern Western languages in contradistinction to the continental names *Seres* and *Serike* which related to the coherent land mass of northern China and spread in the west overland.[43] But Pelliot has conclusively proved that in pre-Christian times China was known to the Hiung-nu of Central Asia as the land of T'sin and the Chinese were called the people of T'sin. He draws our attention to a report on the hardships of an enterprise against the Hiung-nu which resulted in the destruction of the army of Li-kuang-li under emperor Wou (140-87 BC). In this report there is a reference to the tethering of a horse near the rampart of a town, where the Chinese were garrisoned, by the Hiung-nu and their ironical exhortation, "come soon to inform the people of T'sin, we give you a horse for coming soon". In a passage of the *T'ien han shu* the Chinese fugitive Wei Lu is said to have advised the Shan-yu of the Hiung-nu who was bent upon attacking China in 83-82 BC (120 years after the fall of the T'sin) to dig wells, build walls, construct towers and entrust their management to "the people of T'sin". Thus it is clear that in the Hiung-nu period the Chinese were called in Central Asia as "the people of T'sin".[44] Later on China was known in Central Asia as Tabghac or T'o-pa in the age of the T'ang after the name of the T'o-pa (Wei) dynasty that ruled there from AD 386 to 556. After that China became famous in Central Asia as Kitai or Khitai (Cathay) after the dynasty of Ki-tan that ruled her from AD 916 to 1125. Not only in Central Asia but also in Japan the Chinese were sometimes called the people of T'sin. In a passage of the Japanese *Nihongi* there is a reference to the coming of the men of T'sin and of Han in AD 540. All these references show that China and her people were known as T'sin after the great T'sin dynasty that unified and strengthened her. In India this name was transcribed and spelt as Cīna and the fact that this name became current in India shows that the Indians came to know of the exploits of the T'sin dynasty at a time when it was identified with the country as a whole. This knowledge of Chinese affairs long before the discovery of the Central Asiatic routes presuppose a regular intercourse of the Indians and the Chinese along the eastern land routes. It is significant that the eighteenth-century Tibetan writer Dharmasūrya-śrībhadra stated that Cīna was identified by some authors with the Dvīpa Pūrvavideha, which the people of India called Mahācīna. Evidently the region of Yunnan served as a cross-roads of the Indians and the Chinese in ancient times.

[43] Berthold Laufer, *The name 'China'*, T'oung Pao (1912), vol. XIII, pp. 719-26.

[44] Paul Pelliot, *L'Origine du nom de Cbine* T'oung Pao (1912), vol. XIII, pp. 727-42.

In the period of the T'ang an attempt was made to reclaim and reopen the routes of Yunnan. The highways to Yunnan were of Siu-tcheou, Tong-tch'ouan, Yunnan-sen and the valley of Kien-tch'ang. The route of the Red River was used later and that of Kouei-tcheou was extremely difficult. The Chinese of the T'ang period preferred the route of Kien-tch'ang. In the period Tcheng-kouan (AD 627-49) Lieou Po-ying the governor of Kien-tch'ang demanded that the barbarians of Song-wai be punished and suppressed so that the route of Si-eul ho (the river of Ta-li) and T'ien-tchou India be opened. Accordingly some years later the T'ang emperor sent an army under general Leang-kien-fang to reduce the tribes of Song-wai. This army penetrated up to Si-eul-ho and in consequence the tribes settled on the Yang-tsen and the Ta'-li paid tribute to the Imperial court in AD 648-56. But at that time the Tibetans made their début into the history of Asia. At first they were friendly to the Chinese and in 648 their king placed a garrison at the disposal of the Chinese envoy Wang Hiuan-t'so who was driven out from Magadha following the outbreak of a revolution. But after some time they fell out with the Chinese and in 670 war flared up among them. As a result the Tibetans extended their sway over Western Sseu-tch'ouan and the north-western part of Yunnan. In 680 the Chinese were forced to renounce the post of Yao-tcheou which they had set up in Yunnan a little to the north of modern Yao-tcheou in 621. It was then in 688 that they made another bid to resuscitate their hold over those regions and created seven posts to the south of Yang-tsen. In 698 the governor of Tch'eng-ton named Tchang kien-tche sent a report to the Imperial court and drew its attention to the fact that the preceding dynasties established their hold over Yunnan with great advantage through which they could communicate with Ta-T'sin and with Tonkin. He pleaded for the abandonment of the costly defence posts and recommended that an official mission be left to deal with the barbarians. But his plan was not heeded and in 740 another attempt was made to subjugate these regions. It appeared that the routes of Yunnan and India had passed under the control of the Chinese but the conflict of the Chinese and the Tibetans gave birth to the state of Nan-tchao which was an important centre of Buddhist culture.

There is a tradition that Avalokiteśvara came directly from central India to convert the people of Nan-tchao. Towards the end of the eighth century seven religious teachers from India dissuaded the King Yi-meou-siun from his liking for Chinese culture and allegiance to the Ta'ng court. In the first half of the ninth century a monk of Magadha named Candragupta showed remarkable feats of thaumaturgy in Yunnan. He founded a monastery named Yüan-hua-ssu in Ho-ch'ing (four day's journey north-east of Ta-li). Another man called Li (with shaggy eyebrows) who was known as "the wise" went from India and played some part in the construction of Ch'ing-sheng ssu, a monastery outside the walled town of Ta-li. In the first half of the ninth century an Indian community flourished in Nan-tchao. About AD 1000 the patriarch Mahākāśyapa introduced Ch'an Buddhism in Yunnan. The Buddhists of this region were so zealous as to transfer the names of the sacred sites to their habitat and thus to create a new holy land in their country. We learn from the traveller Tch'en Ting that the 300 religious men sent abroad by the Chinese emperor in 964 in search of sacred books in India reported on their return in 976 that they saw the Kukkuṭapādagiri, the stone house of Upagupta, Rājagṛha, the Gṛdhrakūṭa hill, the Stūpa of Ānand and the cave of Pippala in Ta-li. The prevalence of all these holy names of Indian Buddhism in Ta-li is an evidence of the depth of Indian influence in the culture of that country.

The Buddhists of Yunnan developed a distinct legendary lore showing the antiquity of their relations with India. In the *Po-kuo- yiu-yu* we come across the story of the colonisation of this country by Aśoka. He entrusted it to his second son P'ao-hsin-ch'ü. This dynasty was given the family name Chang by the Han. These Chang were driven out by a *rākṣasa* who tyrannised over the country. At last Kuan-yin-p'u-sa arrived and begged of him land as large as the monk's robe. At the time of measurement the robe went on expanding till it covered the whole country. Thus the tyrant was driven out and the Chang ruler was reinstated.

In Yunnan there is a large number of old Pagodas. Some of them are the oldest and the most beautiful in China. Their cornices and corner decoration showing rows of pitchers (*mangala ghaṭa*) betray unmistakable Indian influence. Many bricks of these pagodas bear Sanskrit inscriptions containing Buddhist *mantras* and formulae in a script which is identical with that current in Nālandā and Kāmarūpa in the ninth century.[45] The beautiful bronze statue of Avalokiteśvara from the pagoda of Ch'ung-sheng-Ssu near Ta-li is an index to the high standard of culture and craftsmanship attained by the Buddhists of Yunnan.[46]

The pagodas of Yunnan were copied from the Chang-an pagodas which were built by members of the Wei ch'ih family who came to the court of the T'ang as hostages from Khotan in the seventh century and settled there. It is likely that they contributed to the culture of Yunnan also. Along this Central Asiatic route a stream of colonisation might have reached Yunnan from northern India and Afghanistan. But in earlier times the people of the east, Magadha and Videha, were in contact with Yunnan as the traditions of Pūrvavideha show.

This ancient Indian colony in the south of China was the cradle of Sino-Indian cultural relationships for a long time.[47]

[45] W. Liebenthal, "Sanskrit Inscription from Yunnan", I, *Monumenta Serica* XII (1947); "A Sanskrit Inscription from Yunnan", *Sino-Indian Studies* III, 1, 2 (1947); "Sanskrit Inscriptions from Yunnan", II, *Sino-Indian Studies* V, i (1955), pp. 46-70; "The Ancient Burma Road", *JGIS*, XV, I (1956), p. 16.

[46] Walter Liebenthal, "An Early Buddha Statue from Yunnan", *Indian Historical Quarterly*, XXXII, 2-3 (1956), pp. 352-3.

[47] Besides Buddhism Śaiva cults were also popular in Yunnan as is manifest from the prevalence of the cult of Mahākāla there.

CHAPTER 31

The Pāñcarātra Sect in Ancient Cambodia

KAMALESWAR BHATTACHARYA

The Pāñcarātra (or Bhāgavata or Sātvata) cult "was in its evolutionary stages in the centuries immediately preceding the Christian era. The progress continued in the subsequent times, and the Gupta period was marked by a great development of the creed, when its tenets were systematised. It is in this period that it was gradually transformed into Vaiṣṇavism."[1] The identification of Kṛṣṇa-Vāsudeva, originally one—second in order of precedence—of the five heroes (*vīras*) of the Vṛṣṇi clan, worshipped by the Pāñcarātras, with the cosmic god Nārāyaṇa of the Brāhmaṇas and the Āditya-Viṣṇu of the Vedas, was instrumental in that process.[2] It is not, therefore, by sheer coincidence that the Pāñcarātra or Bhāgavata cult is found to have spread to Cambodia, precisely in that epoch and under the same form.

It is an inscription of Fu-nan, that of Prince Guṇavarman,[3] dated approximately the second half of the fifth century AD, that constitutes our first landmark. This inscription commemorates the erection of a Viṣṇupada, placing the donations to the sanctuary at the disposal of the Bhāgavata priests (*viprair bhāgavataiḥ*).

The next mention of the Bhāgavatas in Cambodia is found in the Baset Stele Inscr.[4] of Jayavarman I (*c.* middle of the seventh century AD). It records the consecration of an image of Viṣṇu under the name of Acyuta, by one Dharmapāla, said to be a Bhāgavata. This inscription is particularly interesting for its mention of the Pāñcarātra cult (*pāñcarātrārcā*), the five sacraments (*pañcabbir yajñaiḥ*), the five diurnal rites (*pañcakāla*) and the five elements (*pañcabbautika*), terms of technical import in the Pāñcarātra.[5]

That the Bhāgavatas flourished during the reigns of Jayavarman II (AD 802-50) and Jayavarman III (AD 850-77), is proved by an inscription of Prasat Kôk Pô,[6] which mentions a *Bhāgavata kavi as* having obtained the complete favour

[1] J.N. Banerjea, Presidential Address, *Indian History Congress*, Patna, 1946, Section I.

[2] Cf. H.C. Raychaudhuri, *Materials for the Study of the History of the Vaiṣṇava Sect*, Calcutta, 1936, pp. 172f.

[3] G. Coedès, "Deux inscriptions sanskrites du Fou-nam", *BEFEO*, XXXI, pp. 2ff.

[4] G. Coedès, *Inscriptions du Cambodge* (*IC*), II, pp. 193-5.

[5] Cf. F.O. Schrader, *Introduction to the Pāñcarātra*, Madras, 1916, pp. 76, 112.

[6] G. Coedès et P. Dupont, "Les Inscriptions du Prasat Kôk Pô", *BEFEO*, XXXVII, pp. 387 ff.

Source: *Journal of the Greater India Society* (XIV/2, 1955, 107–16).

(*ativallabhatāpannaḥ*) of Jayavarman II and having been the *guru* of his Viṣṇuite son, Jayavarman III. The same inscription also shows that Bhāgavatism flourished during the reign of Indravarman I (AD 877-89), for two religious foundations are ascribed to Amṛtagarbha, a descendant of the *Bhāgavata kavi* mentioned above, and himself a Bhāgavata. The second of these foundations took place in AD 883.

During the reign of Yaśovarman I (AD 889-900), the Pāñcarātras figure as one of the principal religious sects in Cambodia, along with the Śaivas, the Pāśupatas, and the Buddhists. An *āśrama* called Viṣṇavāśrama was dedicated to them at Prasat Koṃnap, not far off from the capital city of Angkor. The Śaivas and the Pāśupatas, on the one hand, and the Buddhists on the other, had similarly their *āśramas*, respectively at Prei Prasat and Tep Praṇaṃ.[7] Pāñcarātra, Bhāgavata and Sātvata, are evidently used, in the stele of foundation of the Vaiṣṇavāśrama, as different names of the same sect, also designated by the generic name of Vaiṣṇava. One need not consider the three terms as standing for three different sects as M. Coedès seems to do.[8] The Prasat Koṃnap Inscription is important for a delineation of the Vaiṣṇava practices in the ninth-century Cambodia, especially when they are placed side by side with their Śivaite and Buddhist counterparts, as depicted, respectively, in the Prei Prasat and Tep Praṇaṃ Inscriptions. Strict chastity was enjoined on the Viṣṇuite hermits. The Buddhist of bad morals and ignorant were declared ineligible for dwelling in the hermitage. Similar remarks were not made regarding the Śivaites—a fact which leads M. Coedès to conclude that the latter "seem to have held continence and knowledge less in esteem". The Śivaite and Buddhist hermits used to go out in quest of alms, but not, perhaps, the Viṣṇuites.

During the reign of Rājendravarman (AD 944-61), the Pāñcarātras occupied an important place in Cambodia. In the Pre Rup Stele Inscr. (AD 961),[9] the court poet referred to the fourfold emanation (*catur-vyūha*) of Viṣṇu, the most distinctive feature of the Pāñcarātra. Besides, the Kuk Sla Ket Inscr.[10] referred to a royal servant, "versed in the Pāñcarātra, the quintessence of which lies in the five diurnal rites" (*adhītī pañcarātre . . . pañcāhnikapuñjite*), and "observing the five *kālas*" (*pañcakālavit*).

In the catholic atmosphere of the reign of Jayavarman V (AD 968-1001), Bhāgavatism flourished along with Śaivism, the official creed, as also Buddhism. The fourfold emanation is referred to in an inscription of Prasat Kôk Pô.[11] According to the Prasat Trapang Run Inscription[12] the consecration of the king was performed by a Sātvata priest, Pañcagavya, who continued to be his *ācārya*. Indeed, Jayavarman V, though an ardent Śaiva, extended his patronage to the Viṣṇuites as Well as to the Buddhists, and seems rather to

[7] G. Coedès, "A la recherche du Yaçodharāçrama", *BEFEO*, XXXII, pp. 84ff.
[8] See, on this point, Raychaudhuri, loc. cit., p. 21.
[9] Coedès, *IC*, I, pp. 77 & 105, v. 4. See *infra*.
[10] Ibid., V, pp. 119 ff.
[11] Coedès and Dupont, loc. cit., pp. 400 & 407, v. 1. See *infra*.
[12] L. Finot, *BEFEO*, XXVIII, pp. 58 ff.

have been an eclectic in his religious outlook. (His posthumous name was Paramavīraloka, apparently of Buddhist inspiration.) A rapprochement between Śaivism and Vaiṣṇavism is clearly reflected in the records of the reign. Thus, the Pañcagavya, mentioned above, had a son "profoundly versed in the Śaiva doctrine" (*śaivasiddhānta-niṣṇātaḥ*) but he performed the function of the consecrator (*dhātā*) of an image of Viṣṇu, erected by his father. Nārāyaṇa, the fervent Vaiṣṇava, in the Prasat Kôk Pô Inscription erects a Nandin and a Mahākāla (Śiva) at the door of a sanctuary of Viṣṇu. Viṣṇuvara (Pṛthivīndra-paṇḍita), "the noble Bhāgavata" (*Bhāgavatārya*), author of at least three Viṣṇuite foundations during the reign, is described, in a Banteay Srei Inscription[13] as "a relation and spiritual friend" (*saṃvandhī dharmavāndhavaḥ*) of the Śivaite *guru* of the king, Yajñavarāha. It is, thus, somewhat curious to note that an inscription of the same king should refuse the recognition of the Bhāgavatas as a regular religious order.[14]

The Prasat Kôk Pô and Trapang Run Inscriptions, referred to above, further show that Bhāgavatism flourished during the reign of Jayavīravarman (AD 1002-6). In the latter of these two records, the Sātvata priest Pañcagavya, whom we have already met during the reign of Jayavarman V, is described as "the principal master" (*ācārya-puṅgavaḥ*) and "highly honoured counselor" (*atimato mantrī*) of King Jayavīravarman.

Sūryavarman I (AD 1002-50), the Buddhist king, also patronized the Pāñcarātras, for an inscription, posterior in date, records that a Pāñcarātra priest, Kavīśvarapaṇḍita, was, during this reign, the *guru* of the hermitages at Īśvarapura (Banteay Srei), Śivapura (Phnoṃ Bayang), Sūryaparvata (Phnoṃ Chisor), and Jalāṅgeśvara (Bos Preah Nan), and later on became a *guru* and adviser (*mantrin*) of the king.[15] It is interesting, however, to note that the same person is stated to have erected an image of Bhagavatī and consecrated a *liṅga* of Śiva.

We have traced above, on the basis of the available data, a history of the Pāñcarātra sect in ancient Cambodia. That history, evidently, remains incomplete. But we should remember that the archaeological exploration of Cambodia is "far from being accomplished" and that "new inscriptions are coming forth every year from the soil of Angkor".[16] Even a quantity of inscriptions, so far discovered, still remains to be published. New informations, thus, may be available in future, to enable us to fill up the lacunae of our present-day documentation.

We have seen above how the essential elements of the Pāñcarātra were known in Cambodia. Especially, we have found reference to the fourfold

[13] "Le temple d'Içvarapura", *Mém. archéol. EFEO*, I, p. 93, vv. 2-3. Cf. Coedès, and Dupont, loc. cit., pp. 393 ff.

[14] Coedès, *IC*, II, p. 67, ll. 10-13 & n. 5.

[15] Ibid., pp. 132, 133.

[16] G. Coedès, *Les États hindouisés d'Indochine et d'Indonésie*, Paris: E. de Boccard, 1948, p. 9.

emanation, the most significant feature of the doctrine. It would be useful to quote the verses in which that reference occurs, for, as we shall notice presently, those show some considerable divergence from the orthodox Pāñcarātra. Thus, the verse of the Pre Rup Stele Inscription runs:

pāre satvarajastamaskam api yo nityan niviṣṭaḥ pade
traiguṇyena caturvvidhena vividhābhivyaktir āvirbhavan
viśvākaradharo nirastasakalākaro pi dedīpyate
vandantāṃ bhagavantam ādipuruṣan taṃ Vāsudevaṃ vibhum ||

To Him, who, in spite of having reached for eternity the supreme world in the condition free from *sattva*, *rajas* and *tamas*, appears (in this world) under diverse manifestations, *through the quadruple triad of qualities*, and who, in spite of having abandoned all forms, shines in the form of the Omnipresent, to that god Vāsudeva, primordial and eternal *puruṣa*, let our homage be rendered.

The Prasat Kôk Pô Inscription has the following verse:

Namaś caturbhujāyāstu caturdhā viṣkṛtātmane
nistraiguṇyaguṇāyāpi catustraiguṇyạdhāriṇe ||

Homage to the god with four arms, who is *manifested four times*—to Him, who, in spite of having for quality the fact that He is without the three *guṇas*, *possesses the quadruple triad of qualities*.

In the two verses quoted above, there is no doubt that the four primary *vyūhas*, or emanations of Viṣṇu, are referred to. But the manner in which this doctrine is expressed (*traiguṇyena caturvidhena*, *catustraiguṇyadhāriṇe*), is peculiar. Evidently, the Cambodian poets conceived the four *vyūhas* to be endowed with the three natural qualities of *sattva, rajas* and *tamas*. According to the Pāñcarātra, however, the six ideal *guṇas* of *jñāna*, *bala*, *aiśvarya*, *vīrya*, *śakti*, and *tejas*, make up the body of the first emanation, Vāsudeva; while from Vāsudeva emanates Saṃkarṣaṇa; from Saṃkarṣaṇa, Pradyumna, and from Pradyumna, Aniruddha, each endowed with a couple of those attributes, namely, *jñāna* and *bala*, *aiśvarya* and *vīrya*, *śakti* and *tejas*, respectively. These six ideal *guṇas*, as Schrader points out, "are *aprākṛta*, not belonging to Nature"—for Nature does not exist as yet—and have consequently nothing to do with the three well-known *guṇas* (*sattva*, *rajas*, *tamas*); that is to say, the old dogma that God is necessarily "free from (the three) Guṇas (*nirguṇa*) does not exclude. His possessing the six ideal Guṇas, which, on the contrary, must be ascribed to Him, because without them there could be no Pure Creation, and, all further evolution depending thereon, no creation at all. . . . The six Guṇas are the material, or instruments, as it were, of Pure Creation, in their totality, and by pairs. . . ."[17] The attribution of the three natural *guṇas* to the four emanations of Viṣṇu, is, therefore a divergence that is worth considering. No further light on the question can, however, be thrown in the present state of our knowledge.

[17]Schradcr, loc. cit., pp. 31ff.

One more point may be discussed in this connection. Though the concept of the fourfold emanation of Viṣṇu was not unknown to the Cambodian poets, there is yet no positive evidence to show that the concept of the secondary emanations, giving rise to the twenty-four *mūrtis*,[18] played any part in that country—a fact which remains in spite of M. Dupont's[19] ingenious hypothesis of "an undifferentiated *sthānaka mūrti* of Viṣṇu", contributing to "distinct identifications of detail, according to circumstances".

[18] Cf. T.A. Gopinatha Rao, *Elements of Hindu Iconography*, Madras, 1914, vol. 1, pt. 1, pp. 227 ff.

[19] P. Dupout, "Viṣṇu mitrés de l'Indochine occidentale", *BEFEO*, XLI, pp. 250 ff. The existence of the triads (consisting of three undifferentiated images of Viṣṇu) at Prasat Daṃrei Krap and Prasat Rup Arak on the Phnoṃ Kulen, poses, indeed, as M. Dupont points out, an important problem of religious interpretation. In the absence of epigraphy, it is hardly possible to solve this problem satisfactorily. But to represent these triads as standing for any of the triads of secondary emanation of Viṣṇu, would perhaps be going too far. For, whether the concept itself was known in Cambodia is still doubtful, while, on the other hand, no similar representation exists even for the well-known fourfold primary emanation.

Index